BRUCE BURK
Game Bird Carving

Other books by Bruce Burk:
    Decorative Decoy Designs
    Waterfowl Studies
    Complete Waterfowl Studies

BRUCE BURK
Game Bird Carving

Third Edition

Winchester Press
An Imprint of NEW CENTURY PUBLISHERS, INC.

31   32   33   34   35   36   37   38   39

LIBRARY OF CONGRESS
Library of Congress Cataloging-in-Publication Data

Burk, Bruce.
    Game bird carving / Bruce Burk.—New rev. ed., 2nd revision.
        p.   cm.
    Bibliography: p.
    Includes index.
    ISBN 0-8329-0439-2 : $37.95
    1. Wood-carving—Technique.   2. Decoys (Hunting)   I. Title.
NK9704.B86 1988
745.593—dc19   87-34824
                                                              CIP

Dedicated to

Wendell Gilley
Arnold Melbye
Lem and Steve Ward

Acknowledgments

I must first express my gratitude to my very good friend Wendell Gilley of Southwest Harbor, Maine, whose persuasion, and help, encouraged me to attempt this book on bird carving. His generosity, with not only his time but also his possessions, is impossible to repay.

I am also deeply indebted to those carvers, collectors, and other people interested in birds who, by their conversations and letters, have encouraged and aided me in this undertaking.

I wish to thank, as well, Jim Robertson of Woodland Hills, California, who gave me invaluable assistance in planning this book; Milt Weiler of Garden City, New York, who made helpful suggestions about the carving of working decoys; and Dr. Paul Johnsgard of Lincoln, Nebraska, who shared his extensive experience as a bird photographer.

My most sincere appreciation to Dr. Ken Stager and Jim Northern of the Los Angeles County Museum for their patience in supplying answers to my layman's questions and for permitting me unlimited use of the museum's large collection of skins and mounts.

The game bird dimensions presented in Chapter 11 are the result of a great deal of cooperation and effort given by Dr. Paul Johnsgard; Dave Hagerbaumer, Independence, Oregon; John Carter, Salem, Oregon; Gilbert Maggioni and Grainger McKoy, Beaufort, South Carolina; Wendell Gilley; Glen Smart, Bowie, Maryland; Tom Carlock, Fair Haven, New Jersey; Bruce Buckley, Costa Mesa, California; and others. These men deserve the credit for any benefits that this data may give to the carver. All shortcomings and errors are the sole responsibility of the author.

I would like to thank my two friends and hunting companions, Gene Mellon, Sherman Oaks, California, and Bill Bartha, Rosamond, California, for often and generously allowing me the lion's share of the bag so that I could obtain specimens needed for game bird carvings.

My thanks also to Frank Schultz, Saugus, California, who made all of the original black and white prints used in this book. His patience, cooperation, and excellent work are deeply appreciated.

Last, but by no means last in importance, I wish to thank my long-time secretary, Mrs. Virginia Garhardt, Hermosa Beach, California, for editing and proofreading the text of this book.

B.B.
Sherman Oaks, California
July, 1972

I would also like to give my sincere thanks for the kind and generous words I have received during the past nine years from many happy readers and users of the first edition of this book. Their thoughtfulness is deeply appreciated. Their suggestions and comments have been most helpful in planning this revised edition.

I would especially like to thank Ed and Esther Burns of St. Michaels, Maryland, for their suggestions and their answers to many questions I had about upgrading and updating *Game Bird Carving*.

B.B.
Grass Valley, California
April, 1982

Again, I would like to express my genuine appreciation and sincere thanks for all the letters and first-hand comments I have received from novice, amateur, and professional bird carvers (and some of their wives). Their favorable remarks made all the work worthwhile and the few critical ones were most useful in the planning of this second revision and were equally well received.

Although I have gotten letters over the years from a sizeable number of the more than 120,000 readers of this book, the one I prize most was written by a gentleman in his late sixties who had been forced into retirement. After several years of being exposed to the "golden years", his existence was without purpose and, with nothing to do or to anticipate, he had become despondent. When given a copy of *Game Bird Carving*, he became so completely absorbed in this activity that he wrote, "You have made my life worth living!"

B. B.
Grass Valley, California
1988

Contents

Introduction

Of today's many creative hobbies, wood carving, realistic bird carving particularly, is one of the most fascinating and rewarding. Not only does the carver express himself in three dimensions by sculpturing the wood to the naturally graceful lines of the bird, he also finds great challenge and satisfaction in attempting to duplicate with paint and brush the complexity and elusive coloring of the bird's plumage. Also, this absorbing and satisfying hobby almost immediately leads to additional interests and activities.

Once the beginner starts carving birds, he actually sees these wonderful creatures for the first time. He finds it impossible not to observe in great detail every bird he chances upon. By firsthand observation and by study, he starts learning more and more about their habits and soon acquires a true appreciation of their incredible beauty, their tremendous power and endurance, their marvelous adaptability on the ground, in the air, and, in the case of waterfowl, on and under the water. With this knowledge, it is almost impossible not to become interested in the conservation of wildlife and preservation of habitats.

Quite often the carver, after the experience gained from painting bird carvings, tries his hand at canvas painting and opens the door to another exciting and rewarding pastime.

In many cases, he becomes interested in amateur photography, if only to take pictures of his carvings. This interest easily leads to photographing actual birds, the results of which are invaluable to the carver for detail and natural shape, to say nothing of the enjoyment he experiences in perfecting his photographic skills.

A smaller number of bird carvers will discover at least one more fringe interest: preservation of specimens, or taxidermy. When most game birds are prepared for the table, the plumage is discarded; with little effort, this beauty can be saved for many years and can provide invaluable firsthand information.

The popularity of realistic bird sculpture is growing rapidly. The ever increasing interest people have in this art and other wildlife art can be attributed to a number of factors but probably the most important one is the desire by many to return to realism in art. Most people have good, inborn artistic sense. They have become tired of the abstract and impressionistic works of the past decade or two and having it forced upon them as fine art. They can relate to art depicting a bird for they know what these creatures should look like. They can also relate to art depicting the bird's habitat for they are familiar with the myriad details of which it is composed. It is, therefore, not surprising that so many people today are interested in and appreciate this new, all-American art form.

There is very little room in realistic bird sculpture and paintings for loose, impressionistic work which is usually the mark of incompetence, rather than an "arty" excuse to establish a style. To quote Arnold Melbye, often called the dean of versatile bird carving, "There are among us those who have such a warm feeling for wild creatures, usually coming from a lifelong intimacy, that the urge to create them in one medium or another cannot be resisted. There is no need for interpretation—just long, intense study in an attempt to reproduce what nature has so beautifully perfected." Don Bridell, fine, contemporary bird sculptor, puts this in a slightly different manner. "Our birds (sculptures) are shadows of the real thing. I see no folly in producing shadows. I see no way to produce anything but a shadow. The things of the universe are complete and alive; nevertheless, it is within our nature to create, even if our works are but counterfeits of reality. The appearance of style simply means we missed the mark if creation of a perfect carving is our goal. The more the object of our search looks like what it is intended to be, the less it will look like the one who made it. The object of our art is to point to the beauty of nature, not to our egos as artists. One cannot remove the presence of the carver from his work, but the intention is to move to the forefront the presence of the subject." (Quoted from North American Decoys, Spring and Summer issue, 1982.)

Nature is precise—sloppiness is not tolerated. The relatively few mistakes nature makes are quickly erased by the survival of the fittest. This does not mean that all realistic depictions of nature are artistic, far from it. It is up to the wildlife artist to select the necessary elements which are artistic and assemble them in an artistic manner. His success will then be determined by his technical ability and by how he can 'put it all together'.

The competitive shows of the early 60's, by reviving interest, made an important contribution to the transition from working decoys to decorative carvings. However, the major turning point in the development of decorative bird carving occurred November 4th thru the 6th of 1965 when the first American Bird Carving Exhibit was held in Chestertown, Maryland. This noncompetitive exhibit, the first of its kind, was originated by the late Dr. Daniel Gibson, President of the George Washington College in Chestertown, and was sponsored by the Kent County Chapter of the Maryland Ornithological Society. Twenty four of the nation's top bird carvers were invited to participate and their carvings were assembled in the Parish House—Emmanuel Protestant Episcopal Church, under the supervision of Dr. Gibson and Mrs. Edward Mendinhall. This exhibit was a success in all departments. For the first time, most of the bird carvers of the nation were able to meet each other, exchange ideas, and compare carvings. Every carver left this most important exhibit with an eagerness to return home and improve his techniques. This is exactly what happened. A huge step had been made and the quality of realistic bird carving was definitely on the upswing.

The success of the 1965 Chestertown show inspired this group to host two more exhibits—one in 1967 and another in 1969. Shortly thereafter, many other national and regional exhibits and contests were organized and have been held at regular intervals since.

As was mentioned above, rapid strides in the development of decorative bird carving were made after the first Chestertown show. The carvings of this period were generally stiff and hard in appearance and lacked the texture so necessary for imparting the feeling of softness and realism. Painting, in most cases was amateurish and failed to capture the delicate details, colors, and texture of the bird's plumage. As a result of the Chestertown shows and their informal competition, carvers of this era were exposed to, and inspired by, the work of their fellow carvers. They started improving their techniques and began originating new ones. When the newer and larger exhibits came into existence, they, too, contributed greatly to the state of the art. What began as a craft for utilitarian purposes had blossomed into a full-fledged American art form. However, its practical ancestor—the working decoy—was still very much evident.

Several important carving and finishing techniques were originated, or improved upon, during the late sixties and early seventies. The first important development was the use of burn marks to duplicate the shaft and barbs of the feather. This technique added greatly to the texture of the carving and to creating the illusion of softness, especially when it was used in conjunction with individually carved feathers.

Other texturing methods utilizing gouges and rotary tools were originated and have become very effective ways for simulating texture and making the carving appear to be soft.

In the early 70's, the individual feathering technique, in which a number of individual feathers are painstakingly shaped and detailed and assembled accurately in their proper sequence and position, was developed. By use of these individual feathers, lifelike representation of the actual bird, which previously had been almost unobtainable with carved feathers, became a reality. The feeling of motion was greatly enhanced by the use of thin, but strong, and completely separated flight and tail feathers. Some of these carvings were breathtaking in form, daring in position, and exquisite in detail—masterpieces that had to be seen to be fully appreciated.

Also during the early 70's, the better carvers began to compliment their carvings with more elaborate and beautifully constructed bases, or mounts, usually embellished with handmade, realistic plant and animal life designed to artistically reflect the natural habitat of the bird being depicted. Although this has been carried, in a few cases, to extremes—where the habitat depiction completely overwhelmed and subordinated the carvings—aesthetic mountings have contributed greatly to the development of realistic bird carvings as an art form.

Concurrently with the innovation of more elaborate and aesthetic bases, top artists started giving more thought and spending more time on the overall design of their pieces. Instead of just striving for realism—color, form, composition, and more important, originality were given more and more consideration. Many of these artists had learned how to capture the elusive details of the bird, both in form and color, and how to create the illusion of softness; now, they had become aware of the importance of good composition so that compositional devices such as habitat depiction, bases, and others would be in artistic balance. Realistic bird sculpture, as a respected art form, had finally come into its own and any connection to its decoy parentage had been completely severed.

Frank Hodsoll, senior White House liason for the Presidential Task Force on Arts and Humanities, concluded his interview with U. S. News and World Report (January 17, 1983) by saying, "We must make a special effort to support work that looks promising. On the other hand, fortunately, not everything in the arts depends on outside help. Much that is good and utlimately lasting may come about without any government help. It just happens." He is so right. Realistic bird scupture, as a new American art form, just happened—thanks to the concerted efforts of a small group of dedicated artists and a very large number of realistic bird sculpture enthusiasts.

The late Dr. George Miksch Sutton, renowned ornithologist, author, and artist, ended his foreword to Anne Small's *Masters of Decorative Bird Carving* (Winchester Press) with, "Carvers of birds in America, realizing that there is no need to become abstractionists to prove they are artists, will go on creating objects of beauty that look wonderfully like living birds. What they, the creators, are called is of little consequence. It is what they create that is important." With the respect due Dr. Sutton, I think it is important what they are called, not only to the artists themselves but also to the collectors and the many people who are intensely interested in realistic bird sculpture.

To date, almost all who describe wildlife art refer to those doing two dimensional art (paintings—oils, watercolors, etc.) as "artists" and those doing three-dimensional art (realistic bird scuplture) as "carvers". Even if not meant, an inference certainly is there. The Leigh Yawkey Woodson Art Museum, in Wausau, Wisconsin, which has annually, since 1976, sponsored one of the most prestigious wildlife art exhibits in the country, refer to two-dimensional artists as "painters" and three-dimensional artists as "sculptors". Some purists argue that a sculpture must be sculpted from one piece—that wood may be removed but never added. They are entitled to their opinion, but I know of no hard and fast rule that bears out their contention. Modeling clay into a three dimensional figure most surely is an additive process but is referred to by even purists as sculpting. From a critical standpoint, the terms "sculpture" and "sculptor", when applied to realistic bird sculpture, are actually not quite correct. A realistic bird sculpture must accurately depict the living bird not only in form but also color: therefore, the term "polychrome sculpture" would be more nearly correct but is somewhat unwieldly. Also, the successful bird sculptor is much more than just a sculptor—he must be an accomplished painter, too. However, all in all, the terms as used by the Leigh Yawkey Woodson Art Museum are a great improvement and, in the opinion of this writer, should be adopted by all concerned in this new art form.

There are many publications available today that provide a wealth of information for the bird carver. However, one of the biggest obstacles the carver of realistic birds still faces is the difficulty of obtaining accurate, detailed structural information on the particular bird he is attempting to depict. The scarcity of this data was one of the reasons for the original writing of this book. Another primary reason, of course, was to pass on to the amateur some of the ways a good carving could be produced. However, no claim is made that the various procedures described here are the best ways to get the job done. I am sure that by the time this revision is published, I myself will have discarded some of these methods for better ones. A successful carver should always be on the look-out for newer, better techniques and should never give up trying to improve his work.

The ultimate purpose of this book is to help the carver artist to plan and to produce realistic carvings, as much like the birds they represent as possible. I share with many carvers and collectors the opinion that for man to attempt interpretations and changes in the already graceful forms and exquisite coloring of birds is trying to improve upon perfection itself.

A firm believer in the old adage regarding pictures versus words, I have used graphics as the primary means of conveying information. The drawings and paintings included of the various birds and the photographs of the carvings should be considered only as aids; the birds themselves and actual bird photographs are what the carver should strive to duplicate. In this way the beginner will develop his own style, and the mistakes he makes will be his own, not a copy of someone else's.

I sincerely believe that hard work, study, and most important, *stick-to-it-iveness* can replace so-called inherent talent, if such an attribute exists in man. The only way the novice can learn bird carving is by doing—not just once or twice, but again and again—each time trying to improve the imperfections of the preceding carving. If this procedure is conscientiously followed, the aspiring bird-carver who feels he was endowed with little or no natural carving ability will soon hear his friends saying, "I sure wish I had your talent!"

Beginner's First Project
Mallard Drake

Beginner's Working Decoys

Ringed-Neck Duck Drake   Lesser Scaup Drake

Beginner's Decorative Bufflehead Drake (From the collection of R. K. Guicelman, Lakewood, California)

Floating Decorative Pintail Hen Decoy

"Siesta Time—Green-Winged Teal" 1984 (Collection of author)

"Wolf Creek Woddie", 1987 Wood Duck Drake (Collection of author)

Stretching hooded booded merganser drake, 1981 (Collection of Dr. and Mrs. Silagi, Texas)

"T. L. C." Hooded Merganser Style, 1984 (Collection of author)

"A Family Affair—Canada geese", 1982 (Life-size Taverner's geese) (Collection of author)

Greater prarie chickens, 1980 (Collection of author)

Ringed-neck pheasant, 1968 (Collection of Jon Chaney, California)

High Desert Chukars'', 1983 (Collection of author)

Scaled quail, 1978 (Collection of Dr. Ray Zeigler, Texas)

Bobwhite quail, 1979 (Collection of Mrs. Lillian Wright, Florida)

California quail, 1980 (Collection of Diane Byrnes, California)

PART I

Getting Started

This book explains the techniques of realistic game bird carving. The methods and information covered here aim at helping the carver produce carvings that look as much like the birds they are supposed to represent as possible—not only in shape but also in detail and color.

Depending on the degree of realism desired, the bird carving can be as simple or as complex as the individual carver wishes. Bird carving·is an ideal hobby because the beginner can experience a great deal of satisfaction from the results of his very first effort; and regardless of the number of carvings he does or the degree of perfection he attains, he will thrill to the challenge each new project presents: coming just a little closer to duplicating the beauty and perfection of nature.

Although a large portion of this book covers information the author hopes will help the serious carver to achieve advanced amateur or professional status, Part I is devoted to the beginner who has never attempted carving or painting. In order to give him a chance to make a start without reading endless pages and without becoming involved in making drawings and getting into other more complicated details, several carving projects, complete with drawings and instructions, have been included in Chapter 1. As soon as the beginner has developed some confidence in his carving ability, he should either start making his own drawings or at least introduce some changes to drawings not his own. This is the only way he can project originality into his carvings and develop his own style. Much more on this important subject will be covered in Part II.

CHAPTER *1*

Carving for Beginners

Bird carving is not nearly as difficult as most people anticipate. However, the one and only way the aspiring birdcarver can find this out is to take a block of wood and a knife and start to carve. The most important thing is to start—*now!*

CARVING WOODS

As realistic bird carvings are almost always painted, the appearance of the wood (color and grain) is of secondary importance. Stability, strength, ease of carving, good machining and sanding characteristics, ability to receive detail, and availability are the prime considerations involved in selecting a carving wood. Basswood, jelutong, and water tupelo—in that order—are the most popular woods today for realistic bird carvings. If these woods are not available, white pine, sugar pine, and white cedar may be substituted, usually with good results.

Basswood, as the American variety of linden is commonly called, is abundant in the eastern half of this country; however, this wood is not widely cut and milled because of its limited demand. Basswood is a light colored, usually close grained, fairly strong wood. It does not machine cleanly and is somewhat difficult to sand. If properly dried, it is a stable wood but its hardness and graininess vary considerably, depending on the locality where it is grown and the part of the tree from which it is cut. Like most woods, thicker pieces, two inches and over, are sometimes difficult to obtain.

Jelutong, a wood imported from Malaysia, has been substituted for quite some time by pattern makers for sugar pine. Jelutong is a light-colored wood, stable (if properly cured), medium-grained wood, free from pitch, and easily worked. Compared to basswood, it is more porous and is not quite as strong. However, it is more easily carved, machines and sands cleaner, receives burning detail better, and probably has more consistent quality than basswood. Jelutong does have defects called "latex pockets", which resemble blades of marsh grass about 1/4 to 3/8 inch wide and approximately 1/32 inch thick growing through the tree. These bladelike pieces of latex can be withdrawn easily from the wood and the remaining holes filled with little trouble.

Water tupelo is a very fine grained, white wood, native of the flood plains along the Atlantic and Gulf Coasts and up into the Mississippi Valley where there is standing water for several months of the year. Only the first few feet of the tree is suitable for carving as the rest of the tree is much harder. Although somewhat inconsistent, water tupelo is a very stable wood which generally carves well, machines without the fuzz of basswood, and receives added texture by burning, hand tools, and machining very well. Its availability is quite limited at this time.

Spare no effort in selecting good, dry wood, free from pitch and checks, and reasonably straight-grained and clear. When weighed against the many hours spent on a carving the small amount saved by buying inferior quality wood is a very poor economy.

A few sources for carving woods are shown in the Appendix.

CARVING TOOLS

A fine workshop with a large collection of chisels, gouges, drawknives, spokeshaves, rifflers, a band saw, a Foredom flexible shaft tool, and other power tools may be desirable, but it is certainly not necessary for the beginner to have all of this equipment or to spend much money in order to get started. An abundance of fine, expensive tools are very impressive to admire and to show to friends, but they will not produce beautiful carvings by themselves. Fancy tools can only supplement, not replace, ingenuity, ambition, perseverance, practice, study, and hard work. There is no question that a well-balanced collection of hand and power tools will aid the beginner in his first attempts at carving. However, there is a very strong tendency during these days of affluence for the rankest amateur to be convinced that he must have the very best, the most professional equipment, before he can even think of starting out. As a result of this attitude, the beginner who is short of cash may not try to start out at all; or if the money is available, he will very likely end up with equipment that later proves to have very little practical use. Begin with simple tools and, as your interest and skill progress, add to your collection accordingly, taking the time to find the tools that most closely meet your personal requirements.

Actually, the first few carvings shown here can be accomplished with nothing more than a sharp knife, a piece of sandpaper, and some glue, although it is not suggested that the beginner start out with just these bare necessities. A list of tools has been included here as a guide; other tools will be mentioned in subsequent parts of this book as the aspiring carver progresses into more advanced carvings. Some of the tools suggested now may not be of the very best quality, but they will get the job done until the beginner's interest and ability develop to the point where he is sure that he wants to invest in more expensive tools. He should then buy the very best quality tools that he can afford.

In addition to the equipment listed below, a workbench or a fairly sturdy table upon which to work is most desirable. It need not be anywhere near as elaborate as the one shown (Fig. 1-3), but it should have some storage space for tools. An attached vise, either a woodworker's or metalworker's, is almost a necessity.

Practical Tools for the Beginner

Knife, either carving or replaceable blade (Fig. 1-1)
Coping saw and fine blades
Carving chisels (Fig. 1-2)
Hand drill with a few assorted drills
Rasps (Stanley Surform half-round and round)
C-Clamp, 6 inch approximately (if vise is not available)
Whetstone
Garnet paper (0, 2/0, 3/0, 4/0, and 6/0)
Sanding block
Wilhold glue and/or 5 minute epoxy
Tube or can of Plastic Wood (or similar product)

(It is assumed that the beginner already has the commonly used home-maintenance tools such as a hammer, screwdriver, pliers, handsaw, etc.)

CARE OF TOOLS

To do their job, the carver's hand and power tools must be properly maintained. In the case of power tools, the manufacturer supplies operating and maintenance instructions with each new tool. Should the carver buy used equipment, these manuals are usually available free from the manufacturer on request. There are a number of articles and publications available on the sharpening of tools (some of them are listed in the Appendix). The importance of having all cutting type tools properly sharpened is obvious. Anyone who has ever done any work with a knife or chisel knows what a poor job a dull tool does and how much more effort is required.

There is nothing complicated about the actual sharpening procedure but for some, including the author, knowing how it is done and actually doing it in the proper manner are two entirely different matters. A knife, for example, must be ground and honed at the same correct angle on both sides of the blade—this is where most experience difficulty in producing sharp edges. Having a bench grinder, a powered wet grind stone, and a variety of whet stones will not be of much help if correct sharpening angles are not maintained.

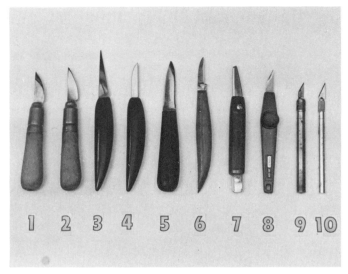

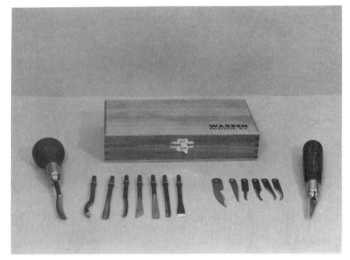

1-1

1-2

1-1 *Knives. (1, 2) Nick Purdo knives; (3, 4) Knotts knives; (5) Wendell Gilley knife; (6) Dastra Tools; (7) Leichtung Inc.; (8) Stanley; (9, 10) Exacto. (See Appendix.)*
1-2 *Removable handle knife and chisel set. Good starting tools for the beginner. Warren Tool Co., Inc.*
1-3 *Some type of workbench is almost a necessity.*

1-3

1-4 *The Lansky Sharpening System.*

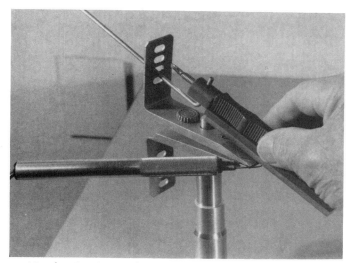

1-5 *Most burning tips can be sharpened using the Lansky sharpener.*

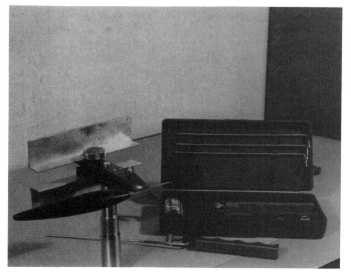

1-6 *A similar, but heavier duty, sharpening clamp made by the author.*

For sharpening knives, skew-type chisels, and most burning tips, the author has found the Lansky Sharpening System (Fig. 1-4) the least expensive, the easiest, and the most foolproof method for getting a razor-sharp edge every time (See Appendix). This system consists of a simple clamp for holding the knife's blade. Incorporated in the clamp are two angles, each with four guide holes. The sharpening stone is built into the hand grip to which a guide rod is attached. The blade of the knife is placed and tightened securely in the clamp. The guide rod of the stone holder is then inserted in the proper hole for the desired sharpening angle (17°, 20°, 25°, or 30°). A sharpening angle of 25° seems to work well for bird carving work. The stone is then placed on the blade and pushed toward it; it is then lifted off at the end of the stroke and returned to the starting point for the next stroke. After the desired edge is obtained on one side, the clamp and knife are flipped over and the same procedure is followed on the other edge of the knife, using the same sharpening angle hole and approximate number of strokes used on the first side. If the blade is dull, or nicked, a coarse stone is first used, followed by a medium stone, and then by a fine stone. If the blade needs only to be 'touched-up', only the fine stone would be used. Five different stones are available. Lansky's standard kit contains the three stones mentioned, complete with guide rods, clamp, and honing oil. The holding post shown in Fig. 1-4 was made by the author. Lansky has two posts available—one is screwed to the bench top and the other can be clamped to the edge of the bench or some other object.

Fig. 1-6 shows a similar, but heavier duty, steel-clamp made by the author. The guide rod of the sharpening stone rides on the upper edge of metal angles and produces a constant 25° sharpening angle along its length.

After the blade is honed with the fine stone, a small wire edge, or burr, probably exists. Leather stropping removes the burr and produces a razor-like edge. Stropping can be accomplished by hand using a leather bench-type strop (Fig. 1-7) or by a power stropping wheel, impreg-

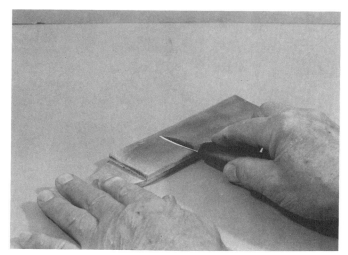

1-7 *Hand stropping the sharpened blade.*

1-8 *Gluing-up individual pieces of leather for a power stropping wheel.*

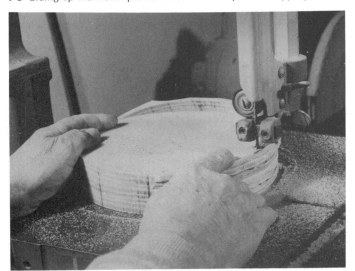

1-9 *The glued-up wheel is cut carefully on a bandsaw and sanded smooth.*

1-10 *The finished product in use.*

1-11 *A small stropping wheel powered by a drill motor. These wheels may be purchased—see Appendix.*

nated with oil and jeweler's rouge, or other fine abrasives. The author uses a 7½ inch diameter leather stropping wheel, which he made, mounted on the head stock of a wood lathe, which will turn as low as 300 rpm (Fig. 1-10). The small 3½ inch diameter leather strop was also made by the author and can be powered by an electric hand drill clamped in a vise, or held by some other means (Fig. 1-11). Three inch diameter leather stropping wheels, complete with arbor and bench type hand strops may be purchased. See Appendix for source.

Cheston Knott, maker of probably the finest carving knives and draw knife available, recommends hand stropping the knife every hour. The hand strops sold by him are double faced. The following stropping instructions were supplied by Mr. Knott.

"On one side of the leather strop, apply a coat of light oil (Neat's Foot or light general purpose oil); sprinkle this with aluminum oxide, working it into the strop. After the strop is conditioned, only an occasional application of aluminum oxide powder will be necessary. Pass the blade back and forth over the surface as a barber strops his razor. Six or eight passes on this side of the strop should be sufficient. Finish stropping on the other side of the strop after applying a few drops of oil to its surface. It is important to hold the blade flat as you strop in order to maintain a straightened edge at all times. Follow this procedure about every hour and you will be richly rewarded with a long lasting, keen-edged tool. A good knife deserves attention".

Note: Mr. Knott also has aluminum oxide powder available. (see Appendix—Carving Tools and Supplies)

USE OF THE KNIFE

There are many ways to remove the excess wood from a carving. The pocketknife or the replaceable-blade knife is the tool usually used by the beginner for carving.

To cut at right angles to the wood, the knife is normally held in a manner similar to that of holding a pencil and is pulled toward the body (Fig. 1-12). Unless the depth of cut desired is quite shallow, considerable downward and pulling forces are necessary. The knife is generally under control when used in this manner. One exception occurs when the cut is made to an edge and off the wood. As the downward and pulling forces applied to the knife are no

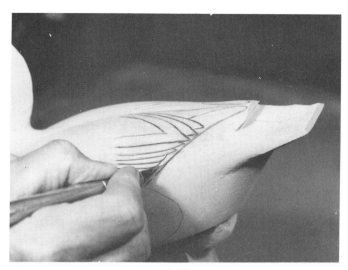

1-12

1-13

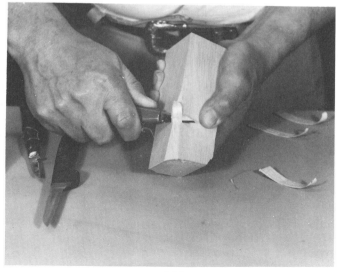

1-14

longer resisted by the wood, the knife is out of control and dangerous. It is usually advisable to make the cut as it comes off the carving into a scrap piece of wood held by the other hand with the fingers out of the way (Fig. 1-13). Using the knife to cut at right angles to the wood is useful for individual feather carving where a cut is made outlining each feather. It is also useful for cutting out the crossed primaries, in carving the bill, and in many other situations.

The knife can also be pulled or pushed with the blade held at a small angle to the surface, so that the wood is cut and removed in a manner similar to wood planing. This method is, of course, commonly known as whittling. A carver using this procedure should give special consideration to control, ease of wood removal, and safety.

Whittling can be done in several ways, three of which are described here. It is suggested that the beginner take some scrap pieces of wood and experiment with these techniques, which are described below for a right-handed person. Reverse the instructions if you are left-handed.

First, try holding the block in the left hand and whittling wood off by moving the knife, held by the closed fist of the right hand, away from the body (Fig. 1-14). It will soon be apparent that it is difficult to control the length and depth of the cut. It will also be obvious that the knife, when no longer removing wood, is difficult to stop, and at this point is out of control and can be very dangerous. This technique is useful when fairly large amounts of wood are to be removed, as when roughing down the body of the carving. If the knife is used in this manner, it is advisable to rest the carving against a scrap piece of wood to arrest the movement of the knife as it comes off the carving.

Next, try holding the block again in the left hand, but this time grasp the knife (with its cutting edge pointed toward the body) by the first and second joints of the fingers of the right hand. Stretch the thumb of the right hand so that it rests against or near the end of the block nearest the body. Now, cut with the knife toward the thumb, using the finger muscles to supply the force in a motion similar to that of closing the hand (Fig. 1-15). Actually, this method is very natural and is exactly like paring a potato. Although the knife is moving toward the thumb, all the power is supplied by the fingers, and there is very little danger of cutting the thumb. This method provides excellent control, not only of the depth, but also of the length of the cut.

The third method of whittling involves holding the block by the left hand and the knife by the four fingers and thumb of the right hand. This time the cutting edge is pointed away from the body. The power is supplied by the thumb muscles of the left hand in the pushing motion (Fig. 1-16). Here, again, the knife and the cut are under good control. This method of whittling works especially well when the carving is held rigidly by a jig or vise, leaving both hands free to remove the wood.

1-12 *Cutting at right angles to the wood.*

1-13 *Cutting off the edge into a scrap piece of wood.*

1-14 *Whittling. Force is supplied by the arm muscles.*

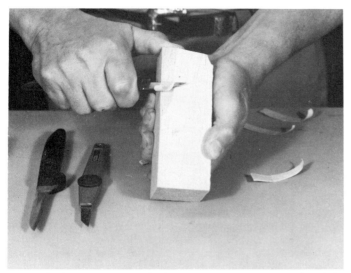

1-15 *Whittling. Force is supplied mainly by the thumb muscles of the left hand.*

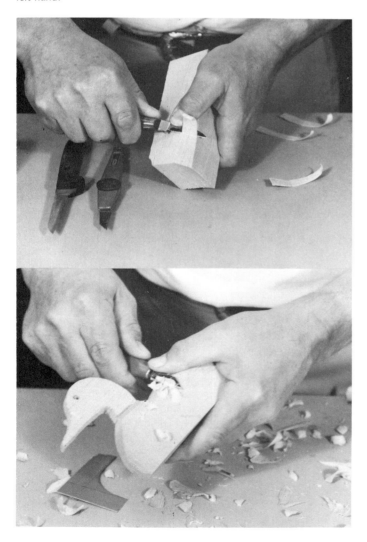

1-16 *Whittling. Force is supplied by the fingers.*

Regardless of the method used, it is essential for good control that the knife edge cuts down at a small angle to the grain of the wood. When the knife or any other sharp cutting tool is used in this manner, the wood is cut cleanly and there is no tendency for the wood to split or tear. This is commonly called, somewhat inaccurately, "cutting with the grain" (Fig. 1-17). If the cut is made angling up toward the grain, or even parallel to the grain, the wood will be split rather than cut. This is called "cutting against the grain," again not an accurate description. Sometimes, when a large amount of wood must be removed, it is desirable to cut up against or parallel to the

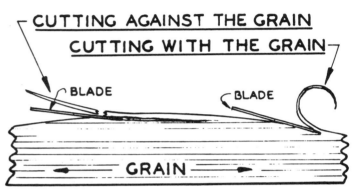

1-17 *Cutting with and against the grain.*

grain and split off fairly large pieces. When this is done, considerable care must be exercised to prevent removing too much wood.

As the beginner progresses, the use of other carving tools will be discussed.

SIMPLE FEATHER CARVING

Simple feather carving can be accomplished with the knife and consists of cutting at right angles along the outline of the feather and whittling in relief with force being usually supplied by the first or the first and second fingers of the left hand. It is suggested that the beginner practice this technique before starting an actual carving.

First, sketch three or four feathers on a piece of scrap wood (Fig. 1-18). Then, using the point of a sharp knife (a #24 Exacto blade works well), cut-in the outline of each feather (Fig. 1-19). Next, remove wood fairly deep from the bottom and right side of the feather group until it stands out (Fig. 1-20). Start carving the first feather by very carefully removing wood at an approximate 45° angle bevel cut next to the adjacent feather (Fig. 1-21). It is important that the knife point cuts just up to the adjacent feather but does not remove any of it. Complete the feather by removing wood at a flatter angle until the beveled cut extends across the entire feather (Fig. 1-22). Repeat this operation for the rest of the feathers and carefully sand each feather smooth (Fig. 1-22A).

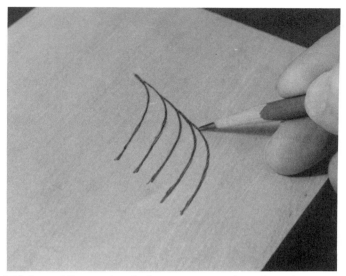

1-18 *Lay out three or four feathers on a scrap piece of wood.*

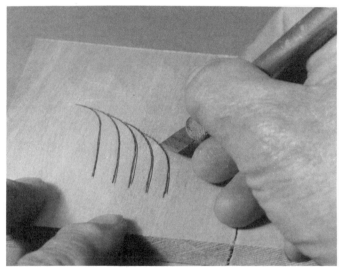

1-19 *Cut-in the outline of each feather.*

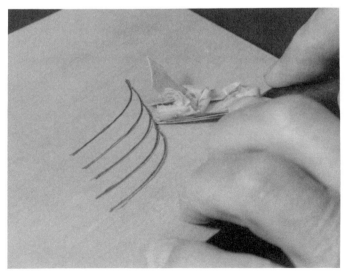

1-20 *Remove wood to make the feather group prominent.*

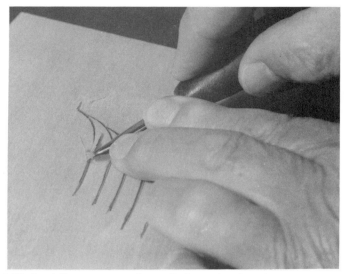

1-21 *Carefully remove wood at a 45 degree bevel angle.*

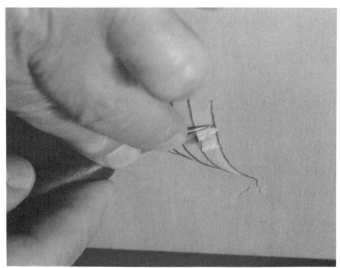

1-22 *Extend bevel cut at a flatter angle across the feather.*

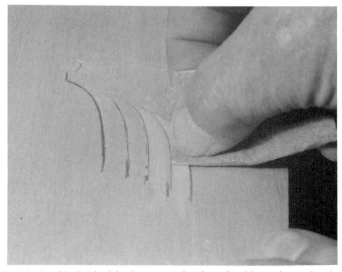

1-22A *Sand individual feathers smooth. They should stand out cleanly.*

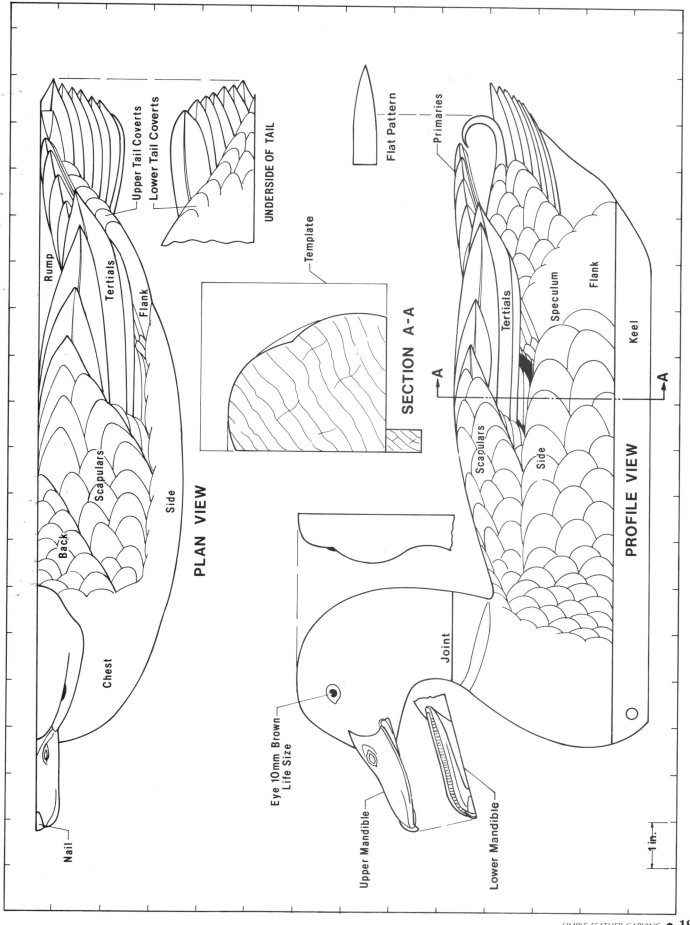

Upper Tail Coverts
Lower Tail Coverts

UNDERSIDE OF TAIL

Flat Pattern

Primaries

Rump

Tertials

Flank

Template

SECTION A-A

Tertials

Speculum

Flank

Scapulars

Back

Scapulars

Side

Keel

A

A

Chest

PLAN VIEW

Side

PROFILE VIEW

Joint

Eye 10mm Brown
Life Size

Upper Mandible

Lower Mandible

Nail

1 in.

1-24 *Mallard drake decoy.*

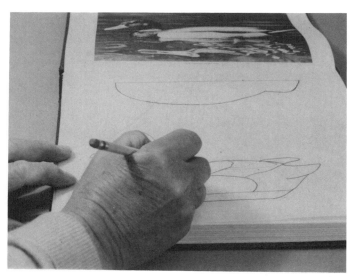

1-25 *Make a tracing of the plan and profile views.*

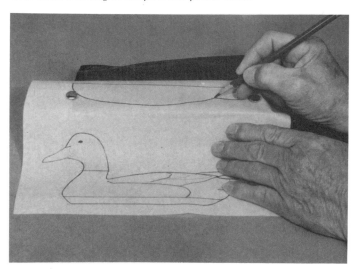

1-26 *Transfer plan view to top of body block.*

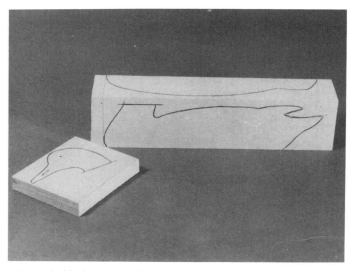

1-27 *Body block and head blank are ready to be cut out.*

CARVING A HALF-BODY MALLARD DRAKE DECOY
(See Fig. 1-23, page 18 and Fig. 1-216, 217, page 73)

Many beginning bird carvers buy all of the books available on the subject and attend many classes and seminars with the idea they can learn bird carving without expending any great effort on their part. Unfortunately, and as was stated in the introduction, the only way a beginner can learn bird carving is by doing—not once or twice, but many times—each time trying to improve upon the mistakes he made earlier. Also, many beginners, in hope they can create a masterpiece on their first attempt, start out on carving projects which are beyond their capabilities and, as a result, become frustrated and discouraged. It is very important that the novice begin with a simple carving—one that can be completed with simple tools and in a relatively short time—and then progress to more difficult carvings as fast as his knowledge and ability will permit.

A half-body decoy has been chosen for the beginner's first project. This is one of the simplest carvings, for problems connected with symmetry are eliminated and the amount of wood that must be removed is considerably less than with a full-body decoy. The project has been further simplified by making it one-half life size, again reducing the amount of wood removal. For species, a mallard drake was selected as mallards are the most common of all ducks and are usually found in most parks where they can be studied at close range.

Three pieces of wood, a block $1\frac{3}{4} \times 2 \times 8$ inches for the body, a piece $\frac{1}{2} \times 2 \times 3$ inches for the head, and a piece $\frac{1}{4} \times \frac{3}{8} \times 6\frac{1}{2}$ inches for the keel are required. If cutting the material to size presents a problem, take the wood to a lumberyard or a cabinet shop and have the pieces ripped to size on a table saw. It is strongly suggested that the beginner have enough wood cut to size for three carvings inasmuch as he may wish to make more than one decoy so that he can correct the mistakes he may make on the first carving or two.

Although an inexpensive set of chisels would be helpful, about the only tools required for this project are a coping saw and knife. Other materials required include a 5-mm brown eye (see Appendix for sources), some 2/0 and 4/0 sandpaper, white glue or 5-minute epoxy, Plastic Wood or a similar product, and a small piece of thin aluminum or other metal for the curled tail feather.

Figure 1-24 as printed is one-half life size and can be copied without the necessity of reducing or enlarging and any required dimensions can be taken directly off the drawing. First, make a tracing of the profile and plan view, also the cross-sectional view, from the drawing (Fig. 1-25).

> Note: Unless the carver plans to make many carvings from a particular drawing or pattern, there is no need to go to the additional work of cutting out a template.

After the tracing is completed, locate the plan view on the top of the body block and fix in place with thumb tacks (Fig. 1-26) and transfer drawing to the block by means of carbon paper. Locate the profile view on the side of the

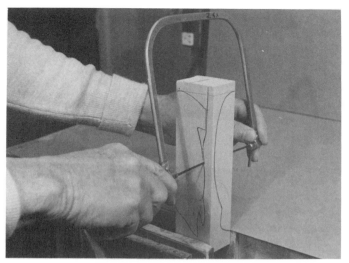

1-28 *Saw out profile view with coping saw.*

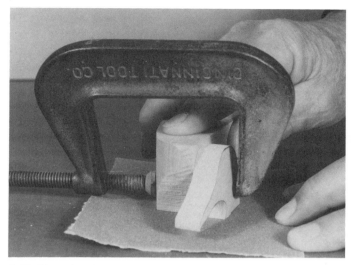

1-31 *Clamp head to body block for accurate sanding.*

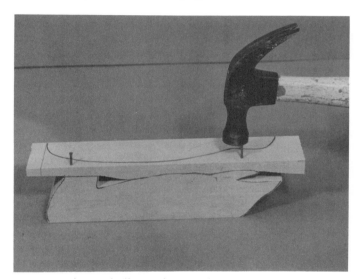

1-29 *Reattach sawed off piece bearing plan view to body.*

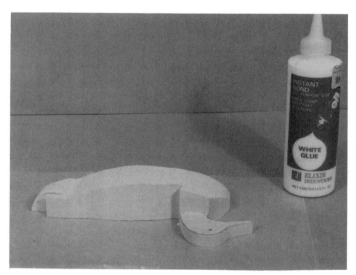

1-32 *Lay parts on waxed paper and glue head to body.*

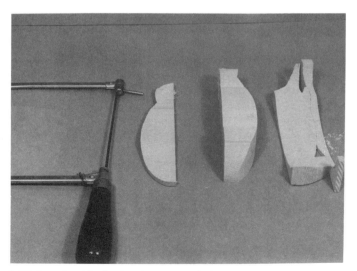

1-30 *Sawed-out body showing removed pieces.*

body block, properly aligned with the plan view, and transfer it to the block in a similar manner. Transfer the head drawing to the ½ inch thick piece of wood, locating the head so that the bill is parallel to the grain (Fig.1-27).

Using a coping saw, carefully cut out the block to the profile layout (Fig. 1-28). Reattach the sawed-off piece (which bears the plan view) to the body with two small nails placed so that they will not interfere with the plan view cut (Fig. 1-29) which is accomplished next. Figure 1-30 shows the sawed-out body with the removed pieces. After the body block has been sawed to shape, cut out the head. If sawing these parts presents a problem, it may be possible to take them to a cabinet shop and have them sawed on a band saw.

It is important that the head-body joint be made in a workmanlike manner. Perhaps the easiest way this can be accomplished is to sand both parts flat and square. One

1-33 *Good rear view of mallard drake. Cross-sectional shape shows well in this photo.*

1-34 *Good profile view of mallard drake's head.*

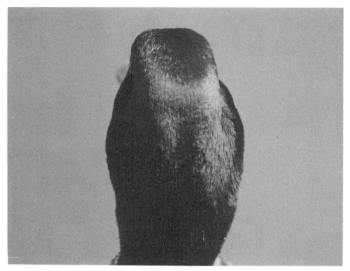

1-35 *Rear view of mallard drake's head.*

1-36 *Bill and eye details show up well in this view.*

1-37 *Considerable bill, head, and body carving information can be gotten from photo.*

way this can be done is to clamp the head to the back side of the body block as shown in Figure 1-31 and sand the parts simultaneously on a piece of sandpaper placed and held on a flat surface.

Place the body block on a piece of waxed paper laid upon a flat surface and glue the head in position with either white glue or 5-minute epoxy (Fig. 1-32). While the glue is setting, transfer the cross-sectional view to a piece of cardboard, or thin plastic, and cut out as shown in Fig. 1-39. A cross-sectional template is not actually necessary when doing a carving that is not symmetrical, but its use provides good experience in working accurately to a predetermined shape.

Before starting carving operations, the beginner should make an attempt to study all available photographs of the drake mallard and, if at all possible, to study the live bird. First, study the profile shape of the duck (Fig. 1-23). See Figure 1-33 and particularly note the cross-sectional

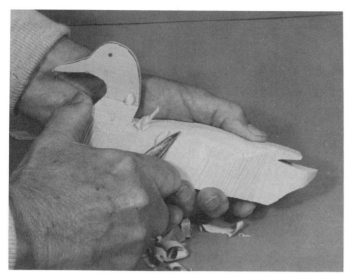

1-38 *Start wood removal from midsection.*

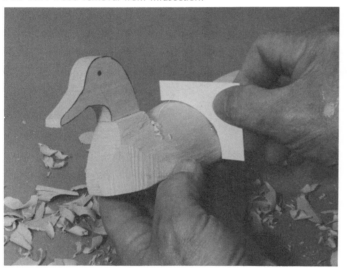

1-39 *Use the template to check body cross-sectional shape.*

1-40 *Sand carving occasionally to check overall progress.*

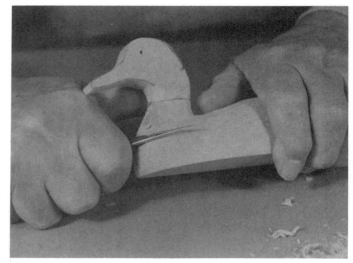

1-41 *Carve the chest by rounding off this area.*

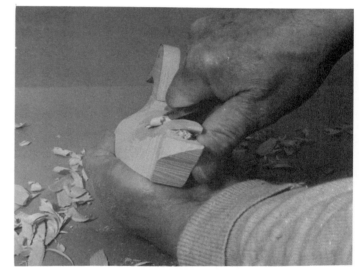

1-42 *Rough-carve the back and upper side of the primaries.*

shape of the body and the shape of the tail as seen from the rear. Refer to Figures 1-34, 1-35, and 1-36 and study the shape of the bill, the profile of the head, the shape of the eye and the shape of the head as seen from the rear. See Figure 1-37 and note the back feathers, the shape of the bill and head, and how the primary groups extend from the body.

Start the carving operation by removing wood from the body near the midsection (Fig. 1-38), checking the body shape with the template to avoid removing too much wood (Fig. 1-39). Make small, unhurried cuts with the grain, which will require turning the carving end-for-end from time to time. Sand the body at intervals as the carving progresses to obtain a better idea of the overall shape (Fig. 1-40). When the body shape matches the template, start removing wood from the chest (Fig. 1-41) and back areas (Fig. 1-42) until the desired shape is approached.

1-43 *Outline the tail location.*

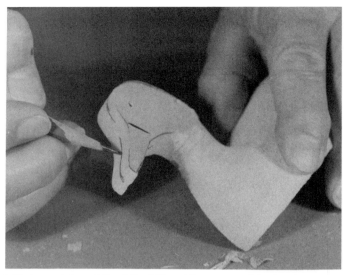

1-46 *Lay out the width of the bill and the crown of the head.*

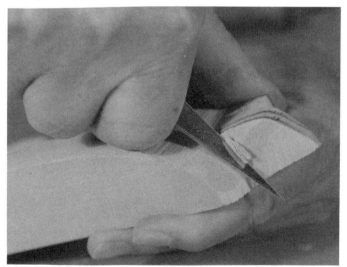

1-44 *Remove wood from the lower tail covert area.*

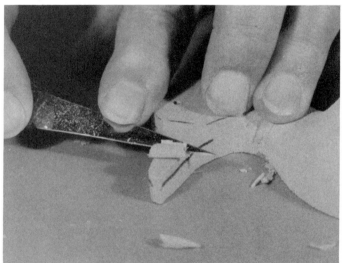

1-47 *Remove wood from the bill area.*

1-45 *Continue by shaping the neck area.*

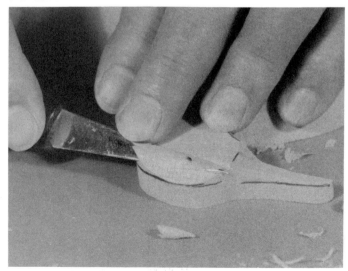

1-48 *Remove wood above the eye down to the crown width.*

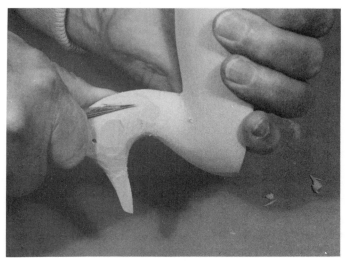

1-49 *Remove excess wood from the back of the head and in the cheek area.*

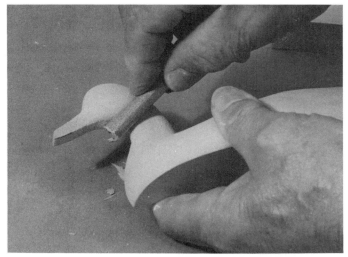

1-52 *Sanding of the neck can be facilitated by wrapping sandpaper around a small dowel.*

Continue by outlining the tail location on the side of the body block (Fig. 1-43) and remove wood from the underside of the tail (Fig. 1-44). Proceed to the neck area and remove wood there after first checking the neck shape on the drawing. See Fig. 1-24, page 19 and Fig. 1-45.

Next, lay out the width of the bill on both the upper and lower sides and mark the appoximate rearward extent of the bill. Also at this time, lay out the width of the crown on the upper part of the head (Fig. 1-46).

Carefully remove wood in the bill area down to the drawn lines (Fig. 1-47). Continue by removing wood above the eye down to the width of the crown (Fig. 1-48) and rough shape the rear of the head after referring to the planform shape of the head shown on the drawing (Fig. 1-24). Rough carve the rest of the head (Fig. 1-49, 1-50 and 1-51) and sand. Sanding the neck and chin areas can be facilitated by wrapping sandpaper around a dowel or pencil (Fig. 1-52).

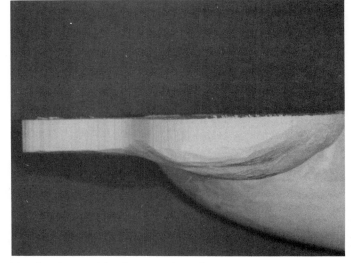

1-51 *Rough-carved head as seen from above.*

1-53 *Lay out the intersection of the bill and head.*

1-54 *Remove wood at the base of the bill to the proper depth.*

1-57 *Remove wood from the underside of the bill in the chin area.*

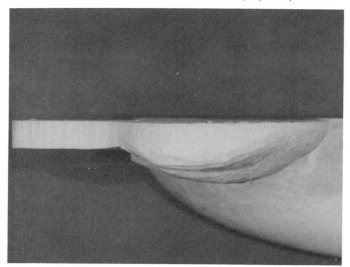

1-55 *Wood removal at the base of the bill as seen from above.*

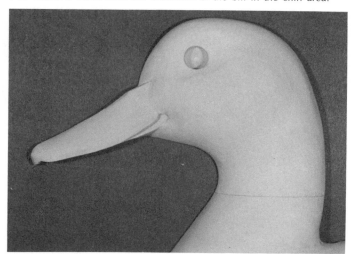

1-58 *Remove excess wood from the chin area and sand smooth. Lay out the lower edge of the lower mandible. Drill for eye.*

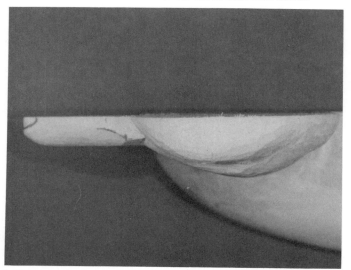

1-56 *Shape cheek area down to the intersection of the bill.*

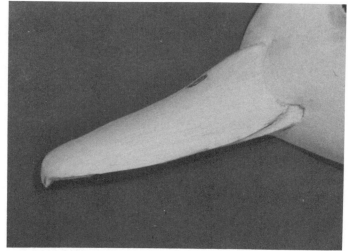

1-59 *Remove wood below the upper mandible down to the lower mandible.*

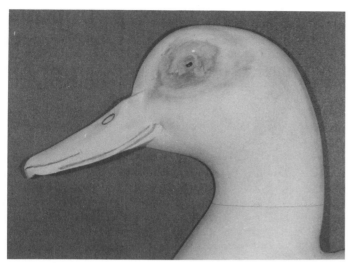

1-60 *Install the eye with Plastic Wood. Add more Plastic Wood around periphery of the eye. Locate the groove on the upper mandible and locate the nostril.*

1-61 *Add bill detail and shape eye.*

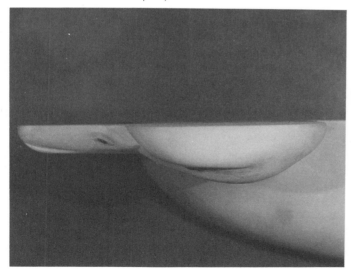

1-62 *Completed head and bill as seen from above.*

Referring to the drawing of the bill (Fig.1-24) and photographs Figures 1-34, 1-36, and 1-37, carefully draw the intersection of the bill and the head (Fig. 1-53) and remove wood from the bill area to the proper depth (Figs. 1-54 and 1-55). Proceed with the carving of the bill by rounding the front of the bill to shape, as seen in the planform (Fig. 1-56). Looking at the drawing of the underside on the bill (Fig. 1-24), note how the chin intersects the lower mandible in the form of a "V". Remove the excess wood in this area (Fig. 1-57). Round-off the chin area and lay out the lower edge of the upper mandible and remove wood down to the lower mandible (Fig. 1-58).

Now is a good time to install the eye so that the Plastic Wood can be drying. Drill a hole of the proper diameter for the glass eye (if a drill is not available, the hole can be made with a pointed knife or a small gouge). Partially fill the hole with Plastic Wood and insert the eye to the proper depth. Add more Plastic Wood around the periphery of the eye and allow to dry thoroughly (Fig. 1-60).

Depending on the beginner's desires and ability, considerably more detail can be added to the bill. Refer again to the bill photographs and Figure 1-24 and draw the groove lines on the upper mandible near the front and along the side (Fig. 1-60). Also, locate and draw the outline of the nail. Carefully remove wood from these areas, referring to the bill photographs from time to time. Sand smooth and round-off the bill's edges with sandpaper. Locate the nostril by taking dimensions from the drawing (Fig. 24). The nostril can be duplicated in several ways. One of the easiest ways is to heat an ice pick and burn the oval-shaped hole. Another way is to make two holes with the point of the ice pick at the forward and rear extremities of the nostril and carefully cut out the opening with a pointed knife. The nostril can then be finished by rubbing the point of the pick around the hole. The nostril can be made to stand out realistically by rubbing the point of the ice pick around the nostril. See Figures 1-34, 1-61, and 1-62.

Using the tip of a small knife, carefully scrape away excess Plastic Wood around the eye until it is realistically shaped. See Figures 1-34 and 1-61. Very carefully sand the area around the eye, taking care that the sandpaper does not scratch the glass eye.

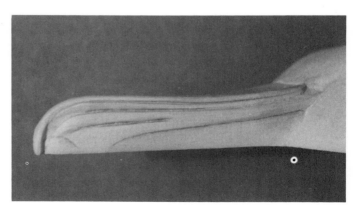

1-63 *Showing completed underside of bill.*

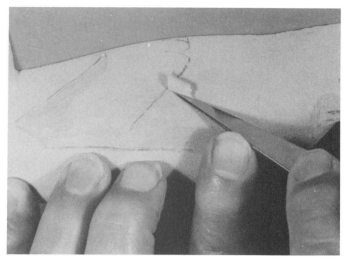

1-64 *Remove wood to make scapular and back feather groups stand out.*

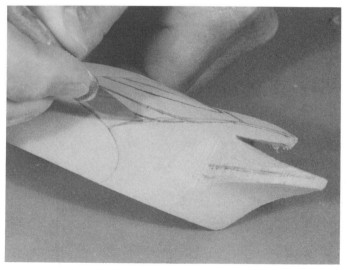

1-65 *Shape primary group and lay out tertials*

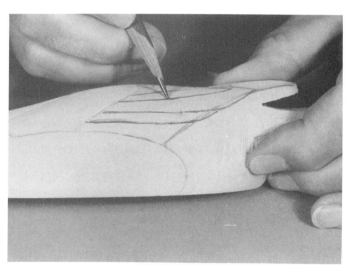

1-66 *Cut around primaries and tertials.*

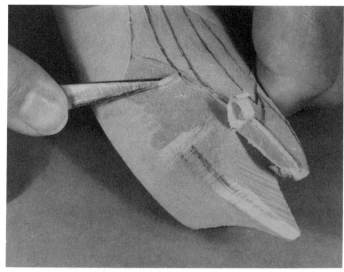

1-67 *Remove wood from the primary and tertial feather group areas.*

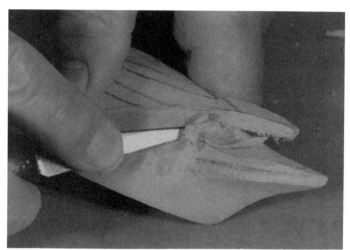

1-68 *Continue by removing wood in the rump and upper tail covert area.*

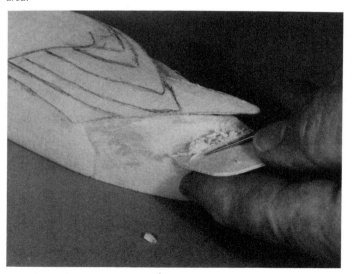

1-69 *Carve the upper side of the tail.*

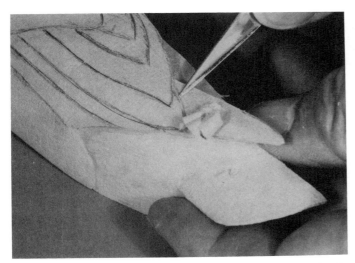

1-70 *Remove wood from the inner side of the tertials to make the primary feather group prominent.*

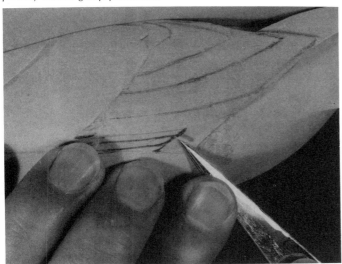

1-71 *Carve the speculum.*

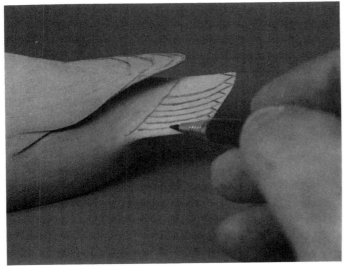

1-72 *Lay out the individual tail feathers.*

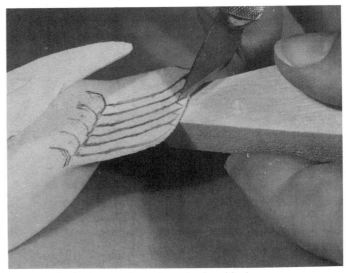

1-73 *Cut the feather notches using a backup block.*

Refer now to the drawing of the underside of the bill (Fig. 1-24) and the photograph of the bill's underside on page 353. Outline the lower mandible on the carving and draw in the lower mandible details. Make shallow cuts along these lines and remove wood to make these details stand out (Fig. 1-63).

Again, refer to the drawing (Fig. 1-24) and lay out the extent of the back feathers, scapulars, and side feathers on the carving. Make knife cuts at right angles along these lines and remove wood so that each feather group stands out (Fig. 1-64).

Next, lay out the folded primaries as they rest over the flank and upper tail coverts. Also draw-in the tertial feathers (Fig. 1-65). Make knife cuts along the rear of the primaries and tertials and also along the inner edges of the tertials and primaries (Fig. 1-66) and start removing wood from these areas (Fig. 1-67).

Continue removing wood from the flank and upper tail covert areas (Fig. 1-68). In order to cut with the grain, it will be necessary to change direction of the cuts when removing wood on the upper side of the tail and in the tail covert area (Fig. 1-69). Remove wood from the rump area and along the inner edge of the primaries until the primary group stands out realistically (Fig. 1-70). Remove wood from the underside of the primaries until they are about $1/16$th of an inch thick. Lay out the secondaries (speculum) and remove wood from them until they are prominent (Fig. 1-71). After the tail has been reduced in thickness, lay out the individual tail feathers (see Fig. 1-24) and cut along these lines. Cut out the notches at the rear of the tail feathers backing up the cuts with a scrap piece of wood (Fig. 1-73) and carve the individual tail feathers (Fig. 1-74). If desired, the underside of the tail may also be carved. Refer to the drawing (Fig. 1-24) and note the flat layout of the curled tail feather (actually, one of the inner upper tail covert feathers). Cut this feather from thin aluminum sheet and bend as shown. Remove a small amount of wood the width and thickness of the curled feather and cement this simulated feather in place

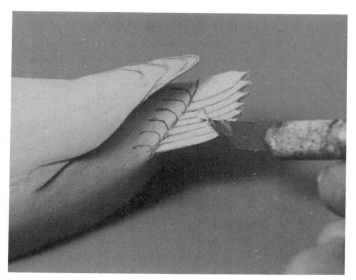

1-74 *Individually carve the tail feathers.*

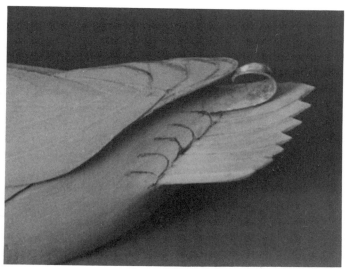

1-75 *Install the curled tail feather with epoxy.*

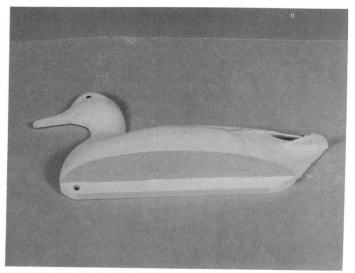

1-76 *Glue the keel to the body.*

1-77 *The carving is now ready for paint.*

using 5-minute epoxy (Fig. 1-75). Cut the keel to shape and glue to the body using waxed paper in a manner similar to the gluing-on of the head (Fig. 1-76). Eliminate all tool marks by carefully sanding the entire carving. The carving is now ready for painting.

The beginner should now look at his creation with a critical eye and also, if possible, have a more experienced carver inspect it. If a particular area of the carving can be improved by removing more wood, this should be done immediately. If there are obvious errors or imperfections that cannot be corrected, the carving should be done over. This is a simple carving—its main purpose is to provide practice. It is much better to learn one's mistakes here, and how to correct them, than to find them out later on a more complicated and time consuming carving. If the novice finds he has done an adequate job, considering his experience, he may wish to consider doing another one-half life size mallard drake but this time making it a full-body decoy and trying to incorporate even more detail. It is a simple matter to go from a half-body to a full-body using the tracing already made. The plan view is transferred to the left side of a body block of twice the thickness. It is then flipped over and is transferred to the right side. Of course, the piece of wood for the head must be twice as thick, too.

Once the novice is satisfied with the carving work on his first piece, he should then turn to Chapter 2, Painting for Beginners, page 81. Even if he has already done some painting, it is strongly suggested that he read the text on paint mixing and matching before attempting to paint his carving. It is very important that he has a thorough understanding of the basics before starting to apply paint. The painting of the mallard drake is covered in detail, starting on page 99. A full color illustation of the painted male mallard is shown in Fig. 2-100, page 121.

ENLARGING OR REDUCING DRAWINGS

All of the drawings for carving projects in this book have marginal marks at intervals that represent one inch on the life-size bird. In most cases, depending upon the scale the carver wishes to use, it will be necessary either to enlarge or to reduce the printed drawing accordingly. There are a number of ways by which this can be accomplished.

The drawing to be changed can be photographed and enlarged, or reduced, to the desired size by the darkroom enlarger, and then printed. The image from the negative (or positive) can also be projected onto a piece of paper by means of a home projector. The projector is moved either closer or further away until the projected image is the correct size, at which time it can be traced.

Drawings can be enlarged, or reduced, by the use of a pantograph (see Appendix for availability). It is, however, very difficult to accurately follow with the stylus the lines of the drawing which is being altered in size. In addition, if the drawing is being enlarged, errors are amplified by the ratio the drawing is being increased in size. Much better results can be gotten if a template is made from the drawing to be enlarged. The template, when used with the pantograph, provides a positive surface for the stylus

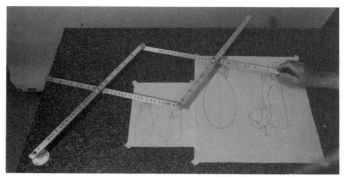

1-78 *Drawings can be enlarged, or reduced, by means of a pantograph.*

to ride against. The enlarged drawing shown in Figure 1-78 has been corrected extensively and darkened so a printable photograph could be made.

Probably the simplest way to alter the scale of a drawing is by the use of squares. First, connect the corresponding marks on the printed drawing in both the horizontal and vertical directions. (Trace the drawing onto thin, translucent paper, or vellum, if marking up the book is objectionable.) Starting from the lower left hand corner, assign numbers to both the horizontal and vertical lines as shown in Figure 1-79.

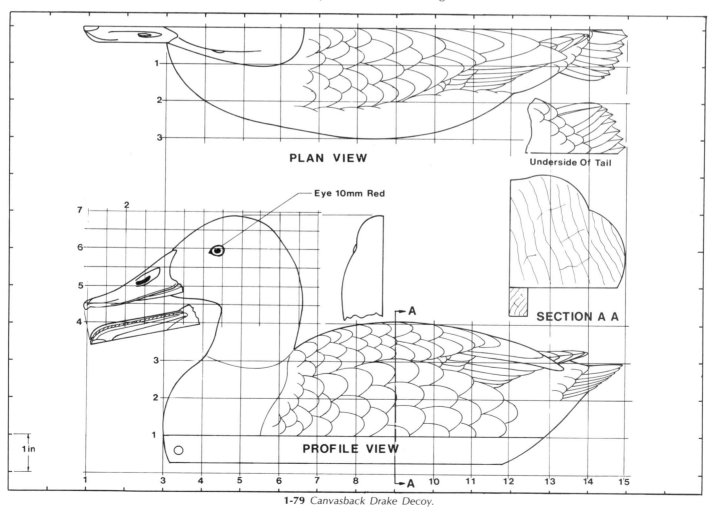

1-79 *Canvasback Drake Decoy.*

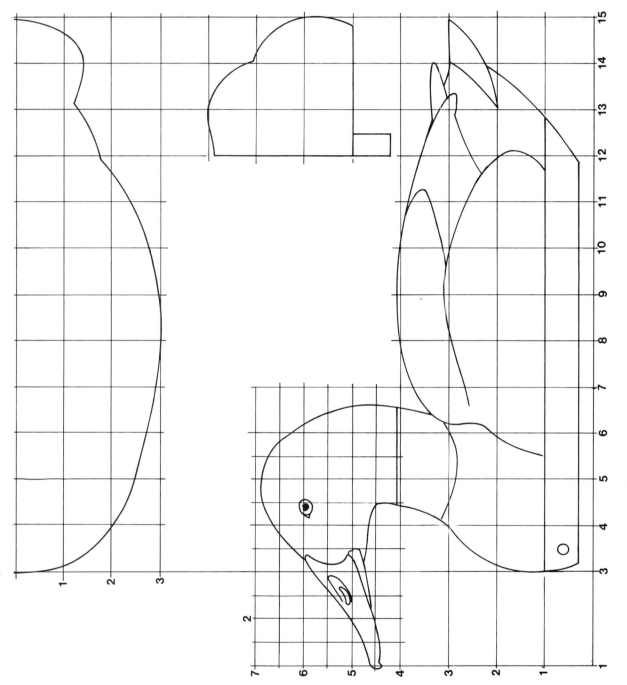

1-80 Canvasback drake drawing enlarged to one-half life size.

To make a life-size drawing, make a layout composed of vertical and horizontal lines forming one-inch squares. An easy way this can be accomplished is to first lay out a rectangle measuring 14 × 18 inches on a large piece of paper. If the construction of an accurate rectangle presents a problem, 22 × 28 inch sheets of graph paper, subdivided into ¼ inch squares are available. (See Appendix for source). Figure 1-81 pictures an enlargement made on this paper. After the rectangle is drawn, add the one-inch marks on its borders and draw lines connecting the corresponding marks. Number the lines exactly the same as the lines on the smaller drawing.

The life-size drawing is now easily made freehand by intersecting the numbered lines in the same manner as those on the drawing being altered (Fig. 1-80). In areas such as the bill and head, where more accuracy is required, it is often advantageous to use smaller squares.

Although enlarging or reducing a drawing by the squares method may sound a little complicated, it is actually quite simple and can be accomplished in a relatively short time.

If a drawing three-fourths life-size is required, the layout is then made up of lines forming ¾-inch squares. If a drawing 80% of life-size is desired, .80 inch squares would be drawn.

Suppose that the carver wishes to make a miniature carving of a canvasback drake with a body length of three inches. The life-size body length of a canvasback drake is approximately 12 inches (see Fig. 1-79). The size of the squares for the drawing of the miniature carving would then be:

$$\frac{3}{12} \times 1.0 \text{ (size of the squares on the life-size drawing)} = .25, \text{ or } \frac{1}{4}\text{-inch.}$$

Game bird drawings of an unknown scale can also be easily enlarged, or reduced, by the squares method. See

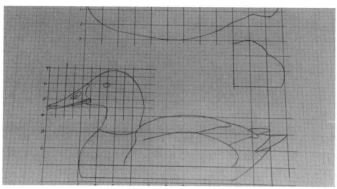

1-81 An enlargement made on graph paper.

accompanying drawing of a female green-winged teal (Fig. 1-82). Start by drawing equally spaced horizontal and vertical lines forming, for example, ½-inch squares. Suppose that the carver wishes to make a life-size carving from this drawing. By referring to the dimensional chart on page 335, the body length of a female green-winged teal is found to be 9 inches. The length of the body as measured on the drawing (Fig. 1-82) is 6 inches. The size of the squares on the life-size drawing would then be:

$$\frac{9}{6} \times \frac{1}{2} \text{ (size of the squares on the small drawing)} = .75 \text{ or } \frac{3}{4} \text{ inch.}$$

DETERMINING DIMENSIONS WITH PROPORTIONAL DIVIDERS

Although proportional dividers have been used for many years by draftsmen, few carvers are aware of their usefulness. The double-pointed legs on this precision tool have a common fulcrum which is movable so that differ-

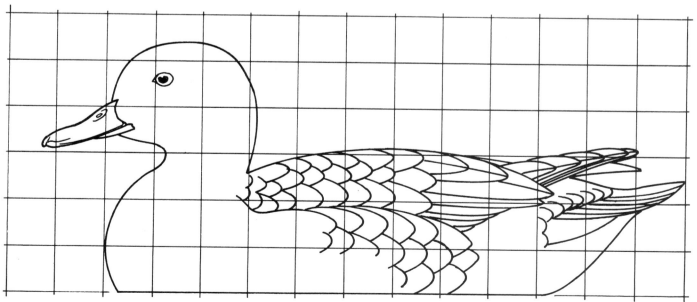

1-82 Female green-winged teal decoy.

ent ratios can be obtained between the leg spreads on either side of the fulcrum. Once the desired ratio is set, dimensions can be taken off an object or a drawing and, by reversing ends of the divider, a constant enlargement, or reduction, can be easily obtained. The proportional dividers pictured (Fig. 1-83) are calibrated to give ratios from 10:1 to ¾:1 and can be easily adjusted to any intermediate ratio. They are available at most drafting supply stores.

Proportional dividers are ideal for obtaining dimensions from actual specimens, or life-size drawings, to be used for smaller-than-life carvings. Suppose the carver wishes to make a ½ size carving and has an actual specimen from which to work. He can then set the proportional dividers at a 2 : 1 ratio and spread the dividers, for example, to the length of the bill on the specimen and, by reversing ends, obtain the length of the bill for the ½ size carving in one simple operation.

Proportional dividers can be used very effectively to determine actual life-size dimensions from photographs of game birds. Fig. 1-102 shows a good, true profile of a canvasback drake. First, it is necessary to set the proportional dividers to the correct ratio. Refer to the life-size photograph of the canvasback male's bill on page 357. The length of his bill, as measured on this photograph is 2½ inches. Place two marks on a piece of soft scrap wood exactly 2½ inches apart. Spread the lower legs of the proportional dividers to this amount and force the points firmly into the wood on the marks, as shown in Fig. 1-84. Next, measure the length of the bill in the canvasback photograph, Fig. 1-102, which is found to be 1¼-inches. Now, loosen the nut and carefully move the fulcrum upward, equally on both legs, until the distance between the upper points corresponds exactly to this length; then tighten the fulcrum nut securely.

It is now possible to easily determine such dimensions as the life-size distance from the tip of the bill to nostril, the length of the nostril, the distance from the tip of the bill to the eye, the overall length of the head, the fore and aft width of the neck, the length of the tail and the distance from the tip of the tail to the side feathers. The capacity of the proportional dividers pictured here is not quite sufficient to measure the overall body length.

This dimension can be gotten, however, by making a mark halfway between the tip of the tail and the forward line of the chest, determining this dimension with the dividers, and then multiplying it by 2.

There is one limitation to determining life-size dimensions from a photo in the manner just described—the dimensions desired must be in the plane of the paper, i. e. the photo must not have been taken at an oblique angle.

HOLDING FIXTURES

Before starting the next project, a very useful home-made tool, the holding fixture, will be introduced. A holding fixture does the work of a third hand (actually, it does the job much better than a third hand). It is simply a rigid support that can be easily attached to the carving by means of wood screws. The fixture is in turn attached to

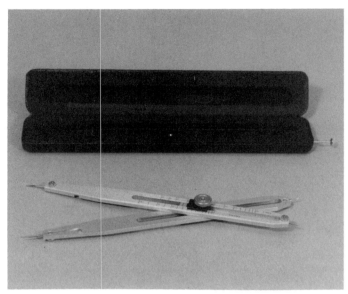

1-83 *Proportional dividers are an extremely useful tool.*

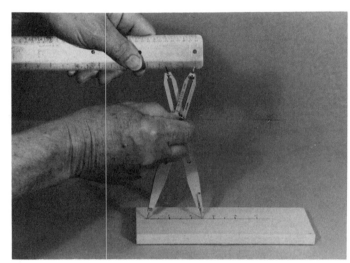

1-84 *An easy way to set the proper ratio.*

the workbench, or table, by a vise or clamp.

Simple holding fixtures can reduce carving time and effort drastically and can actually improve the quality of the carving by freeing both hands for guiding wood-removal tools. In addition, a much greater selection of carving tools can be utilized when both hands are unhampered and when the block is rigidly held by the fixture. Efficient and less tiring wood-removing tools, such as the drawknife, Surform rasps, and the spokeshave can be used—tools which are operated by the combined efforts of both arms and hands instead of tools like the knife or chisel where the force is supplied by one hand or even the fingers of one hand. Power tools, such as the Fore-dome flexible shaft tool and the die grinder can be used with greater accuracy when guided by both hands. Furthermore, the larger the carving, the more important the holding fixture, for more wood removal is entailed. Last,

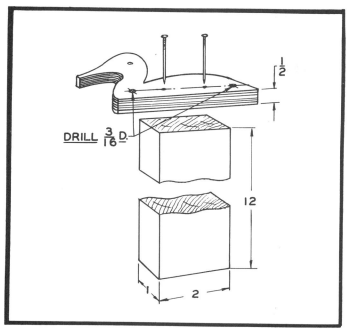

1-85 *Holding fixture for half-body decoys.*

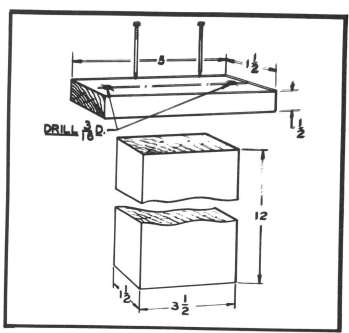

1-88 *Holding fixture for full-body decoy.*

1-86 *The carving is attached with woodscrews.*

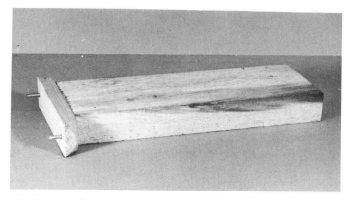

1-89 *Completed holding fixture for full-body decoy.*

1-87 *Half-body decoys installed on holding fixture.*

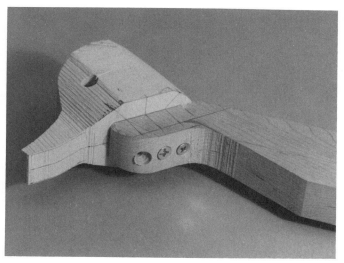

1-89A *Simple holding fixture for carving heads.*

and of considerable importance, the risk of accidently cutting oneself is greatly reduced when the carving is not hand held. See Figures 1-85 through 1-89A.

The author has not hand-held a carving, even a head, during the carving operation for many years. He feels that the use of his left arm and hand is much too valuable to waste doing a job that can be done much better by a couple of pieces of scrap wood. Recently, when re-doing the half-body mallard decoy project for this revision, he was forced to do this carving without benefit of a holding fixture and was amazed to find how much more difficult it was to shape even such a simple piece working in this manner.

1-90 The Mechanical Power Arm—an excellent holding fixture.

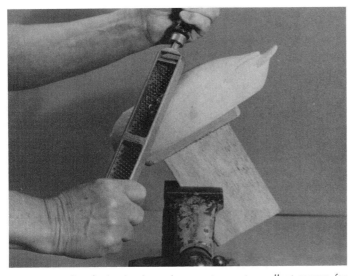

1-91 A metalworker's vise is an inexpensive and excellent means for supporting a carving when used in conjunction with a homemade holding fixture.

Although not cheap, the Mechanical Power Arm (Fig. 1-90) is an excellent holding fixture for the carver who plans to concentrate mainly on decoy-type carvings. It is well designed, strongly made, will hold large carvings rigidly, and has considerable flexibility. Two different sizes are available—the larger is a much more useful tool. (See Appendix for availability).

The Power Arm, like all holding fixtures, is no better than the table or bench supporting it. It is strongly recommended the aspiring birdcarver make every effort to build, or buy, a strong, rugged workbench. See Figure 1-3.

A vise, either a metalworker's or a woodworker's, is an essential piece of equipment for the carver. The author uses a quick-release woodworker's vise for most carving operations. For carving metal feet and for some other operations, he prefers a metalworker's vise (Fig. 1-91).

USE OF OTHER CARVING TOOLS

The drawknife, Stanley Surform rasps, and the spokeshave are excellent tools for removing the wood down to the approximate final shape and are much more efficient and less tiring to use than a knife. Both hands are required to use these tools effectively; therefore, a holding fixture must be employed.

Drawknives are available with blades approximately six, eight, ten, and twelve inches long. (Refer to the Appendix for tool suppliers.) For roughing down the smaller-scale carvings, the six-inch blade is preferred. For larger, life-size carvings, the eight- or ten-inch blade can be used to advantage. Drawknives are normally pulled toward the body, with the blade at a small angle to the surface (Fig. 1-93). Rather than turning the carving end-for-end so that the cut can be made with the grain, it is sometimes easier to reverse the tool and make the cut by pushing the drawknife away from the body (Fig. 1-94). Controlling the depth of cut with the drawknife is a little tricky, so its use should be limited to roughing operations only.

Once the carving has been cut down to its approximate rough shape, use a tool whose depth of cut can be more accurately controlled. The Stanley Surform rasp is excellent for removing wood down to the final shape. These fine rasps were introduced a number of years ago by Stanley Tools. They are made from very thin, hardened and tempered Sheffield steel and provide constant depth of cut, predetermined by design, which makes it possible to remove wood easily and quite safely from a surface that is curved in both directions, a difficult operation by almost any other means, except for sandpapering. In construction and manner of cutting, they are very similar to a kitchen grater. The many formed and sharpened teeth act as tiny wood planes, and each has an opening for the shavings to pass through, thereby eliminating clogging and assuring a clean cut with every stroke.

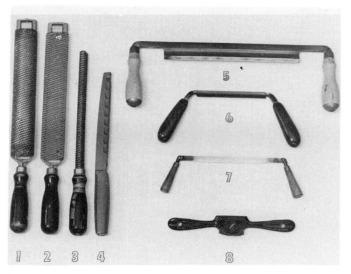

1-92 (1-4, Stanley Surform rasps; (5) Greenlee drawknife; (6) Knotts Knives drawknife; (7) homemade drawknife; (8) spokeshave. (See Appendix.)

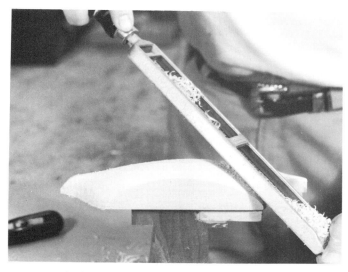

1-95 Using the half-round Surform rasp to shape the chest.

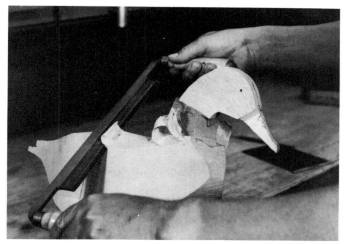

1-93 Use drawknife to rough out the body.

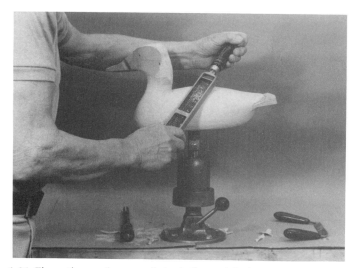

1-96 The author prefers to pull the half-round Surform rasp.

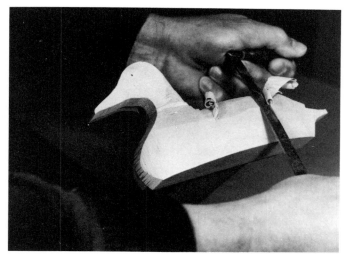

1-94 The drawknife can also be pushed with good results.

These rasps, like the conventional solid rasps, are normally pushed (Figs. 1-90, 1-95). However, if the direction of the grain permits, the author prefers to pull the rasp toward the body, with a motion similar to that used with the drawknife (Fig. 1-96). When the Surform rasp is used in this manner, the force required to remove the wood is more evenly divided between the arms and can be applied with less fatigue than when pushing. The Surform rasps are available in three basic shapes: flat, half-round, and round. The flat-rasp probably is the least used for bird carving; however, an unmounted flat Surform rasp (or a broken piece) is useful for removing wood in tight places.

The spokeshave is very similar to the wood plane, except that its shorter base permits the tool to cut on a curved surface. The spokeshave is normally pushed by two handles located on either side of the blade. The depth of cut is determined by the exposed amount of blade, which is adjustable in a manner similar to that of a

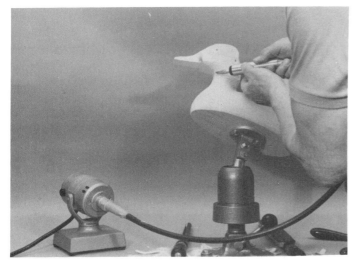

1-97 *The very popular Foredom Flexible Shaft power tool.*

1-98 *Rear view—canvasback drake.*

wood plane. The author prefers using Surform rasps rather than the spokeshave, mainly because the Surform rasps are more easily controlled and will cut end grain somewhat better than a spokeshave. This is strictly a personal preference, however, and not shared by all carvers.

In recent years, the Foredom Flexible Shaft tool (Fig. 1-97) has become very popular, not only for delicate detailing, but also for general wood removing (see Appendix for availability). Like all power tools utilizing high speed rotary type cutting tools, they are very dirty and it is advisable to wear some sort of a filtering face mask to prevent inhaling the fine wood dust.

When used with tungsten carbide burrs, this tool will remove wood fairly fast. Although the author uses the Foredom for some operations, he prefers the more powerful die grinder. More on this subject will be covered in Part III, Advanced Game Bird Carving.

1-99 *Bill and head shape show clearly in this photo.*

OTHER HALF-BODY DECOY PROJECTS

All of the drawings included in this first chapter, "Carving for Beginners", can be used as half-body decoy projects. Actually, any decorative decoy drawing shown in this book may be easily adapted and used for half-body decoys. Conversely, the half-body patterns may also be used for full-body decoys.

The half-body patterns included in this chapter are: mallard drake, canvasback drake, cinnamon teal drake, shoveler drake, and green-winged teal drake. The full-body patterns shown are: ring-necked duck drake, lesser scaup drake, bufflehead drake and wood duck drake. Painting instructions for these decoys are covered in Chapter 2. Painted illustrations, printed in full color, for these projects are also included, starting on page 121.

The half-body decoys featured here may be carved in the manner described earlier for the mallard drake. If a holding fixture, such as the one shown in Fig. 1-85, is available, the easier and faster methods of wood removal discussed previously can now be used.

1-100 *Close-up shows bill and eye detail.*

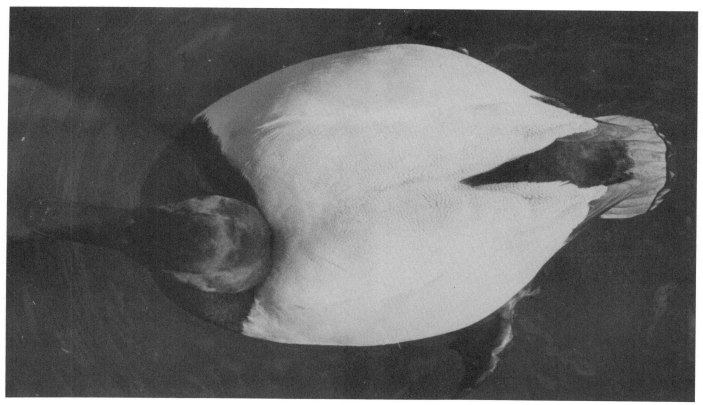

1-101 *Overhead shot—canvasback drake.*

1-102 *Good profile of a canvasback drake.*

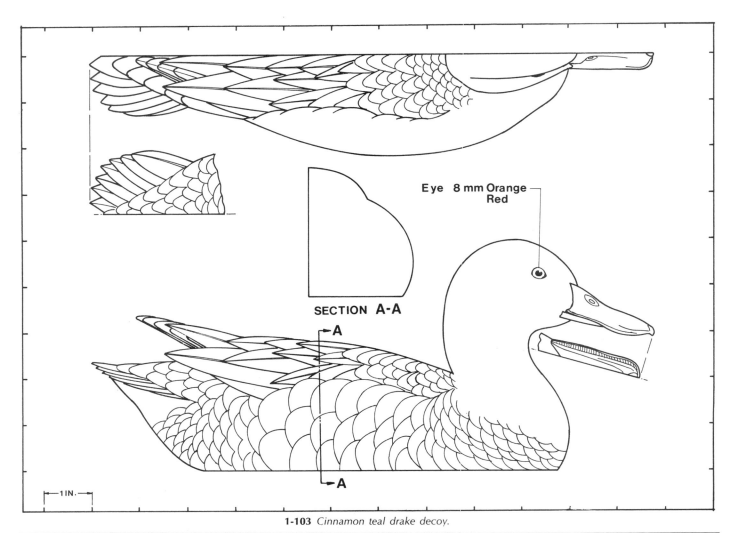

Eye 8 mm Orange
Red

SECTION A-A

1-103 *Cinnamon teal drake decoy.*

1-104 *Good plan view photo—cinnamon teal drake.*

1-105 *Cinnamon teal drake.*

1-106 *Rear view—cinnamon teal drake.*

1-107 *Close-up shows eye and bill detail.*

1-108 *Cinnamon teal plaque (c. 1964).*

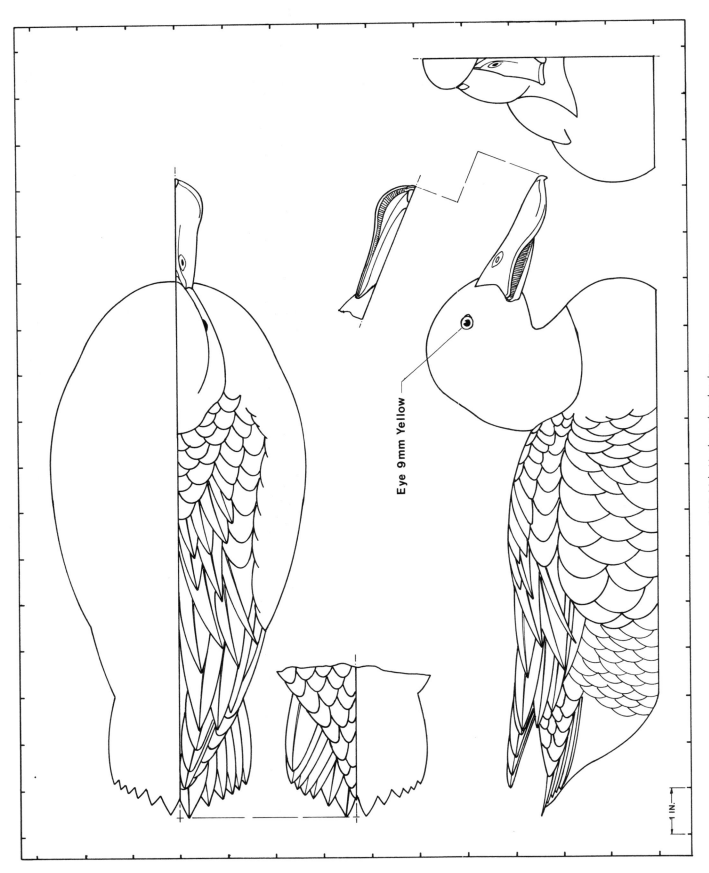

Eye 9mm Yellow

1-109 *Male Northern shoveler decoy.*

⊢1 IN.⊣

1-110 *Good profile of a Northern shoveler drake.*

1-111 *Overhead shot of a male shoveler. His back, scapular, and tertial feathers show well in this view.*

1-112 *Rear view of the male shoveler. Especially note body and head shape.*

1-114 *Front view of a male shoveler.*

1-113 *Good profile of a resting shoveler.*

1-115 *Profile of a male shoveler in an interesting pose.*

1-116, 117 *A group of Northern shovelers dabbling.*

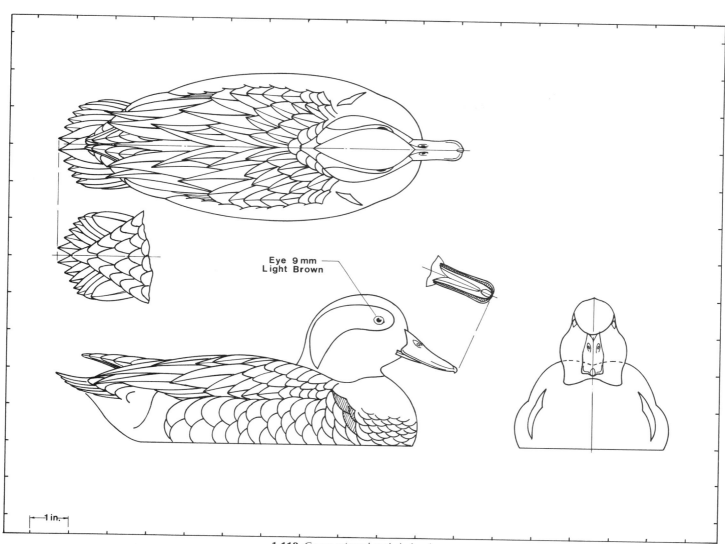

Eye 9mm
Light Brown

1-118 *Green-winged teal drake decoy.*

1-119 *Good overhead shot of the little greenwing.*

1-120 *Profile view of a relaxed green-winged teal.*

1-121 *Front view of the little drake.*

1-123 *Another profile of a relaxed greenwing.*

1-122 *Head and bill shape show clearly in the photo.*

1-124 *Profile of head and bill show many details.*

CARVING WORKING DECOYS

The carving of a full-body decoy is the next important, and logical, step forward for the beginner. If detail is kept simple, full-body carving is not much more difficult than carving a half-body decoy. This type of carving gives the novice experience in obtaining symmetry, in carving the complete head and bill, and in carving the primaries of both wings when they are folded and fitted closely together. A working-type decoy was selected for the first full-body project inasmuch as there is considerably less detail required for this type of carving.

Although few hunters in this age of plastics still use wood decoys, the revival of competitive decoy contests in 1960, along with the appearance of many publications, plus the great popularity of antique decoy collecting have promoted the strong comeback of this American art form. Thousands of working decoys are now entered by novices, amateurs, and professionals in a large number of annual competitions held in many parts of this country. Many other decoys are carved and sold to collectors, and a fewer number are carved and sold as actual decoys, to be put into the water and shot over.

Probably every decoymaker, hunter, and collector has his own personal idea of what a good working decoy should look like. When some method of communicating directly with the ducks is developed, their reaction to different decoys can be polled, and if the ducks themselves agree, it will then be possible to design the "perfect decoy". However, until that time, the designs of duck decoys, like those of fishing lures, will be influenced almost as much by their aesthetic appeal as by their ability to attract game. If there is disagreement on the design of working decoys, there is even more dispute on just what constitutes a good competition decoy.

During the '60's, competition decoys still resembled old working decoys. More and more detail was added in recent years and they were so beautifully carved, textured, and painted that they became indistinguishable from decorative decoys. Eventually, and with considerable logic, competition decoys were divided into three different categories, namely: Decorative Floating Decoys, Service (or Gunning Stool) Decoys, and Decorative Non-Floating Decoys. To further interest in competitive decoy shows, a definite distinction was made in regard to experience and proficiency. Most shows have divided this competition phase into Novice, Amateur, and Professional Classes. There are variations in the rules set up by the different contests and carvers who are not in the professional class should establish their personal status prior to entering.

The following overall standards for working decoy design are a guide for the beginner. I believe they meet generally accepted criteria for competition Service Class decoys. No attempt has been made to cover some of the more controversial aspects of working decoy design, such as the extent of carving and painting detail, the most desirable attitudes of the bird to duplicate, and others.

The working decoy must bear an unmistakable likeness, in form and color, to the species (and sex) they represent. They must be constructed and finished to withstand hard usage. It follows that certain parts, such as the bill and tail must be stronger and usually thicker than those on decorative decoys. Primaries and other feathers must not be raised, or undercut, from the body. The head-neck joint must be strong and withstand the adverse effects of water and weather. The decoy must be carved so as to prevent water from collecting or pooling on the upper side of the body.

The decoy must float realistically—it must not list; the body must be at the correct fore-and-aft angle to the water; and the proper amount of the body must be exposed. Both the flotation angle and the correct amount of exposed profile vary with different species.

The decoy must have static stability, i.e., it should be capable of righting itself from any position. Static stability is usually obtained by locating a ballast weight under the body, normally in the keel. The decoy should also have reasonable stability around its fore-and-aft axis, which means that any rolling motion should be quickly self-damping. The most important factors contributing to good antiroll characteristics are the cross-sectional shape and weighted keel. Some decoymakers also obtain additional roll stability by exaggerating the width of the body.

The decoy should neither yaw nor drift sideways excessively. Adequate directional stability and drift restraint are usually supplied by the keel if it is of sufficient depth and of a length almost, or equal to, that of the decoy body. Generally speaking, decoys used in deep, open water should have deeper keels than those used on ponds.

Provisons must be made for the attachment of the anchor line to the decoy.

The wood of both the interior and exterior should be adequately sealed to prevent the absorption of water.

The painted finish of the decoy must be as nonreflective as possible.

Competitive working decoys are usually judged on four characteristics: shape and form (likeness to species); seaworthiness (behavior in water); construction and workmanship; and painting and finish. Present-day workmanship has reached such a degree of perfection that the contest judges in many cases are forced to make their final selections on how the decoys look and perform in the tank. To the experienced eye, many species of waterfowl are recognizable at a distance just by the way they sit on the water. The position of the tail relative to the water and the amount and actual shape of the body profile exposed are some of the characteristics by which a particular species is identified. Most judges are experienced in these details and are quick to note inconsistencies. Most of them also consider each entry on the basis of static characteristics (the ability of the decoy to right itself) and dynamic characteristics (usually referred to as roll and yaw stability).

The beginner who aspires to enter a winner in one of the many contests should start by obtaining the rules for the particular contest in which he is interested. He should study every winning decoy (actual decoys or photographs) that he possibly can. He should endeavor to attend some shows and gain first hand exprience on how the decoys are judged and the winners chosen. He will find that his fellow competitors are a most friendly group and will, in most cases, go out of their way to help in any problem he may be experiencing. In addition, he will have the opportunity to acquaint himself with the quality of workmanship required for the different class levels. From this exposure, he will be able to set realistic goals and proceed with a singleness of purpose to become a winner himself.

Drawings (Figures 1-127, 1-175, and 1-180) of a male ring-necked duck, a male lesser scaup, and a wood duck drake have been included in this section to show the construction of typical working decoys. Their general configurations are also representative of many competition decoys.

Because it is less detailed, the carving of a working decoy is simpler than that of a decorative non-floating decoy. However, the body of the working decoy (and most floating decorative decoys) is normally hollowed out, an operation requiring a few changes to the carving procedure.

Over the years, decoymakers have removed wood from the interior of decoy bodies in a number of ways. Figure 1-126 shows six different ways this can be accomplished.

Method A. The bottom is made from a separate piece of wood, rabbetted into the body of the decoy.

Method B. The bottom is made from a separate piece of wood, mitered into the decoy body.

Method A and *B* require careful workmanship in the removing of wood and the fitting of the bottom piece. These two methods are often used for floating decorative decoys as there are no joints showing. Joints are difficult to hide on textured carvings because the glued seam does not burn the same as the surrounding wood.

Method C. The body of the decoy is rough-shaped and is then cut into two pieces on the bandsaw. After the body is hollowed out, the bottom piece is cemented to the body and the decoy is the carved in the normal manner.

Method D is similar to *Method C*, except that the bottom is a separate piece of wood.

Method E is similar to *Method C*, except that the joint is made above the waterline, usually just under the tail of the decoy. In this method, hollowing must be accomplished on both body pieces.

In *Method F*, the body is made from two pieces of wood and is temporarily cemented together with two or three small spots of epoxy. After the body is rough-shaped, the two halves are broken apart and hollowed. They are then cemented together permanently and the body is finished for carving.

1-125 *Male ring-necked duck.*

A variation of Method E would be to make the decoy body from two pieces, temporarily stick them together with epoxy (as was decribed in Method F), hollow the two parts and then cement them together permanently.

Method A will be used on the lesser scaup decoy and Method E will be used on the ring-necked duck decoy.

Most carvers hollow their decoys by means of a Forstner bit (see Appendix for availability), powered by means of a drill press. These bits remove wood quickly and efficiently. They are available in different sizes from 1/4 inch to 2 inches in diameter. After as much wood as possible is removed with the Forstner bit, gouges and rotary cutters are used to smooth the hollowed surface. (See Figures 1-145, 1-146, and 1-147).

CARVING A RING-NECKED DUCK DECOY

A male ring-necked duck was chosen for the first working decoy project because of his relatively small size and also because he is somewhat easier to paint than most ducks.

The following materials are required for the carving: 3 3/8 × 5 1/2 × 11-inch block for the body; 2 × 3 1/2 × 5-inch block for the head; 7/8 × 1 1/8 × 8-inch piece for the keel; two 9-mm eyes; sandpaper; automotive body filler; five-minute epoxy; wood screws; and lead for the ballast weight.

Drawing (Fig. 1-127), as printed, is one-half life-size. The first step in this project is to enlarge it to life-size (see section entitled "Enlarging or Reducing Drawings," page 31). After the drawing has been enlarged, transfer it to the body block in the manner previously described. The body will be sawed-out on the bandsaw using a slightly differ-

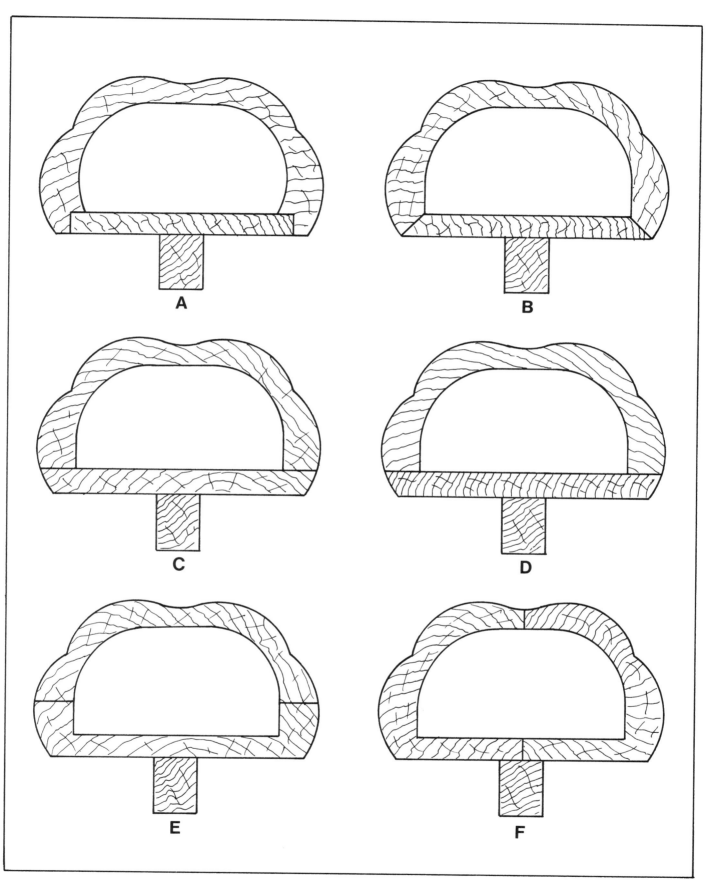

1-126 *Six different methods of constructing the decoy body.*

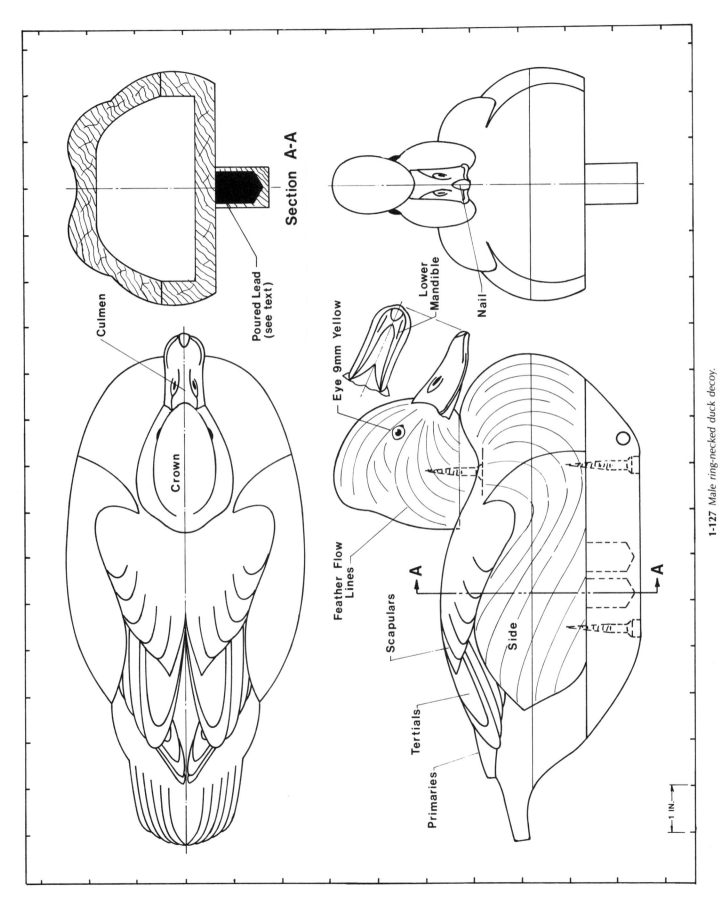

Section A-A

Culmen

Poured Lead
(see text)

Crown

Eye 9mm Yellow

Lower
Mandible

Nail

Feather Flow
Lines

Scapulars

Side

A

A

Tertials

Primaries

1-127 *Male ring-necked duck decoy.*

1 IN.

1-128 *Good profile view of the drake ring-necked duck.*

1-129 *Rear view shows head and body shape.*

1-130 *Front view—note head shape.*

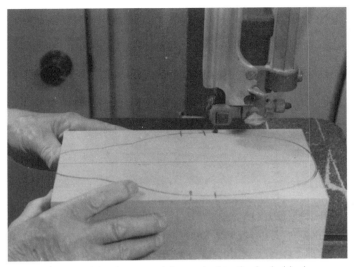

1-131 *The two side pieces are left attached to the body block.*

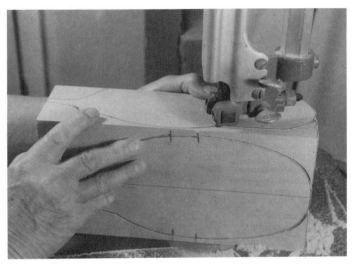

1-132 *The profile view is sawed next.*

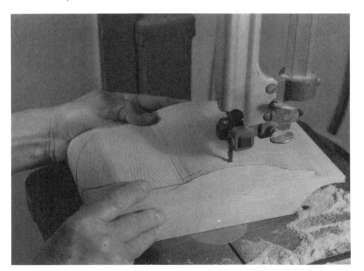

1-133 *The two side pieces are now cut from the body block.*

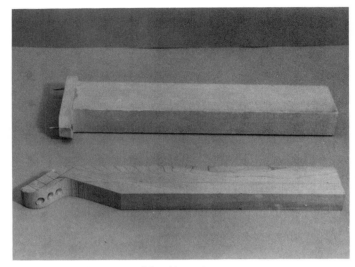

1-134 *Holding fixtures used for this project.*

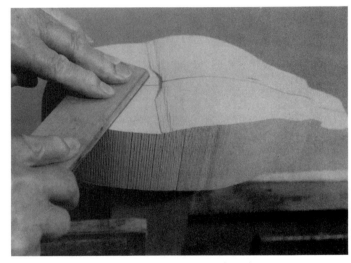

1-135 *Sand the head attachment area smooth and true.*

ent procedure than was used when cutting out the half-body decoy, one that eliminates the necessity of nailing one of the pieces back onto the block.

Saw the plan view first, leaving about one-inch uncut, near the maximum width on either side of the body (Fig. 1-131). Cut out the profile view completely next (Fig. 1-132). Then, place the body block back on the bandsaw and make the two one-inch cuts on the plan view (Fig. 1-133).

Transfer the head drawing to the head block making the length of the bill parallel to the grain. Cut out the entire head in the profile view—also remove some of the excess wood in the plan view.

Simple fixtures will be used to hold the body block and head during the carving operations (see Figures 1-88 and 1-134). After attaching the holding fixture to the body block, sand the head attachment area smooth and true. This may be accomplished by means of sandpaper glued to a small, flat piece of wood (Fig. 1-135). True the head

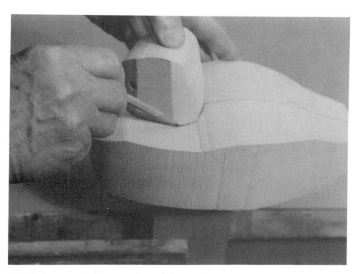

1-136 *Locate the head and mark its outline.*

1-139 *Check cross-sectional shape with a template.*

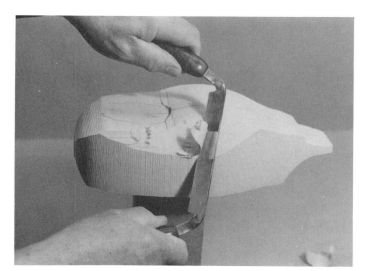

1-137 *The drawknife is used to remove some of the excess wood.*

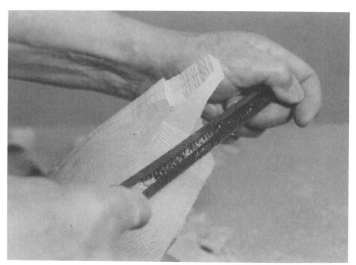

1-140 *Shape the undertail area with the round Surform rasp.*

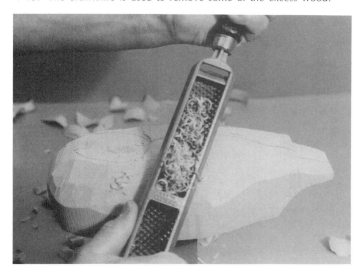

1-138 *Final shaping is accomplished with a half-round Surform rasp.*

1-141 *Remove tool marks with coarse sandpaper.*

at the joint area in a similar manner. Next, locate the head on the body block and outline the head shape onto it with a pencil (Fig. 1-136).

Now, start removing excess wood from the body being careful not to take off any wood inside the head outline (Figs. 1-137 and 1-138). Check the body shape from time to time with a template until the proper shape is obtained symmetrically (Figure 1-139). Remove the excess wood from under the tail area (Fig. 1-140). After the body has been roughly shaped, remove tool marks and sand smooth with coarse sandpaper (Fig. 1-141).

The roughly shaped body is now ready to be cut into two pieces so that it can be hollowed. The joint, as measured on the pattern, is 1⅛ inches from the bottom of the decoy. Cut a small piece of wood 1⅛ inches in thickness and use it to support a pencil and move the decoy around on a flat surface until a continuous line, to be used for the saw cut, is made (Fig. 1-142).

Now, place the decoy body on its side against a square

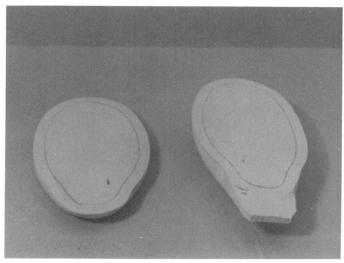

1-144 *Mark areas to be hollowed on body pieces.*

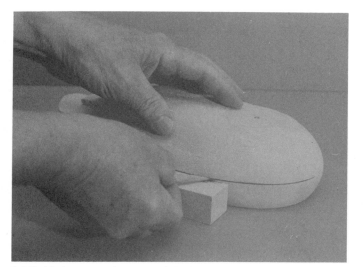

1-142 *Mark saw cut line around the body.*

1-145 *Remove as much wood as possible with the Forstner bit.*

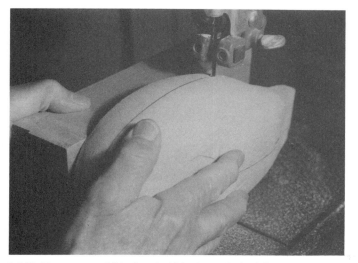

1-143 *Use a squared block to hold body vertical while sawing.*

1-146 *Remove excess wood left by the Forstner bit with a gouge.*

1-147 *Smooth upper body half with a spherical-shaped rotary file, or burr.*

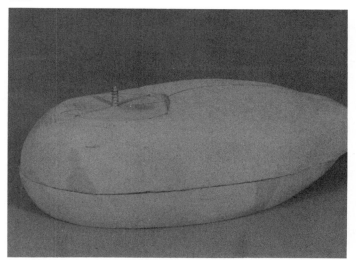

1-148 *Drill a hole for the head attaching wood screw.*

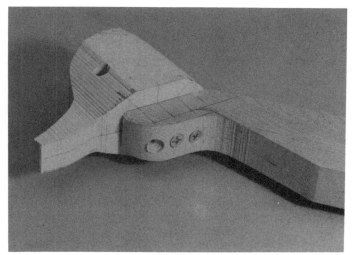

1-149 *Attach head to the holding fixture.*

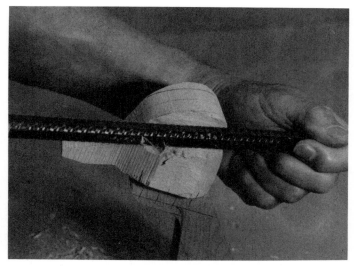

1-150 *Mark crown width and remove wood in this area.*

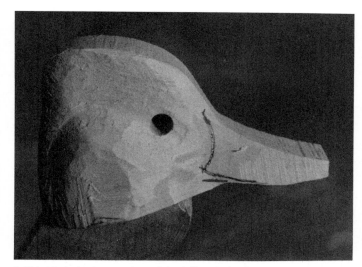

1-151 *Mark the intersection of the bill and cheek.*

block of wood and saw the body in two with the bandsaw (Fig. 1-143).

Next, draw a line one-half inch inside the perimeter of the two body pieces (Fig. 1-144) and remove as much wood as possible with the Forstner bit in a drill press (Fig. 1-145). Using a hand gouge, remove the excess wood left by the Forstner bit (Fig. 1-146). A spherical rotary file, or tungsten carbide burr, powered by a die grinder or electric hand drill, is most useful for removing excess wood and generally smoothing the upper body half (Fig. 1-147).

After the hollowing operations are completed, drill a hole at the center of the head location for a wood screw (Fig. 1-148).

> Note: The two body pieces should not be cemented together until the head has been permanently attached.

The head should be carved next. Attach it to the hold-

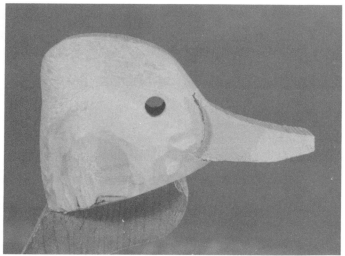

1-152 *Remove wood until proper width of the bill is established.*

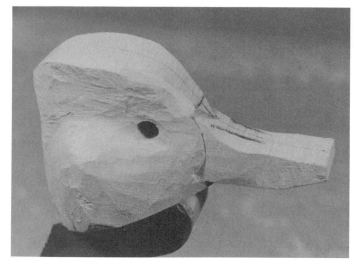

1-155 *Carve hill in the forehead area.*

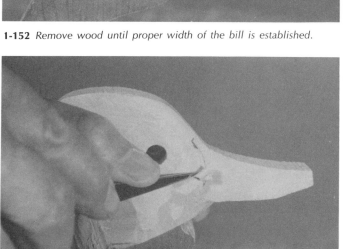

1-153 *Remove excess wood in the cheek area.*

1-156 *Remove excess wood in the forehead area and lay out the lower edge of the upper mandible.*

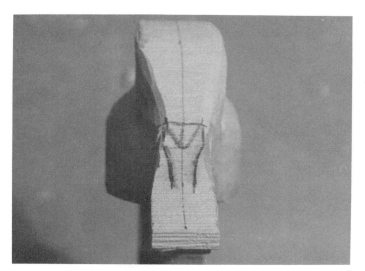

1-154 *Lay upper side of bill, or culmen.*

1-157 *Remove wood below the upper mandible until the proper width of the lower mandible has been established.*

ing fixture with two screws as shown in Fig. 1-149. Lay out the width of the crown and remove the excess wood in this area (Fig. 1-150). Sketch the intersection of the bill and head in the cheek area (Fig. 1-151) and remove wood forward of this line until the proper width of the bill is established (Fig. 1-152). Continue by removing the excess wood from the cheek area (Fig. 1-153). Now lay out the culmen (the upper surface of the bill). See Fig. 1-154. Remove wood from the intersection of the culmen and the forehead (Fig. 1-155) and round-off the forehead area. Next, lay out the lower edge of the upper mandible (Fig. 1-156) and remove wood in this area down to the width of the lower mandible (Fig. 1-157). Continue by locating the nostrils, nail, and grooves on the side of the bill (Fig. 1-158). The finished bill and rough-carved head is shown in Fig. 1-159.

Apply five-minute epoxy to the head and cement it to the body using the wood screw to pull the parts closely together (Fig. 1-160).

1-160 *Attach head to the upper body half with epoxy.*

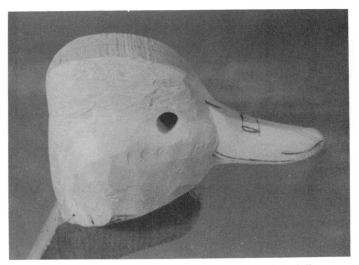

1-158 *Locate nostrils, nail, and grooves on the sides of the bill.*

1-161 *Cement body halves together with automotive body filler.*

1-159 *Sand bill smooth.*

1-162 *Lay out the extent of the side feather group.*

Thoroughly seal the interior of the decoy with thinned lacquer sanding sealer; it is advisable, however, not to apply sealer to the joint areas. The two body parts can now be cemented together permanently. It is imperative that a waterproof cement or glue be used for this very important joint. Although there are probably a number of products that would work equally well, automotive body filler, a two-part polyester, does a very adequate job; it is readily available, inexpensive, and easy to use. (I kept a test joint soaking continuously in water for one year without any separation). It sets up fairly fast, therefore it is advisable to mix plenty and to work quickly (Fig. 1-161).

The decoy is now ready for final carving. Reattach the holding fixture and pencil-in the outline of the side feather group (Fig. 1-162). Using a gouge, remove wood above and to the rear of this line (Fig. 1-163), referring to the pattern for the depth of cut. Now, round the side feather group down to the bottom of the gouged groove (Fig. 1-164) and shape the scapulars in a similar manner (Figs. 1-165 and 1-166). Using the gouge again, remove wood along the centerline of the back, forming a rounded

1-165 *Remove wood to establish the shape of the scapular area.*

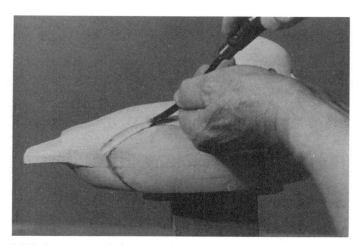

1-163 *Remove wood above the side feathers with a gouge.*

1-166 *Sand sides and back smooth.*

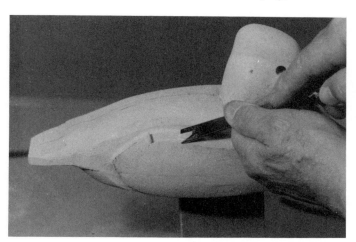

1-164 *Round-over the side feathers.*

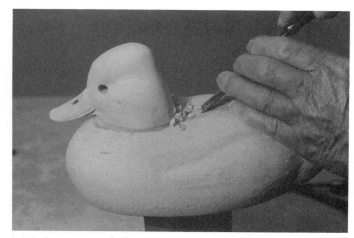

1-167 *Remove wood along the centerline of the back to form the rounded "V"-shaped depression.*

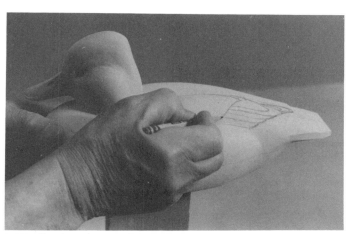

1-168 *Sketch-in the scapular, tertial, and primary feathers.*

1-170 *Attach the keel temporarily by means of rubber bands.*

1-169 *The carving is now finished except for installing the keel.*

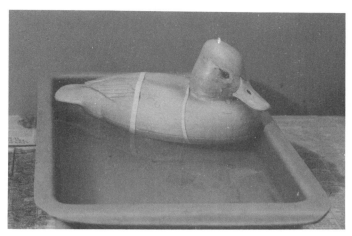

1-171 *The location of the keel, ballast, and the amount of ballast must be determined by floating the decoy.*

"V" (Fig. 1-167). Proceed by laying out the scapular, tertial, and primary feathers (Fig. 1-168) and carve these feathers individually (Fig. 1-169). The tail feathers can also be drawn-in and carved. Install and shape the eyes at this time.

Fill the two screw holes in the bottom of the decoy with body putty. Sand the entire exterior of the decoy smooth and seal all surfaces with thinned lacquer sanding sealer.

Next, make the keel. To get more weight below the body, some decoymakers use a denser wood, such as oak or maple, or one of the other hardwoods. The amount of weight required to obtain static stability (self-righting) depends on the location of the weight below the decoy body. Therefore, it is somewhat more efficient to use a lighter keel and to meet the static stability requirement by locating the necessary weight in the form of lead, or some other heavy material, at or near the bottom of the keel. However, if ballast weight is installed by pouring molten

lead directly into a hole in the keel, it is desirable to use the harder, tougher wood to withstand the heat.

The amount of ballast, and its location, must be determined by trial and error—it may be necessary to make more than one keel, possibly several, to achieve the desired results. A logical start would be to attach the un-weighted keel near the centerline of the body with two heavy rubber bands (Fig. 1-170). Now, float the decoy and note whether it rides tail too high or too low (Fig. 1-171). If it rides about the correct fore-and-aft angle, remove the keel and drill a ⅝th inch diameter hole near its fore-and-aft center. Fill the hole with molten lead (discarded tire balancing weights can be substituted for this purpose). See Fig. 1-172. Attach the keel as before and float the decoy again. If the carving is not symmetrical, or if the head is turned to one side or the other, the decoy will list. If the decoy does list, move the keel in small increments to the high side until the list is corrected and carefully mark its final location. Hold the head of the

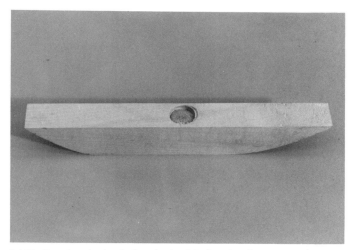

1-172 *Showing the keel after the lead ballast has been poured.*

CARVING A LESSER SCAUP DECOY
(See Figures 1-173, 1-174, 1-175, 1-176)

Although method "A" body hollowing (see Fig. 1-126) is shown on the lesser scaup decoy pattern (Fig. 1-175), it would be simpler for the beginner to hollow this decoy in the manner covered for the preceding ring-necked duck decoy or to use method "C" or "D". Except for the possible use of a different hollowing method, this decoy is carved in a similar manner to the ring-necked duck decoy.

When floated, this decoy was found to require an additonal small amount of lead (see Figures 1-177 and 1-177A), due to the fact that probably less wood was removed from the body.

See Chapter 2, page 118, for painting instructions.

decoy under water, release it, and see if it will right itself. If it does not, either more ballast is required or a deeper keel must be made so the ballast can be located farther from the decoy body. Before adding more weight, check to see if the decoy floats at the proper fore-and-aft angle. Also see if the correct amount of profile is exposed above the water. Both of these features can be checked by using photographs of a ring-necked male duck for comparison. The fore-and-aft angle (tail too high or too low) can be corrected by relocating the weight to the high side, or by adding an additional weight. Correcting the amount of exposed profile is somewhat more difficult to accomplish. If the decoy rides too high, the obvious solution would be to add more weight. Making a correction to a decoy that rides too low requires either lightening the decoy or adding more height to it. Since the amount of ballast is usually determined by the self-righting requirement, it is not possible to lighten the decoy by reducing this weight.

One way the decoy can be lightened is to cut it in two again and remove more wood from the interior. An easier solution to the problem would be to add another piece of wood to the bottom. If only a small correction is required, the keel can be replaced by a wider one. This will increase displacement, making the decoy ride slightly higher.

In the case of the decoy pictured in Fig. 1-170, the location and the amount of ballast (see Fig. 1-172), proved to be very close—this was strictly a matter of luck. The decoy was self-righting, it floated at about the correct fore-and-aft angle, and the amount of exposed profile appeared to be similar to that shown in photographs of floating male ring-necked ducks. It was necessary, however, to locate the keel to the left of the body centerline in order to correct the slight list caused by the turned head.

Locate the keel on the marks made previously and attach it to the bottom of the decoy with two wood screws (see Fig. 1-127).

The decoy is now ready to be painted. Painting instructions are included in Chapter 2, page 109.

1-173 *Rear view—lesser scaup drake.*

1-174 *Front view—lesser scaup drake.*

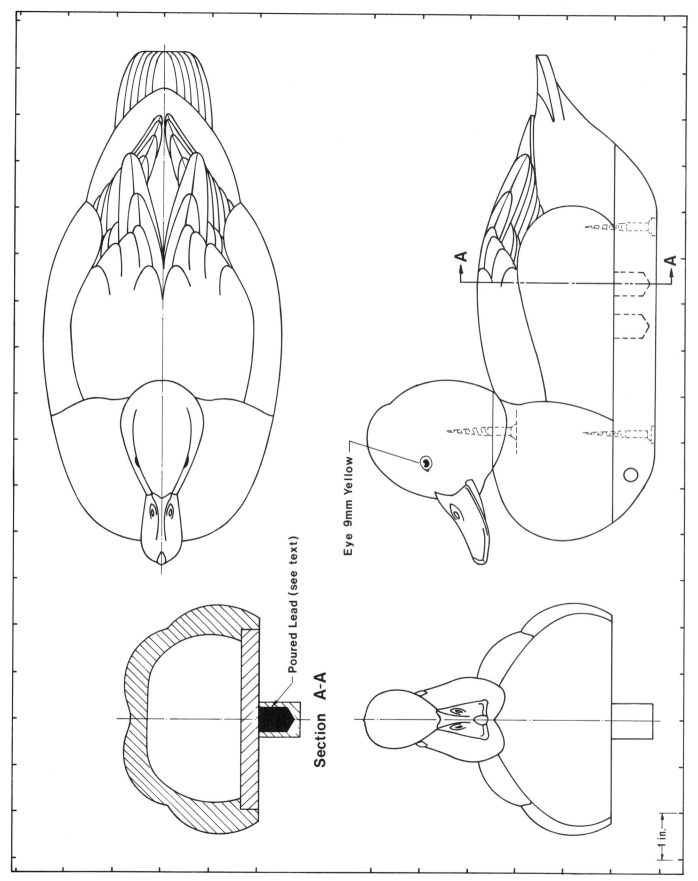

Eye 9mm Yellow

Poured Lead (see text)

Section A-A

1 in.

1-175 *Lesser scaup drake decoy.*

1-176 *Profile view of a male lesser scaup.*

1-177 *Floating decoy to determine ballast requirements.*

CARVING A WOOD DUCK DECOY
(See Figures 1-179, 1-179A, 1-180)

Method "D" body hollowing (see Fig. 1-126) is shown on the wood duck decoy pattern Fig. 1-180. In this case, the height of the normal body block is reduced by one-half inch. After the wood is removed from the interior, a one-half inch piece of wood is attached to the body by means of automotive body putty. Other carving details are similar to those described previously.

See Chapter 2, page 120, for painting instructions.

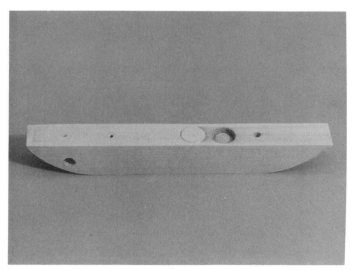

1-177A *Showing ballast in keel.*

1-178 *Three-quarter rear view of a male wood duck.*

1-179 *Profile of an alert male wood duck.*

1-179A *Many of his feathers are clearly shown in this top view of a male wood duck.*

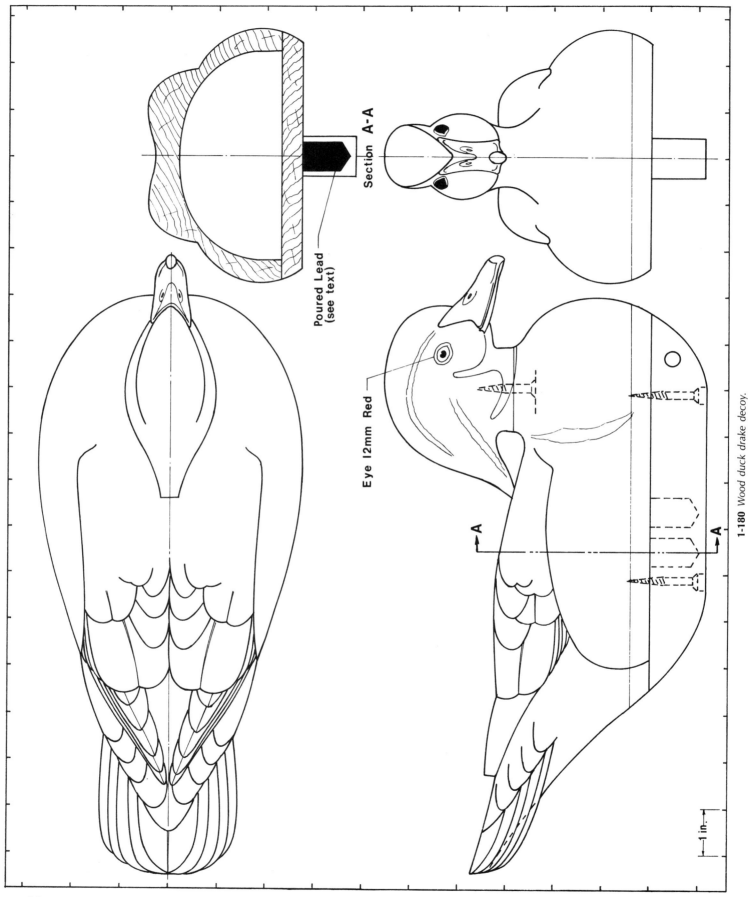

Section A-A

Poured Lead
(see text)

Eye 12mm Red

A

A

1-180 *Wood duck drake decoy.*

1 in.

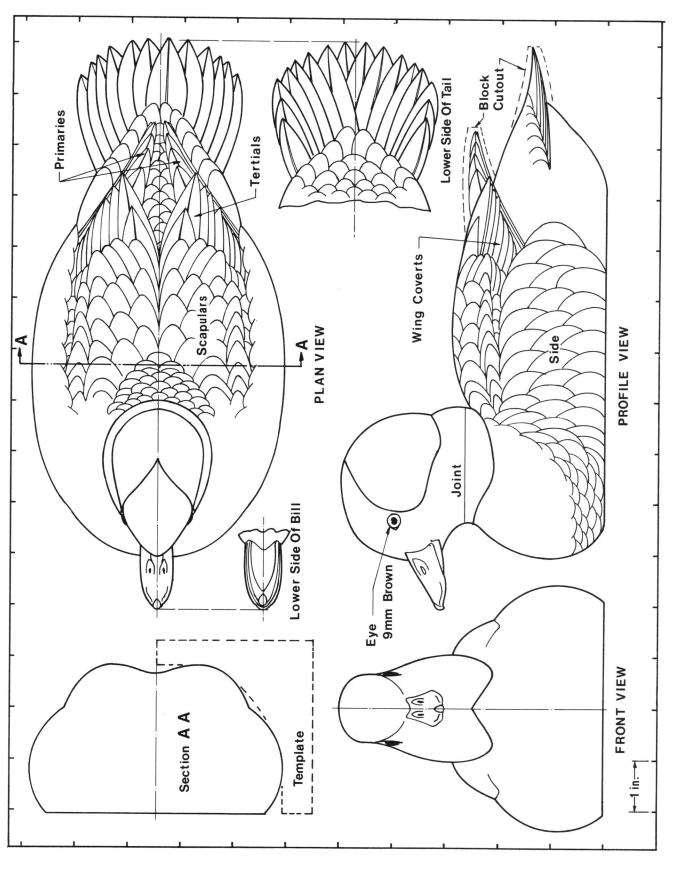

Primaries

Tertials

Scapulars

A

A

PLAN VIEW

Lower Side Of Tail

Block Cutout

Wing Coverts

Side

Joint

Eye 9mm Brown

PROFILE VIEW

1-181 *Bufflehead drake decoy.*

Lower Side Of Bill

Section A A

Template

FRONT VIEW

1 in.

1-182 *Bufflehead drake.*

1-183 *Rear view—bufflehead drake. Note body and head shape.*

1-184 *Front view—bufflehead drake.*

CARVING A DECORATIVE BUFFLEHEAD DRAKE DECOY

The carving of a full-body decorative decoy is the next logical step for the amateur carver who wishes to advance his carving techniques.

A bufflehead drake was chosen for this project as he, like the ring-necked duck drake and the lesser scaup drake, is one of the smaller ducks and is somewhat easier to paint than many of the others.

The following materials are required for the carving: 3¼ × 5 × 10½-inch block for the body; 2 × 3 × 4½-inch block for the head; two 9-mm brown eyes; garnet paper, and five-minute epoxy.

First, enlarge Figure 1-181 to life-size. Transfer this drawing to the body block and cut out the body using the procedure described for the ring-necked decoy. Transfer the head drawing to the 2-inch block. Be sure the bill is located parallel to the grain. Drill a hole of the proper diameter through the head for the eyes.

1-185 *Interesting profile of a male bufflehead.*

1-186 *Three-quarter rear view of the little bufflehead.*

As shown by the step photographs, the head was permanently attached to the body before it was carved. The author prefers to do the carving of the bill and most of the head prior to attaching it to the body, as was done in the previous project. The beginner should proceed with whichever method suits him best. It is recommended, however, that he carve the neck after the head has been attached. In this way more realistic neck lines can be developed when the neck and body are carved as one. If extreme head positions make it difficult or impossible to carve the lower side of the bill, it should definitely be completely carved prior to the head being installed.

True the head attachment area by sanding flat and true (*see Figure 1-135, page 52*). Also true the head at the joint area in a similar manner.

After the centerlines of the head and body have been established and drawn-in with a pencil, locate the head and neck fore and aft and sidewise (also, if desired, turned to one side or the other) and mark this location with pencil lines. If the head (and bill) are to be carved separately, care must be taken that no wood is removed inside the head outline.

Attach the body block to the holding fixture. See Fig. 1-134, page 52. Start removing wood from the midsection of the body (Figs. 1-188 and 1-189) until both sides match the body template (Fig. 1-190). Continue roughing the body by removing wood from the chest, flanks, and under tail coverts (Fig. 1-191 and 1-192). Sand the body occasionally to check the overall progress.

To insure symmetry, it is important to retain the penciled centerline on the body and head until all detail has been completed. Whenever a centerline is partially removed by the wood-removing operations, it should be redrawn before it is completely lost.

When the overall body shape has been established, make the plan view layout of the bill, cut to shape, and rough out the head (Fig. 1-193). Sand the entire carving smooth.

Now, draw-in the outline of the side feather group (Fig.

1-187 *Locate and attach head with epoxy.*

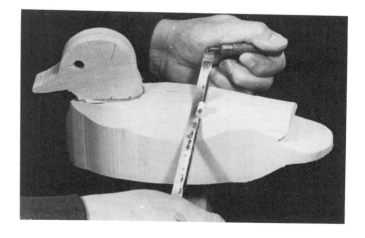

1-188 *A small drawknife can be used to rough-shape the body.*

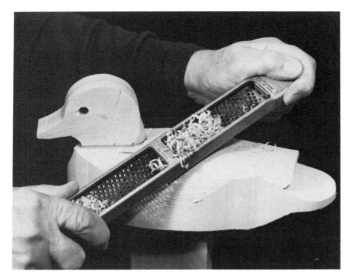

1-189 *Blend the body contours with the half-round Surform rasp.*

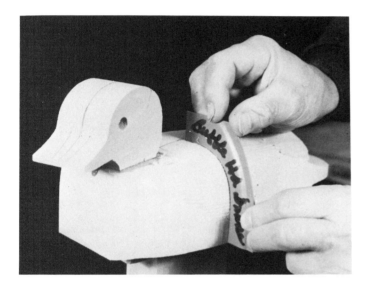

1-190 *Periodically check the cross-sectional shape of the body.*

1-191 *Shape the breast by using the Surform rasp in the pulled position.*

1-192 *Shape the flanks and undertail coverts with the round Surform rasp.*

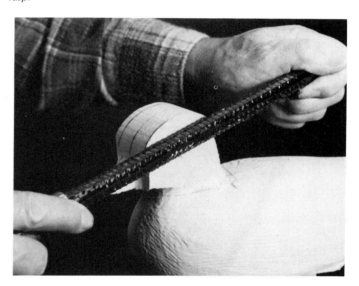

1-193 *Rough form the upper part of the head.*

1-194). Using a gouge, remove wood above and to the rear of this line. Continue using the gouge to shape the concave intersection of the scapulars along the centerline of the back (Fig. 1-195). Also with the gouge, carve the intersection of the neck and body (Figs. 1-196 and 1-181, Finish shaping the head (Fig. 1-197).

Now, lay out the individual tertial, secondary, and primary feathers on one side of the carving (Fig. 1-198). Trace this layout on a piece of transparent paper and transfer the layout, using carbon paper, to the other side of the carving (1-199).

With the tip of a sharp knife, cut around the outline of the primaries and start removing wood with a chisel (Fig. 1-200 and 1-201). Cut underneath the primaries, down to the rump, with a coping saw (Fig. 1-202) and remove this wedge-shaped piece of wood. Using a knife and chisels, carefully remove the wood from under the primaries until

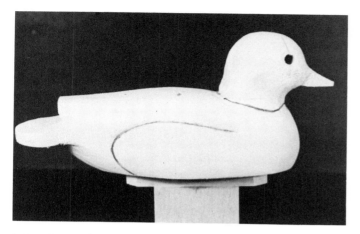

1-194 *The overall shape of the carving has now been established. The head-body intersection and the extent of the side feathers are drawn in.*

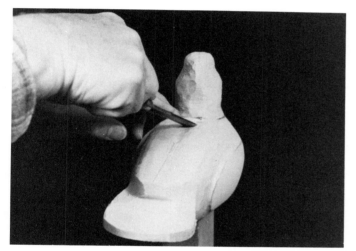

1-195 *Gouge out the rounded v-shaped depression at the centerline of the body.*

1-196 *Using a gouge, carve the intersection of the head and body.*

1-197 *Carve the head to its final shape.*

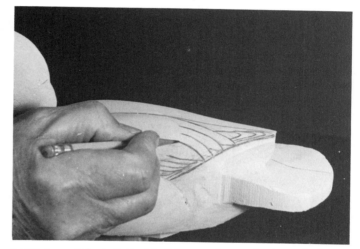

1-198 *Lay out the individual tertial, secondary, and primary feathers.*

they are about ³⁄₃₂ to ¹⁄₈th inch thick. Continue working in this area until the rump is smoothly shaped (Fig. 1-203). The primaries should now stand out realistically from the body. Carvers who wish to incorporate more detail may draw in the individual scapulars, exposed wing coverts, and other feathers. Cut around the individual tertial feathers and carve down the upper side of the primaries until they stand out from the tertials (Fig. 1-204). Continue by carving each feather of the tertial and secondary groups (Fig. 1-205), scapulars, and other feather groups (1-206) if desired.

Lay out the tail feathers as shown in Fig. 1-206. Support the tips of the tail feathers with a scrap piece of wood and cut them to shape (Fig. 1-207). Cut around the outline of each tail feather and carve them individually (Fig. 1-208).

Referring to Fig. 1-181 and also the bufflehead bill pictured on page 357, lay out the ridge of the bill (culmen) and carve the cheeks and bill roughly to shape (Fig. 1-209). Now, lay out the intersection of the bill and cheek on both sides of the carving (Fig. 1-210) and carve the bill and cheeks down to this line (Figs. 1-211 and 1-

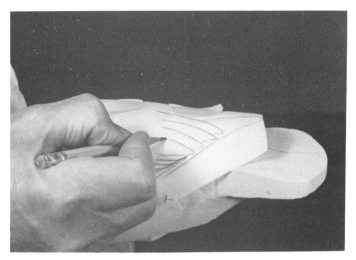

1-199 *Trace off the feather pattern layouts and transfer them to the other side.*

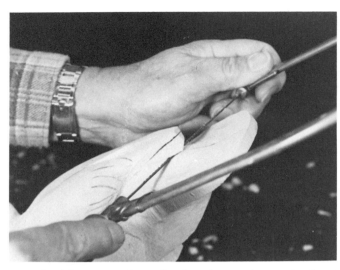

1-202 *Carefully saw out the wedge-shaped pieces from under the primaries.*

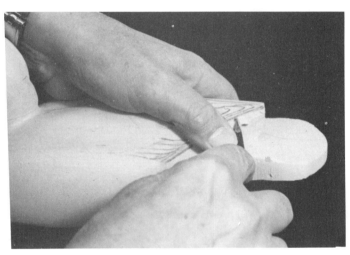

1-200 *Remove the wood from the rear side of the primaries.*

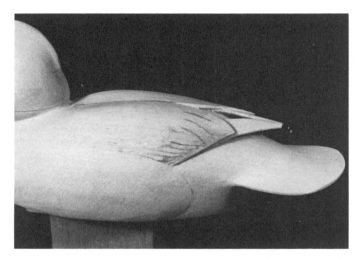

1-203 *Carve the primaries until they stand out realistically from the body.*

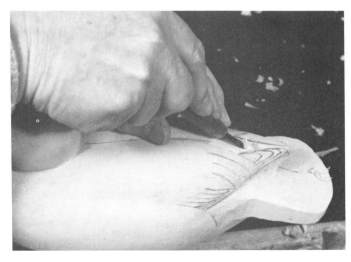

1-201 *Shape the rump with a small chisel.*

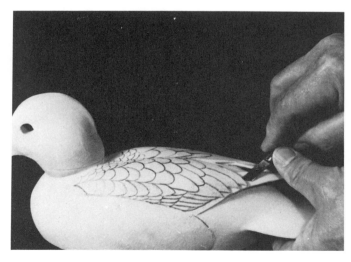

1-204 *Carefully carve the upper side of the primaries.*

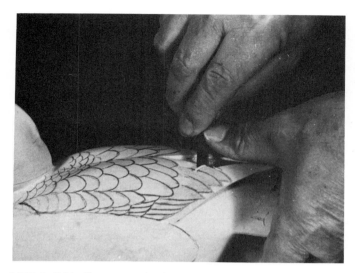

1-205 *Individually carve each of the secondary and tertial feathers.*

1-208 *Individually carve all of the tail feathers.*

1-206 *If desired, additional feathers may be carved.*

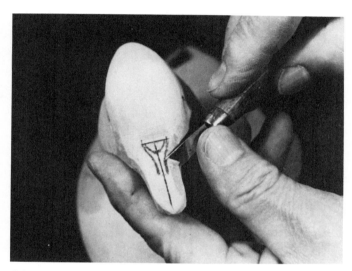

1-209 *Lay out the culmen and carve the bill down to this line.*

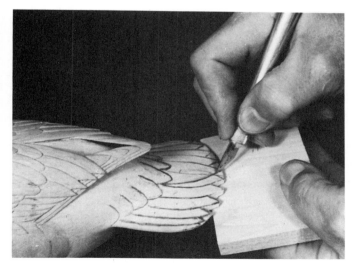

1-207 *Support the tail with a scrap piece of wood while cutting the v-shaped notches.*

212). Lay out the lower edge of the upper mandible and remove wood in this area until the proper width of the lower mandible is established. Locate and mark the nostrils on both sides of the bill. The nostrils can be duplicated several ways. One easy way is to burn them in with a hot ice pick. Another way is to make holes at their extremities with a sharp tool such as an ice pick and remove the wood in between with a small knife. The nostrils of most waterfowl lie at the bottom of a small oval-shaped depression which can be realistically reproduced by using a small gouge (Fig. 1-213). Make a shallow cut around the outline of the nail and make it just barely visible by removing a small amount of wood around the cut. Carve the underside of the bill by referring to Fig. 1-181 and the pictures on page 357. Complete the head by installing the eyes in the manner described on page 27.

Check the entire carving for toolmarks and sand smooth where necessary. The carving is now ready to be sealed and painted. See Chapter 2, page 114, for painting instructions.

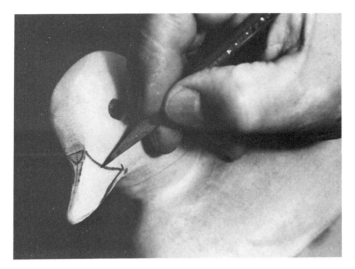

1-210 *Lay out the intersection of the bill and cheek.*

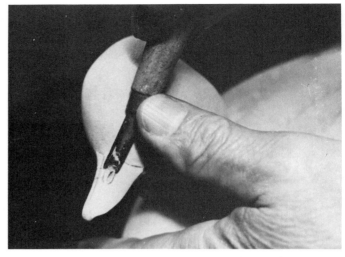

1-213 *Gouge out the small depression around the nostril.*

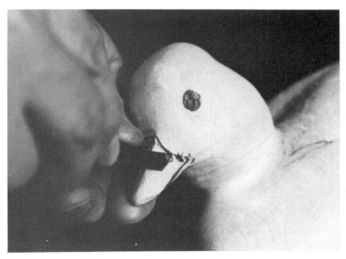

1-211 *Carve the bill down to the bill-cheek intersection line.*

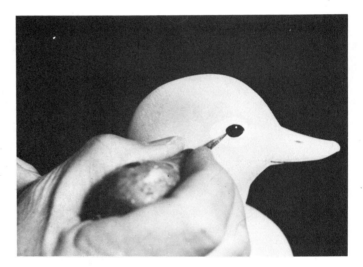

1-214 *Carefully shape the eyes.*

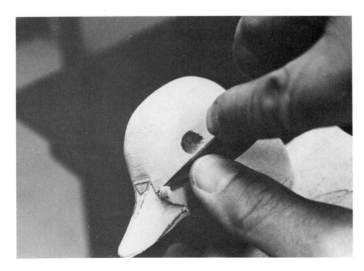

1-212 *Carefully shape the cheek in the bill area.*

1-215 *The carving is now ready to be painted.*

Common Mallard, males.

Canvasback, males.

1-220

Northern Cinnamon Teal, males.

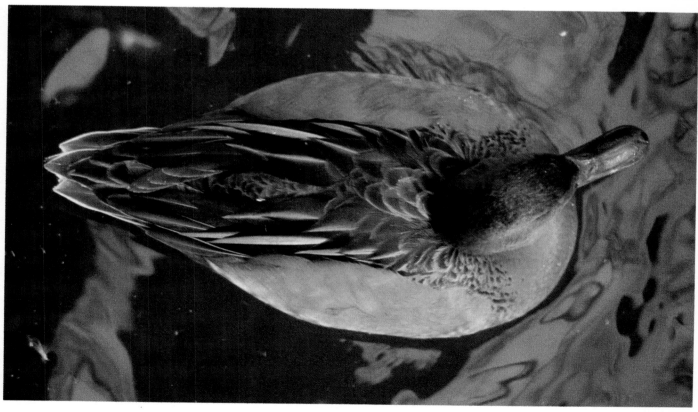

1-222

Northern Shoveler, males.

1-223

1-224

Green-Winged Teal, males.

1-226 *Ringed-Neck Duck, male.*

Lesser Scaup, male. **1-227**

1-228

Bufflehead, males.

1-229

Carolina Wood Duck, males.

2

Painting for Beginners

Painting the carving can be every bit as interesting and absorbing as doing the actual carving. A bird's plumage is beautifully complex, not only in color, but also in texture and pattern; even to approximate its subtleties is difficult and time-consuming. This should not discourage the beginner, but only make him aware of the unlimited creative possibilities and the great challenges connected with this phase of realistic bird carving.

The painting of a bird carving can be very simple or extremely complicated, depending on the desires, ability, and patience of the individual carver-artist. If the beginning bird carver has never done any painting, it is wise on his first attempts to keep the painting detail as simple as possible; otherwise he will become frustrated and discouraged. As soon as he has developed some confidence, he should try to add a little more detail with each new attempt. Painting birds can only be learned by doing and by studying the actual bird and trying each time to come a little closer to the real thing. The novice (and also the advanced amateur and professional) should never be completely satisfied with his work; there will always be room for improvement.

This chapter covers only some of the easier techniques involved in the painting of realistic game birds. Those with some experience in painting should immediately turn to Chapter 8 ''Advanced Finishing Techniques.''

However, it is strongly recommended that he review some of the color basics covered in the section entitled PAINT MIXING AND MATCHING, page 83, before attempting more advanced types of painting.

The techniques involved in painting a realistic bird carving are not unlike those used by the illustrator-artist in painting very detailed, lifelike bird portraits with oils on canvas. The illustrator-artist must resort to shading and the use of highlights and shadows in order to create a three-dimensional effect. Although the carver-artist is already working on a three-dimensional object, he, too, has to use highlights and shading on occasion to make the painted bird appear natural. A *good* realistically painted carving generally requires more detailed work, extending over the bird's entire body, than a bird painted on canvas. The canvas painting can be viewed only from one side and normally at a distance; the painted carving is frequently subjected to very close inspection from all angles over its entire surface.

Much of the carver-artist's available time is spent doing the actual carving work and getting the piece ready for paint. As a result, he paints infrequently and has plenty of time to forget what he learned during the previous painting session. A lot about painting a bird carving can be learned, and a great deal of uninterrupted practice can be gotten in a short time by working directly on canvas or paper surfaces. The beginner may feel that time is wasted by not painting on a carving but actually, in the long run, the learning process for handling paints will be shortened appreciably. He should start out in this manner and then switch to the actual carving as soon as he has built up confidence in his painting ability. Painting, like almost everything else, requires practice, study, and more practice, and a great deal of patience. He should not expect to become an expert overnight—no one else has.

MATERIALS AND EQUIPMENT

As there are a number of ways to go about painting a bird carving, few carvers agree completely on which are the best techniques and materials. The materials and equipment listed below and the techniques described here and in Chapter 8 are certainly not the only ones. Although practically all realistic bird carvings are painted with either artist's oils or acrylic paints, the author has listed only oil paints. For the beginner, who has never painted, the slower-drying oils are easier to use than acrylics and it is recommended that he start with them. It is further recommended that Grumbacher's Pre-Tested Oils be used inasmuch as the exercises and the color samples done here are based on this brand.

Most carver-artists now use acrylic paints, and some obtain excellent results. On the other hand, some of the very finest bird carvings done today are painted with oils. About the only advantage acrylics have over oils is their faster drying time, although to some of us this is a disadvantage. Acrylics dry in just a few minutes, giving the artist very little time to blend colors. They also have a disconcerting property of drying somewhat darker than the mixed color, and compared to oils, have poorer covering qualities. Oils are slow drying and give ample time for mixing and blending of colors and for the duplication of feather detail and brush marks. They dry the same color as mixed and the colors on the palette remain usable for hours—a distinct advantage over acrylics. When oils are used, there is plenty of time to make corrections which is an important feature expecially for beginners. If the carver-artist is not satisfied with some of his painting, the paint can be easily wiped off for a second attempt. Acrylics are usually dry, and difficult to remove, by the time the decision is made that a particular area should be done over.

Painting with acrylics, as done by the experts, is a complicated procedure involving much detail work and often involving many thin coats, or washes, as they are called. The procedure must be carefully planned in advance and accomplished with considerable speed. Blending acrylics requires quick and skillful strokes. It is very questionable if any great amount of time is saved by the use of these fast drying paints.

Painting with oils, in the author's opinion, is simpler especially when painting over textured surfaces which largely eliminates the need for duplicating feather barb lines with brush marks or individual strokes.

After the beginner has gained some experience in handling paints and has acquired some confidence in his painting ability, he can then explore the feasibility of switching to acrylic paints.

In actual practice, however, many carver-artists become frustrated and impatient waiting for oil paints to dry. Instead of giving up, discarding the oil paints, and going out and buying acrylics, they should become acquainted with the ways in which the drying time of oils can be drastically reduced. There are at least four ways this can be accomplished.

1. Modifying certain slow drying colors with fast drying colors. For example, black and white are two of the slower drying colors. Black, straight from the tube, is rarely (if ever) used to duplicate the color of a bird. It can always be modified to a more natural shade by the addition of burnt umber, a fast drying color. Although some birds appear to be very white, or have some white colors, their whites are actually much grayer, or brownish gray, than white from the tube. Raw umber, also a very fast drying color, subdues the starkness of tube white into a more realistic color when added in small quantities. The drying time of these two often used colors will be reduced approximately 50% when modified as described above.

2. By the use of fast drying mediums. Oil paint from the tube is almost always reduced in consistency by the use of a medium (see Mediums and Drying Agents). Some mediums are much faster drying than others. The author uses turpentine and copal medium, mixed about equally. Both turpentine and copal medium are fast drying and reduce the drying time of all oil colors considerably.

3. By the use of a drier. The drying time of all oil colors can be reduced to overnight (often to three or four hours) by the addition of a very small amount of Grumbacher's Cobalt Drier. Grumbacher claims there are no adverse effects resulting from the use of this drier. It should be added in minute quantities only to the paint as it is actually being used as it will obviously shorten the time a color will remain usable on the palette. This method can also be used to further decrease the drying time of the modified colors described in Paragraphs 1 and 2.

4. In 1976, Winson and Newton, a British company who have been supplying artists with oil paints since the 1880's, introduced a new medium called Artist's Alkyd Colours. All colors of this paint dry in four or five hours and combine the advantages of both oil and acrylic paints. These paints are of high quality, are made with alkyd resin instead of linseed oil, and are completely compatible with oil paints and oil paint mediums. Unfortunately, they have never become popular in this country and, as a result, their availability is limited. For those carvers who prefer not to use a drier, some of the slower drying oil colors (black, white, yellows, and reds) could be replaced by alkyd colors with excellent results.

By using the four methods covered above, most of the objections to the drying time of oils are eliminated. It is strongly recommended that the beginner experiment with them before making any judgment regarding the use of oil paints.

Except for those situations in which acrylics can be used easily for undercoats or when no blending of colors is required, the painting instructions in this book assume the use of oil paints. Some of the basic materials and equipment required for painting realistic bird carvings are listed below. More can be added as the novice progresses.

Sealer
    1 pint lacquer sanding sealer
    (Deft Clear Wood Finish similar)
Undercoat—Grumbacher's Hyplar or equivalent
    8 oz. white   2 oz. burnt sienna
    2 oz. black   2 oz. raw sienna
    2 oz. burnt umber
Oil paint
    150 ml. Titanium white   37 ml. cadmium red
                                            (deep)
    37 ml. cobalt blue   37 ml. burnt sienna
    37 ml. Ivory black   37 ml. vermillon
    37 ml. cadmium yellow
    (medium)   37 ml. yellow ochre
    37 ml. burnt umber   37 ml. alizarin crimson
    37 ml. cadmium orange   37 ml. Thalo blue
    37 ml. raw sienna   37 ml. Thalo red rose
Brushes
    sable flats, sizes 1, 2, 8
    round sables, sizes 0,00,000
    sable flat, 3/4 inch wide
    white bristle fan blender, small and medium
    1/4 inch white bristle angular
Other equipment
    palette knife
    palette (multiple sheet, throw-away type)
    turpentine
    medium
    Grumbacher's Cobalt Drier

brush cleaner—Silicoil jar and Cleaning Fluid (manufactured by the Lion Co., 428 Ormsby, Louisville, KY)

SEALERS AND UNDERCOATS

Before applying any paint to the sanded carving, the wood should be sealed. While sealer does not actually hermetically close off all the wood pores, it does reduce considerably the rate at which the wood gains or loses moisture, which is important in the prevention of checks. Sealing also helps prevent the wood from exuding pitch. In addition, when sanded or steel-wooled, the sealer helps fill the open grain of the wood.

A number of wood sealers are available at paint stores. The author prefers lacquer sanding sealer, which can be either sprayed or brushed on, thinned about 50%-50% with lacquer thinner. Under normal temperatures, lacquer sanding sealer dries and is ready for sanding in less than one half hour. "Deft", a brushing-lacquer, is quite similar to lacquer sanding sealer.

After the wood is sealed and sanded (or steel-wooled) apply either an oil paint or an acrylic paint undercoat to the carving. The color of the undercoat should approximate that of the final coat. The author prefers to use an acrylic base paint, not only because it dries in a few minutes, but also because it has excellent bonding characteristics. Grumbacher's Gesso, tinted to the desired color, may also be used as an undercoat. The undercoat, regardless of type, should be thinned to reduce brush marks to a minimum.

MEDIUMS AND DRYING AGENTS

Oil paint from the tube is normally mixed with a painting medium. The painting medium can modify the oil paint in one or all of the following ways: reduce the consistency of the paint for easier application; make the paint more translucent; affect the flatness or the gloss of the dried paint; and decrease drying time. There is probably more disagreement among carver-artists on the selection of painting mediums and the amount to use than on any other point.

Turpentine and linseed oil, or a mixture thereof, are the most popular painting mediums. Turpentine tends to make the dried paint flatter (less shiny) and reduces drying time. Linseed oil adds sheen to the dried paint and increases drying time. The author prefers to use Copal Painting Medium, made by Grumbacher, mixed equally with turpentine. This mixture produces a very slight sheen and reduces drying time considerably. If alkyds are used, Winsor and Newton have a medium called Liquin that complements the fast drying time of Alkyd Colours.

As previously stated, Grumbacher's Cobalt Drier can drastically reduce the drying time of oil paints without causing any adverse effects.

A number of painting mediums and drying agents are available at artist's supply stores. Experiment with these products until you obtain the finish you prefer.

MIXING AND MATCHING COLORS

To the beginner, the mixing and matching of colors is, without much doubt, one of the most perplexing phases of realistic bird carving. Invariably, aspiring bird carvers will say they are experiencing no insurmountable problems doing the actual carving but that they are completely confused when it comes to mixing, matching, and applying the paint to the carving. Most successful bird carvers in this country have had little or no art training and have had to learn the intricacies of handling paints the hard way. So, it can be done. I am firmly convinced that so-called inherent talent plays only a minor role in the development of one's abilities. I believe hard work, stick-to-it-iveness, plus a sincere and strong desire to excell are *the* important factors. I have addressed a number of challenges in my life with the question, "If Joe Blokes can do it, why can't I?" The novice painter should roll up his sleeves, get out his paints, and take this same approach.

In an attempt to present some easy way for the beginner to go about mixing and matching colors, I have gone through what I can find on the subject. After reading books and articles which purported to take the mystery out of this troublesome, but necessary, operation, I was unable to find any simple method that would benefit the novice.

Most of the material I read had to do with mixing colors for flat work such as landscapes and seascapes where many colors were determined by personal interpretation, often based on unusual or extreme lighting conditions, and further affected by overall color composition. Unfortunately for the bird carver-artist, this "looseness" is not permitted in painting of realistic bird carvings. Color must closely match those of the actual bird as seen under normal lighting conditions, making color matching a great deal more critical and obviously much more difficult. However, on the plus side, the bird carver-artist does not have to be concerned with color composition on the bird itself as nature has beautifully performed this task for him.

The only way the novice can learn to mix paints and match colors is by actually doing it; however, if he goes about this in a haphazard manner, either the learning process will be much longer or he will throw up his hands and give up. All discussions and explanations on this subject included here have been kept as simple as possible, without the use of confusing technical terms, and involve practical applications wherever possible. It is assumed that the reader knows very little about handling paints so this presentation starts with the very basics and proceeds in logical steps. It is strongly recommended that the beginner get out his paints, palette knife, and palette and follow along by actually mixing some of the different colors described, or specified, in the following discussions.

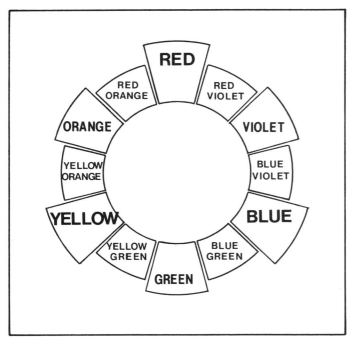

2-1 *Color wheel showing primary, secondary, and intermediate colors.*

First, the beginner should become thoroughly familiar with the classic "color wheel" (see Figures 2-1 and 2-3). Color can be broken down into three *primary* colors: *red*, *yellow*, and *blue*. If these three colors were pure "rainbow" (spectrum) colors, all other colors could be derived from them (plus the use of black and white, which are theoretically not considered colors). When red and yellow are mixed, orange will result; yellow and blue will produce green; and blue and red will produce violet. *Orange*, *green*, and *violet* are referred to as *secondary* colors. When adjacent primary and secondary colors are mixed, *intermediate* colors are created, namely: *red orange*, *yellow orange*, *yellow green*, *blue green*, *blue violet*, and *red violet*.

The beginner should go through at least a few of the steps involved in making the color wheel. The following tube colors will simulate reasonably well the three primary colors: Thalo red rose, French ultramarine blue, and cadmium yellow, light. Inasmuch as colors made from pigment have different characteristics than pure spectrum colors, the different mixtures cannot always be made on a 50%-50% basis.

Start the color wheel by removing a sheet from the disposable-type palette, draw a cirle on it, and divided it into twelve equal parts (see Figure 2-3, page 89). Squeeze out fairly large piles of the three primary colors onto the palette. Now, with the palette knife, slice off approximately equal parts of red and yellow. (Always wipe the palette knife clean after transferring each color). Mix these two colors together, identify it as "orange", and transfer about one-third of it to the proper spot on the color wheel. Next, take approximately equal parts of the orange mixture and red and mix them together. Identify this mixture as "red orange" and transfer it to the correct

spot on the color wheel. Using the same orange mixture, add an approximately equal part of yellow, mix, and identify as "yellow orange" and transfer this to the color wheel. Repeat this procedure for the rest of the color wheel. After all of the colors have been mixed and identified, save this color wheel for future use.

At this point, the novice is undoubtedly thinking this is all very good if you should want to paint a rainbow but just how does it apply when painting ducks? Very shortly, when he attempts to paint the head of a drake mallard, he will use the two primary colors, yellow and blue; the secondary color green; and the intermediate colors, yellow green and blue green (see Figure 2-9, page 95). A little later, over one half of the colors shown on the color wheel will be used when painting the iridescent head of the bufflehead drake—from yellow green, through green, blue green, blue, blue violet, and to red. Another practical application will occur when painting the male wood duck which involves the direct use of almost all of the colors shown on the color wheel.

Using the primary colors on the palette, another exercise can easily be performed at this time. Mix about equal amounts of red, yellow, and blue together. The resulting color should be very dark, approaching black. If true spectrum colors were used, instead of colors made from pigments, the mixed color would be black.

When mixing colors, it is often necessary to lighten them or darken them. Lightening a color is accomplished by adding more of the lighter color (or colors) which was used to create it, or by adding white, or both. Darkening, or graying-down, a color can be accomplished in three ways: by adding more of the darker color (or colors) which was used to create it; by adding black; or by adding its *complimentary* color. Although usually somewhat more complicated, the latter method is preferred by purists because the basic color tends to retain its vitality rather than becoming muddy in appearance. The color wheel is a necessity for determining the complimentary color which is found *diametrically* opposite the color to be darkened. For example, the complimentary color for red is green; the complimentary color for yellow is violet; and so on. Usually, this method for darkening a color is simple; however, for some colors, mixing the complimentary color can be as complicated as mixing the original color.

Refer again to the color wheel (Figure 2-3). The inner group of colors shown on this color wheel shows the primary, secondary, and intermediate colors grayed-down by the complimentary color method.

It is suggested that the beginner follow through two examples which have practical applications. The bill of a mallard drake, which will be painted very shortly, is a dull, yellow color. Squeeze a small amount of cadmium yellow (medium) onto the palette and add a very small amount of black. Note that the yellow is now darker but that it has acquired a greenish cast. By referring to the color wheel, the complimentary color for yellow is found to be violet. Mix a very small amount of alizarin (a violet color) to the cadmium yellow (medium). Notice that the yellow is now darker but has retained its rich color.

The body of a male cinnamon teal is a rich cinnamon

color. Burnt sienna from the tube is too light in color to duplicate it accurately. Try adding a small amount of black to the burnt sienna and mix. Then, do the same thing but add a small amount of cobalt blue (the approximate complimentary color) instead of the black. Note how much more vibrant the latter mixture is as compared to the one obtained by the use of black.

Using the colors aready mixed for the color wheel, the complimentary color method of graying can be easily demonstrated. As was stated previously, the complimentary color can be found diametrically opposite of the color in question. Starting with red, the complimentary color is seen to be green. Mix a small amount of the green mixture into the red. Note that the red has become grayer but has retained its rich color. By adding more green, the red becomes progressively darker. Repeat this procedure for all of the colors on the wheel and place a daub of each grayed-down color in its proper place on the color wheel. Save this chart for future reference.

As an aid to the beginner who has limited color reference material, paint mixing instructions have been included for all of the carving projects in this book. Except for the first few projects, where painting and paint mixing is described in detail, paint mixing instructions will be given using the "color formula", explained below. Although it is difficult to specify the exact proportions of two or more colors required to produce a given color, the method used here, with a little practice, will usually give fairly consistent results.

When a color is described as "white, black", these two tube colors should be mixed in equal amounts, i.e., the pile of white should be the same size as the pile of black. In this case, the amount of white is considered a *basic* amount and the amount of black is considered a *basic* amount.

When a color is described as "white, ••raw umber, •burnt sienna", the amount of white is the basic amount. The amount of raw umber specified by "••raw umber" is approximately one-tenth of the basic amount. The amount of burnt sienna, specified by "•burnt sienna" is about one-half of the above amount or approximately one-twentieth of the *basic* amount. When the amount is specified by "•–burnt sienna" (for example) would be an even smaller amount. When an amount is specified by "•+burnt sienna" (for example), it would be a somewhat larger amount than "•burnt sienna" but smaller than the amount specified by "••burnt sienna".

When a color is described as "white, black, yellow ochre, ••raw umber, •burnt sienna", the amounts of white, black, and yellow ochre are equal and each is considered a *basic* amount. The amounts of raw umber and burnt sienna are the same as in the above example.

When a color is described as "white, white, cobalt blue" the amount of white is doubled and each portion of white is considered a *basic* amount.

Considerable time can be saved when recording paint mixtures using the "color formula" if abbreviations for the tube colors are used. The following abbreviations will be used hereafter in this book:

| W | titanium white | UB | French ultramarine blue |

B	ivory black	Rl	cadmium red (light)
BU	burnt umber	Rm	cadmium red (medium)
RU	raw umber		
BS	burnt sienna	Rd	cadmium red (deep)
RS	raw sienna	RR	Thalo red rose
Y	cadmium yellow (medium)	AC	alizarin crimson
		cV	cadmium vermilion
Yl	cadmium yellow (light)	O	cadmium orange
YO	yellow ochre		
TB	Thalo blue		
CB	cobalt blue		

The beginner should practice using this "color formula" system. It is suggested that he select several colors shown on Fig. 2-6, page 92. Suppose the first color selected is described "W, ••RU, ••RS". First squeeze out small amounts of white, raw umber, and raw sienna onto the palette. Next, with the palette knife, slice off an amount of white about the size of a navy bean. Wipe the palette knife clean and then slice off an amount of raw umber about one-tenth the size of the white pile. Again, wipe the palette knife, and then slice off an amount of raw sienna equal to the amount of raw umber. Now, mix the colors thoroughly with the palette knife and then holding the palette knife flat, press it down on the paint mixture with a wiping motion so that the end of the knife is thinly coated with the mixture. Hold the palette knife closely to the color sample and compare the two colors. If the mixture on the knife is too grayish in color, try mixing again with a smaller amount of raw umber. If the mixture is too yellowish in color, try again using less raw sienna. If the mixture is generally the right color, but is too dark, add more white. If the mixture is too light, add more raw umber and raw sienna. With a little practice, the novice should be able to match the described color quite closely on the first attempt.

When the beginner uses these color formulas, it is suggested that he check his mixtures against the paintings included in this book, or preferably, against the corres-

2-2 *Palette arrangement used by author.*

ponding colors on a study skin, or mounted bird. If there is disagreement, the necessary corrections should be made and noted. When matching colors to the printed paintings, it may be easier to cover the page with Saran wrap (or a similar product) and apply a daub of paint directly on the color being used for comparison.

A given color can often be reproduced by two, or more, different combinations of tube color or it may be that the desired color can be mixed easier with fewer tube colors. The color formulas included in this book certainly should not be considered the only way, and the best way, to obtain a given color.

The mixing and matching of colors can be greatly facilitated by being methodical, establishing good procedures and religiously following these procedures. One of the first procedures the beginner should establish is the layout of his palette. There are no set rules for this—it is mainly a matter of locating the different tube colors in a convenient manner determined by personal choice, using this same arrangement each time he prepares to paint. As shown in Fig. 2-2, the palette layout used by the author starts with a fairly large pile of white followed below by much smaller piles of black, burnt umber, raw umber, raw sienna, and a very small pile of burnt sienna. Colors such as yellow ochre, cadmium yellow (medium), Thalo blue, cobalt blue, and others are added individually when needed.

A consistent palette arrangement will not only save time, it will help prevent errors caused by reaching for and using the wrong tube color.

Fortunately for the carver-artist, a large percent of the colors of all game birds can be matched, usually fairly easily, by using only a few tube colors. As a result of supplying paint mixing instructions for my recent book DECORATIVE DECOY DESIGNS, Volume I "Dabbling and Whistling Ducks," I found that approximately 80% of the different color mixtures required the use of only four tube colors (in addition to black and white), namely: burnt umber, raw umber, burnt sienna, and raw sienna—often referred to as the "earth colors". Inasmuch as burnt sienna was used infrequently, over 75% of the different colors were made from only three tube colors. It is probable that these percentages would apply to all game birds. It is very important that the beginner become very familiar with these colors. Figures 2-4, 2-5, and 2-6 were designed specifically to help this familiarization process. It is strongly suggested that the novice follow along by mixing these various colors on his own.

The color samples on these three pages will often prove to be very useful for determining the basic color from which to start when attempting to match certain colors.

The tube colors burnt umber, raw umber, raw sienna, and burnt sienna are located on the color wheel between red and yellow. This statement may be checked easily by mixing varying amounts of red and yellow and adding black. Figure 2-4, page 90 shows the effect of lightening the above mentioned four colors, plus black, by adding different amounts of white. It will be noted that when white is added to black, the mixtures become grayer, actually becoming a bluish gray. Burnt umber, from the

tube, is a dark brown. When white is added to it, the brown becomes more evident and, as more white is added, beige tones result. Raw umber is a dark, grayish brown. When white is added, the gray becomes more apparent. Raw sienna is a yellowish brown and becomes a cream color when white is added in predominent amounts. Burnt sienna is a dark tile-colored red and acquires a pinkish cast when a considerable amount of white is added.

The lightness or darkness of a particular color is referred to as "value", white having the highest value and black the lowest. Lightening a color is generally expressed as "increasing its value" and darkening a color, "decreasing its value". The term "value" is used often and its meaning should be understood and remembered by the amateur painter.

In Figure 2-4, the value of the five basic colors used is increased by the addition of white—the color samples in Column IV having the highest values.

Figure 2-5, page 91 shows the effect of adding black to these four most used colors. When black is added on a 50%-50% basis (Column I), there is very little difference between these colors. Even when white is added equally to the other two colors in the mixture (Column II), there still is little difference between the colors. It is only when white is added in predominent amounts that these colors regain their individuality (Columns III and IV).

Columns VI and VII show a comparison of graying down by the addition of black (Column VI) versus graying down by the complimentary color method (Column VII).

The approximate complimentary color for burnt umber and raw umber is blue. Raw sienna is a yellowish-brown; therefore its approximate complimentary color would be blue plus a small amount of red. Burnt sienna is a dark tile-colored red; therefore its complimentary color would be blue plus a small amount of yellow.

It will be noted that the corresponding color samples in Columns VI and VII have been grayed-down about the same amount. However, the color samples grayed by the complimentary color method are definitely on the "cool" side, i.e., are bluer (blue, green, and gray are referred to a "cool" colors). The various colors on game birds are generally on the "warm" side (yellow, orange, and red are considered "warm" colors). Therefore, the graying down of these colors, especially raw umber and raw sienna, by the addition of black appears to be more desirable than by graying them using the complimentary color method.

Figure 2-6, page 92 shows the results of mixing each of these four most used colors with the others and then adding different amounts of white. Without the addition of white, the colors are all quite dark as would be expected. It is only when white is added in substantial quantities that the new colors make themselves evident.

The amateur painter, by now, has had a chance to get his feet wet, so to speak, and should have acquired some proficiency in mixing colors as specified, or described, by the color formulas in this book. The mixing of colors, so far, has been purely mechanical and has required very little perception on his part. If he is to progress, it is of the utmost importance that he learn how to match a particular color working on his own—without being prompted as to what tube color to use.

There are three important steps involved in the mixing and matching of a particular color.

1. Determine its basic color as compared to the tube colors which are available.

There obviously has to be a starting point—unless the beginner's eyes are insensitive to certain colors, he should be able to determine whether the color to be matched is, for example, brownish, reddish-brown, yellowish-brown, or grayish-brown. If it is determined that the color appears to be brownish, or reddish-brown, burnt umber would be the logical choice for the basic color. If the color appears to be yellowish-brown, raw sienna would be used as the basic color. If the color appears to be grayish-brown, raw umber would be used.

2. Determine whether the color to be matched is "light" or "dark".

For example, colors in Columns I and II, Figures 2-4, 2-5, and 2-6 are "dark" colors inasmuch as dark colors predominate their mixtures. Colors in Columns III and IV (see Figures 2-4, 2-5, and 2-6) are "light" colors due to the fact that white is predominant. If the color to be copied appears to be a dark color, the lighter color, or colors, would be added to the dark basic color. If the color in question appears to be a light color, the basic color used would be white and the darker color, or colors, would be added to it.

3. Determine the necessary modifying color, or colors.

The mixing problem becomes more complicated at this point because perception is required to detect the existence of secondary colors and experience is required to anticipate the effect of their addition to the mixture. It is often difficult to perceive the necessary additive colors and their identification can only be determined by trial and error. When this procedure becomes necessary, it is very important that some sort of a record, or notes, be kept so the artist can see where he has been and to help prevent duplication of effort. The recording of paint mixing can be greatly facilitated by the use of abbreviations for the tube colors (see page 85) and by the use of the color formula, which has been described previously.

As was stated earlier, color mixing and matching has to be learned by doing. It is most important that the amateur artist follow along on these next paint matching exercises. The color samples on page 94 have been included without their color formulas so they can be used for practice matching. Color sample #1 will be used for the first example.

Starting out with Step 1, our sample is a warm, grayish-brown. Step 2, it is a light color; therefore white will be used as the basic color. Referring to Figure 2-4, page 90, burnt umber appears to be the tube color which would most closely match the sample. So, we will add a small amount of this color, making the color formula "W, •BU". It appears we have made a correct choice as the resulting color is definitely in the right direction but is too light. We can try four different ways to darken this mixture: add more burnt umber; add black; add its complimentary color (blue); or add some other dark color. For this discus-

sion, let us try all four. Divide the mixture into four parts (it may be necessary to a mix an additional amount of W, •BU in order to have usable amounts in each pile). Adding another •BU to the first pile results in a color of about the correct value but is too brown. Adding •B to the second pile results in a color too cool (gray). Adding •CB to the third pile results in another cool color, this time on the bluish side. Referring again to Figure 2-4, page 90, raw umber appears to be a much warmer gray. So, let us add •RU to the fourth pile. This time the resulting color matches Sample #1 closely. The final color formula is W, •BU, •RU.

Color sample #2, page 94, seems to be a light brown with a hint of red. It appears to be a light color. Starting with a basic amount of white let us add •BU. Inasmuch as the color sample seems to have a slight reddish tinge, let us also add •BS. The resulting mixture is fairly close but is somewhat lighter than the desired color. Again, let us hedge our bets and divide the mixture into two piles, labeling them W,•BU,•BS. It appears that this mixture could be grayer, so we will add •RU to the first pile and change its formula to W,•BU,•BS•RU. The color of this mixture is now very close but is still slightly light. We will decrease its value by adding an additional •RU but now find that the resulting mixture is too dark and gray. We can now go to the second pile and add an additional •BU, making the formula W,••BU,•BS,•RU, and find that we have matched the color sample very closely. Suppose we added too much burnt umber on this second try. We could start from scratch or we could add more white and just a little more burnt sienna and raw umber and would probably end up with the desired color.

Color sample #3 appears to be yellowish-brown with some red. It is a light color. Referring again to Figure 2-4, page 90, raw sienna from the tube is quite similar but is a little too dark. Starting out with a basic amount of white, let us add a similar amount of RS, making the color formula W, RS. The resulting color is too light and needs the addition of some red. •BS is added but, although the resulting color is in the right direction, it is still too light. So, we will add another •BS, making the color formula W, RS, ••BS. The resulting color this time is quite close but could be slightly grayer. Again, divide the mixture into two piles and try adding •B to the first pile and •RU to the second pile. The second pile matches the color sample more closely. The final color formula becomes W,RS,••BS,•RU.

Sample #4 duplicates the color of the back and scapulars of a California quail and appears to be a bluish-gray. However, upon looking more closely, it seems to be somewhat on the warm side, or have a warm tint (this is more evident when looking at the feathers of the actual bird). Referring again to Fig. 2-4, page 90, black and white, mixed equally, appears to be a good choice from which to start, making our color formula at this point B,W. After mixing the two colors, we find the resulting color is too dark and cool. We now warm the mixture by adding •RS but find the mixture is still too dark and cool. We add another •RS which improves the mixture but it is still too dark and cool. Suppose we start over with B,W,RS and after mixing these three colors in equal parts find that the mixture has been warmed sufficiently but is now too light. It is obvious that the correct mixture is somewhere between B,W,••RS and B,W,RS. Let us go back to the original mixture and add an additional small amount of RS and we find that the color matches the sample quite closely. The final color formula is B,W •• + RS.

Color sample #5 duplicates the upper chest of a male Carolina wood duck and is a rich, purplish-chestnut color. It is obviously a dark color. In looking over the available red colors, we find we have at least three choices for the basic color: burnt sienna, alizarin crimson, and Thalo red rose.

For a first try, let us start with burnt sienna as the basic color. Burnt sienna, from the tube, is too light and lacks the necessary purplish shade. First, we will try darkening it with its approximate complimentary color, blue, and add ••CB, making the color formula BS,••CB. The resulting color is about the correct value but still lacks the purplish shade. Starting over again, we add a small amount of alizarin to the burnt sienna, making the color formula BS,•AC, but find the mixture still needs more purple. We double the amount of alizarin crimson, making the color formula BS,••AC. We now have the desired purplish shade but the mixture is still too light and too red. Again, we will try darkening it with a small amount of cobalt blue, making the color formula BS, ••AC, •CB and we find we have matched the color sample quite closely.

We will now try another approach, using alizarin crimson as the basic color. Alizarin crimson, from the tube, is a very transparent color, one that dries quite dark. In the above example, we found that burnt sienna, a reddish-brown, worked well with alizarin crimson. We already have red in the alizarin crimson so, instead of adding burnt sienna, we will try adding burnt umber, making the color formula AC,BU. The resulting color is too red so we will try darkening it with its complimentary color, green. We add a small amount of cadmium yellow (medium) and a smaller amount of cobalt blue, making the color formula AC, BU,••Y,•CB and find we have a good match.

We will try still another approach, again using alizarin crimson as the basic color but this time we will add an equal amount of burnt sienna, making the color formula AC,BS. This mixture is too light and too red. We try adding •CB and have a color which is quite close but still slightly light. We add another •CB and obtain a mixture that matches color sample #5 closely and the final color formula is AC,BS,••CB.

Our fourth, and last approach involves the use of Thalo red rose as the basic color. When adding an equal amount of burnt umber, we find the resulting mixture to be too dark. Instead of starting over with less burnt umber, we will try adding a small amount of cadmium yellow, medium, making the color formula RR,BU,••Y. The mixture is now approaching the desired color closely but is slighly light. We can now decrease its value by adding •CB and obtain the desired results. The final color formula is RR,BU,••Y,•CB.

In this exercise, we have shown that a given color, at least sometimes, can be obtained in more than one way.

Color sample #6 duplicates the color of a blue-winged teal's head and is a dark gray with a hint of warmness (this is more obvious on the actual bird). As in example #4, black and white, mixed equally, seems to be a good choice from which to start. The resulting color in this case is too cool and too light. Raw umber, from the tube, is a dark grayish-brown and would be a likely color for darkening the mixture and also warming it. We try adding ••RU and find that the resulting mixture has been warmed but is still too light. Starting over, we try mixing B,W,RU and see that the mixture is now quite close to the desired color. The next step is difficult to justify except to those who have seen the actual bird, or a mounted bird. The head of a male blue-winged teal has a slight reddish-violet iridescence; therefore, we will add a small amount of alizarin crimson (AC), making the color formula B,W,RU,•AC. The resulting color now matches the sample closely.

Again, it takes a great deal of practice to become proficient in duplicating colors. Eventually, if the beginner seriously applies himself, he will often reach instinctively for the correct tube color. He will seldom get a good color match on the first attempt but he usually will be close and can then make the necessary modifications quite easily or start again in the correct direction.

The beginner should be aware that there are some variations in the coloring and markings of feathers of the same species and sex. Some of these dissimilarities, but not all by any means, can be attributed to age and molt. For example, first year female ducks vary some from adult females. The considerable variation of the side feather coloring of female widgeons is a good example of the color differences between adult birds of the same species and sex. Also, some adult ducks of the same species and sex have differences in the coloration of their bills and feet. Kortright's fine book, *The Ducks, Geese, and Swans of North America* covers some of these variables in his excellent written descriptions.

The carver-artist has one problem that most flat artists do not have. As was previously mentioned, a great deal of time is spent doing the actual carving of wood and getting the carving ready for paint. This means the carver has plenty of time to forget what he learned painting the previous carving—in many cases several weeks or even months may go by before the carver even thinks about painting and much he had learned has now been forgotten. Colors, and their compositions, are very difficult to remember. It is sometimes very disconcerting to try to duplicate a color he spent some time in perfecting on a previous occasion. It is strongly suggested that the carver-artist start his own notebook of color samples, including their formulas, and where they were used. It is advisable to assign consecutive numbers to these color samples so they can be easily referred to at a later date. These numbers can then be added to the drawing or pattern of each bird carving, making a permanent record of each color that was used on the various parts of the bird carving.

The amateur painter, who has now learned the rudiments of mixing paints so they will match the colors on a bird, is now ready to try his hand applying these paints. The application of paints is the second of the two most

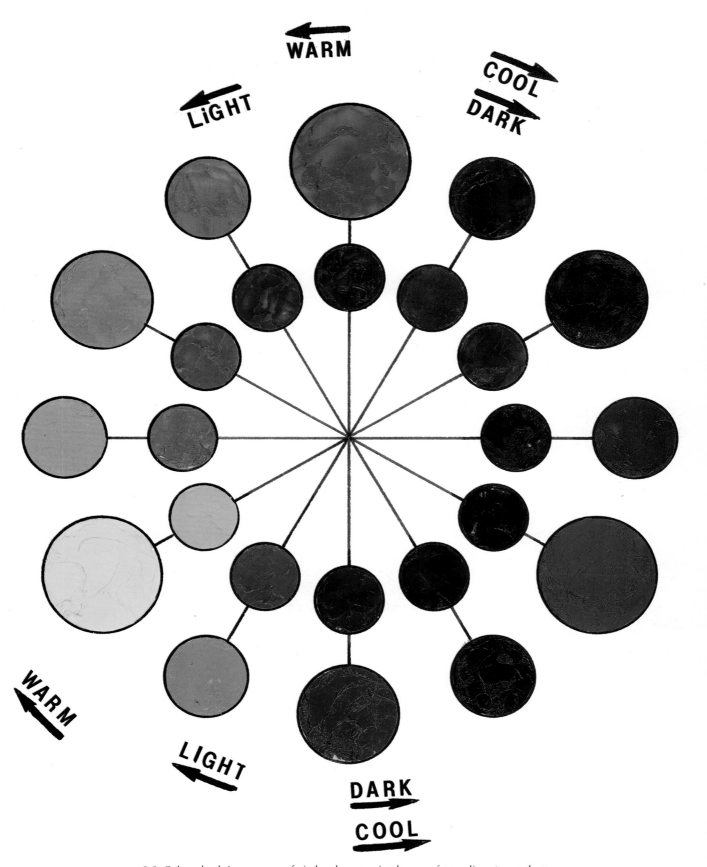

2-3 Color wheel. Inner group of circles show graying by use of complimentary colors.

Dark ← → Light

I	II	III	IV

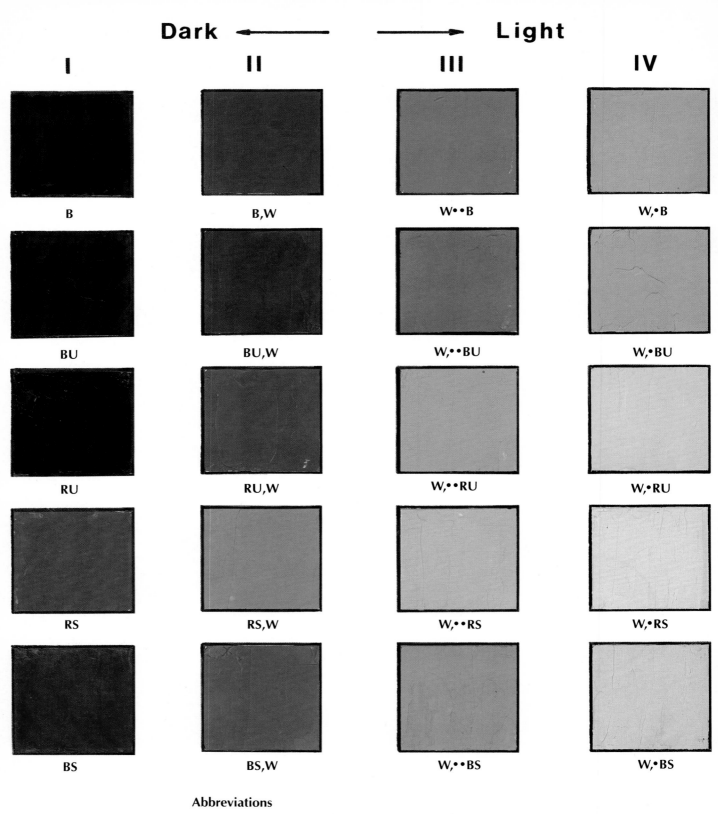

I	II	III	IV
B	B,W	W••B	W,•B
BU	BU,W	W,••BU	W,•BU
RU	RU,W	W,••RU	W,•RU
RS	RS,W	W,••RS	W,•RS
BS	BS,W	W,••BS	W,•BS

Abbreviations

B	Black	**RU**	Raw Umber
W	White	**RS**	Raw Sienna
BU	Burnt Umber	**BS**	Burnt Sienna

Fig. 2-4 *Showing the effect of adding white to black, burnt umber, raw umber, raw sienna, and burnt sienna.*

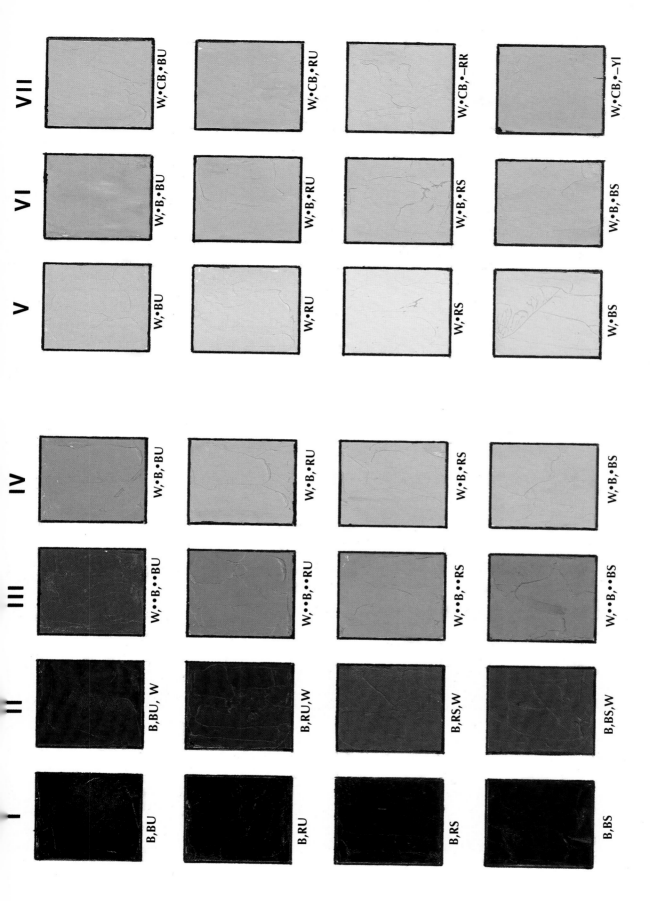

Fig. 2-5 *Showing the effect of adding black to burnt umber, raw umber, raw sienna, and burnt sienna (Col. I thru IV). Columns V thru VII show a comparison of graying with black versus graying with the complimentary color.*

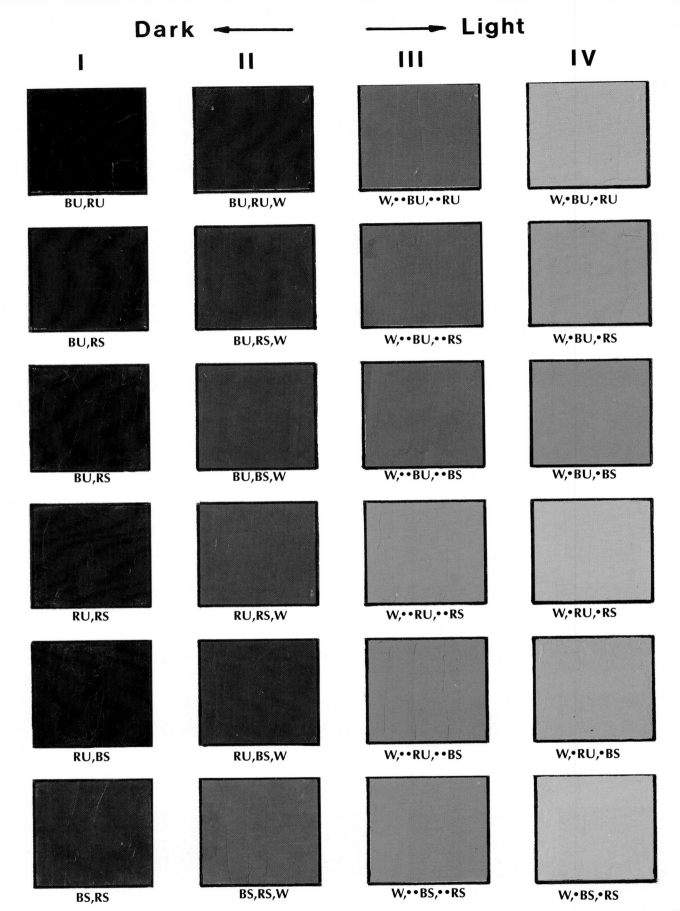

Fig. 2-6 *Showing the four "earth colors" mixed with each other and the effect of adding varying amounts of white.*

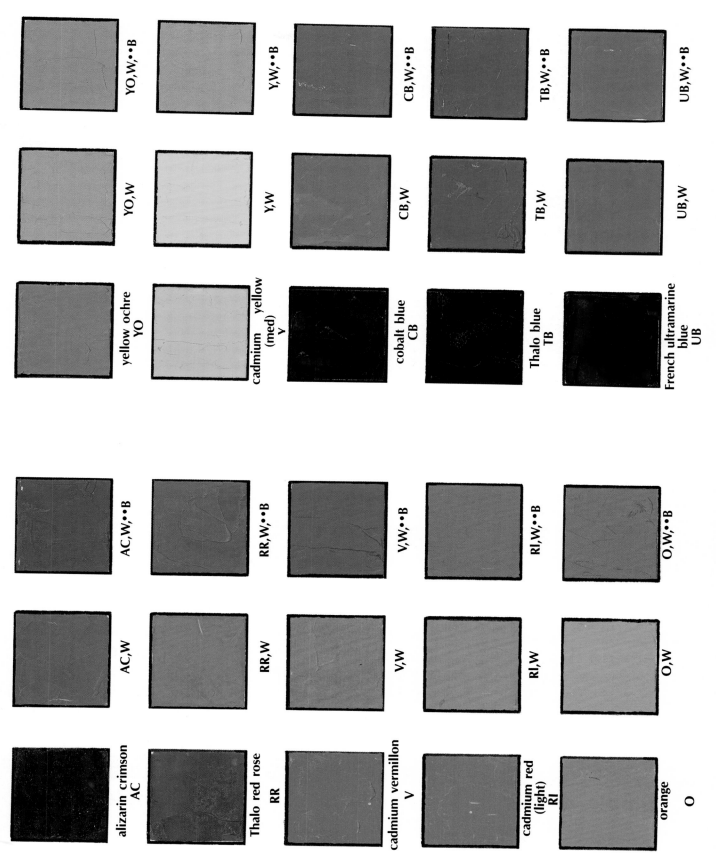

Fig. 2-7 *Showing occasionally used colors and the effect of adding white and adding white and black.*

YO,W,••B

YO,W

yellow ochre
YO

Y,W,••B

Y,W

cadmium yellow (med)
Y

CB,W,••B

CB,W

cobalt blue
CB

TB,W,••B

TB,W

Thalo blue
TB

UB,W,••B

UB,W

French ultramarine blue
UB

AC,W,••B

AC,W

alizarin crimson
AC

RR,W,••B

RR,W

Thalo red rose
RR

V,W,••B

V,W

cadmium vermillon
V

RI,W,••B

RI,W

cadmium red (light)
RI

O,W,••B

O,W

orange
O

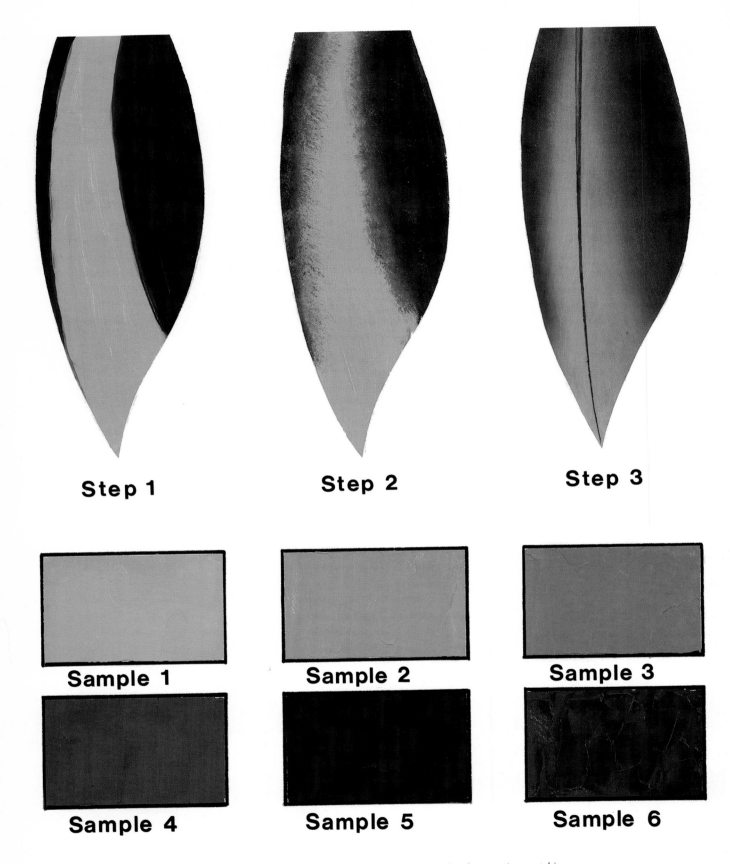

Step 1

Step 2

Step 3

Sample 1

Sample 2

Sample 3

Sample 4

Sample 5

Sample 6

2-8 *Painting a mallard's tertial feather and color samples for practice matching.*

2-9 *Painting the mallard and canvasback drakes' heads.*

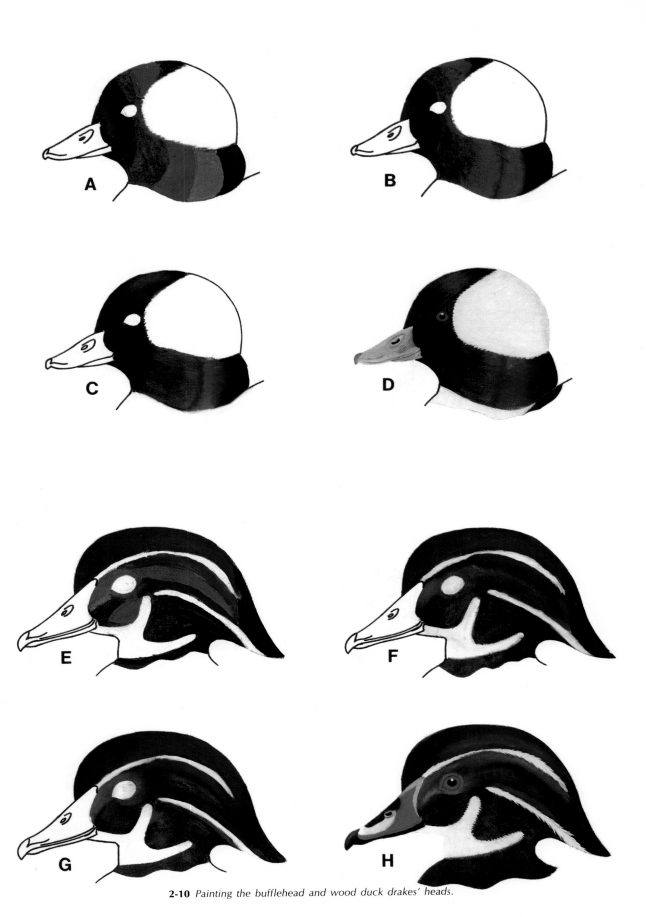

2-10 *Painting the bufflehead and wood duck drakes' heads.*

troublesome problems confronting most beginning bird carvers. Before attempting to paint an actual carving, the author strongly recommends he practice first on a flat surface. A great deal of time can be saved and much can be learned in this manner. Art stores carry a variety of paper pads which are suitable for oils and are ideal for practice painting.

The aspiring artist should first practice blending two colors. When he has mastered this seemingly simple procedure, he will have made his first step towards the successful handling of paints. First, draw a line on a practice sheet and brush burnt umber paint on one side of the line and yellow ochre on the other. (Fig. 2-11)

Note: On this exercise and all other exercises and instructions on painting it will be necessary to mix a small amount of painting medium into the paint from the tube.

2-13 *Brush the yellow ochre into the burnt umber.*

2-11 *Paint burnt umber on one side of a line and yellow ochre on the other.*

2-14 *Brush the burnt umber into the yellow ochre.*

2-12 *Stipple the two colors along their junction.*

2-15 *Finish blending the two colors with a fan blender.*

Now, blend the two colors together along their junction by stippling (Fig. 2-12). Stippling is accomplished by lightly tapping a dry brush held perpendicular to the surface. Wipe the brush clean and dry every few stipple strokes. After roughly blending the two colors in the area where they meet, further blend them by lightly brushing, from the dark into the light and the light into the dark, using a #4 or #6 sable flat brush wiped clean and dry after every stroke or two (Figs. 2-13 and 2-14).

Further blend the two colors with a larger flat sable brush, or a fan blender using light brush strokes parallel to the original line of intersection between the two colors until a gradual change from dark to light is obtained. It may be necessary to work more of the darker color into the lighter, or vice versa, to attain a smooth transition from burnt umber on one side to pure raw sienna on the other side.

Start out by sketching the outline of one of these feathers (Fig. 2-8, page 94) on the practice paper. Life-size, they are about one and 3/4 inches wide and four inches long (Fig. 2-16). The center part of the web is a grayish-brown. The outer part of the feather is a dark brown and shades into the gray center. Paint the outer part of the feather and the narrow stripe on the inner edge with burnt umber and raw sienna, mixed about equally (BU,RS). Paint the center portion of the feather with white and a small amount of raw umber (W,••RU). See Fig. 2-8, Step 1. Using the procedure already covered, blend these two colors together. After the blending has been completed, and the paint has dried, the aspiring artist might try his hand at painting-in the feather shaft, using a round 0 sable brush and some of the outer web paint mixture.

The second practical application of color blending will be the duplication of the beautiful, iridescent head of the

2-16 A mallard drake's large tertial feather.

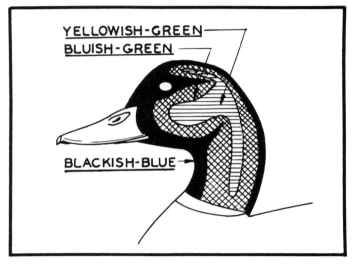

2-17 Approximate location of the head colors—mallard drake.

Repeat the above exercise but this time mix burnt umber and yellow ochre about equally and, using this mixture, paint a strip about one-half inch wide between the two colors. Proceed with the blending as before until a gradual transition is made. Note how much easier it is to blend two colors when an intermediate color is used.

Do this exercise one more time using black and white. It will quickly become apparent that it is much more difficult to blend colors having such a difference in value and still retain the pure original colors on the extreme sides of the transition. In this case, an intermediate color, or colors, will greatly facilitate making a clean transition from black to white.

The two most important things to remember when blending colors are to keep the brush dry and clean and to use very light, smooth brush strokes.

The male mallard's large tertial feathers are a beautiful example of the blending of colors by nature. A painting exercise duplicating one of these feathers provides a practical application of what has been learned so far.

mallard drake. As was pointed out previously, this will involve the direct use of two primary colors and one secondary color and two intermediate colors—straight from the classical color wheel!

The painting of the drake's head will be accomplished using black (B), burnt umber (BU), Thalo blue (TB), and cadmium yellow, medium (Y). Squeeze out a small amount of each color onto the palette. Trace off the outline of the mallard's head from Fig. 1-124, page 19, and transfer this to the practice paper. Next, referring to Fig. 2-17 and Fig. 2-9A, page 95, lightly sketch the areas of different colors. Paint the area marked "blackish-blue" with B,••BU,•TB. Next, mix the bluish-green color, Y,•• +TB, and apply this mixture to the rest of the head and neck and blend into the blackish-blue paint (Fig. 2-9 B). Now, add more yellow paint, Y, to the area marked "yellowish-green", Fig. 2-9 C. The addition of this yellow paint (when blended into the bluish-green paint) will produce a bright, rich green color, similar to the highlighted iridescent color on the mallard's head. The location and

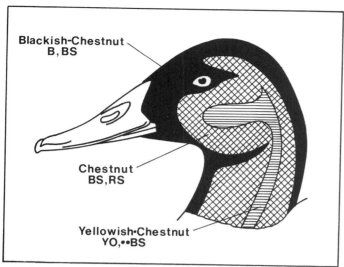

2-18 *Approximate location of the head colors—canvasback drake.*

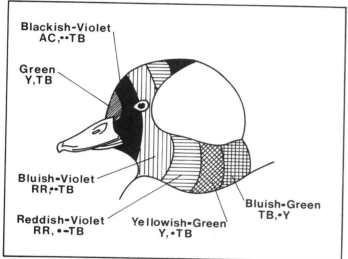

2-19 *Approximate location and mixture of the head colors—bufflehead drake.*

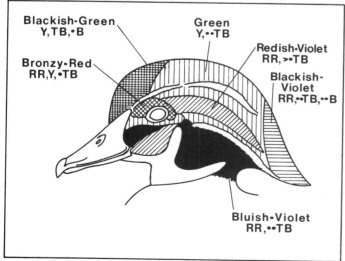

2-20 *Approximate location and mixture of the head colors—wood duck drake.*

extent of this iridescent area will vary, depending on the angle of the sun's rays (see Fig. 1-216, page 73). When there is no reflection from the sun, the mallard's entire head appears to be bluish-black.

The third practical application of color blending will involve the drake canvasback's head. See Figure 1-79, page 31, and Fig. 2-18. This exercise is very similar to the preceding one, except there is no duplicating of an iridescent color involved.

Four tube colors are required for this exercise: black (B), burnt sienna (BS), raw sienna (RS), and yellow ochre (YO). Referring to Fig. 2-18, and Fig. 2-9D, page 95, mix equal parts of burnt sienna and raw sienna (BS,RS) for the area marked chestnut; mix equal parts of black and burnt sienna (B, BS) for the area marked "blackish-chestnut"; and mix yellow ochre and a small amount of burnt sienna (YO,••BS) for the highlighted areas on the cheek and neck. Apply and blend these colors in the manner previously described. See Fig. 2-9D, E and F.

The next practical application of mixing and blending colors will be somewhat more difficult and will involve duplicating the bufflehead drake's colorful head. See Figures 2-19 and Fig. 2-10, page 96. This exercise will require the following tube colors: white (W), raw umber (RU), Thalo red rose (RR), alizarin crimson (AC), Thalo blue (TB), and cadmium yellow, medium (Y). As before, start out by making a tracing of the head (Fig. 1-181, page 65); transfer it to the practice paper. Referring to Figures 2-19 and 2-10, lay out the areas of different colors—the color formulas are also shown in this figure. Mix them and apply them as shown in Fig. 2-10A. Next, stipple the different colors at their junctions.

Note: It is especially important that the brush, or brushes, be kept very clean and dry, otherwise the brilliant colors will be muddied.

Continue by very delicately brushing and blending these colors. If a particular color becomes muddy, wipe it off and apply new. As with the mallard drake, the bright colors are a result of the reflection of the sun's rays—without the sun, the bufflehead drake's head is quite dark, except for the large white patch. It is difficult to paint the head patch while the bright head colors are still wet. After the paint has dried, mix a very small amount of raw umber into white and apply this to the head patch.

The fifth, and last, practical exercise for the mixing and blending of colors will be the duplication of the incomparable male wood duck's head. As with the bufflehead drake, the addition of the white markings should be done after the bright head paints are dry.

The painting of the male wood duck's head (see Fig. 1-180, page 64) involves the following tube colors: white (W), black (B), Thalo red rose (RR), Thalo blue (TB), and cadmium yellow, medium (Y). Refer to Figures 2-20 and 2-10E for the location of the different colors and their color formulas. Most of the male wood duck's head colors are iridescent and the colors that are seen vary with the angle of the sun's rays—they have to be seen under actual conditions to be fully appreciated. Again, the painting of the wood duck's head requires very careful and delicate blending. It may be necessary to touch-up the colors after the original paints are dry, or almost dry.

PAINTING THE MALLARD DRAKE
(See full-color illustration, Fig. 2-100, head painting illustrations, Fig. 2-9, and color photos, Figs. 1-216, 217).

Preparatory to any actual painting, assemble all photographs of mallard drakes, especially those in color, that you possibly can. In addition, make every attempt to study the actual bird. Then familiarize yourself with the basic colors of the plumage, giving special attention to areas such as the tertials, where colors blend.

Some means must be provided to support the carving while it is being painted and to facilitate handling while

2-22 *Seal the wood with lacquer sanding sealer.*

2-21 *Simple holding fixture for painting a half-body decoy.*

2-23 *After sealing, sand the carving lightly.*

the paint is wet. A holding fixture (Fig. 2-21) is simple to make; almost any scrap of plywood larger than the carving will suffice. Add another piece of plywood, smaller than the carving, for spacing the carving away from the holding fixture. Attach the carving by means of two woodscrews.

Seal the wood before applying the undercoat. Lacquer sanding sealer, thinned about 50 percent with lacquer thinner, works well, dries in a very short time, and can be applied with either a brush or a cloth (Fig. 2-22). When the sealer is dry, sand lightly with 6/0 sandpaper or 3/0 steel wool (Fig. 2-23). Be careful not to scratch the glass eye.

It is usually desirable to make the undercoat approximate the final colors of the different areas, but in order to simplify these first painting projects, an undercoat of white Hyplar acrylic paint will be used. Thin the Hyplar with water and apply evenly over the entire carving (Fig. 2-24). Work carefully to eliminate brush marks or build-ups. Allow about twenty minutes for the undercoat to dry.

2-24 *Apply a thin coat of white Hyplar.*

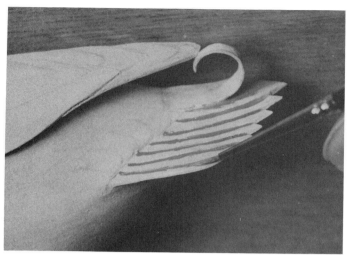

2-25 *Paint the inner part of each tail feather.*

(Wet brush bristles thoroughly with water prior to painting. Wash brush in soap and water when finished.)

Because of the overlapping of feathers, the finished painting must usually start at the tail and proceed forward. The upper edges of the side feathers overlap the scapulars, tertials, and secondaries; therefore, these areas must be painted before the side feathers.

The upperside of the tail will be painted first. Mix equal amounts of white and raw umber (W,RU) and add a small amount of medium (equal parts of linseed oil and turpentine will do nicely for this first painting attempt). If desired, a very small amount of Cobalt drier may also be added to speed drying time.

Note: Although it will not be mentioned in future paint mixing instructions, medium (and possibly drier) should be added to all paint mixtures.

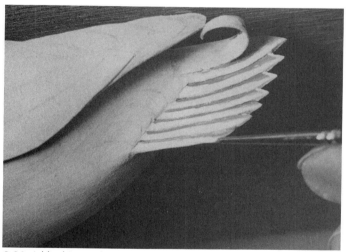

2-26 *Add white to the outer edge of each feather.*

2-28 *An excellent way to clean brushes.*

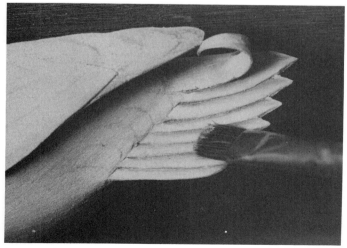

2-27 *Carefully blend the two colors.*

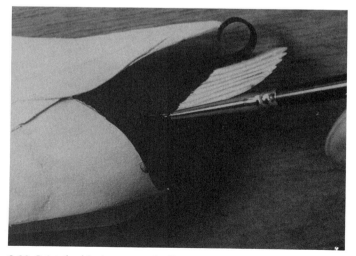

2-29 *Paint the black rump and tail coverts.*

2-30 *Paint the primaries next.*

Using a #2 round sable brush, apply a stripe of the above described paint along the inside of each carved tail feather (Fig. 2-25). Now, mix a very small amount of raw umber into white (W,•RU) and brush this paint onto the outer edges of each feather (Fig. 2-26). Blend the two colors along their junction lightly and smoothly with a clean dry brush so that there are no ridges of paint (Fig. 2-27). Paint the underside of the tail with the lighter colored mixture (W,•RU). See Fig. 2-100, page 121.

Use a brush for each color, if desired, or quickly clean the brush for the next color. When cleaning a brush, first wipe off the excess paint on a paper towel or cloth. Then stroke the bristles across the coils of a Silicoil brush cleaning jar filled with Silicoil brush cleaning fluid until they are clean (Fig. 2-28). Wipe the bristles dry. Clean all brushes thoroughly after each painting session. The Silicoil jar is highly recommended for fast cleaning and conditioning of the brush. If it is not available, almost any jar

2-31 *Paint the white neck band so that it can be drying.*

2-33 *Paint the dark areas of the tertials.*

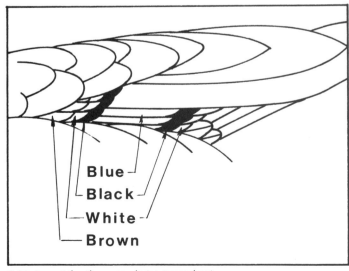

Blue
Black
White
Brown

2-32 *Layout for the secondaries (speculum).*

2-34 *Paint the light areas next.*

filled with turpentine or paint thinner can be used. In this case, stroke the brush bristles against the side of the jar and wipe with paper towels or a cloth until clean.

Continuing with the painting of the mallard, sketch the forward extent of the black on the rump and under tail covert area. Mix black and a small amount of burnt umber (B,••BU) and paint this area including the curled tail feather (Fig. 2-29). Carefully paint back to the tail feathers. Using a 00 or 000 round sable brush, drag the black paint with single brush strokes, back into the tail feathers to duplicate the feathery edges of the tail coverts. When making these fine lines, wipe the brush clean after every stroke. If desired, this could be done after the tail paint is dry; however, as the amateur progresses he will be using the *alla prima* (wet-on-wet) technique more and more. Adding these feathery edges will give him his first experience with this technique. Brush the forward extent of the black paint to eliminate any ridges of paint.

Proceed now to the primaries. Paint this group, including the edges and underside, with burnt umber and raw umber, equally mixed, and lightened with a small amount of white (BU,RU,•W). See Fig. 2-30. The fine, light-colored edgings of these feathers will be added after the paint has dried.

Add a very small amount of Cobalt drier to the whitish mixture used for the tail feather edges (W,•RU) and paint the white neck band area (Fig. 2-31). This area is painted now so that it will be dry when the neck and chest are painted. Yellow is a slow drying paint so it would be advisable to paint the bill at this time (see text, page 84). The mallard drake's bill is a dull, yellow color. Cadmium yellow (medium) will be used and darkened, or grayed, by its complimentary color which is violet. Add a very small amount of alizarin crimson to the yellow (Y,•AC); also add a very small amount of Cobalt drier. Paint the entire bill with this mixture.

Referring to Fig. 2-32, sketch-in the secondary feathers (speculum). The blue area is a mixture of white and alizarin crimson, mixed equally, with a small amount of

2-36 *Finish blending the two colors using a large, camel's-hair brush.*

2-37 *Showing the finished tertials.*

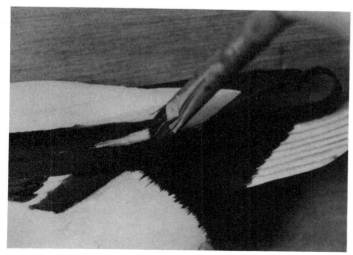

2-35 *Blend the two colors by stippling.*

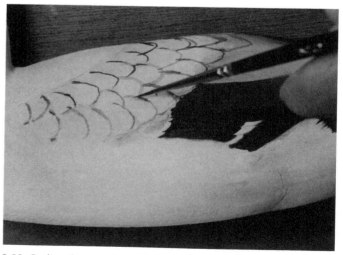

2-38 *Outline the scapulars with a small brush.*

Thalo blue added (W, AC,••TB); the black edgings are a mixture of black and a small amount of burnt umber (B,••BU); and the white markings are white plus a very small amount of raw umber (W,•RU). Paint the white areas first, then the black, and finish by painting the blue area. Delineate each feather with fine black lines. The speculum requires very careful painting. It may be necessary to retouch this area after the paint has dried.

Move along to the painting of the tertial feathers. The painting of one of the mallard's tertial feathers was included previously as a painting exercise—see Fig. 2-16, the text on page 98 and Fig. 2-8. There are two paint mixtures involved: burnt umber and raw sienna, mixed equally (BU,RS) for the darker areas and white mixed with a small amount of raw umber (W,••RU) for the lighter areas. Paint the darker areas first (Fig. 2-33) and then apply the lighter paint (Fig. 2-34). Blend the two colors along their junction by stippling (see page 86 and Fig. 2-35). Further blend the two colors with light, smooth brush strokes, keeping the brush dry and clean (Fig 2-36). Fig. 2-37 shows the painted tertials.

Now, proceed with the painting of the scapulars. Referring to drawing Fig. 1-24, page 19, outline each of the

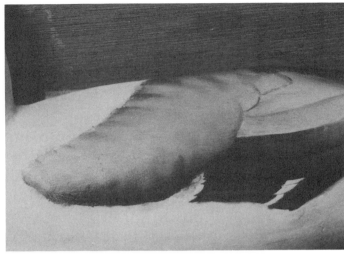
2-41 *Blend the two colors by stippling and brushing.*

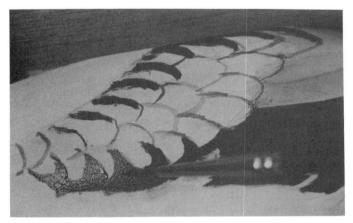
2-39 *Paint the dark areas first.*

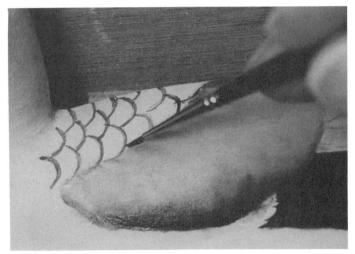
2-42 *Outline each of the back feathers.*

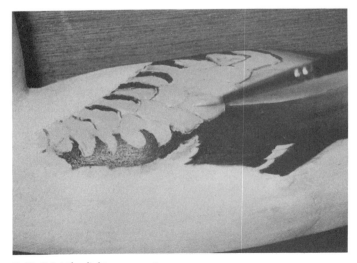
2-40 *Paint the light areas next.*

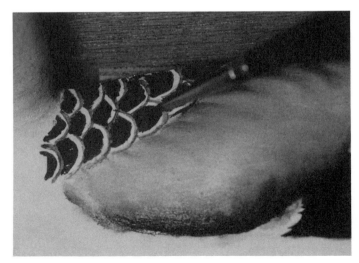
2-43 *Paint the dark areas, leaving the edges unpainted.*

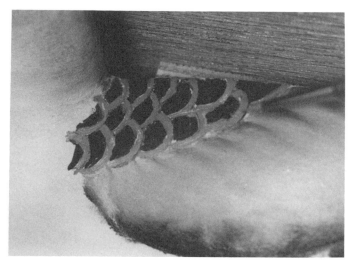
2-44 *Paint the lighter edges next.*

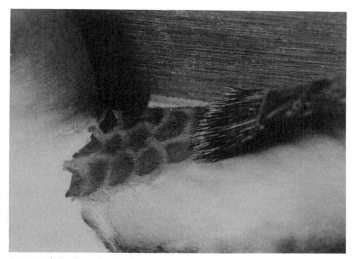
2-45 *Lightly drag the dark paint into the edges.*

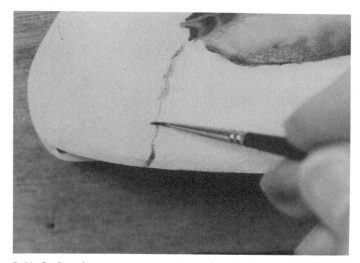
2-46 *Outline the rearmost extent of the chest feathers.*

scapular feathers. The method of outlining shown in Fig. 2-38 is a most useful one. Pencil marks are often difficult to cover with light-colored paints; also the indentation of these marks is sometimes visible through the paint. A better method is to outline the feathers with a small 00 or 000 round sable brush dipped in a darker colored paint that has been thinned considerably with turpentine. Errors can be corrected by simply wiping the markings off with a piece of paper towel or cloth dipped in turpentine. Paint the outer edges of the outer feathers and the inner edges of the inner feathers with the same dark brown mixture used on the scapulars (BU,RS). See Fig. 2-39. Mix a light gray paint using white and very small amounts of raw umber, raw sienna, and black (W,•RU,•RS,•B). Mix a somewhat larger amount of this paint as it will also be used for the side of the body. Apply this mixture to the unpainted areas of the scapular feathers (Fig. 2-40). Carefully blend these two colors by stippling and brushing (Fig. 2-41).

Paint the back feathers next. Referring again to Fig. 1-24, page 19, outline each of these feathers (Fig. 2-42). Mix raw sienna and a small amount of burnt umber (RS,••BU) and apply it to the back feathers leaving their

2-47 *Paint the rump area.*

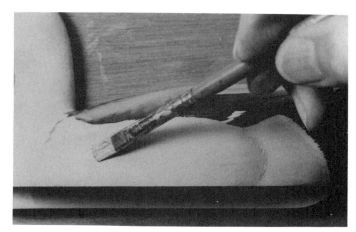
2-48 *Paint the side feathers.*

edges unpainted (Fig. 2-43). Now, mix white and small amounts of raw sienna and burnt umber (W,••RS,••BU) and carefully paint the feather edges (Fig. 2-44). Drag the bristles of a fan blender *very* lightly over these feathers. If this technique is done with care, a very realistic, feathery effect can be gotten (Fig. 2-45).

Add more white to a small portion of the gray mixture (W,•RU,•RS,•B) used for the scapulars and paint the flank area. Drag this paint into the black to give a feathery effect (Fig. 2-46).

Sketch the rearmost extent of the chestnut-colored chest feathers (Fig. 2-47). Paint the side feathers with the un-lightened mixture (Fig. 2-48).

Mix burnt sienna and a small amount of cobalt blue (BS,••CB) for the mallard's rich chestnut-colored chest feathers. Carefully drag this paint into the gray side feathers and upward into the white neck band in the manner previously described (Fig. 2-49).

Paint the head and neck next. Refer to Figures 2-9 and 2-17. Mix black and very small amounts of Thalo blue and burnt umber (B,•TB,•BU) for the areas designated blackish-blue. For the bluish-green area, mix cadmium yellow (medium) and a small amount of Thalo blue (Y,••TB). First, apply the blackish-blue mixture (Fig. 2-50)

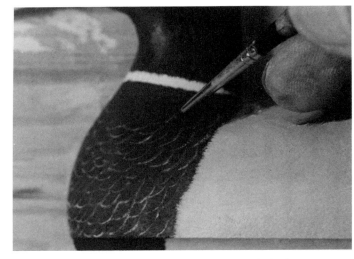

2-51 *After the chest paint is dry, lightly outline each feather.*

2-52 *Delineate each primary feather.*

2-49 *Apply paint to the chest area.*

2-50 *Paint the dark areas of the head first.*

2-53 *Showing the finished mallard drake.*

2-54 *Finished mallard, when framed, makes an attractive wall hanging.*

and then apply the bluish green mixture to the rest of the head and neck (Fig. 2-9A). Stipple and blend these two colors (Fig. 2-9B). Next, apply cadmium yellow (medium), from the tube, to the highlighted area designated yellowish-green (Fig. 2-17). Stipple and blend the yellow paint carefully to give the iridescent effect seen when the sunlight is on the mallard drake's head. Drag the green paint into the white neck band to produce a feathery effect.

Add more raw umber into the side feather paint mixture and very lightly outline each of the chest feathers (Fig. 2-51).

Delineate each primary feather with white mixed with a small amount of raw umber (W,••RU). See Fig. 2-52.

Paint the nail of the bill and the nostril with black mixed with a small amount of burnt umber (B,••BU). Carefully scrape away any paint that may have gotten onto the glass eye accidently.

Inspect the entire carving for missed spots and touch up any areas that may have gotten muddied. Allow the paint to dry thoroughly before removing the carving from the holding fixture.

PAINTING THE CANVASBACK DRAKE

Painting the male canvasback is very similar to painting the mallard drake. In this instance, however, the entire bird will be painted *alla prima*—without permitting certain areas to dry before proceeding.

Attach the carving to the holding fixture and seal the wood with lacquer sanding sealer, thinned with lacquer thinner. Sand lightly or rub with 3/0 steel wool. Brush an undercoat of white Hyplar, thinned with water, over the entire surface of the carving.

Supplement these instructions by referring to the canvasback full-color illustration (Fig. 2-101, page 122) and color photos Figures 1-218 and 1-219, page 74.

After laying out the rearmost extent of the tail coverts and the individual tail feathers, paint the upper and lower surfaces of the tail with a mixture of burnt umber, white, and a small amount of black (BU,W,••B). Make the indi-

vidual tail feathers prominent by painting a fine line of burnt umber just outboard of each upper tail feather and just inboard of each lower tail feather and lightly blend the burnt umber into the tail paint. Lay out the forward extent of the black tail coverts and rump areas and paint with black mixed with a small amount of burnt umber (B,••BU). Drag the black paint into the wet tail paint to create the feathery edges of the tail coverts.

Mix a medium gray color using white and a small amount of black (W,•• + B), and paint the secondaries, but do not paint the edges of the three upper secondary feathers. Paint these edges with the black mixture used for the tail coverts. The upper and lower surfaces of the bill may also be painted with this same black at this time.

Now, mix a small amount of black into white (W,•B) to duplicate the basic body color of the male canvasback. Add a very small additional amount of black to a small portion of this mixture and paint the flank area. Drag some of this paint, with fine, careful brush strokes into the black tail covert paint.

Paint the exposed wing covert feathers next. These feathers are finely vermiculated with a brownish-black, giving them a brownish overall effect. If they are not to be vermiculated, paint them with white, mixed with very small amounts of burnt umber and black (W,•BU,•B). If they are to be vermiculated, paint them with the basic body gray paint. Lightly delineate the individual feathers with a slightly darker mixture. Paint the primaries with burnt umber and raw umber, mixed with a small amount of white (BU,RU,••W). Finely paint the edges of these feathers with white mixed with a very small amount of raw umber (W,•RU).

Using the light gray mixture (W,•B), paint the entire area of the tertials, scapulars, and the back. Apply a small amount of the medium gray mixture (W,•• + B) just above the side' feathers to delineate the two feather groups. Blend this paint into the scapulars.

Paint the side feathers with the light gray mixture (W,•B).

Lay out the line separating the chestnut-colored neck from the black chest and back. Carefully paint the black chest, using black mixed with a small amount of burnt umber (B,••BU), just back to where it touches the gray body paint. Again, using light brush strokes, drag the black paint into the gray body paint.

Refer to page 99 and Fig. 2-9, page 95, for painting the canvasback's head and neck.

The painting of the carving can be considered finished at this point unless the beginner wishes to add vermiculations. See page 289 for some of the ways these fine markings can be duplicated.

PAINTING THE CINNAMON TEAL DRAKE

The beautifully colored cinnamon teal drake is an interesting bird to paint. Paint mixing instructions for this project (and for most of the subsequent projects) will be given by color formula. See page 85 for an explanation of this paint mixing method and for the abbreviations used. Also, refer to the full-color illustration of the cinnamon

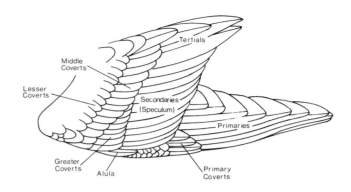

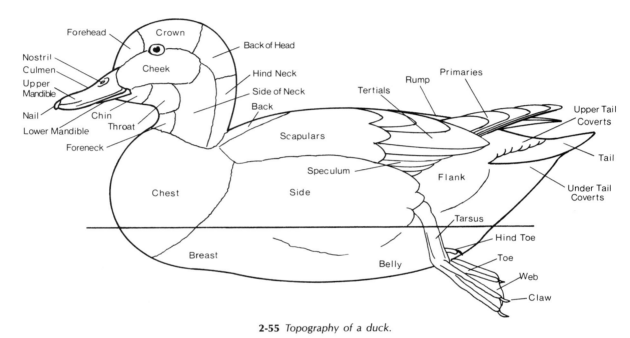

2-55 *Topography of a duck.*

teal drake, Figure 2-102, page 123, and color photos Figs. 1-220, 221.

Head and Neck
Bill: B,•BU,•W
Forehead and crown: B,•BU; small feathers edged with BS,••CB.
Rest of head: BS,••CB
Eye: 7-mm orange red.

Body
Back and forward scapulars: BS,Y0; marked with B,BU.
Rear scapulars: B,•BU,•Y,•TB; streaked with W,RS,•BS.
  Outer web of one scapular—W,••B,•CB.
Sides and chest: BS,••CB.
Upper flanks: B,BS; faintly edged with BS,YO.
Rump: BU,RS; edged with W,RS,•BU.
Upper tail coverts: BU,RS; edged with W,RS,•BU.
Lower tail coverts: BU,B; faintly edged with W,•RU.

Tail
Upper surface: BU,RS; edged with W,RS,•RU.
Lower surface: W,•RU,•BU; edged with W,•RU.

Wing
Primaries: BU,RU,••W; faintly edged with W,•RU.
Tertials: Outer webs—B,•BU,•Y,•TB; edged with W,R-S,•BU.
Inner webs—BU,RS. Tertials streaked with W,RS, •B-S,•BU.

PAINTING THE NORTHERN SHOVELER DRAKE
(See full-color illustration, Figure 2-103, page 124, and color photos, Figures 1-222, 223, page 75.)

The Northern shoveler drake is closely related to the cinnamon teal and is also an interesting painting subject.

Paint Mixing Instructions

Head and Neck

Bill: B,••BU,•W.
Crown, forehead, chin, and throat: B,••BU; small feathers edged with W,BU,RS.
Cheeks, sides and back of neck: Y,••TB. Add more Y in

areas where iridescent effect is desired such as on the highlighted areas of the cheek and side of neck.
Eyes: 9-mm yellow.

Body
Back: W,BU,RS; edged with W,•RU.
Long, rear scapulars; B,••Y,•TB. Streaked with W,•RU. Outer vane of one long scapular—W,••B,•CB.
Forward scapulars: W,BU,RS; streaked with W,•RU.
Outer scapulars: W,•RU.
Sides: BS,•CB. On upper and rear side feathers, lighten mixture with raw RS,W. These feathers are lightly vermiculated with B,••BU (vermiculations are more prominent on some birds than shown). Feathers edged with W,•RS,•RU.
Upper flanks: W,•RU.
Lower flanks: W,RS; marked with BU,•W.
Upper and lower tail coverts: B,••BU. Highlighted with Y,•TB.
Chest: W,•RU.

Tail
Upperside: BU,••W; edged with W,•RU.
Lower side: W,••RU; edged with W,•RU.

Wing
Primaries: BU,RU,••W.; faintly edged with W,•RU.
Secondaries (speculum): Y,•TB.
Tertials: Outer webs—B,••Y,•TB. Inner webs—BU,RS,W; streaked with W,•RU.

PAINTING THE GREEN-WINGED TEAL DRAKE
Refer to the full-color illustration of this duck, Figure 2-104, page 125, and color photos, Figures 1-224, 225.

The tiny green-winged teal drake, in the eyes of many, is one of our most beautiful ducks.

Paint Mixing Instructions

Head and Neck

Bill: B,••BU,•W.
Forehead, crown, back of head, cheeks, and neck: BS,••YO,•BU.

Chin: add black to the above mixture.
Eye patch: Y,•TB. Shades into B around eye; edged on lower side with W,•RS.
Lower crest feathers: B,••BU,•TB.
Eyes: 7-mm brown.

Body
Back and sides: W,•B,•RU; vermiculated with B,••BU.
Scapulars, forward and outer: Same as back. Feathers streaked with BU,RU,W. Outer webs of some outer scapulars—B,••BU,•TB. Outer webs of large scapulars—W,RU. Inner webs—BU,RU,W.
Chest: W,••RS,•RU,•BS; spotted with B,••BU.
Flanks: same as sides but lighter—add W. Also add RS to area just forward of black stripe.

Upper tail coverts: B,••BU,•TB; edged on inner webs with W,RS,•RU. Highlighted with Y,•TB.
Lower tail coverts: B,••BU,•TB. Outer feathers—W,••RS; bordered on the front with B,••BU,•TB.

Tail
Upper side: BU,RU,RS,W; edged with W,•RU. Highlighted with Y,•TB.
Lower side: W,••BU,••B; edged with W,•RU.

Wings
Primaries: BU,RU,••W; faintly edged with W,•RU.
Secondaries (speculum): Y,•TB.
Tertials: BU,RU,W; streaked with BU. Outermost tertials broadly edged with B,••BU,•TB.

PAINTING THE RING-NECKED DUCK DRAKE
(See full-color illustration Fig. 2-105, page 126, and color photo, Fig. 1-226, page 78)

The jaunty little ring-necked duck drake is another interesting painting subject. Painting both sides of this full-body working decoy will give the beginner experience in applying the paint symmetrically.

A simple holding fixture, made from ¼-inch plywood

2-56 *Simple holding fixture facilitates handling of the carving.*

2-57 *Sketch the outline of the different feathers.*

will facilitate handling the carving while the paint is wet (Fig. 2-56).

Attach the decoy to the holding fixture with two wood screws and seal the wood with thinned lacquer sanding sealer. Sand lightly or rub with 3/0 steel wool. Coat the entire surface of the carving with white Hyplar, thinned with water.

Refer to drawing, Figure 1-127, page 50, and lay out the scapular feathers and the rearmost extent of the black chest (Fig. 2-57). Burnt umber or raw umber, thinned with turpentine, and applied with a small brush is a good way to make this layout.

Start by painting the upper surface of the tail. First, paint a stripe of black just outboard of the outer edge of each carved feather. Mix a very small amount each of raw sienna and white into raw umber (RU,•RS,•W) and apply it to the rest of each tail feather (Fig. 2-58). Next, brush a stripe of white paint along the outer edge of each feather, wet-on-wet (Fig. 2-59) and blend the three colors with an angular white bristle brush, moving the brush diagonally to the rear to simulate the feather's barb lines (Fig. 2-60). Paint the underside of the tail with burnt umber and white (BU,W).

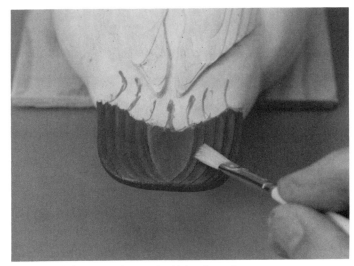

2-60 *Blend the two colors and add brush marks.*

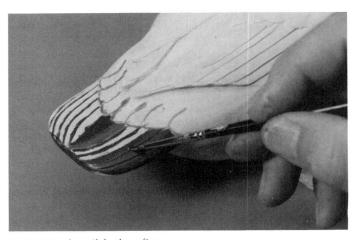

2-58 *Paint the tail feathers first.*

2-61 *Paint the rump and tail covert areas.*

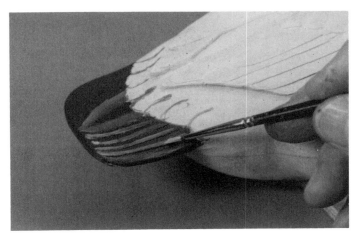

2-59 *Lighten their outer edges by adding white.*

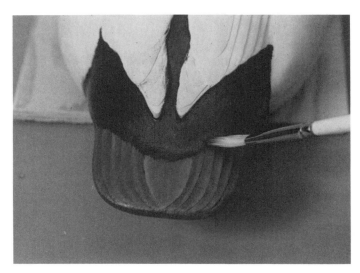

2-62 *Add brush marks and drag the black paint onto the tail feathers.*

Mix black and burnt umber, about equally (B,BU), and apply this mixture to the rump, flanks, and tail covert areas (Fig. 2-61). Clean the angular white bristle brush and add brush marks to simulate feather texture and drag the blackish paint back onto the tail feathers to create a feathery effect (Fig. 2-62).

Paint the primaries next using a small amount of white mixed into burnt umber and raw umber (BU,RU,••W) and faintly outline each feather with white to which a small amount of raw umber has been added (W,••RU). Delicately blend this light-colored edging into the darker paint. Continue by painting the secondaries and tertials. Mix raw umber and white (RU,W) and paint the outer-most secondary (speculum) with this mixture. Paint the outer tertials with cobalt blue, mixed with small amounts of black, cadmium yellow (medium), and white (CB,••B, ••Y,••W). Edge these feathers narrowly with black and burnt umber (B,••BU). The inner tertials are painted with black and burnt umber (B, BU) (Fig. 2-63).

The scapulars are painted next. Outline each feather with white mixed with small amounts of black and burnt umber (W,••B,••BU) (Fig. 2-64). Paint the rest of each feather with black and burnt umber (B, BU) (Fig. 2-65). Add only a small amount of Cobalt drier to these mix-

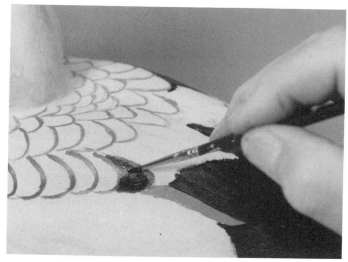
2-65 *Paint the rest of the feather with the black paint.*

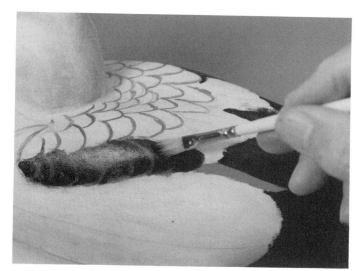
2-66 *Blend the two colors and add brush marks.*

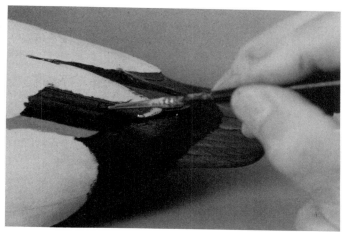
2-63 *Paint the tertials next.*

2-64 *Paint the edges of the scapulars.*

2-67 *Highlight each scapular feather with the greenish paint.*

tures. Now, blend these two colors, making brush strokes to duplicate the feather barbs (Fig. 2-66). The scapular feathers, also the inner tertial feathers of male ring-necked ducks have a slight greenish iridescence. Mix cobalt blue with small amounts of black, burnt umber, cadmium yellow (medium), and white (CB,••B,••BU,••Y,••W). After the paint on the scapulars has dried, or is almost dry, highlight each of these feathers with the greenish mixture (Fig. 2-67).

Now, paint the chest. Mix black with a small amount of burnt umber (B,••BU). Add Cobalt drier only—no medium. Using a white bristle brush, make brush strokes to duplicate the feather texture (Fig. 2-68). See drawing, Fig. 1-127 for the approximate flow lines of feathers.

Paint the head and neck with the black mixture used on the chest and again add brush strokes to simulate feather texture (Fig. 2-69).

Continue by painting the bill. First, add the white band near its tip and the white markings at its base, using white mixed with a very small amount of raw umber (W,•RU). Next, paint the black tip and nostrils using the black chest

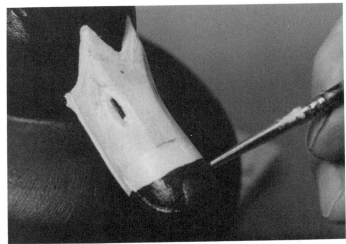

2-70 *Paint the light-colored stripe first and then paint the black tip.*

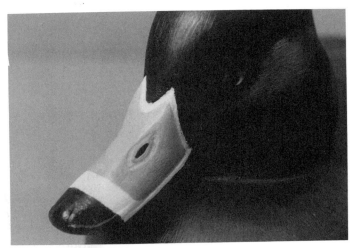

2-71 *Showing the finished bill.*

2-68 *Paint the black chest next.*

2-69 *Apply black paint over the entire head and neck.*

mixture (Fig. 2-70). Paint the rest of the bill with white mixed with a small amount of black and a very small amount of cobalt blue (W,••B,•CB) (Fig. 2-71).

The painting of the ring-necked duck drake is now complete except for the side feathers. The painting of these feathers will provide a most important step forward for the beginner. It is imperative that he thoroughly understand the technique about to be shown as it will be used often to help achieve the feeling of softness on areas of the bird that appear to be of the same basic color.

The side feathers, also the breast feathers, of a male ring-necked duck appear to be a uniform grayish-white color. When these feathers are studied more closely, very delicate differences in color along their length can be detected.

As was explained earlier in this chapter, the lightness or darkness of a color is often referred to as its "value", white having the highest value and black the lowest. The value on light-colored feathers usually increases moving rearward along the length of the feather. On dark-colored feathers, the reverse is often true. When there is a change in value along the length of each individual feather, high-lights and shadows result, which in turn create the feeling of a soft, undulating surface. This subject will be covered in greater detail in the advanced painting section of this book.

The differences of color values of the side feathers will be exaggerated slightly so they will be discernible in the photographs. Mix a very small amount of raw umber into white. Add Cobalt drier but do not add any medium inasmuch as a fairly thick paint is required to make the brush marks required to simulate feather texture. Add brush marks in the direction shown in Fig. 1-127 and allow this paint to dry (Fig. 2-72). Now, using white and raw umber, make three different mixtures: mixture #1 is white, plus a small amount of raw umber (W,••RU); mixture #2 is white plus a very small amount of raw umber (W,•RU); and mixture #3 is white from the tube. Add medium and drier to these mixtures. First, sketch-in the outline of each feather (Fig. 2-73). Next, paint a stripe of the #1 mixture on the rear of the feather layout lines (Fig. 2-74). Continue by painting the forward one-half of each feather with the #2 mixture (Fig. 2-75). Now, paint the

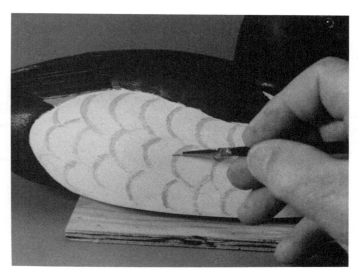
2-73 *Outline each side feather.*

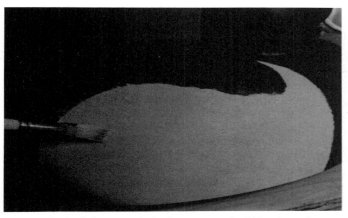
2-72 *Apply the light gray side feather paint and add brush marks.*

2-74 *Add the darker paint to the side feathers first.*

remaining rear of each feather with white (Fig. 2-76). Using a white bristle brush, blend these colors. Make the brush strokes in the same direction as the brush strokes in the undercoat (Fig. 2-77).

After the chest paint has dried, outline each chest feather lightly, using black mixed with white (B,W). Add no medium. If the mixture is quite dry, and if very light brush strokes are used, these outlines will have feathery edges (Fig. 2-78).

The head of the male ring-necked duck is highlighted with purplish iridescence. Mix a small amount of cobalt blue and a very small amount of white into alizarin crimson (AC,••CB,•W) and apply, and blend, in the areas shown on the full-color illustration (Fig. 2-105).

The male ring-necked duck has very fine vermiculations on most of his side feathers—see full-color illustration Fig. 2-105. For those who would like to add these feather markings read the section entitled "Adding Vermiculations" page 289.

2-75 *The center parts of the feathers are painted next.*

2-76 *Add white to the rear edges last.*

2-79 *Showing the finished ring-necked duck decoy.*

2-77 *Blend the three colors on each feather.*

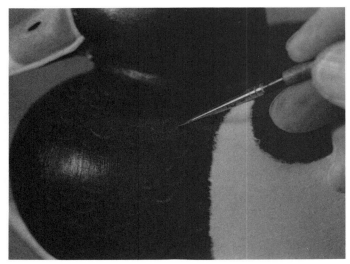

2-78 *Lightly delineate each chest feather.*

PAINTING THE BUFFLEHEAD DRAKE
(See full-color illustration, Fig. 2-106 and color photographs, Figures 1-228, 229, page 79.)

The handsome, vivacious little bufflehead drake is another interesting painting subject. With the exception of his beautifully iridescent head, he is no more difficult to paint than the ring-necked duck drake.

The painting procedure used, as shown in the following step photos, is similar to the one used for the ring-necked duck drake. If the beginner would prefer to try a slightly more advanced procedure, he may wish to follow the method used in the following project for the lesser scaup drake—where feather texture is added to the entire carving by means of brush marks; or better still, he may prefer at this point to study Chapter 8, "Advanced Finishing Techniques" and incorporate even more realistic texturing and painting methods.

After sealing the carving, apply thinned white Hyplar over the entire surface. When the white Hyplar has dried, lay out the areas of dark color lightly with a pencil (Fig. 2-80) and paint them with black Hyplar (Fig. 2-81).

Note: If a heavy oil base coat has been used for feather texturing, do *not* apply acrylic paint over oil paint. Use black oil base paint, mixed with burnt umber and thinned with medium, instead.

Add some white in the upper tail covert area and blend this gradually into the black rump area. Again, the undercoats should be thin, and brush marks and build-ups in the paint should be carefully eliminated.

Mix raw umber and a small amount of black into white (W,RU,•B). Apply this gray paint to the tail feathers, on both the upper and lower surfaces and diagonal brush marks to duplicate the barbs of the feathers (Fig. 2-82). Repeat this operation for the underside of the tail. Using a small sable brush, add white to the tips of the tail feathers (Fig. 2-83). Mix a small amount of burnt umber and black (BU,B) and paint the exposed feather shafts (Fig. 2-84).

2-80 *Lay out the areas of the dark colors lightly with a pencil.*

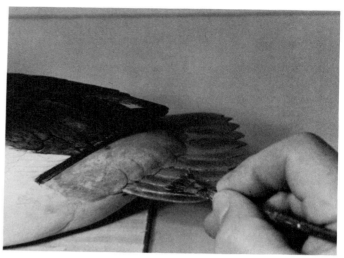

2-82 *Add brushmarks to duplicate the barbs of the feathers.*

2-81 *Make the undercoat approximate the final colors.*

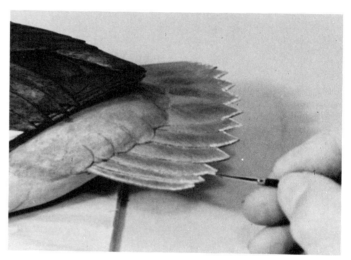

2-83 *Add white to the tips of the tail feathers.*

Add a fair amount of black and a very small amount of burnt umber to white (W,•• + B,•BU) and apply this paint to the upper tail covert area. Mix black with a small amount of burnt umber (B,••BU) and paint the forward rump area. Blend blackish rump paint into the grayish upper covert paint, making a gradual change in color. Add white to the edges of the upper coverts (Fig. 2-85) and blend (Fig. 2-86). Add a small amount of raw umber into white (W,•RU) and paint the under tail coverts and flank areas on both sides. Blend the white into the gray upper covert and rump areas.

Mix a small amount of white into burnt umber and raw umber (BU,RU,••W) and paint the primaries, both upper and lower surfaces. Delineate each of these feathers by adding a small amount of white on their edges and blend into the darker paint. Paint the primary feather shafts with black and burnt umber (B,••BU).

Mix a small amount of raw umber into white (W,•RU), add medium and Cobalt Drier and paint the outer scapulars, exposed wing covert feathers, and secondaries. Add

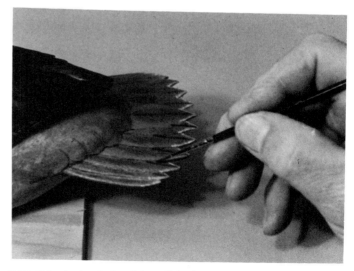

2-84 *Paint in the shafts of the tail feathers.*

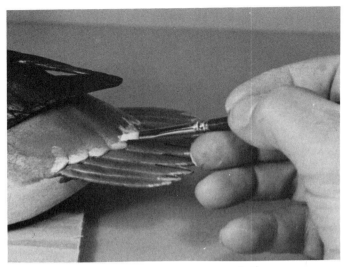

2-85 *Add white to the tips of the upper covert feathers.*

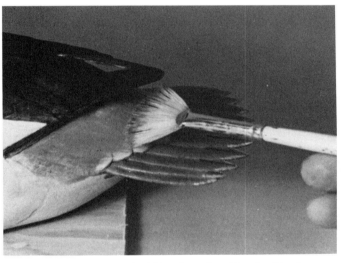

2-86 *Blend these areas and add brush marks with a fan blender.*

brush marks with an angular white bristle brush. Delineate these feathers with a small amount of raw umber, blended into the white paint. Allow this paint to dry.

Mix a small amount of raw umber into white (W,•RU), add drier but no medium and paint the side feathers and chest and add brush marks to simulate feather texture as has been previously described (Fig. 2-87). Allow this paint to dry.

Now, mix a small amount of burnt umber into black (B,••BU,) and paint the inner scapulars and tertial feathers. Carefully drag the black paint onto the white outer scapulars to create a feathery effect. Very faintly delineate each scapular feather with a very small amount of white blended into the black paint.

After the white undercoat on the sides and chest has dried, mix three values of the side paint; W,••-RU;

W,•RU; and W. Apply this paint as was described when painting the ring-necked duck drake.

Paint the head next. Refer to page 99, and full-color illustrations, Figs. 2-10A through D, and 2-106.

Mix a very small amount of black and an even smaller amount of cobalt blue into white (W,•B,•–CB) for the bluish-gray bill. Lighten the forward part by adding more white. Paint the nail a dusky color by adding a little more black and a very small amount of raw umber to the bill mixture. Paint the nostril black (B,••BU).

The upper side feathers and lower outer scapulars are delicately edged with black (B,••BU). Duplicate this black edging with individual strokes of a small sable brush (Fig. 2-88).

2-87 *Paint the sides and chest and add brush marks with the fan blender.*

2-88 *Paint the black edging of the upper side feathers with individual strokes.*

2-89 *Finished bufflehead drake.*

2-90 *The bufflehead drake has been stripped, additional carving detail has been added, and it has been repainted. (Collection of R. K. Guicelman, Maywood, California)*

PAINTING THE LESSER SCAUP DRAKE

(See full-color illustration Fig. 2-107, page 128, and color photo, Fig. 1-227, page 78.)

The lesser scaup drake is painted in a very similar manner to the ring-necked drake with one exception—a heavy undercoat is painted over the entire carving and brush marks, simulating feather detail, are added. With some practice, fairly realistic feather texture can be added with little effort by use of this technique.

Using a small brush and thinned-down raw umber, sketch in the individual scapular, side, and tail covert feathers, referring to drawing, Figure 1-175 (Fig. 2-91). Mix a small amount of raw umber into white (W,•RU), add Cobalt drier, but no medium, and paint this mixture, quite heavily, over the entire carving, except the bill. Where the feathers are outlined, paint them individually so that at least some of outline remains. Starting at the

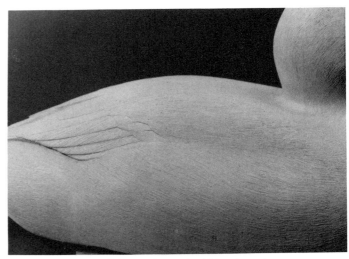

2-93 *Paint the rest of the carving and add brush marks.*

2-91 *Outline each scapular feather.*

2-94 *Showing brush marks on the head.*

tail, and using the angular white bristle brush, add brush marks to simulate the feather barbs. This must be done quite lightly and the brush must be wiped clean after every few strokes. Make the brush strokes the length of the individual feather (Fig. 2-92). If the brush strokes over a particular area appear to be too rough, smooth them by brushing very lightly with a large, dry, sable brush. Refer to the feather flow lines on drawing Figure 1-127, when making brush marks on the side, chest, neck, and head feathers (Figures 2-93 and 2-94).

After the undercoat is dry, again add the individual feather layouts (Fig. 2-95). The scapular and side feathers are painted using three different values on each feather, as was done when painting the side feathers·on the ring-necked drake (Figs. 2-96 and 2-97).

While the addition of vermiculations on the ring-necked duck drake was optional, the addition of these markings, at least on the scapulars and tertials, is mandatory on the lesser scaup drake if any degree of realism is desired. As shown in Fig. 2-98, the vermiculations were

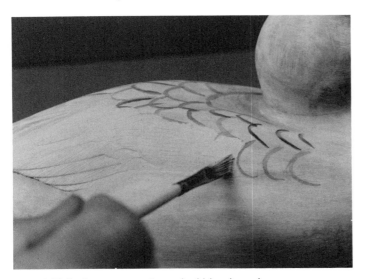

2-92 *Add the heavy gray paint and add brush marks.*

2-95 *Outline all of the feathers again.*

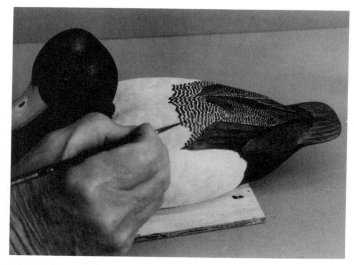

2-98 *Add vermiculations with a small, round sable brush.*

2-96 *Paint the scapulars using three different values of colors.*

2-97 *Blend the three colors.*

added by means of a small brush (#2 round white sable) using paint thinned with medium. It is very advisable to practice making these vermiculations on paper before attempting to add them to the carving. Study a mounted bird, if possible, or photographs and also refer to the section entitled "Adding Vermiculations" on page 289.

Paint Mixing Instructions

Head and Neck
Bill: W,••CB,•B
Entire head and neck: B,••BU; highlighted with AC,••C-B,•W.

Body
Back and scapulars: basically, W,•RU. Use three values: W,••RU, W,•RU, and W. Broadly vermiculated with B,BU.
Sides: same as scapulars; upper and rear side feathers vermiculated with W,••BU,•RU.
Chest: B,••BU; feathers lightly edged with B,W. Flanks and upper and lower tail coverts: B,BU; feathers faintly edged with B,BU,••W.
Rump: B,BU.

Tail
Upper surface: RU,•RS,•W (see painting tail on ring-necked drake).
Lower surface: BU,W.

Wing
Primaries: BU,RU,••W; faintly edged with W,•RU.
Tertials: the color of the long, inner tertials seem to vary. On some birds, their basic color is the same as the scapulars. On others, they are much darker—W,••RU. On most birds, they are vermiculated with B,BU.Outer tertials—BU,••Y,•AC; narrowly edged with B,BU.

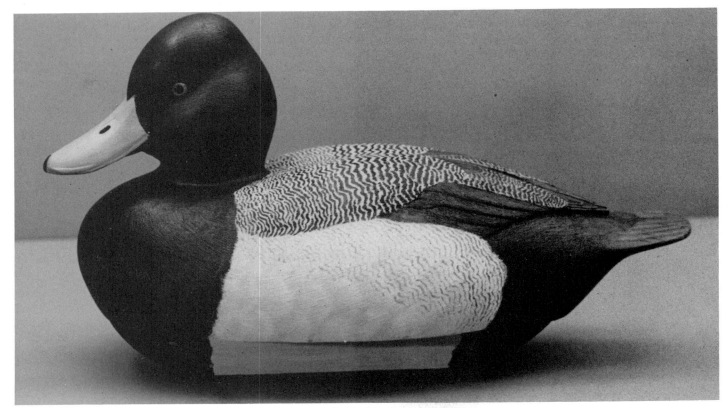
2-99 *Showing the finished lesser scaup drake.*

PAINTING THE WOOD DUCK DRAKE

(See full-color illustration Fig. 7-263, page 259, and color photos Figs. 1-230, 231, page 80.)

The duck species to be carved by the beginner up until now have been selected primarily because their coloring can usually be duplicated reasonably well by the inexperienced painter. The painting of the male wood duck is not easy and will provide a real challenge to the amateur artist. Many of the wood duck drake's colors are iridescent, i. e., they are the result of the bird's feather structure refracting light waves in such a way that a particular color of the spectrum is seen. The color of these feathers can change depending on the angle of the sun's rays. The colors obtained from the following paint mixtures will approximate the colors on the actual bird when the lighting is from a fairly high angle.

Paint Mixing Instructions

Head and Neck: See page 99 and full-color illustration, Figure 2-10,E,F,G,&H for paint mixing and painting instructions.
Eyes: 12-mm red.

Body
Back: BU,••Y,•–TB.
Scapulars: B,••BU,••TB. Inner webs of outer scapulars highlighted by adding white to above mixture. Outer

webs of inner scapulars—highlight by adding Y to above mixture. Inner webs of inner scapulars—Y, • +AC,•–TB.
Sides: YO,•RU; vermiculated with B,BU. Upper feathers edged with B,••BU,••TB. Stripes between black edgings—W,•RU.
Rump: BU,••Y,•–TB.
Upper tail coverts: B,••BU,••TB. Highlight feathers with Y,•TB. Hairlike projections from outer tail coverts—V,0,•B.
Lower tail coverts: BU,••B,•W.
Flank patch: Rd,CB. Highlight feathers with streaks of 0,BU. Blend into patch.
Chest: AC, BU,••Y,•CB. Triangular chest markings—W,•RU.

Tail
Upper side: B,••BU,••TB. Highlight center feathers by adding small amounts of white. Highlight other feathers by adding Y,•TB.
Lower side: BU,••W.

Wing
Primaries: Outer webs—W,•B,•RU. Inner webs—BU,•W. Highlight tips with B,••BU,••AC,••TB,••W.
Tertials: B,••BU,••TB. Highlight inner webs with AC,TB,W. Outer tertials edged on rear with W,•RU.
Speculum: W,TB,B,Y. Edged on rear with W,•RU.

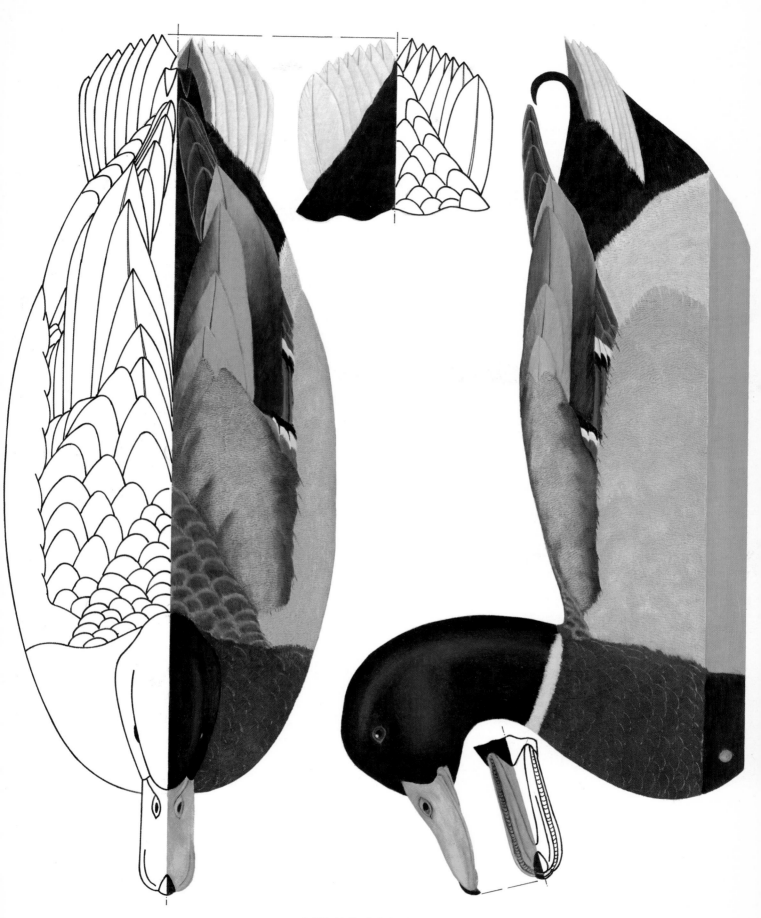

2-100 *Mallard drake decoy.*

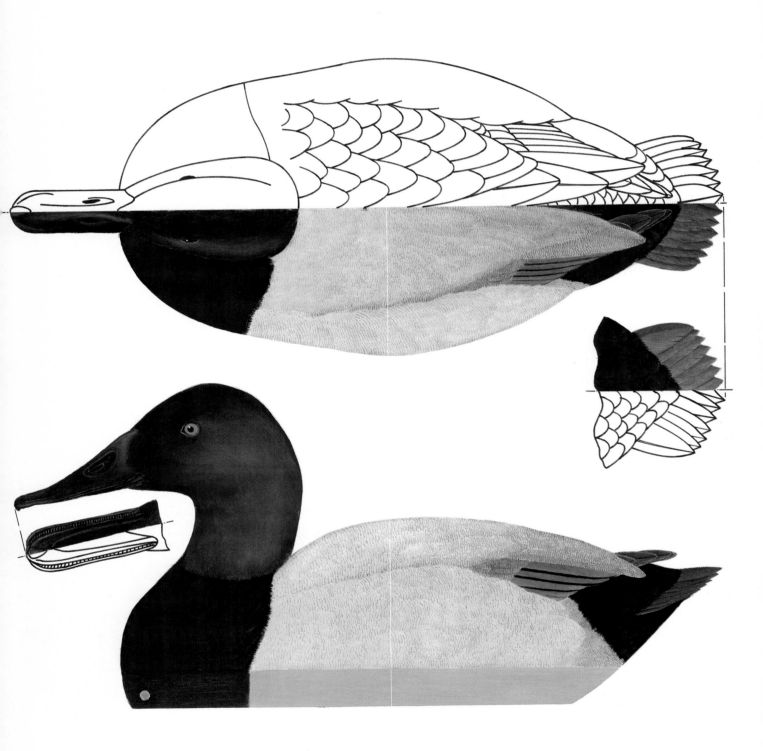

2-101 *Canvasback drake decoy.*

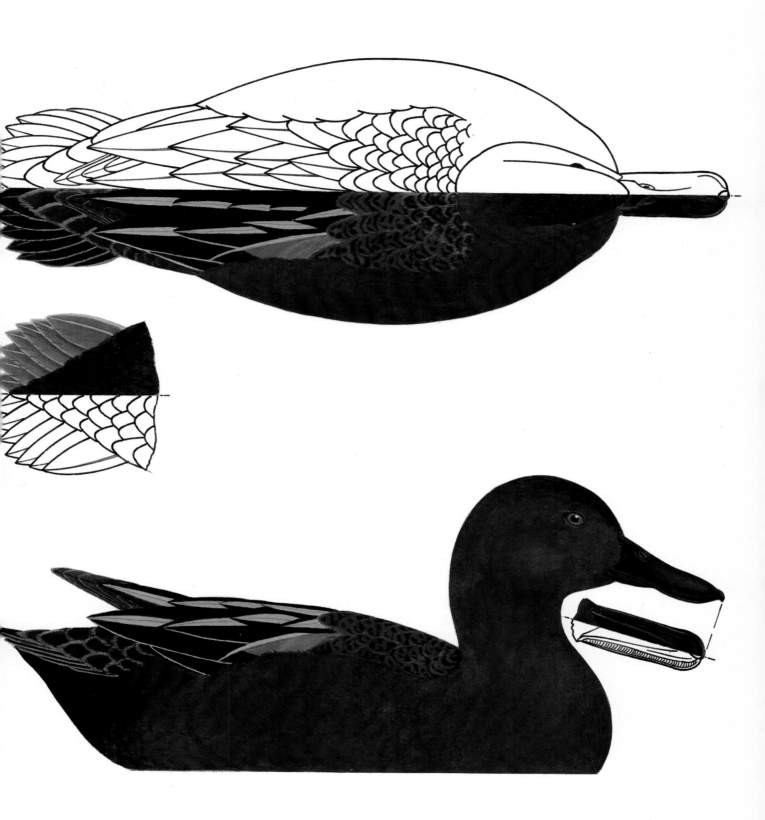

2-102 *Cinnamon teal drake decoy.*

2-103 *Northern shoveler drake decoy.*

2-104 *Green-winged teal drake decoy.*

2-105 *Ringed-neck duck drake decoy.*

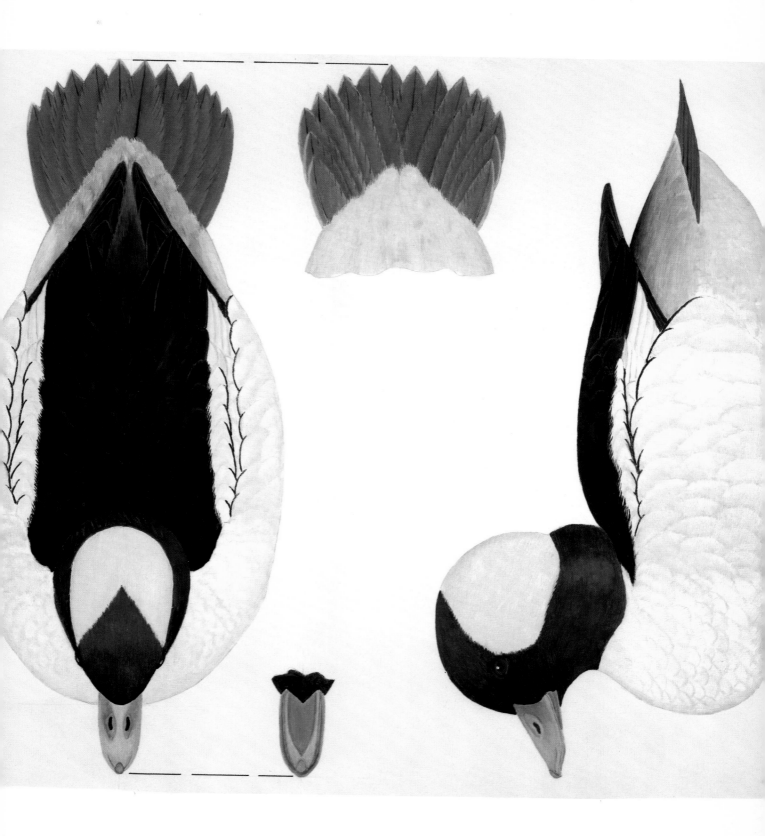

2-106 Bufflehead drake decoy.

2-107 *Lesser scaup drake decoy.*

PART II

Planning the Carving

Once he has developed some skill and confidence in his work, the resolute carver should never knowingly copy another's carvings or use another carver's drawings. All man-made creations, including artists' drawings and paintings, should serve only as aids. Make every effort to work from actual birds and photographs. This is the only way to develop your own style and produce carvings that truly represent your creativity. With the exception of the first few projects for the beginner, all of the drawings and photos of carvings in this book are presented only to help the carver plan his own work. Obviously they will not serve this purpose if they are directly copied.

The success of a realistic bird carving primarily depends on four factors: how well the carving is planned during the drawing stage; how expertly and accurately the actual carving procedure is executed; how realistically the carving is painted; and how artistically the carving is displayed.

The planning and drawing stages that precede any actual work on the wood block are every bit as important as the actual carving and painting. Unfortunately, this all-important part of carving is often relegated to a minor role. Lack of originality, awkward poses, inaccurate dimensions, anatomical errors, and other undesirable characteristics can usually be traced back to improper planning.

A realistic bird carving must obviously be dimensionally and anatomically accurate. A good realistic bird carving must also capture a graceful, natural pose. An infinite number of bird positions may be completely natural; however, some are not graceful and, if duplicated, will not make pleasing carvings. The carver's success largely depends on his ability to select and accurately duplicate the poses that accentuate the naturally graceful and beautiful lines of the bird he is attempting to depict.

The serious carver must acquire a comprehensive knowledge of the various positions of game birds: relaxed, alert, sleeping, preening, stretching, displaying, landing, taking off, and others. Whenever possible, study the live bird from every aspect and record all observations, preferably on the spot. Sketches may be made, but photography is the only method by which important structural details and position can be accurately discerned and recorded. Much more on the subject of photography will be included in Chapter 4.

Information and suggestions presented here and in subsequent parts of this book will aid the game bird carver in working out some of the planning problems mentioned above and, in addition, will help him to consolidate these ideas into a drawing. Again, remember that the planning of a carving, like everything else, reflects the amount of study, research, and effort that went into it.

(3A) *Five pintail drakes and one hen—courtship flight.*

3

Bird Anatomy for Carvers

Some knowledge of bird anatomy is necessary for planning a successful realistic bird carving and for the proper execution of the carving work itself. Even a smattering of bird anatomy will help the carver to improve his carvings and also to appreciate more fully the absolutely fantastic physical adaptations and the superbly efficient and beautiful construction of these marvelous creatures.

As there are few anatomical differences between game birds and other birds, a great deal can be learned about game bird anatomy while dressing domestic fowl or even when carving the Thanksgiving turkey. Much more can be learned, however, by carefully skinning a game bird specimen, studying the feather groups on the removed skin, and then, by dissection, becoming acquainted with the important bones, joints, and muscles.

From one viewpoint, the exterior anatomy of birds is somewhat more complex than the corresponding anatomy of mammals. In most mammals, except for some very longhaired or wooled species, the skin and hair do not contribute greatly to the overall shape. On most birds, waterfowl especially, the contour feathers, including the down feathers, are quite thick over much of their bodies and modify the skeletal-muscular-skin configuration considerably. The extent of this modification varies, for the bird, by using an estimated twelve thousand feather control muscles, can at will alter its overall exterior body shape by fluffing out or pulling in part or all of its body-contour feathers. The strutting turkey gobbler is a familiar example of this exquisite feather control. The exterior appearance of a bird is further complicated by the fact that the overall body shape is modified by the wings when they are in the folded position.

From another viewpoint, the overall body shape of the bird is simplified to a degree in comparison to the mammal's in that the feathers refine the rather irregular basic body form, in most cases, into more smoothly flowing lines.

Although the game bird carver's knowledge of bird anatomy need not be extensive, it should at the very least cover individual feather construction, major feather groups, and the more important bones, joints, and muscles.

FEATHERS

The intricacy of bird plumage almost defies description. Since a great deal of the time spent on a realistic bird carving is devoted to the simulation of feathers, the construction of the individual feather will be described briefly (Fig. 3-1).

The exterior part of the feather is called the vane. The main structural member is called the shaft. It runs lengthwise from the quill, which is embedded in the skin, to the tip of the vane. Branching out from the shaft at an angle on both sides are the many barbs, each a minute feather in itself. On one side of the barb, too small to be seen with the unaided eye, are the straight barbules. On the other side of the barb, projecting out in a similar manner, are the barbules with tiny, hooklike projections called barbicels. The barbicels hook themselves to the straight barbules of the adjacent barb and hold the vane together in an amazingly strong, continuous, and flexible manner. If the barbs become separated, they will rejoin not just once, but time and time again. It is well worth the time and effort to examine a bird's feather under a high-power magnifying glass or microscope.

On the flight feathers, tail feathers, and certain other feathers, the barbs are held together along their entire length by the tiny barbicels. On most of the body-contour feathers, the barbules apparently do not have the barbicels (or at least they are ineffective) out near the edges of the vane. As a result, the barbs separate and are seen as fine lines, giving the feather's edge a very soft and delicate effect. Both wing and body feathers, which are more or less solidly vaned, are generally referred to as contour feathers.

Making an accurate layout of feather groups and individual feathers is one of the most difficult phases of realistic bird carving. Many feathers are hard to discern in photographs and even on live birds. This is especially true when groups of feathers are of the same color. Individual feathers are even harder to distinguish on some study skins and mounts where the normal pattern has been disturbed. To further complicate matters, the bird has many more feathers (a pintail duck has approximately

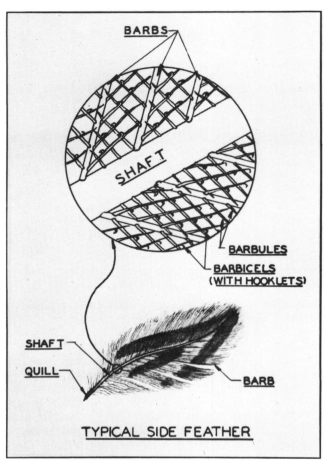

3-1 *Feather details.*

waves by the different surfaces of the barbules while pigment granules located below the surface of the barbules absorb the light waves not reflected. More will be said on this subject in Chapter 7.

It is interesting to note that when the bird's feathers are dark, their bases are of a lighter color and vice versa. Using this change in color value along the length of the vane when painting a carving can be most helpful in creating the illusion of softness.

FEATHER MOLTS

Birds from time to time replace their worn feathers by molting. This is of little consequence to the carver except in the case of ducks. In the Northern Hemisphere, a special, or eclipse, molt occurs after the females start incubating their eggs. At that time the bright breeding plumage of most male ducks is replaced with a plumage very similar to that of the females. Shortly after this molt is completed, a second molt starts, and the female-type plumage is very gradually replaced over a period of several months by the breeding plumage.

Male ducks are almost always carved and painted in breeding plumage. However, the ruddy duck is one exception as his most attractive plumage occurs during early summer. Many duck specimens taken during the normal hunting seasons have not yet gotten their full breeding plumage. The carver should be aware of this and the molting process when using male duck specimens for feather pattern and coloration. F. H. Kortright's fine book, *The Ducks, Geese, and Swans of North America*, thoroughly covers this subject.

FEATHER GROUPS

At first glance, the contour feathers of the game birds appear to be quite evenly distributed over their entire bodies. A closer inspection reveals that the contour feathers originate from groups, or tracts, on the skin and that there are certain other areas with no contour feathers, although they may be covered with downy feathers. This distribution of the contour feathers, called pterylosis, is complex and varies somewhat between the different groups of birds.

The serious carver need not be familiar with all of the feather tracts (pterylae) and the areas where there are no contour feathers (apteria) inasmuch as the contour feathers overlap and appear to be continuous. He should, however, be familiar with some of the more prominent feather groups, both wing and body, for several reasons. First, the external shape of the bird's body is modified greatly by its feathers. Second, in some cases, the overall shape of the feather group must be carved prior to the carving of the individual feathers. Third, it is sometimes difficult without this information to distinguish feathers of one group from those of another. A good example of a

15,000 feathers) than can be possibly drawn and carved. Therefore, on carvings some feather patterns have to be simplified and the total number of feathers reduced.

Although they may appear at times to be similar to shingles on a roof, feathers are not flat. With the exception of the flight feathers (primaries and secondaries), all feathers are *convex* in cross-sectional shape. Their edges form a seal which traps air for buoyancy and insulation and helps prevent water from getting under the individual feathers. The flight feathers, in addition to being curved along their lengths, have a flattened S cross-sectional shape (see Fig. 7-218, page 246). This shape serves a dual purpose. One, it forms an effective air seal between adjacent feathers during the downstroke. Two, during at least part of the upstroke, when the individual flight feathers are opened slightly, air flows between them and, by virtue of their airfoil-like shape, lift is produced.

The coloring of the feathers is just as complex as their structure. Blacks, browns, most reds, and yellows are produced by pigments. Blues, some yellows and reds, violets, glossy blacks with a bluish or greenish tint, and whites are structural colors. Structural colors are produced by the microscopic surface structure of the feather reflecting portions of the color spectrum. The iridescent colors, which are structural, are produced by the interference of light situation of this kind would be the overlapping of the scapulars with the tertials and, in turn, with the primaries and secondaries of the folded wings of a green-winged teal (Figs. 3-2, 3).

If available, an actual fresh or unfrozen specimen can be a great help in acquainting the beginner with the different feather groups. The feather groups on a specimen should first be studied with the wings outstretched. Particular attention should be paid to the position of the scapulars and tertials in this position. Next, the wings should be correctly folded and the new position of the feather groups noted.

The position of the folded wing and the amount of wing exposed vary not only with the different game birds but also on a particular bird, depending on its activity. In the case of waterfowl, the wings are normally neatly folded under the side feathers and scapulars. The long primaries extend on back under the secondaries and tertials and normally lie crossed above the tail or upper tail coverts. (On some of the smaller geese, the crossed primaries actually extend beyond the tail.)

Compared to waterfowl, upland game birds have much shorter and broader wings. Although their folded wings normally lie under the side feathers and scapulars, the primaries of upland game birds are not crossed but rest along the bird's flank, sometimes extending to the upper tail coverts, and are covered to a large extent by the secondaries, tertials, and scapulars. The folded wings of pigeons and doves remain almost completely outside the body-contour feathers. On these birds, the primaries, which are largely covered by the secondaries, tertials, and scapulars, normally meet at a point above the tail coverts.

Folding the wings of a specimen also graphically shows the carver how the wings should appear in this position and, very roughly, the movements required of the bird to accomplish this remarkable feat. Of equal importance, this exercise clearly shows how the shape of the bird's body is modified by the folded wings. As mentioned, waterfowl, especially geese, have much larger wings relative to their body size than, for example, upland game birds. The shape of the goose's body will be altered to a greater extent by the folded wings than that of a quail's.

After noting these exterior features, carefully skin the specimen and identify and study the feather groups on the removed skin.

Primary Flight Feathers

These large, strong-shafted feathers, always ten to each wing, are the most important flight feathers. In the flight configuration, they are also the most prominent feather group on most game birds. The primaries are attached to the ''hand'' part of the wing structure and are controlled individually and as a group by a complex system of muscles and tendons. During the upstroke, the individual feathers are rotated and are opened to permit the air to pass through them; on the downstroke, they close and overlap to prevent the flow of air. Movement of the individual primaries is accompanied by the movement of the wing as a whole and the primaries as a group through

3-2 *Showing attachment of primary and secondary feathers with coverts removed. Left wing.*

wrist movement. These movements of the wing and of the individual primary feathers are so complex that even experts do not fully understand how they contribute to the bird's flight. The above oversimplified statements were not intended to describe the flight of a bird, but only to point out some of the detail the carver must consider when attempting to duplicate the bird's wing in the flight configuration. Consideration must also be given to the bending or deflection of the primary feathers caused by the high air loads developed during the downstroke. Many fine pictures that stop the fast-moving wing in its various flight positions are now available in a number of publications. The carver should familiarize himself with the basic wing and feather movements of the bird in flight.

Even when the wings are folded, the primaries significantly affect the overall shape and detail of the bird's body. Because the primaries of waterfowl, pigeons, and doves lie under the secondaries and tertials, and extend to or beyond the bird's plan-view centerline, they affect the overall contour of the back more than in the upland game birds.

Secondary Flight Feathers and Tertials

The secondary flight feathers are attached to the forearm of the wing and are in effect a continuation of the primaries. Unlike the primaries, they are not individually controlled, and they act more like the wing on an airplane to maintain lift and to stabilize flight. The two or three innermost secondaries, usually longer and/or different in shape and color, are the tertials. On many ducks several of the secondary feathers are brightly colored, more often than not iridescent, and are referred to as the speculum. The secondaries and the tertials form a prominent feather group when the wings are outstretched.

When the wings are folded, varying amounts of the secondaries are exposed, depending on the species.

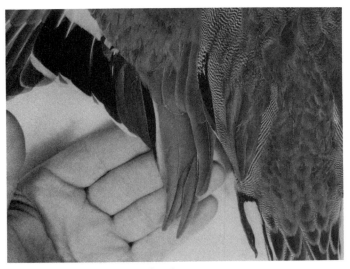

3-3 *Tertials on a green-winged teal.*

3-4 *Scapulars on a Canada goose.*

Ducks display all of the tertials and often some of the speculum, although in many cases, the side feathers completely cover all of these secondary feathers. Most of the secondaries and all of the tertials of the different goose species are exposed when the wings are folded. Some of the secondaries on the upland game birds, pigeons, and doves are usually exposed; on quails and partridges, however, the secondaries are almost all covered by the scapulars. The tertials are much more conspicuous on waterfowl than they are on the other game birds.

Wing Coverts

The wing coverts, on both the upper and lower wing surfaces, are arranged in rows and are overlapped like the shingles on a roof (Fig. 3-6). The primary coverts overlap the primary feathers, and the greater coverts extend over the secondary feathers. The primary and greater coverts are in turn overlapped by the middle coverts, which are partially covered by the lesser coverts. The wing coverts, especially the primary and the greater, are usually quite

3-5 *Wing of a common Canada goose.*

3-6 *Scapulars on a green-winged teal.*

3-7 *Back feathers on a Canada goose.*

distinct when the wing is outstretched and, on geese, are always noticeable when the wings are folded.

Alula (Spurious Wing)

The alula is composed of three feathers attached to the articulated "thumb" of the wing. These feathers act in a manner similar to that of a slat on the leading edge of an airplane wing, which reduces the stalling speed by locally speeding the airflow over the upper surface of the wing. These feathers are important to flight and are discernible during certain conditions of flight, at which time they are extended forward of the wing's leading edge.

Axillars

The axillars are a fan-shaped group of feathers located on the underside of the wing in the "armpit" area. These feathers, usually elongated, help close the gap between the inboard wing feathers and the body during flight. This feather group is, of course, seen only when the wings are outstretched.

Scapulars

The scapular feathers, often elongated and sometimes differently colored and/or marked, are located on either side of the back in the "shoulder" area, just inboard of each wing. The scapulars overlap the tertials in the flight configuration and help streamline the wing-body intersection; in addition, they help cover the folded wings. The overall body shape is modified somewhat by the scapulars, depending on the position of the wings and also by muscular control of the scapulars themselves. Regardless of the bird's position, the scapulars as feather groups can never be ignored by the carver.

Head and Neck Feathers

The feathers of the head and neck are small, long, and narrow. The barbs separate, making these small feathers appear to be more like hair than feathers. The head and neck feathers can be partially erected causing the head and neck at times to appear to be larger than normal. The head and neck feathers of most female dabbling ducks, and some diving ducks, are finely marked along their centers with a darker color, causing a streaked effect.

The head and neck feathers of some duck species such as the male and female wood ducks, male green-winged teal, male and female bufflehead, male and female hooded mergansers, and the female American merganser are very long and narrow. These crest feathers can be raised at will by superb muscular control. Some of the upland game birds also have crest feathers.

3-8 *Female blue-winged teal's tail feathers with coverts removed.*

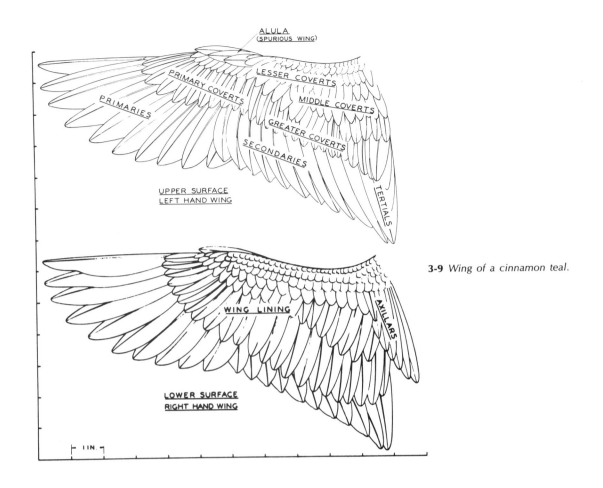

3-9 *Wing of a cinnamon teal.*

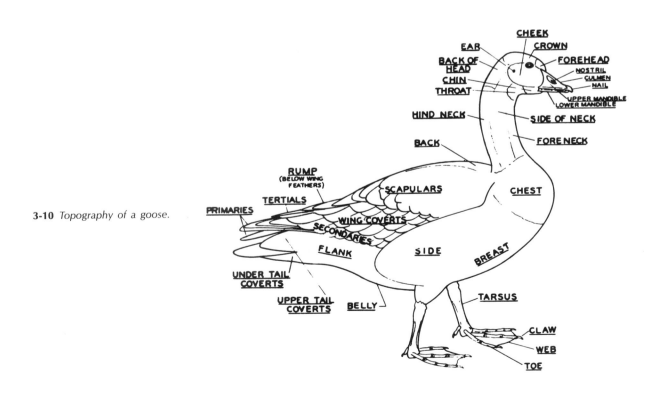

3-10 *Topography of a goose.*

3-11 *Canada goose's tail and upper tail coverts.*

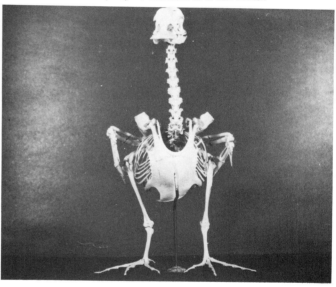

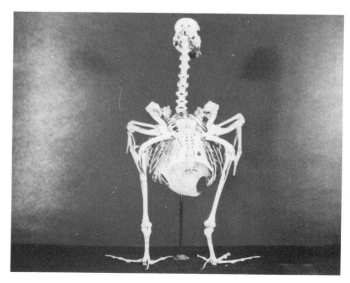

3-12, 13, 14 *Skeleton of a surf scoter.*

Chest, Breast, and Belly Feathers

Below the foreneck, the feathers become progressively larger. These feathers are quite long; however, only the rounded lower part of the vane shows. The breast feathers are a continuation of the chest feathers but their size remains about the same. The breast and belly feathers on most waterfowl are light in coloration and are very thick. They are most important to waterfowl as they provide insulation and waterproofing below the bird's waterline.

Back Feathers

The back feathers are a triangular-shaped group of fairly large feathers located between the neck and the rump and extend back between the forward part of the scapulars. They are much more evident when the bird is stretching his neck forward as in flight; however, they can normally be seen when the bird is in the sitting or standing position.

Side Feathers

This conspicuous group of large feathers, often strikingly marked, not only cover the bird's side and legs, but they also help cover the folded wings.

Tail Coverts

The tail coverts overlap the tail feathers and complete the streamlining of the bird's body. These feathers, especially the upper tail coverts, often have distinctive color and markings. The upper tail coverts of the wood duck and pheasant are outstanding not only for their coloration but also for their length.

Tail Feathers

The tail feathers are extended or fanned out during certain flight maneuvers (see Chapter 5). At other times

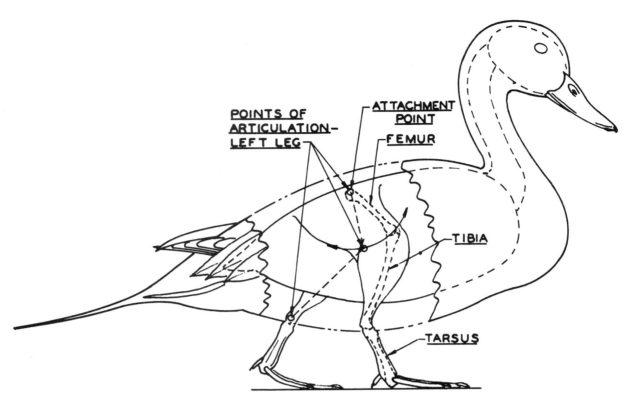

ATTACHMENT
POINT

FEMUR

TIBIA

TARSUS

3-15 *Leg movement and leg musculature of a pintail.*

and when the bird is at ease on either ground or water, the tail feathers are normally compressed together and are much less conspicuous. (The tail feathers on brant and on some of the quails and partridges are often almost, or completely, covered by the tail coverts.) This feather group is of special importance to the carver, because its position almost always reflects the activity of the bird: jumping, landing, flying, turning, stretching, preening, or displaying.

BONES, JOINTS, AND MUSCLES

The bird's skeleton is a remarkably strong and extremely lightweight structure (Figs. 3-12, 13, 14). Nature has fused most of the back vertebrae to provide strength and rigidity for flight, and compared to man's, the bird's skeletal structure (except for neck and tail) is quite rigid. The main part of the bird's skeleton is somewhat analogous to the fuselage of an airplane: it provides a rigid structure between the wings and tail, articulated points of attachment for the wings, legs (landing gear), and tail, and a rigid structure for the attachment of the heavy pectoral flight muscles (engine mount and engine).

A bird stands on its two legs, as does man, but there is little similarity between the two as far as posture is concerned (Fig. 3-16). For a human to simulate a bird's posture, he would have to stand on his tiptoes, draw his knees close to his chest, and bend his body forward until

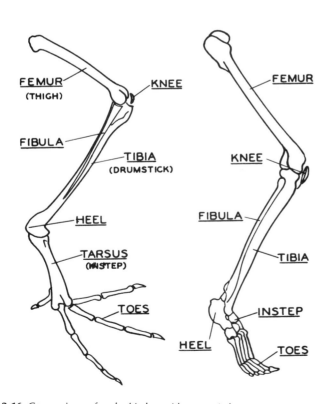

FEMUR
(THIGH)

KNEE

FIBULA

TIBIA
(DRUMSTICK)

HEEL

TARSUS
(INSTEP)

TOES

FEMUR

KNEE

FIBULA

TIBIA

INSTEP

HEEL

TOES

3-16 *Comparison of a duck's leg with a man's leg.*

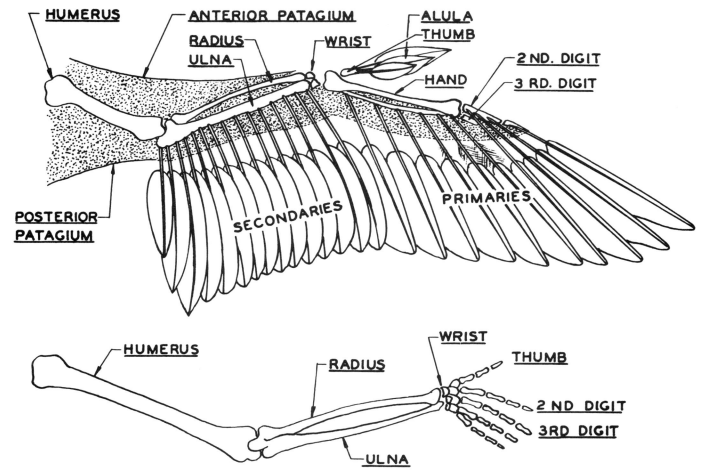

3-17 *Comparison of a duck's wing with a man's arm. The attachment of the flight feathers is also shown.*

it was almost parallel to the ground. Obviously, this posture, if assumed by man for more than a few moments, would become quite uncomfortable. The bird assumes this position easily by virtue of its almost rigid back structure, long pelvis, short and heavily muscled forward-pointing thighs, and long, highly developed toes. Some birds (the partridge and quail families are good examples) can also stand, walk, and run, seemingly without effort, in an almost erect manner. However, with most birds, this upright position is usually assumed in an attempt to gain more visibility when they are alerted.

Unlike man's, the bird's thighbone (femur) is quite short and is articulated in a limited forward and backward direction only (Fig. 3-15). The thighbone is in turn articulated with the shinbone (tibia) at the knee in a similar manner to that of man's; however, due to the very short, forward-pointing thighbone and its high attachment point, the bird's knee is located against its body and, being completely covered by the side feathers, is never seen. The bird's thighbone superficially appears to be more a part of the body than of the leg. In the case of game birds, the muscled shinbone, or drumstick, is also almost completely covered by the side feathers when the bird is

standing. When the bird is walking or running, a larger part of the shinbone is exposed. Under most conditions, the unexposed part of the muscled shinbones modifies the overall body shape and, for that reason, must be noted by the carver.

The bird walks on its toes; the actual heel joint (commonly but erroneously referred to as the knee) is located close to the body, in some cases actually touching or hidden by the body-contour feathers. The metatarsal bones (the arch of man's foot) are fused on the bird into a single bone called the tarsus, which is almost always incorrectly called the leg. All game birds have three forward-pointing toes. Including the attachment joint, the outer toe has four joints, the middle toe three, and the inner toe two. On game birds, doves and pigeons excepted, the fourth toe, called the hind toe, is relatively undeveloped and serves very little useful purpose.

Because of the large number and shape of the cervical vertebrae, the bird's neck is remarkably flexible in all directions; a common Canada goose has approximately twenty vertebrae compared to a giraffe's seven. A bird can move its head almost 180 degrees in either direction and can reach practically any part of the body with its beak. Since the bird's eyes are immovable, this flexibility of the neck is of great importance in detecting danger. It also aids the bird in obtaining food, feather-preening, and many other tasks. The long neck of a duck or goose is the ultimate in gracefulness; unfortunately, this attribute is seldom accurately duplicated in carvings. The carver should study these smoothly flowing, almost serpentine convolutions, at every opportunity.

The tail is supported and articulated in all directions by six caudal vertebrae terminating in a flattened bone (pygostyle) to which the tail feathers attach. The bird, by adept muscular control, can not only move its tail in any direction, it can fan out or compress its individual tail feathers, make them concave or convex, and can raise one side and lower the other (see Chapter 5). Understanding the significance of these various tail configurations is important in duplicating the bird's activity and imparting the feeling of motion.

The bird's wing, with its incomparable structure and matchless muscular control, represents one of nature's most marvelous adaptations. It is almost inconceivable that something so very light in weight, so superbly functional and durable, and so beautiful could have evolved over eons of time from the foreleg of the bird's reptilian ancestors.

The wing's skeletal structure is incredibly small in comparison to its total area and is located well forward, almost at its leading edge. The upper arm (humerus), the forearm (composed of two bones, the radius and the ulna), and the elbow are quite similar to man's (Fig. 3-17). The joints of a bird's wing also articulate in a manner very similar to man's. The bones of the bird's hand have been reduced to the second and third fingers, fused together, and a small thumb.

The ten primary feathers are attached to the hand and second and third fingers. The secondary feathers originate from the rearmost bone of the forearm (ulna). The thumb is articulated and bears the three feathers of the spurious wing, or alula. The primary, greater, middle, and most of the lesser coverts are attached to a long, flat membrane lying behind the bones of the hand and forearm. Stretching between the shoulder and wrist is another membrane

(anterior patagium), which forms the leading edge of the wing in this area and is covered by small covert feathers. To the rear of the upper arm, a third membrane (posterior patagium) stretches from the elbow to the body.

The muscular control of the wing as a whole and of the individual flight feathers is extremely complex. How a bird instinctively masters the intricacies of flight is almost incomprehensible. There are muscles that extend, retract, and fold the wing; others control the wing fore and aft; and still others can rotate the wing as required. Small muscles and tendons located in the membrane along the rear of the fused fingers control the individual primary feathers. The major pectoral muscle—the large breast muscle that supplies the tremendous power for the downstroke—attaches to a ridge on the front face of the upper arm near where it is articulated with the body. The minor pectoral muscle, which supplies the much smaller, but vital, power for the upstroke, is located between the major pectoral muscle and the keel. How can a muscle located well below the wing possibly raise it? Nature has ingeniously supplied this muscle with a long tendon that passes up through a hole formed by the three shoulder bones and attaches to the top side of the upper arm. This hole acts as an efficient pulley for the tendon to work over. The pectoral muscles, both in weight and dimension, comprise a very large percent of the bird's body. They are important to the carver, for they can, and do, modify the body shape, especially in the bird's flight configuration.

4

Collecting Data

A certain amount of basic information on the particular bird to be carved is an absolute necessity before planning any serious carving. Ideally, this information should include overall dimensions of the bird and certain detail dimensions; the characteristic shape of the head, bill, neck, body, wings, tail, and feet; the color and markings of the plumage; the color of the bill and feet; and actual photographs of the bird showing its natural configuration in the pose to be duplicated. Unfortunately, most carvers are almost always forced to work with considerably less information. In too many instances, carvings are planned, carved, and painted from information limited to only one or two photos or illustrations. Obviously, the more information available for the planning, carving, and painting stages, the better the finished product will be.

COLLECTING PICTURES

First, acquire and save every actual game bird photograph that you can. *Audubon, National Wildlife, Ducks Unlimited, National Geographic*, many official state magazines, and the various sports magazines are all potential sources of good bird photographs. Many excellent bird books are available now (some of which are listed in the bibliography) which feature actual photographs, rather than artist's illustrations. This is not to suggest that you should not collect books illustrated by drawings and paintings, for many of these books can be very helpful. Most artists and illustrators make every effort to portray the bird accurately, but small errors and a little artistic license are inevitable. It must be remembered, too, that the artists until recently had relatively few good action photographs to work from and had to rely completely on their ability to retain what they saw. Use actual photographs whenever possible. Man-made illustrations and photos of others' carvings should be used only as an aid for working out details difficult to obtain from actual bird pictures.

Conscientiously search for good game bird pictures and save all you find, and you will be amazed at the fast growth of your collection. Obviously, some systematic means of filing these pictures must be provided if they are to serve their purpose.

Don't attempt to save complete magazines with good bird photos, not only because of the storage problem involved, but also because of the difficulty of finding a particular picture in a large pile of publications. Instead, cut out important pictures and attach them by means of rubber cement or other adhesives to a fairly heavy 8½ × 11-inch sheet of paper and insert these sheets into loose-leaf notebooks. The pictures of the male and female of only one species are put on a page. When the cut-out pictures are pasted up in this manner, the pages showing one species can easily be filed in one section of the notebook or in a separate notebook covering that species or a group of similar species. At present, the author has separate notebooks for geese, ducks, upland game birds, marsh birds, and shorebirds. These will be further broken down as the present books become full.

As you increase the number of bird books and other bound publications in your collection, it becomes very difficult to remember the location of the various good pictures of a certain game bird. One way to overcome this problem is to have a blank page, or part of a page, assigned to each species and to insert it in the notebook next to the corresponding page on which the pictures of that species are pasted. The location by publication and page number of each good picture of this species is then written on this page. The same could be accomplished with a small card file. Another method is to photographically copy the better pictures and paste the prints in the notebooks along with the cut-out pictures.

Another very important aspect of data collection is a systematic filing of all pertinent information used to make a particular carving. The author uses a file consisting of 9 × 12-inch envelopes, one for each game bird species, containing all drawings and sketches, detail feather-pattern drawings, and cross-sectional templates required to make the carving. If several carvings of a particular species have been made, the individual sketches and drawings are identified and dated accordingly.

BIRD SPECIMENS

There is no better source for data than an actual specimen (Figs. 4-1, 2, 3). Game bird carvers have one advantage over other bird carvers—specimens can be collected legally during the open hunting seasons. Specimens can also be purchased from game bird farms. Even the carver who does not hunt usually has hunter friends who normally are glad to help out. Heads, wings, feet—some of the most difficult parts of the bird to carve—are discarded when the bird is cleaned.

When a specimen becomes available, stuff the throat of the bird with cotton or Kleenex type tissue, wash off any blood with cold water, and blow dry wet feathers with a hair dryer. Place the bird carefully into a plastic bag being careful not to ruffle or bend the feathers. Remove as much air from the sack as possible and seal it tightly. Specimens and parts can be preserved for some time, probably several years, by freezing; however, providing the necessary freezer space and thawing and refreezing them a number of times eventually presents problems.

The serious carver who wishes to retain specimens for use over the years should make a special effort to learn how to permanently preserve the whole bird and bird parts he acquires. Several publications on this subject are listed in the bibiliography.

For those who do not wish to become involved in taxidermy, there are, of course, many professional and amateur taxidermists who will mount the bird in either a standing or flying position. Many taxidermists will also make study skins for a somewhat reduced charge. A study skin, when properly made, will supply most, if not all, the information found on a standing mount and has the advantage of requiring considerably less storage space, a very important consideration for most carvers.

Next to having a live bird at the carving or painting bench, a bird preserved by taxidermy is the best information source available for color, feather shape, and feather pattern. However, some very valuable information is lost when the bird is mounted due to the fact that during the mounting process the bird's skin is often stretched, or shrunk, and the feather patterns and groups are affected accordingly. Also, the bird's bill, feet, and legs lose their natural color in a very short time.

When a carver has a fresh specimen available, he should immediately make color notes or actual color samples of the bill (both upper and lower sides) and the legs and feet.

In addition, he should take the measurements shown

4-1 Study skin, with one wing exposed, prepared by author.

4-2 Study skin, skinned head, and dried feet prepared by author.

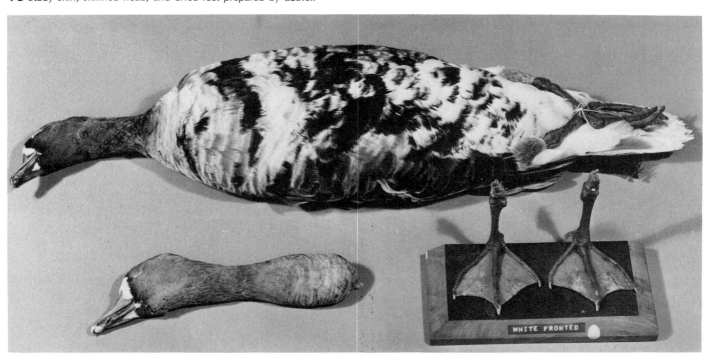

WHITE FRONTED

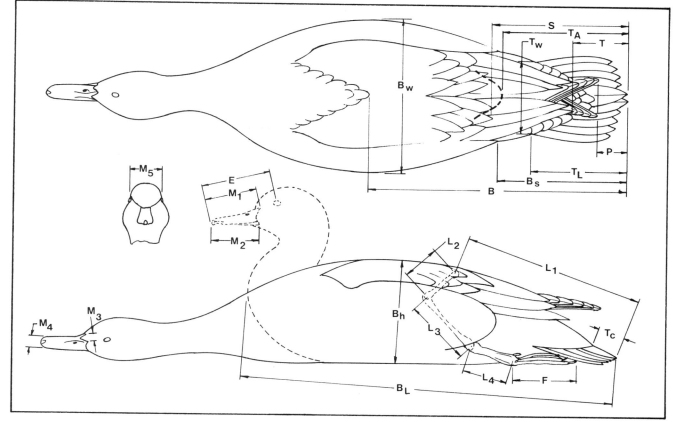

4-3 *Information which can be supplied by a specimen.*

on the figures in Chapter 11, page 334 and in Fig. 4-3. It is advisable to compare the overall length of the specimen with the overall length given in Chapter 11 for that species and sex, which is an approximate average. If the specimen is appreciably larger or smaller than the average, it may be desirable to compensate for this difference when planning the carving.

Explanation of the symbols used in Fig. 4-5.

B   Distance from back feather group to tip of tail.

BL   Body length. This dimension is determined by raising the bird's head and neck to a natural position.

BS   Distance from tip of tail to rearmost extent of side feathers.

BW   Body width. Measurements should be taken with the wings carefully folded and again with the wings extended. The side feathers on a dead bird are normally compressed and it is usually necessary to add about one-half inch to the body width to compensate for this.

BH   Body height. Here, again, approximately one-half inch should be added to compensate for the compressed breast feathers.

E   Distance from tip of bill to center of eye.

F   Foot length. It is advisable to measure and record the length of all four toes—also, the width of the foot with the toes spread in a normal manner.

L1   Distance from femur attachment to tip of tail. This dimension, in addition to L2, L3, and L4, is important for determining proper leg positions when planning standing carvings.

L2   Length of the femur.

L3   Length of the tibia.

L4   Length of the tarsus.

M1   Length of the upper mandible.

M2   Length of the lower mandible.

M3   Width of the upper mandible near the forehead.

M4   Maximum width of the upper mandible.

M5   Width of the crown at the eye location.

S   Distance from rear of scapular group to tip of tail.

P   Distance from tips of primaries (when carefully folded) to the tip of the tail.

TA   Distance from tip of tail to tail attachment point.

TC   Distance from tip to tail to rearmost extent of tail coverts (upper and lower).

TL   Length of tail.

TW   Width of tail at tail-body intersection.

BIRD VIEWING

The serious bird carver should make every effort to view and study live birds at every opportunity. Indentification of species, typical attitudes, movements, habits, idiosyncrasies, and much more can be learned in this manner. Even if nothing more is gained, bird viewing will help the carver-artist more fully appreciate these wonderful creatures who have so marvelously adapted themselves to their different environments.

It is very difficult to view wild birds in their natural habitats from close distances. Most wild birds, game birds especially, will not permit a viewer to approach within gun shot (forty or fifty yards) without moving away or taking off; therefore almost all viewing must be done from a considerable distance and, even with binoculars, the amount of information that can be obtained, and retained, is very limited.

Fortunately, some wild birds can be viewed under better circumstances. Many parks have a large menagerie of tame, or domesticated, waterfowl of different species and mixtures which attract wild birds who, after a period of handouts, become relatively tame and can be viewed and photographed from close distances. Wild Canada geese, mallards, widgeon, scaup, redheads, shovelers, teal and other species are often seen at these places. Also, native species propagated by game bird breeders can be seen at zoos and private aviaries, or at the bird farms themselves.

The bird carver who is sincere about improving his carvings should take advantage of all the sources that are available to him for viewing live birds. If he is fortunate enough to be able to view a live bird of the species he wishes to carve during the planning, carving, and painting stages, a great deal more information can be obtained due to the fact that he will be looking for specific details, rather than generally viewing the overall bird. When this procedure can be followed by the carver a few times, a more purposeful and systematic approach to live bird study will evolve and he will instinctively look for important details that are necessary for the completion of a good carving.

There are, however, practical limitations as to the amount of detailed information that can be acquired by just viewing a live bird. Contemporary realistic bird carvings require so much accurate detail that it is impossible to obtain all the necessary information by simply studying a live bird from a distance. For example, there is no way of taking measurements from a live bird (especially, a wild one) without somehow trapping it or killing it. Although some dimensions can be taken from photographs by using simple ratio and proportion (see pages 34 and 164) almost all structural information has to be derived from specimens.

Most people do not have photographic memories and find it difficult to remember more than a few details from one viewing. Unless it is possible to go back again and again to check various details on the live bird, assistance gained in this manner will be limited. In order to more efficiently take advantage of viewing opportunities, the carver should make a list of the details he wishes to check and record his findings by either notes or sketches.

Natural feather shapes and arrangements are, of course, best seen on a live bird, provided it can be closely approached. Even when viewed from a few feet, it is usually necessary to use binoculars to perceive these details with any degree of clarity. Retaining, or recording, this information is another matter. Fresh, or frozen, specimens and study skins, or mounts, are the best source for feather shapes. Fresh specimens, if they have been carefully handled and the feather patterns have not been disturbed, and study skins and mounts, if prepared by expert taxider-

mists, are the best sources for feather patterns. Some mounted birds which have been done by top taxidermists can be helpful in determining shapes and positions. However, generally speaking, the carver should treat them as suspect and rely on live birds, or refer to photographs, for these most important features.

The best possible way to augment the knowledge the carver has gained by studying live birds is by taking photographs of them. Using the fine equipment that is available today, amateur photography is not nearly as difficult, or as expensive, as it may sound. Many carvers use this means of making a permanent record of the bird's form or shape, posture, and some feather shape and arrangement details. Bird photography will be covered in more detail in the next section.

Due to the difficulty in remembering color accurately, the live bird viewed at a distance is of little assistance when trying to duplicate its colors. Color transparencies and color photographs are also of little help due to the many variables involved in color photography and printing. Lighting and film exposure are only two of the several critical factors in color photography. The bird is three-dimensional and, even under the best of conditions, certain parts receive more light than others. These highlights and shadows cause considerable differences between the color recorded on the film and the actual colors on the bird, as underexposure darkens colors and overexposure bleaches or lightens them. Another problem in color photography involves film sensitivity to certain colors. There are also several variables in color processing which can affect the final colors on positives or negatives. A completely new set of problems which can affect final colors occurs when color separations are made and when color photographs are printed for publication.

A live bird standing on the painting table obviously would be the best possible color reference. Although this has been done in a few cases, it is usually not possible or feasible. For most carver-artists, fresh (or frozen) specimens, good study skins, and mounts are the best practical color reference available.

PRIVATE AVIARIES

The private aviary is the ideal solution to the problem of having live birds available for studying and photographing. Birds of almost all species, which have been raised on game bird farms, are readily available and, except for some diving ducks, can be obtained quite reasonably. As an added bonus, a private aviary can be a source of entertainment for the whole family and can further provide nature lessons for the young ones who often have little exposure to such things in our modern way of life.

However, like most desirable and worthwhile things, a private aviary does not materialize easily or cheaply. The original cost of the aviary, depending on its size and complexity, can be considerable—usually much more than the cost of the birds. Proper maintenance of the aviary requires almost daily attention.

Aviaries for waterfowl must be provided with a pond,

4-4 *Author's aviary.*

or pool—a necessity which usually represents the most expensive part of the project. Waterfowl, unfortunately, do most of their defecating when in the water; therefore, the pool must be drained and cleaned every few days, depending on its size and the number of birds using it. Maintenance is reduced drastically when a natural pond, with a dirt bottom and fed with sufficient fresh water to prevent stagnation, is available.

The birds must be protected from animals and rapacious birds with a good, predator-proof fence and some overhead covering which is usually in the form of nylon netting. Aviaries located in cold climates are even more expensive, both originally and maintenance-wise, because of the necessity of providing pool heaters and warm enclosures for the birds.

Many birds raised on game bird farms are "pinioned". Pinioning involves permanent removal, on one wing, of the bird's wing structure from which the ten large flight feathers (primaries) grow, making the bird incapable of flight. While pinioning is necessary for many aviaries with large, uncovered ponds, it is certainly not desirable on birds which are kept primarily for study and photography. In the author's opinion, it is almost sacrilegious to permanently cripple these beautiful creatures so they can no longer function in the most remarkable way nature intended. Although not as plentiful as pinioned birds, full-winged birds are available and the carver should very carefully ascertain that he is not buying a pinioned bird. Game bird breeders usually clip the primary feathers on unpinioned birds to prevent them from escaping. The clipped feathers can be easily and painlessly removed, permitting new feathers to grow in a very short time.

Inasmuch as the primary purpose of the private aviary is for viewing, studying, and photographing the birds, it should be carefully planned so that these activities can be accomplished in the best possible manner. The pond, or pool, is normally the focal point of the aviary and should be located so that it will be in sunlight at least part of the day. Good lighting is a prerequisite to getting good pictures.

If only a part of the pool is in sunlight, invariably the bird to be photographed will be in the shadows. The use of telephoto lenses, which have fairly long minimum focusing distances, is necessary even in small aviaries for getting good, detailed bird photographs. Depending on the minimum focusing distance of the lens to be used, space must be provided so that the photographer can bring the birds into focus. Although birds can be photographed through holes in the fence, it is much better not to be restricted in this manner. It is usually necessary to use binoculars to see certain details on the bird; therefore, the minimum focusing distance on them should also be considered.

Figure 4-5 shows typical aviary construction. The following is an explanation of the symbols used.

A. *Pool.* If a natural pond is not available, some type of a manmade tank (concrete, fiberglass, or metal) must be constructed or purchased. It must be capable of being

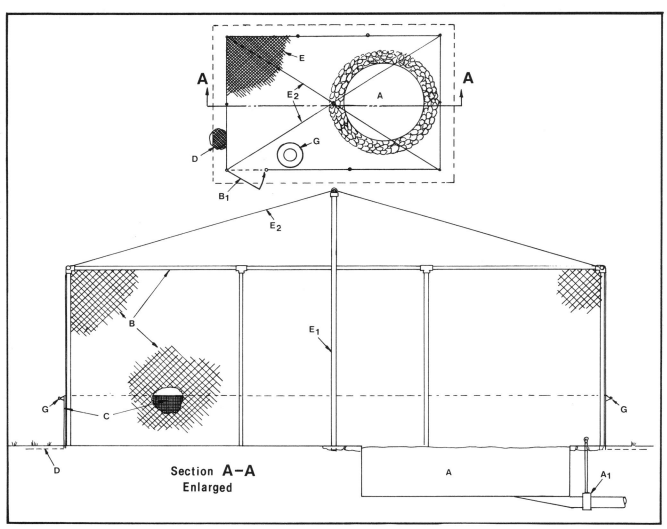

4-5 *Typical aviary construction.*

easily and quickly drained for cleaning; therefore, a drain valve (A1) must be incorporated in the tank or in the drain plumbing leading from it. Provisions must be made for disposing of the dirty water. Fresh water for filling must be available.

B. *Fence.* The aviary must be enclosed by a strong, predator-proof fence. A six or seven foot high chain link type fence provides excellent protection and long life. A close fitting gate (Bl), capable of being locked, must be provided.

C. Inasmuch as small predators, including snakes, can crawl through the chain link fencing (fabric), the addition of ½ inch mesh hardware cloth, 24 inches wide should be installed over the fencing from the ground level.

D. One-inch mesh chickenwire, two feet wide, attached to the ½ inch mesh hardware cloth and chain link fabric, will prevent predators from burrowing under the fence.

E. Nylon netting (see Appendix), supported by means of a center pole (E1) and diagonal wires (E2) attached to each corner post, and attached to the chain link fabric, will provide excellent protection from owls and hawks and will also prevent the aviary birds from escaping.

F. Some type of all-weather feeder is usually desirable.

However, if the birds are hand fed, they will be more dependent on humans and will become tamer.

G. An electric, single wire, fence is usually desirable to prevent predators from climbing the fence and possibly chewing through the nylon netting.

AMATEUR PHOTOGRAPHY

Amateur photography can aid in collecting carving data in at least two ways. First, the serious carver will soon want either to give some of his carvings to friends or to sell them. Once the carving is gone, it is amazing how soon the pertinent details of the carving are forgotten. With photographs of his carvings for reference, the carver can see where he has been, so to speak, and these pictures can help immeasurably in improving future work. Also, it is almost a necessity to have photos of his work available if he intends to exhibit or sell.

Second, by amateur photography the carver can build a file of live bird pictures to which he can refer for planning and carving data. As previously mentioned, it is practically impossible to recreate by sketching or to retain in memory the myriad details of a bird's structure, position, feathering, and coloration. Only the camera can capture and accurately record these all-important features.

The photographing of wild birds in their natural habitat can be very difficult, time-consuming, and expensive; however, taking pictures of these same bird species in parks, zoos, private aviaries, game refuges, and game farms is much easier, and good results can usually be obtained with considerably less effort and expense.

Considering original cost and availability of the body, lenses, and accessories, cost of film and processing, and portability, the 35-mm camera, featuring interchangeable lenses and focusing screens is, without much doubt, the best single piece of equipment for photographing both carvings and live birds. Many of the newer SLR (single lens reflex) cameras incorporate automatic exposure control. On the better cameras, this automatic feature can be overridden, and the shutter speed and aperture adjusted manually to obtain the correct exposure. On some cameras, the automatic feature can be compensated to adjust for extreme conditions. Most cameras with automatic exposure incorporate either shutter-preferred exposure or aperture-preferred exposure (on a few models, either method can be selected). With the shutter-preferred system, the desired shutter speed is selected manually and the aperture (diaphragm) is controlled automatically. On the aperture-preferred system, the aperture is selected manually and the shutter speed is controlled automatically. Regardless of whether the exposure is manually or automatically controlled, the behind-the-lens exposure meter should be "center-weighted", i.e., the meter should read the amount of reflected light at the center of the viewing screen, instead of reading the average reflected light over the whole area being photographed. When photographing live birds, also carvings, the exposure reading should be based on the light reflected from the bird, not the bird plus the background. If birds, or carvings, are photographed with cameras whose exposure meters measure the average overall light, the subjects will be often underexposed on the negatives, or transparencies.

When taking pictures of birds that seldom remain still for long, the amateur photographer needs every advantage he can get for proper exposure control.

At the time of this writing, there are several cameras that feature automatic focusing and there are now a few fairly long focal length lenses that can be used with at least some of these cameras. The author was unable to ascertain the effectiveness of these cameras when used with long lenses for general bird photography and especially for photographing birds in flight. If there are any shortcomings with this first generation of auto focusing cameras, it will probably be only a matter of time before accurated auto focusing with long lenses on fast moving objects becomes a reality.

Sharp focusing with long lenses is without any doubt the most difficult part of taking good bird photographs. Automating this operation will revolutionize bird photography.

Selecting Camera and Lenses

So much 35-mm camera equipment is available today and at such a range in price that the selection of a camera and lenses becomes very confusing. Take your time and become thoroughly familiar with some of the different popular makes of cameras. Visit a number of camera stores, if possible, state your specific needs, and obtain recommendations from a number of camera salesmen. Using the actual recommended equipment, try focusing on objects of the size and at the distance that will exist under actual conditions; familiarize yourself with the exposure control; try changing lenses; and perform any other operation that may be necessary for the particular camera. In addition, it is strongly advised that the amateur rent the camera and lens of his choice (many camera stores rent equipment) for a short time and use the equipment in the field before buying.

In selecting a camera and a standard lens (usually 50- to 58-mm focal length), an important point to consider is how close to the subject the lens will focus. This minimum focusing distance varies considerably with different makes of cameras. It is almost always desirable to fill the negative, and it is also desirable or necessary at times to take detailed, close-up pictures—for example, the head and bill or feet of the carving. The amateur should try to anticipate the smallest object he may wish to photograph and try to pick a camera-lens combination that will handle the situation. To photograph quite small objects, it may be necessary to buy accessories such as macro lenses or even extension bellows.

Before deciding on a particular camera and lens, the amateur should test the camera's viewing and focusing capabilities with a telephoto lens of at least 400-mm focal length. Focusing screens that work well with the normal lenses (50- to 58-mm) are usually inadequate for use with longer lenses. Most bird photographers prefer to use plain ground-glass focusing screens. The split-image microprism focusing feature, which is standard on most SLR cameras, tends to black out when used with lenses whose focal length is 200- to 250-mm or more. A few SLR cameras have interchangeable focusing screens, and there are usually a number of screens from which to choose. When selecting a camera, the amateur should definitely pick one whose focusing screens can easily be interchanged.

For photographing live birds, a telephoto lens of at least 200-mm focal length for the 35-mm camera is normally required. The amateur should not overestimate the magnifying power of the long lenses. For example, when using a 35-mm camera equipped with a 200-mm focal length lens, it is necessary to be within ten feet of a bird the size of a mallard in order to fill the negative. This distance would increase to twenty feet when a 400-mm focal length lens is used and to approximately thirty-five feet with a 640-mm lens. Minimum focusing distance is also a very important consideration when selecting the telephoto lens. There is nothing to be gained by going to a 400-mm lens, if, because of minimum focusing distance it becomes necessary to back away from the object being photographed until only one half of the negative is used. The same results could be obtained much less expensively with a 200-mm lens, provided that this lens has a minimum focusing distance one half that of the 400-mm lens.

The minimum focusing distance on some telephoto lenses can be reduced somewhat by the use of an extension tube inserted between the camera body and lens. This reduction in minimum focusing distance is gained at the expense of not being able to focus on objects at distances that approach the infinity end of the focusing range. For example, the 400-mm Novoflex Nesting Tele Lens has a minimum focusing distance of approximately fourteen feet. When an extension tube 21-mm in length is inserted between the lens and camera body, the minimum focusing distance is reduced to approximately eleven feet. The maximum focusing distance is reduced from infinity to approximately sixty feet.

Zoom lenses have been improved greatly during the past few years, and many good ones are available in the 80- to 250-mm range. There are now a few in the 75- to 300-mm range and at least one each in the 100- to 400-, 500-, and 600-mm ranges. Zoom lenses are ideally suited for photographing birds in close quarters for two reasons: first, most of these lenses have relatively short minimum focusing distances; and, second, if the bird approaches the camera to the point where it more than fills the viewing screen, the photographer can in effect "back off" by decreasing the focal length of the lens.

Also improved are tele-converters, or extenders, which are small, optical devices that can be inserted between the camera and the lens to increase the focal length of the lens. These extenders double (2X) or triple (3X) the focal length of the lens on which they are used. There are advantages and disadvantages connected with use of extenders. On the plus side: great increases of focal length with small increases in size, weight, and cost and without increasing the minimum focusing distance (very important for close-up photography). On the minus side: decreased speed of the lens (with a 2X extender, the lens speed is cut in half) and the magnification of the optical deficiencies of the lens plus the addition of some new ones. On the whole, the better extenders do a fair to good job. Some of the higher priced zoom lenses have matching extenders that are designed to give optimum performance. If the lighting conditions permit a lens with a 2X converter to be stopped down to f/8 or smaller (the effective diaphragm opening thus becoming f/16 or smaller), satisfactory results can be gotten. However, although a converter is inexpensive, light, and convenient, it will not produce results comparable to a telephoto lens whose focal length is the same as the telephoto-converter combination.

A number of SLR camera manufacturers now have power winders (autowinders) available at a reasonable cost. These battery-powered units are capable of advancing the film and releasing the shutter at speeds up to about three frames per second. They are very useful for bird photography and permit the amateur photographer to get many shots he would normally miss while manually advancing the film.

Owing to the magnifying ability of the long focal length lenses, any camera movement is also magnified; therefore, it usually becomes necessary, unless a very fast shutter speed is used, to provide a support for the camera when lenses longer than 150-mm focal length are required. Even when the camera is mounted on a sturdy tripod, some shake or vibration can still exist, and it is advisable to use a shutter speed of 1/125 second or faster when using lenses with focal lengths in excess of 300 mm.

Because of practical limitations of size, weight, and cost, long focal length lenses are much slower than standard focal length lenses. The terms "fast" or "slow" when used in reference to a lens indicate in general terms the light-gathering ability of the lens. The speed of the lens (not to be confused with the shutter speed) is dependent on the diameter of the lens, or more accurately, the maximum aperture of the lens. For example, if a 400-mm focal length lens were designed to have the same light-gathering capability, or "speed," of a standard 50-mm, f/1.8 lens, the 400-mm lens would be in excess of nine inches in diameter. This lens would obviously be a costly and heavy piece of equipment.

Under actual usage, it soon becomes very apparent that the slow, long focal length lenses, combined with the necessary faster shutter speeds, have very definite limitations in regard to available light. This limitation can be offset, to a degree, by using films with fast emulsion speeds (high ASA ratings). Generally speaking, however, the faster the emulsion speed, the grainier the film, and the smaller the amount the negative can be enlarged and still produce a usable print.

All of the normal focal length lenses purchased as standard equipment on SLR cameras have automatic diaphragms. An automatic diaphragm permits the photographer to compose the picture and focus with the lens at its maximum opening. With the lens at maximum opening, the image is at its maximum brightness and the depth of field (the distance in front of and behind the subject within which all objects are in focus) is at its minimum. These are conditions for optimum focusing. When the shutter is released, the diaphragm stops down to a preselected opening.

Most older telephoto lenses, and even a few newer ones, do not have automatic diaphragms. The automatic diaphragm is a most important feature. Opening the diaphragm for focusing, and resetting it after focusing, takes considerable time—time that is much better spent following the bird and bringing it into focus. Also, the shutter-preferred automatic exposure control, available on some newer cameras, is not compatible with a lens that does not have an automatic diaphragm.

The most important considerations in selecting a telephoto lens, in addition to general overall quality, are ease and accuracy of focusing, diaphragm control, minimum focusing distance, and lens speed (maximum aperture). The amateur should be very deliberate in his selection, and, again, he should try to use the lens of his choice under actual field conditions before buying.

Photographing Bird Carvings

While it is important to photograph the carving from an angle that will produce the best picture for sales or publicity purposes, it is necessary to take pictures from several different angles so that a complete photographic

4-6 *Photographing a bird carving with natural light.*

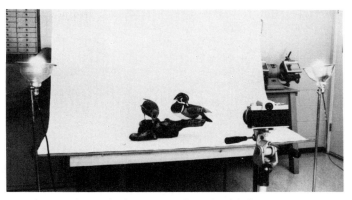

4-7 *Photographing a bird carving with artificial light.*

record of the carving is made. The pictures should include a direct profile view, three-quarter front and rear views, front view, rear view (preferably taken from a fairly high angle so that the back of the carving will be shown), and any detail shots that seem important.

There are at least two simple, popular ways of photographing a bird carving. One is to photograph the carving against a perfectly plain background, attempting to eliminate distracting shadows. When taking black-and-white pictures, it is also desirable to eliminate or reduce any differentiation in shade between the horizontal surface upon which the carving rests and the vertical surface forming the background. This may not always apply when photographing in color. The other method is to photograph the bird carving in a natural background (Figure 4-8). In this case, shadows are usually desirable, provided they do not detract from the carving itself.

One of the simplest ways of lighting the subject is to photograph the carving in the shade, using only available outdoor light (Fig. 4-6). When this method is used, shadows are subdued or reduced to a minimum. For black-and-white pictures, a light-colored background (light gray works well) should be used. For color pictures, a background paper of a contrasting color, which adds interest to the photograph, may be desirable.

When it is not convenient to take pictures outside, or if the weather does not cooperate, the amateur has to resort to an artificial light source, such as the popular electronic flash. However, unless the flash is bounced off the ceiling or some other reflective surface, the resulting picture will be quite flat and there will often be harsh, distracting shadows.

Good, consistent results can be quite easily obtained with the use of two inexpensive floodlights and reflectors (preferably supported by stands) when the camera, lights, and subject are arranged as shown in Figure 4-7. The background paper is continued from the vertical onto the table as before. The floodlight reflectors are pointed straight up and the light is bounced off the ceiling. If the ceiling is reasonably reflective, the carving will receive a soft light and shadows will be practically eliminated. If shadows are desired, the floodlights (or light) can be placed and directed at the subject in many ways, giving a variety of effects. Also, a combination of indirect and

4-8 *Photographing a bird carving using natural background.*

direct lighting can be used to give pleasing and sometimes dramatic effects. However, direct lighting is generally harsher and produces a picture with more contrast that often does not show the carving to its best advantage.

When taking pictures in artificial light, the exposure time is increased, requiring slower shutter speeds. Therefore, a tripod or some other support for the camera is an absolute necessity.

It is almost always desirable to photograph the carving in color. However, it is difficult at times to record on film the true colors of the carving. This is due to a number of variables, the two most important being the type of film used and its exposure.

The type of lighting dictates the type of color film that may be successfully used. Daylight-type film can be used for natural, outdoor light and for electronic flash type lighting. It cannot be used with floodlights or other types of artificial lights without the use of corrective color filters. When Tungsten 3200K floodlights are used for artificial lighting, both negative (print-type) and positive (transparency-type) films, which are color balanced for this particular light source, are available at most camera stores. Regardless of the type of film and lighting used, it is most advisable to "bracket" the exposures, i.e., both overexpose and underexpose the film. Color is affected

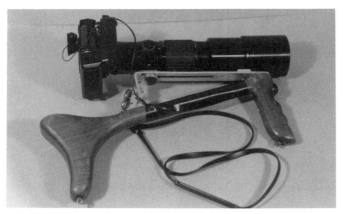

4-9 *Homemade gunstock-type mount for 400-mm lens.*

by exposure—bracketing greatly increases the chances of getting accurate color.

Photographing Live Birds

Before attempting to photograph live birds, thoroughly familiarize yourself with your equipment. Practice focusing on objects the size of a bird located at a distance likely under actual conditions. Focusing the long lenses is extremely critical, and birds seldom stand still for long, if at all; learn to focus quickly and accurately. Also, practice using the exposure controls (diaphragm and shutter speed) until all of these operations become more or less automatic.

The long lenses and the camera must be supported by a tripod or by some other means. As the birds are generally moving, the camera cannot be locked into one position on the tripod. It is usually desirable to tighten the pan control (azimuth) and the elevation control until there is a slight restraint to movement. The camera can then be moved the necessary amount to follow the bird's movements. The shutter release should be carefully squeezed—like the trigger on a rifle—to reduce movement of the camera.

Unless the photographer is operating from a fixed position, such as a blind, a tripod is very cumbersome to transport, set up, and use. Furthermore, in many instances a tripod does not provide sufficient flexibility, for example, when photographing birds in flight—a difficult task even under the most ideal conditions. When the subject is moving rapidly, better pictures can be gotten by mounting the camera and lens on a structure similar to the stock of a gun, which is held by both hands and braced against the shoulder, thereby reducing unwanted camera movement (Fig. 4-9). When this equipment is used, shutter speeds of 1/250 second, or faster, must be maintained. Shutter speeds of 1/250 second, or faster, are required to stop the rapid wing movement of birds in flight.

While the gunstock mount is a necessity for photographing birds in flight, it also works well for photographing sitting, standing, or swimming birds and gives the photographer much greater mobility. When photographing birds, ease of movement is of great importance; if the photographer is loaded down with equipment, he will spend more time moving this equipment than taking pictures. The author learned this the hard way and now limits his equipment to the gunstock mount, one lens (usually an automatic diaphragm 500-mm telephoto), two camera bodies (one loaded with black-and-white film and the other with color), and plenty of film.

If the carver has actual specimens available for color reference, there is not much to be gained by taking color pictures. Black-and-white film generally has more latitude (greater allowance for error) than color film and is, of course, much cheaper to use. Contact-size proofs can be inexpensively made of all the black-and-white film that has been exposed, and if a magnifying glass is used for making the selection, only sharp, well-exposed pictures need be enlarged. Two popular American black-and-white films produce good results: Kodak Plus X (ASA speed 125) and Kodak Tri X (ASA speed 400). For most lenses with focal lengths of over 400 mm, it is often mandatory to use the faster Tri X film so that shutter speeds of 1/125 second or faster can be used in conjunction with smaller apertures which produce greater depths of field and in turn make focusing somewhat less critical.

Ektachrome 400 and Fujichrome 400 are two popular color films used for bird photography. It is desirable, when light conditions permit, to use slower, finer grain films. However, light conditions can change rapidly at times and it can be very disconcerting to miss some good shots by having a slower film in the camera at the wrong time. The author carries only Fujichrome 400 color film and Tri X black and white film.

When taking pictures of a particular bird, try to get shots from different angles: profile, front and rear, three-quarters front and rear, and from overhead, if possible. Also try to get pictures of the bird in different poses: alert, swimming, preening, sleeping, stretching, and others.

MUSEUMS AS SOURCES

Another source of information commonly overlooked is the natural history museum. Museum curators and preparators are especially helpful in passing a wealth of information on to the carver.

Many museums not only have fine reference libraries, they usually have on display mounted specimens of all the game birds, and, in addition, a large collection of study skins. In some cases, if the proper contacts are established, it may even be possible to borrow some of their study skins. Some museums are in need of certain specimens to complete or to provide more depth to their collections. It is possible that the carver can reciprocate the museum's generosity by supplying some of these specimens when they can be legally taken.

5

Making the Drawing

The success of a realistic bird carving greatly depends on how well it was planned in the drawing stage. Unless the original cut out of the rough block is made from a drawing based on accurate dimensions and proportions and a graceful, natural pose of the bird, no amount of good carving and painting will save the finished product from looking amateurish. It is possible to make some corrections during the carving procedure by removing more wood than originally planned; however, adding wood is often a real problem. Some carvers attempt to work out the important lines and details of the carving as they proceed with the actual wood removal. While this "by guess and by golly" method of carving may occasionally turn out fairly well, depending on the carver's experience, ability, and luck, more often than not the end product betrays the lack of early thought and planning. This does not mean that every detail of the carving has to be worked out on the drawing prior to doing any work on the carving itself. Such details as feather-pattern layouts can usually be more easily accomplished on the curved surface of the carving after its overall shape has been established. The drawing does not have to be a thing of beauty in itself. Its primary purpose is to produce a good carving; its secondary purpose is to provide a record for possible future use.

There are now a number of books on bird carving, several video tapes, and many instructional classes and seminars making the learning of the various techniques involved much easier. The serious carver of today can learn in a relatively short time what it took some of us years to learn. This ease of learning how to carve and paint birds has been generally a great benefit to the amateur carver but, in many cases, has been at the cost of lost initiative and originality. There is a strong tendency these days to follow the path of least resistance and to just copy rather than spend the time and effort doing one's own research. The carver who uses little initiative is missing one of the most satisfying aspects of bird carving—that of being able to say, "This carving is actually my own creation".

The aspiring bird carver does not use his full creative ability until he plans his own carvings and makes his own drawings. As long as he uses other carver's drawings and attempts to duplicate other carver's work, his carvings will not be truly original, and his own distinctive style will not develop.

ALTERING EXISTING DRAWINGS

If the beginner has little drawing experience and possesses limited dimensional and structural information on game birds, it may be to his advantage to start by altering other carvers' drawings before attempting a completely original drawing. However, this practice should be discontinued as soon as he has gained some confidence in his own ability to plan a carving. Carving planning, like the actual carving, can only be learned by doing.

When altering an existing drawing that is not your own, realize that you may be copying another's mistakes; therefore, attempt to check such important points as overall dimensions, shape, etc., as thoroughly as possible within the limits of the data you possess.

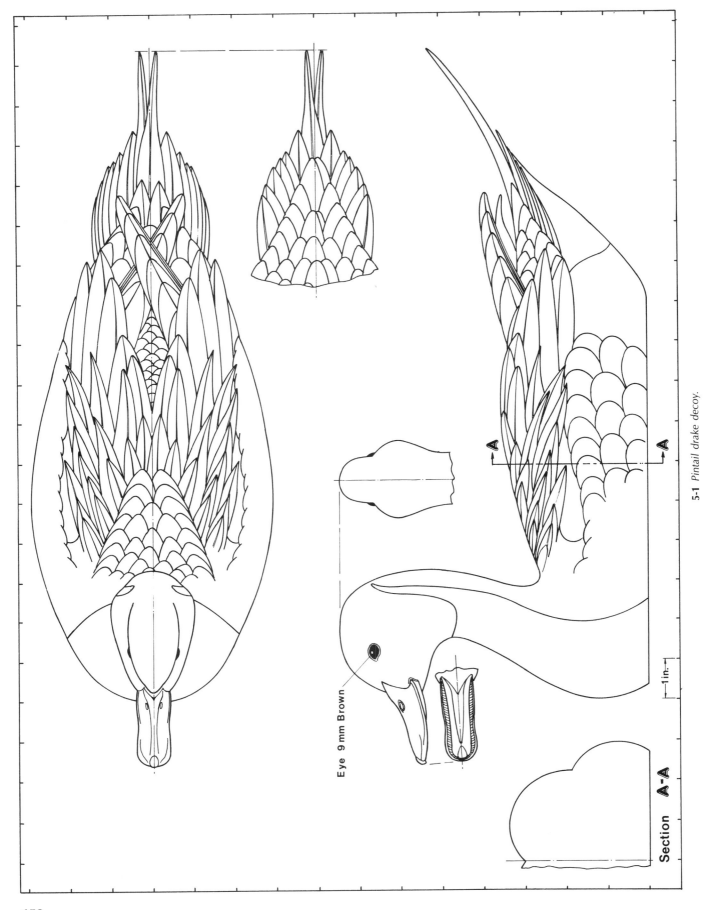

Eye 9 mm Brown

Section **A·A**

5-1 *Pintail drake decoy.*

1 in.

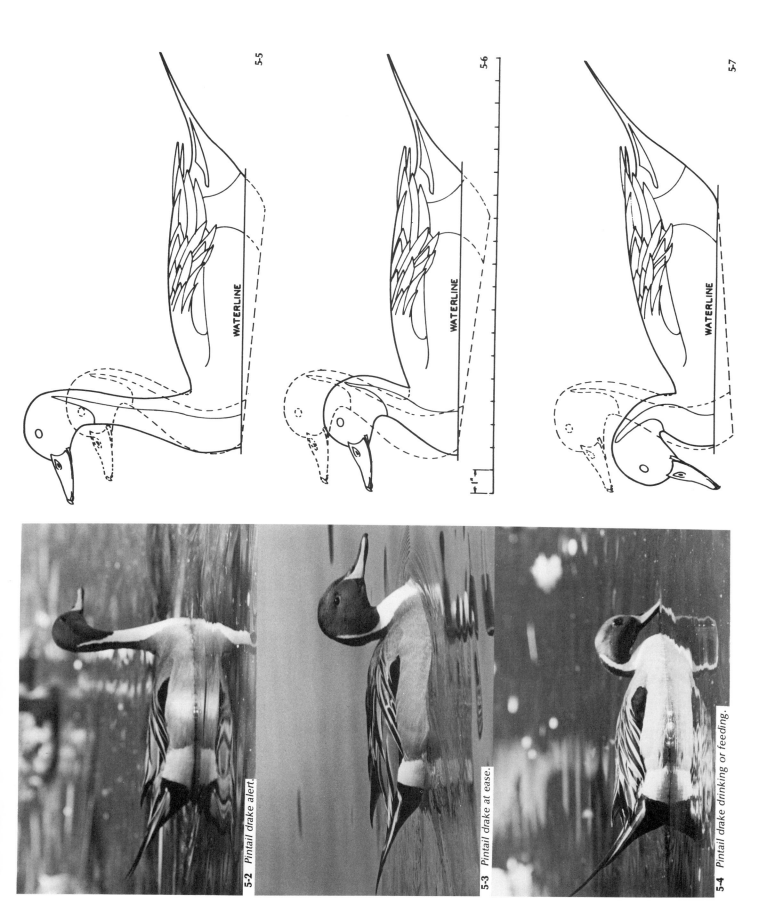

5-5

5-6

5-7

WATERLINE

WATERLINE

WATERLINE

5-2 Pintail drake alert.

5-3 Pintail drake at ease.

5-4 Pintail drake drinking or feeding.

For all practical purposes, the position of the head on a decoy carving establishes the activity of the bird: relaxed, alert, sleeping, preening, feeding, drinking, displaying, attacking, or others.

A simple change in the head position of the bird is probably one of the most common alterations to an existing drawing and suitable for a first attempt. Extreme head positions are very difficult to work out accurately on paper, and usually some cutting, fitting, and other alterations are required during the actual carving procedure.

Head rotation is the easiest modification to make. Instead of making it straight ahead, the head can be rotated up to about 30 degrees in either direction without greatly affecting the neck lines. If the head is to be rotated, make the head-body joint parallel to the base of the carving. When this is done, the head can be rotated without introducing another, often undesirable, angle. If the head is rotated more than approximately 30 degrees, the neck lines are affected and must be altered. Considerable alterations are required when head rotation angles of over 90 degrees are made.

The next easiest pattern change is to alter the head position. Start out by making a tracing of the duck's profile on vellum or thin tracing paper. Make another tracing of the head and part of the neck. Now, place the head tracing under the profile drawing and move the head around until the desired head position is attained. Trace off the head onto the upper drawing. Next, blend the neck and chest lines from the original drawing into the new head location. Photographs of live birds can be most helpful in developing new head positions and working out new neck and chest lines.

To provide an example, a drawing of a pintail drake (Fig. 5-1) has been altered to portray three different head positions shown in Figures 5-2 through 5-7.

Raising or lowering the tail relative to the water, with a resulting change in angle, is also a simple modification. Raising the tail can usually impart a feeling of alertness or

5-9 *Female pintail in an aggressive pose.*

5-10 *Canvasback hen exposes her wing as she preens.*

5-8 *Ducks lower their chest into the water when feeding or swimming.*

5-11 *Male shoveler about to scratch his bill.*

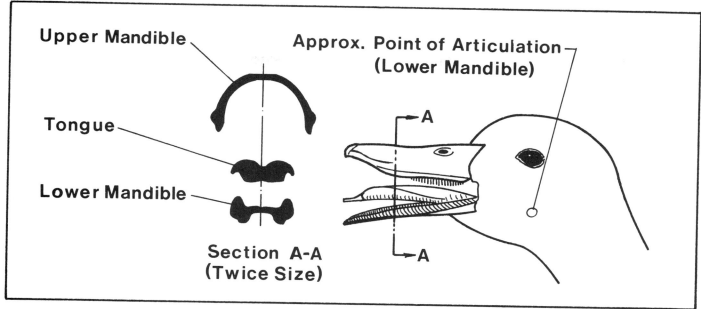

Upper Mandible

Approx. Point of Articulation
(Lower Mandible)

Tongue

Lower Mandible

A

A

Section A-A
(Twice Size)

5-12 *Open bill details—typical for ducks.*

jauntiness, while lowering the tail can give a more re-laxed effect.

Changing the angle of the duck's body relative to the water is still another easily accomplished alteration. Ducks, when swimming or feeding, usually submerge more of their chests and expose more of the rear of their bodies (Fig. 5-8).

Raising the folded wing feather groups can impart the feeling of alertness and aggressiveness (Fig. 5-9). Ducks, when relaxing, often lower their wings, sometimes un-crossing them.

Although somewhat more complicated, interesting de-tail can be added by exposing more of the wing. Ducks often expose part of their wing when preening (Fig. 5-10).

Ducks sometimes scratch their heads and bills while in the water. Although this is a rather difficult pose to dupli-cate, it can result in an interesting and unusual carving (Fig. 5-11).

Opening the bill can further enhance the feeling of aggressiveness obtained by lowering the head and raising the wings. See Fig. 10-7, page 305. When opening the bill, it is very important to pivot the lower mandible about its proper articulation point, which is located fairly far back on the head (Fig. 5-12).

Waterfowl have interesting courtship displays. Some of their various poses and attitudes can make interesting, out of the ordinary, carvings (Fig. 5-13).

Opening, or closing, the tail is another relatively easily performed modification. When on the water, the duck usually has his tail compressed. The tail is expanded.

5-13 *Pintails display to gain the attention of a rather indifferent female.*

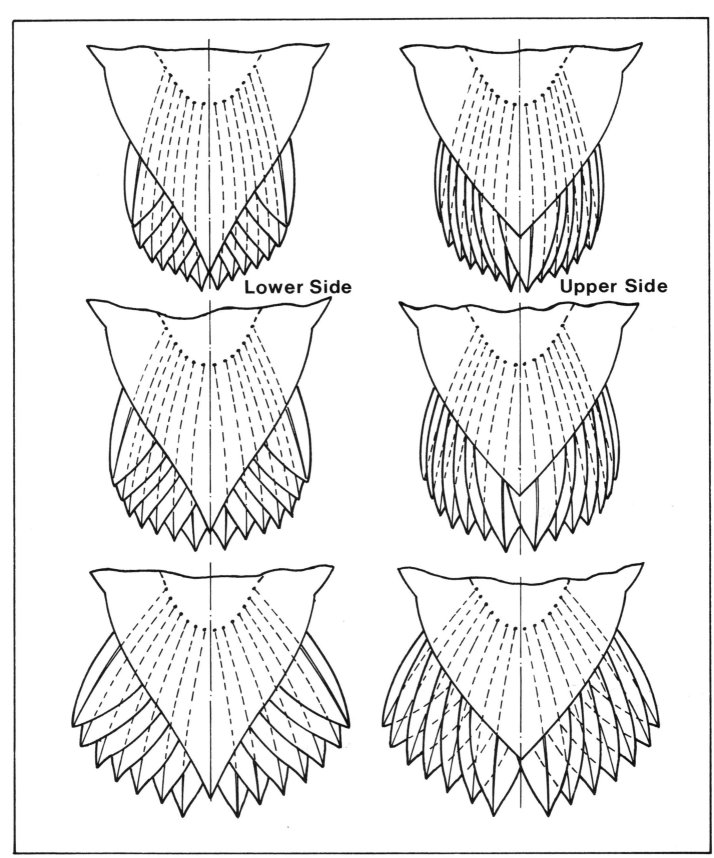

Lower Side

Upper Side

5-14 *Showing the mechanics involved in duplicating the expanding of a duck's tail.*

however, during some activities such as preening, attacking, stretching, and others. The duck's tail is composed of a right hand group and a left hand group—usually seven or eight feathers in each group. These feathers can be moved as a group or individually.

To accurately expand, or compress, the tail feather groups, it is most desirable to have a specimen available, not only for individual feather size, shape, and location, but for establishing the point from which the tail feathers originate. See Fig. 3-8, page 135. When this information is available, the attachment point for each individual tail feather can be located, which is also the point about which it moves when the tail is expanded or contracted. If the carver does not have a specimen, the tail feather attachment points can be approximated.

Assuming that it is desired to expand the tail, first, make a drawing (or make a tracing from an existing drawing), showing the shape and location of each feather. Next, establish the overall width, complete with centerline, of the new tail configuration on another piece of paper and place it over the above mentioned drawing. Now, trace off the innermost feather, locating it slightly further outboard from the centerline by rotating it about its attachment point. Continue by rotating the outermost tail feather about its attachment point until its outer edge touches the outer limits of the new tail configuration and trace its outline onto the new drawing. Locate the tips of the remaining feathers between the inner and outer tail feathers at more or less regular intervals, rotate them at their attachment points and trace them. Figure 5-14 shows the tail of a green-winged teal drake in an approximately normal compressed configuration and two other configurations in which the tail has been expanded. Take particular note that the shafts of all the tail feathers are curved.

MAKING ORIGINAL DRAWINGS

Although existing drawings, generally referred to by carvers as "patterns", are a most useful aid to the beginner, the serious aspiring bird carver does not utilize his creative talents until he starts designing his own carvings. This is not meant to imply he should ignore existing patterns and carvings of others completely—he should use them as just another of many sources of information, or as stepping stones, to achieve his goals and to help him from making time-consuming mistakes. When starting out, the amateur bird carver has much to learn—benefiting from the experience of others will obviously reduce the learning time considerably.

Compared to just a few years ago, there is now a tremendous amount of material available to the carver that can aid him in planning and designing his carvings. Over thirty years ago, the author's first carving (a landing mallard with outstretched wings and feet) was planned and carved from only one source of information—a borrowed copy of Kortright's *Ducks, Geese, and Swans of North America*. Today, with a little research, he could find a number of actual photographs (also artists' conceptions) of landing mallards taken from different angles. He now would have study skins and parts (wings, feet, and a cast study bill) from which to obtain accurate shapes and dimensions. In addition, if he wished to spend the money, he could acquire a remarkably accurate bird mounted in the landing configuration.

One of the better ways to work out a good drawing is to obtain dimensions from a fresh specimen and to determine natural shape and position from actual photographs. For those who do not have access to actual specimens, some of the more important dimensions (based on approximate averages) have been included in Chapter 11. Mounted birds and study skins are excellent for establishing feather patterns, shapes, and colors. Great improvements have been made in the art of taxidermy in recent years. A few top bird taxidermists have become so skillful that their work could be used as a reliable source of three-dimensional information for form and position. Generally speaking, however, mounted birds and artists' drawings (including those in this book) should be treated as suspect and should be checked against the real thing whenever possible.

Before starting a drawing, it is very important to assemble all of the reference material (specimens, actual photographs, artists' drawings and paintings, patterns, etc.) available for the particular species to be portrayed.

The four most important photographs required for making an accurate drawing are: a true profile, a rear view, a front view, and an overhead or top view. Good profile views are fairly easy to find. Good rear and front views are not nearly so available. Photographs taken from overhead are considerably harder to obtain as they almost always have to be taken under controlled conditions. In addition to the top views of thirteen duck species shown in this book, LeMaster's *Wildlife in Wood, Waterfowl* and *A Gallery of Ducks* (see Bibliography) have others. If a top view is not available for the species to be carved, approximations which will produce reasonably accurate plan view drawings can be made based on similar species and from good, rear view photographs.

Depending on the equipment and/or services which are available to the carver, there are several ways of making a lifesize drawing from a photograph.

1. If the negative for the photograph to be enlarged is available, it can be blown up to the correct size on a darkroom enlarger and printed.
2. If the negative is not available, the photograph can be copied with a camera and the resulting negative can be used to make a life-size print in the manner described above.
3. The photograph (also drawings) can be projected by means of an opaque projector onto a screen, or the wall. By varying the distance from the projector to the screen, the image from the photo can be enlarged to the correct size and traced.
4. If the photograph is in the form of a transparency, it can be projected onto the screen with a home projector and traced as described above.
5. The photograph (or the photo in the book) can be

taken to a printing shop, copied, and enlarged to the correct size.

6. The photograph can be enlarged directly to the correct size by means of a zoom-type copier, available at some print shops.

Although the author has some of the equipment referred to above and has access to the others, he usually finds it easier and quicker to sketch or trace the profile and plan view photographs and enlarge the drawings by means of squares. This method is fast, produces good results, and requires no special equipment. It will be used in the following exercise of making an original drawing.

Since it is easier to make a drawing for a decoy carving, this type of carving will be used for the step-by-step example. In the event the beginner would like to carve a pair of ducks, a female pintail has been selected for the subject, inasmuch as a male pintail has already been featured in this chapter.

When planning a carving, the carver should take advantage of all the reference material he can lay his hands upon. In the following example, however, the drawing will be made only from information contained in this book.

The profile (side) view should be worked on first. As Fig. 5-15 shows a direct side view of a pintail hen, an accurate profile drawing can be made either by tracing, or sketching, directly from this photograph.

Note: When selecting a profile view photograph, it is very important that the picture is actually a true profile view, i.e., the film plane of the camera must be parallel to the centerline of the bird. If the picture is taken at an angle, the bird will be foreshortened. If this angle is small, the overall length of the bird will be affected some but its general shape will not change greatly.

In the case of the pintail female shown in Fig. 5-15, the body profile appears to be true (note that the tips of the primaries of each wing lie on a vertical line). However, the head appears to be turned slightly to the right (note that the lower forehead at the centerline of the bird's head is not visible between the two pointed projections of the upper rear of the bill). The shape of the head will be affected only slightly, but the length of the bill is definitely foreshortened and must be corrected.

It is not necessary at this time to add much detail nor does the drawing have to be a work of art. The primary purpose of this drawing is to eventually provide a pattern from which the body block can be sawed. It is desirable, though, to show the extent of the side feather group, the primaries, and the extent of the scapular and tertial feather groups. Particular attention should be given to accurately duplicating the profile shape of the head and neck.

The same procedure described above for making the profile drawing will be used for making the plan view drawing. Fig. 5-17 shows the top view of a female pintail.

5-15 *Pleasing profile of a female pintail.*

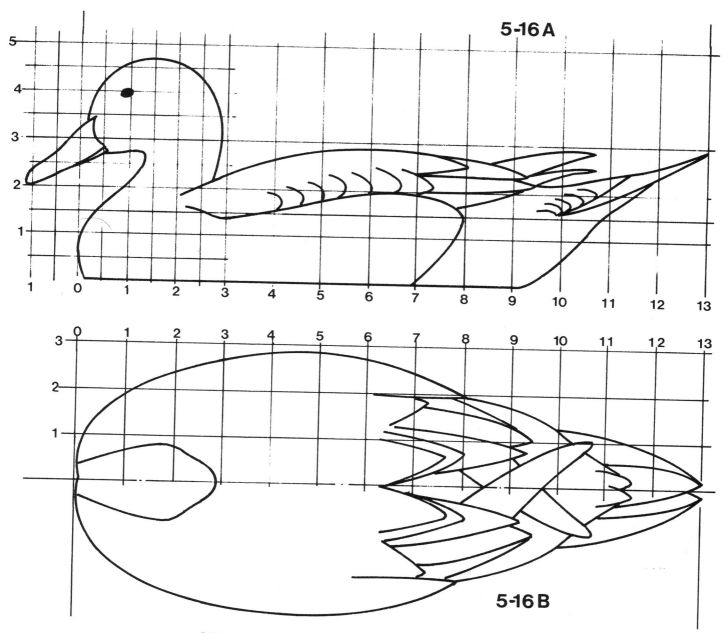

5-16 A

5-16 B

5-16 *Drawing of female pintail from Figures 5-15 and 5-17.*

Make a tracing, or sketch, of this photograph and establish a centerline.

Note: Figure 5-18 shows another top view of a female pintail. Especially note the differences in the feather patterns of the back and of the scapulars near the centerline of the bird. This second top view was included here to show how feather patterns can vary from one time to another, as these two photographs are of *the same bird* but taken at different times, possibly two weeks apart. In this example, the scapular pattern shown in Fig. 5-18 will be followed more closely than the feather pattern shown in Fig. 5-

17. There is no distinct back feather pattern visible in either top views (the topographical location of the back feathers is shown in Fig. 2-55, page 108). However, the left side of the back feather pattern shows fairly clearly in Fig. 5-9.

Fig. 5-19 shows still another top view photograph. In this picture, the bird's head has moved forward, similar to the position shown in the profile photograph, Fig. 5-20. Notice how the planform body shape has changed in the chest area.

The plan view of the head shows reasonably well in Fig. 5-18. Due to muscular feather control, the width of the bird's head can vary considerably. Most carvers tend

5-17 *Top view of a pintail hen.*

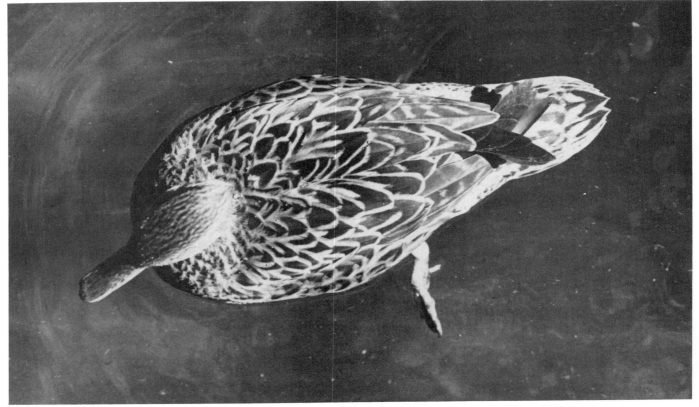

5-18 *Note difference in feather patterns.*

5-19 *Planform of the forward body can change with different head positions.*

5-20 *Approximate head position of pintail shown in Fig. 5-19.*

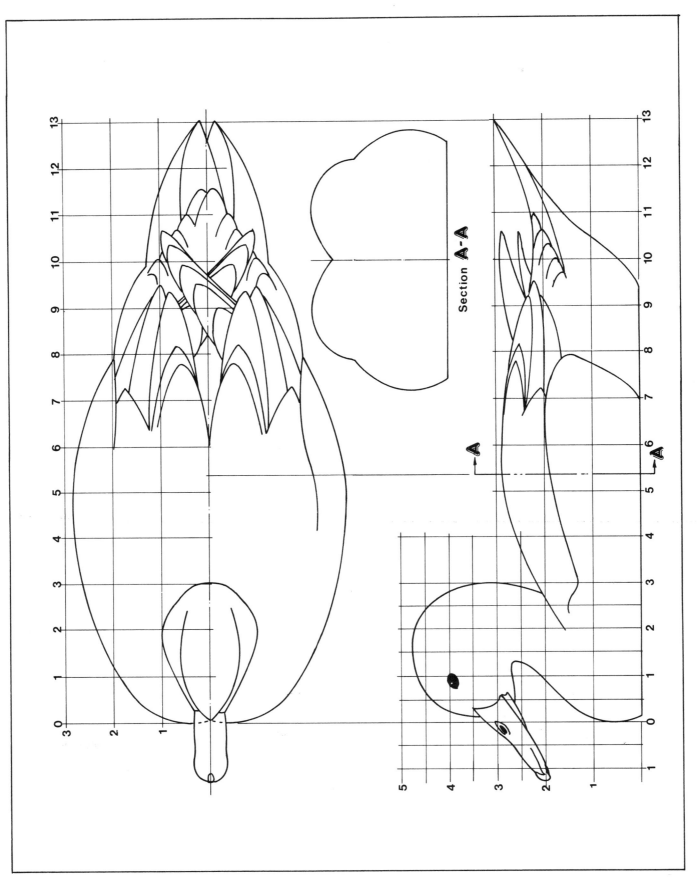

Section A-A

5-21 *Original drawing for female pintail decoy in its final form.*

to exaggerate the head widths. Based on the actual life-size width of her bill, the maximum head width of the pintail hen pictured in Fig. 5-18 is approximately 1.7 inches. Inasmuch as she appears to have her head feathers pulled in, it would probably be desirable to add upwards to ¼ inch to this dimension, making the maximum life-size head width approximately 2.0 inches.

After the profile and plan view drawings have been made from the photographs, they must be enlarged to the desired size of the carving which in this case will be life-size. This enlargement will be accomplished by means of squares, a procedure described previously on page 31.

First, lay out horizontal and vertical lines on the profile drawing forming .5 (½) inch squares (the squares could be larger or smaller but in this case this size gives about the number of lines required to make an accurate enlargement). Number both the horizontal and vertical lines as shown in Fig. 1-79, page 31. See Fig. 5-16A.

Next, lay out lines on the plan view drawing forming .5 inch squares. See Fig. 5-16B.

The approximate average body length of a female pintail as given in Chapter 11, page 335, is 13.0 inches. The body length as measured on the profile photograph (Fig. 5-15) is 6.5 inches. 13 divided by 6.5 equals 2.0, or the number of times the squares used on the profile drawing (Fig. 5-16A) must be enlarged. 2.0 multiplied by .5 equals 1.0, or the size of the squares which will produce a life-size drawing.

A drawing composed of 1.0 inch squares can now be made and the horizontal and vertical lines numbered in the same sequence as on the smaller drawing. Now, draw in the life-size profile of the bird freehand in the manner described in Chapter 1, page 33. See Fig. 5-21.

If the decoy is to be floated, an additional amount must be added to the body height. This amount depends on the kind of wood used and whether or not the body is hollowed. In most cases, one-half to one inch must be added.

The drawing of the bill should now be corrected. The bills of mounts and study skins dry in a very short time and some of their cross-sectional dimensions are affected. Plastic study bills, cast from fresh specimens, are now available for most waterfowl species (see Appendix for source) for those carvers who would like a more accurate reference. It is recommended that they be used for competition and for professional carvings. Actually, the changes caused by drying are rather minor from a beginner's standpoint and, in most cases, satisfactory results can be gotten from dried bills. The dried bills of all game birds are pictured life-size in Chapter 13. The female pintail's bill, shown on page 354, is quite accurate with two exceptions—approximately ¹⁄₁₆ inch should be added to the width, and the tip of the lower mandible should be lowered a small amount (in other words, the bill should be opened slightly).

If a study bill is not available, trace the profile and plan views from the photographs in Chapter 13, and transfer the profile view to the life-size profile drawing (Fig. 5-21).

Note: In order to simplify this first example of making an original drawing, top view photographs, Figures 5-17 and 5-18 were enlarged and printed so that the body lengths pictured would correspond to the body length of the bird shown in Fig. 5-15. Normally, there would be differences in body lengths, which would require different size squares for the plan view enlargement.

5-22 *Rear view of a floating pintail hen.*

5-23 *Front view of a floating pintail hen.*

Establish a centerline in the upper part of the life-size drawing (Fig. 5-21) and draw in the right side of the plan view, duplicating the intersection of the horizontal and vertical lines of the smaller drawing (Fig. 5-16B). Extend a vertical line upwards from the rearmost extent of the side feathers on the profile view. If these two views are not in agreement, which often happens, it may be advisable (as it was in this example) to compromise and alter both the plan and profile views. When a pleasing planform contour has been established on the right side of the plan view drawing, lay a piece of tracing paper over the drawing, trace it off (including the centerline), flop it over, and transfer this contour to the left side of the drawing.

Now, rework the planform shape of the head, making its maximum width approximately 2.0 inches, a dimension which was previously determined.

It is desirable at this time to establish the cross-sectional shape of the bird. First, draw a vertical line on the profile drawing at a point where the body height is the greatest. Extend this line upward across the plan view. Now, draw a rectangle whose width is the width of the body at the cross-sectional line and whose height is the height of the body at this same line. Now, draw a horizontal line across the rectangle located at a height corresponding to the height of the side feather group at the cross-sectional line. Referring to Fig. 5-22, draw the cross-sectional shape free hand. If desired, the cross-sectional shape could be traced and enlarged by means of squares as was done when establishing the profile and plan view drawings.

The carver should now go over his drawing carefully and critically. If possible, he should compare it to other photographs picturing similar poses or, even better, to a live bird. If any part of the drawing is not pleasing to his eye, he should try changing it. Changes are very easy to make on paper—they are usually difficult, if not impossible, to make on the actual carving. Does the drawing seem to project the character of the bird? Is the head shape correct? Are the neck and chest lines graceful? Does the bill emanate from the head at the correct angle? Is the eye located properly? Could the drawing be improved with a different head position? Could the pose be improved by changing the waterline, making the tail higher or lower? Should the primaries be raised or lowered? Are the back lines pleasing? These are some of the questions the carver should ask himself. It is a simple operation to place a piece of tracing paper over the drawing and make configuration changes. If it appears that the drawing has been improved, these changes should then be transferred to the original drawing. Planning a successful carving requires experience which can only be gotten by actually going through the whole procedure, not just once, but many times.

The primary purpose of the drawing is, of course, to provide a basis from which to start the actual carving process. Its secondary purpose is to provide a record for future use. Any changes that are made during the wood removal should be noted on the drawing. If it appears that improvements could have been made, they, too should be noted on the drawing.

Drawings, or tracings, of feather patterns should also be saved for future reference. If possible, photographs of the finished carving should be taken from different angles and these prints should be filed with the drawing. Once a carving is sold, or otherwise disposed of, it is amazing how quickly important details are forgotten. Records that show mistakes, as well as successes, are an important part of the unending learning process.

This original female pintail drawing (Fig. 5-21) was developed from good reference material. However, ideally, this material would also have included a good study skin, a cast study bill, and additional photographs showing a number of different positions, taken from different angles. Unfortunately, most carvings are planned and their drawings are made from much less information. It is most important that the carver learn to make the most of the information he has available and that he become acquainted with some of the ways of determining dimensions in a less direct manner and making intelligent approximations when necessary.

During the planning and actual carving stages, it is often desirable to ascertain a certain dimension from a photograph without making a drawing and enlarging it to life size. One way this can be accomplished—by the use of proportional dividers—has already been explained on page 34.

Life-size dimensions also can be obtained from photographs, or drawings of an unknown scale, by the use of simple arithmetic involving a procedure referred to as "ratio and proportion". Actually, this method was used previously when determining the size of squares which would produce a life-size drawing in the above discussion and on page 33. The use of ratio and proportion is a valuable tool, one that the author uses often. It is a very easy procedure to employ, especially when the simple mathematics are solved by means of an inexpensive calculator. Two examples will be covered here step-by-step. It is strongly suggested that the beginner follow through these few steps.

Referring to the profile photograph of a female pintail's

5-24 *Female pintail's head and bill details.*

head (Fig. 5-24), it is desired to determine the life-size distance from the tip of the bill to the center of the eye. In order to use this method, *one life-size dimension must be known*. In this case, the "known dimension" is the length of the upper mandible which can be determined from a study bill, or a specimen, or from the life-size bill pictured on page 354. This dimension is determined to be 2.0 inches.

> Note: It is much simpler to use decimal, or metric, dimensions. If fractional dimensions are used, they must be converted to decimal equivalents in order to use a calculator. Engineer scales, calibrated in tenths and one-hundreds of an inch are readily available at drafting supply stores.

The length of the upper mandible as measured on Fig. 5-24 is 1.42 inches. The distance from the tip of the bill to the center of the eye as measured on Fig. 5-24 is 2.1 inches. 2.0 (the life size length of the bill) divided by 1.42 equals 1.41 or the number of times the dimension from the tip of the bill to the center of the eye must be multiplied to obtain the life-size dimension, or 2.1 × 1.41 equals 2.96 inches. To state this in another way, the measured distance on Fig. 5-24 must be increased by 141%. This figure is a constant and can be used to determine other dimensions on this photograph. For example, the measured width of the neck is .93 inches. The life-size width of the neck is found by multiplying .93 by 1.41 or 1.3 inches.

For a second example, suppose we wish to know the life-size dimension from the tip of the tail to the rearmost side feather as determined from photograph Fig. 5-15. The distance measured on this photograph is 2.85 inches. The measured body length on this picture is 6.5 inches. Assuming that the average body length of a female pintail is 13.0 inches, we calculate the desired life-size dimension as follows:

$$\frac{13.0}{6.5} \times 2.85 = 5.7 \text{ inches}$$

As was previously stated, one life-size dimension must be known in order to be able to calculate other life-size dimensions that are in the same plane as the known dimension. The length and width of the bill are often used as "known dimensions". When the length of the bill is known, many other dimensions in the profile view can be calculated. When the width of the bill is known, dimensions such as body width, head and crown width and other dimensions in the top view can be determined. However, compared to the length and width of the bird's body, the length and width of the bill are quite small—if the dimensions of these parts are only slightly incorrect, sizeable errors can result. When the body length and width are known with some degree of accuracy, they should be used rather than calculated dimensions based on bill size. In any case, it is advisable to cross-check all calculated dimensions whenever possible with other sources. Other sources include fresh specimens, other photographs, the tables in Chapter 11, pattern books, etc.

When checking similar dimensions taken from different sources, it is often difficult to establish agreement. First, and most important, birds and their different parts vary appreciably in size. When dimensions are taken from a fresh specimen, the overall length of the bird (from tip of bill to tip of tail) should be checked against the average overall length of the same bird given in Chapter 11. The average lengths of waterfowl shown in Chapter 11 were taken from Kortright's *Ducks, Geese, and Swans of North America*.

The lengths given in this reference book were calculated from the known lengths of a number of birds and can be considered very reliable. By comparing the length of the specimen to the average length, the relative size of the specimen can be determined, i. e., small, medium, or large. Any dimensions taken from the specimen can then be corrected accordingly. Second, disagreement between dimensions obtained from photographs can be caused not only by size variations between the birds photographed but also due to the fact that many photographs have been taken at an oblique angle to the bird rather than straight on. When dimensions are calculated from photographs using a known body length as the "known dimension", fairly consistent results should be obtained even if the photographs are somewhat oblique, inasmuch as every dimension obtained is based on a percentage of the body length. When dimensions are gotten by using the length of the bill as the "known dimension", the bill in the photograph may not lie in the same plane as the rest of the bird and sizeable errors can result.

The making of the original drawing in this exercise has been quite straightforward because of the availability of good profile and top view photographs. As was previously mentioned, direct top view photographs of waterfowl are scarce and many carvings are planned without their benefit.

Assume than an overhead photograph had not been available. A good rear view photograph is the best

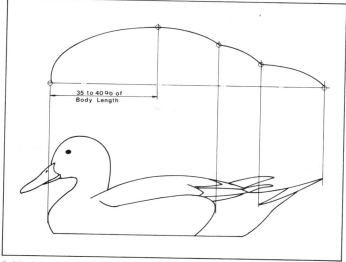

5-25 *Approximating the plan view using dimensions taken from a rear view photograph.*

substitute—see Fig. 5-22. Two very important dimensions can be obtained from this photograph, namely: the width of the body at the rearmost extent of the side feathers and the width of the body at the foremost extent of the tail. These two dimensions can be determined either by making a drawing from Fig. 5-22 and enlarging it to life-size and measuring these dimensions, or they can be gotten by calculation using the procedure just covered.

Suppose we elect to calculate these dimensions. The approximate average maximum body width for a female pintail as given in Chapter 11 is 5.75 inches. The maximum body width as measured on Fig. 5-22 is 2.68 inches. 5.75 divided by 2.68 equals 2.14 or the amount any measured dimension must be multiplied to obtain a life-size dimension. The measured body width just behind the rearmost side feather is 1.9 inches. 1.9 multiplied by 2.14 equals 4.0 which compares quite closely with the dimension measure on the life-size drawing Fig. 5-21. The measured width of the tail is 1.1. 1.1 multiplied by 2.14 equals 2.35. This is somewhat less than the tail width on the life-size drawing; however, it is possible the bird shown in Fig. 5-22 has its tail compressed more than the bird in Fig. 5-17.

The plan form shape can now be approximated. First, draw a centerline for the plan view, located above the profile view. Now, project the following points on the profile view upwards across this centerline: the fore and aft extremities of the profile body, the rearmost feather in the side group, and the intersection of the tail with the body—see Fig. 5-25. Also draw a vertical line across the plan view centerline at 37.5% of the body length (the maximum body width occurs at about 35-40% of the body length on most puddle ducks and about 40-45% on diving ducks). Next, lay out each of the calculated dimensions on their corresponding vertical lines. The rough planform body shape can now be drawn, making the forward body one-half of a rather blunt-shaped ellipse, or oval. As was pointed out, the planform shape of the for-

5-26 *Front view—blue-winged teal drake.*

ward body can vary, depending on the head position. Approximating the plan form shape of the tail is another matter. It is almost necessary to have a specimen for accurately establishing this shape, especially if the tail is expanded. However, the planform shape of the pintail hen's compressed tail is strongly suggested in Fig. 5-8. (The planform shape of the forward body is also fairly obvious in this picture of a feeding pintail hen). The tails of puddle ducks (with the exception of wood ducks) are roughly triangular in shape when compressed, while the tails of diving ducks more nearly resemble a rectangle.

Profile, plan, and front views of a male blue-winged teal (Figures 5-27, 28, and 29) have been included here to provide the beginner with the necessary reference material for making an original drawing.

Top views of several duck species are shown on pages 168, 169, and 170.

5-27 *Good profile view of a blue-winged teal drake.*

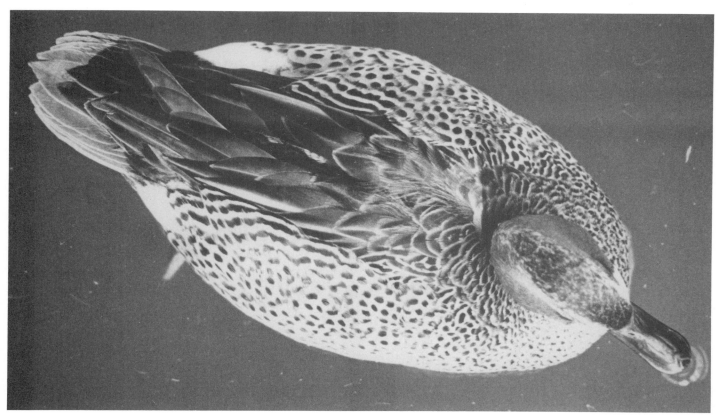

5-28 *Top view of a male blue-winged teal.*

5-29 *Top view of a male pintail.*

5-31 *Female widgeon.*

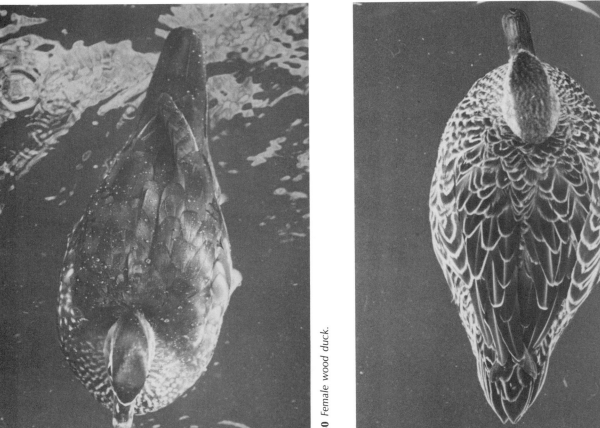

5-30 *Female wood duck.*

5-33 *Female cinnamon teal.*

5-32 *Female blue-winged teal.*

5-35 *Female gadwall.*

5-37 *Female green-winged teal.*

5-34 *Male gadwall.*

5-36 *Female shoveler.*

5-38 *Male redhead.*

5-38A *Female redhead.*

5-39 *Female hooded merganser.*

5-40 *Male ruddy duck—winter plumage.*

DRAWINGS FOR STANDING CARVINGS

Next, attempt a drawing for a standing carving. These drawings are not much more difficult to make than drawings for decoy carvings, except that some knowledge of the placement and size of the bird's tarsi and feet is required.

The direct, profile view of a male pintail shown in Figure 5-41 can be copied and enlarged by using the procedure described earlier (See Fig. 5-42).

In this example, the tarsi location is easily obtained from Fig. 5-41. However, it is sometimes necessary to rework a decoy drawing into a drawing for a standing carving or to work from a picture of a floating bird. As an aid to the carver, the length of the tarsus and the overall length and width of the feet are included in Chapter 11. The approximate tarsi locations are shown in Chapter 12. The tarsus length given is the distance from the bottom of the foot up to the first joint. On most waterfowl and also marsh and shore birds, the entire joint and some of the lower part of the tibia (drumstick) is usually exposed. About 10 to 20 per cent of the tarsus length given in Chapter 11 should be added to obtain the approximate overall length of the exposed "leg" of these species. The tarsus length for the pintail drake is given as 1.87 inches, to which 20 per cent, or .37 inches, is added, giving an overall length of exposed "leg" of 2.25 inches. This dimension is now used to establish the groundline in the profile of the drawing.

The feet and tarsi of birds of the same game bird family are similar, except for size. By using dimensions given in Chapter 11, in conjunction with photos or sketches shown in Chapter 12, it is fairly easy to approximate the size and shape of the tarsi and feet. However, more realistic results can be obtained with much less effort if actual specimens are available for reference. Avoid making feet of water fowl in an exactly triangular shape, so often seen on standing carvings; under the bird's weight, the toes spread out to the extent the web will permit and, being jointed, form anything but straight lines. Most birds are pigeontoed; take this into consideration when locating the feet on a carving. Also, the tarsi of most birds are cambered, i. e., closer together at the ground than at the body. The camber angle is approximately 3 to 5 degrees, measured from the vertical. This angle should be duplicated when the leg holes are drilled.

The proper positioning of the tarsi and feet relative to each other can be very important in imparting the illusion

5-41 *Pintail drake.*

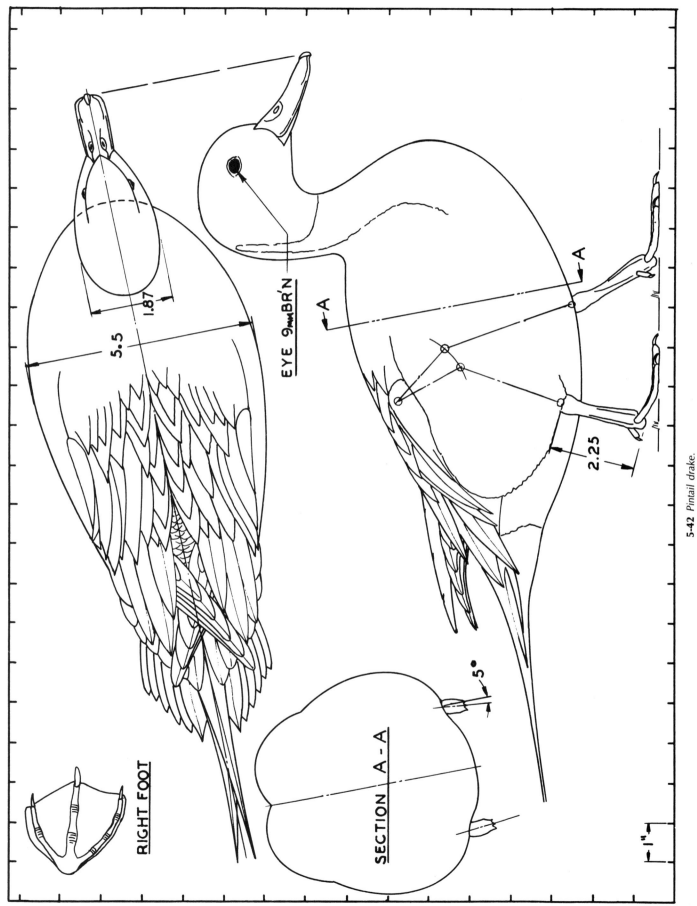

EYE 9mmBR'N

RIGHT FOOT

SECTION A - A

5°

5.5

1.87

2.25

1"

5-42 Pintail drake.

of movement, or inactivity, as in carvings of sleeping birds. The static or stiff appearance of some standing carvings is often caused by the improper positioning, and sometimes the improper location, of the tarsi and feet. Generally, both tarsi should not be located at the same angle and position. When extreme leg positions are used, it is advisable to locate points of articulation and lines representing the position and location of the femur and tibia on the drawing, in addition to showing the tarsus and foot. See Figure 3-15, page 138. A careful study of photographs and live birds will help eliminate the problems caused by incorrect positioning of tarsi and feet.

When working out the tarsi angles and positions of the feet, consider also how the carving is to be mounted. This is usually of secondary importance if the carving is mounted on a flat surface, but is very important if the carving is mounted on an irregular surface such as a piece of driftwood or another similar mount. In almost all cases, it is advisable to select the actual base or mount while the carving is still in the drawing stage. If this is done, the location and angles of the tarsi and feet can be accurately determined to fit the mount. Furthermore, the carving itself, both its pose and positioning, and the mount can be selected to complement each other. (See Chapter 9.)

By referring to Figures 5-41, 5-43, 5-44, and 7-267, the body width dimension in Chapter 11, the plan view and the cross-sectional view can now be constructed, and the head and neck width can be determined in a manner similar to the procedure described in the preceding section.

Figure 5-45, an alteration of Fig. 5-42, duplicates the pose shown in Fig. 5-46. This pose does not compliment the bird; it is not pleasing to the eye, and it looks stiff.

The long neck of a pintail is very graceful and its beauty should be accentuated. Figures 5-47 and 48 show the same basic pose except that the neck has now been curved. Much of the stiffness has been eliminated, and the effect of motion has been created by a simple change in the position of the feet and tarsi.

By altering Fig. 5-42 again, Figure 5-49, which duplicates the pose in Fig. 5-51, is obtained. Here, the bird is about to enter the water, and by opening the bill, the feeling of aggressiveness was added to this already dynamic position. Figure 5-50 shows still another alteration, this one duplicating the relaxed, striding pose shown in Fig. 5-52.

For practice, make a drawing depicting the female pintail's pose shown in Fig. 5-53, aided by Figures 5-54, 5-55, and 5-56.

5-43 *Rear view of a standing pintail drake.*

5-44 *Front view—pintail drake. Especially note the camber of his legs.*

5-46 *Pintail drake in an alert pose.*

5-48 *Pintail drake in a semi-alert, graceful pose.*

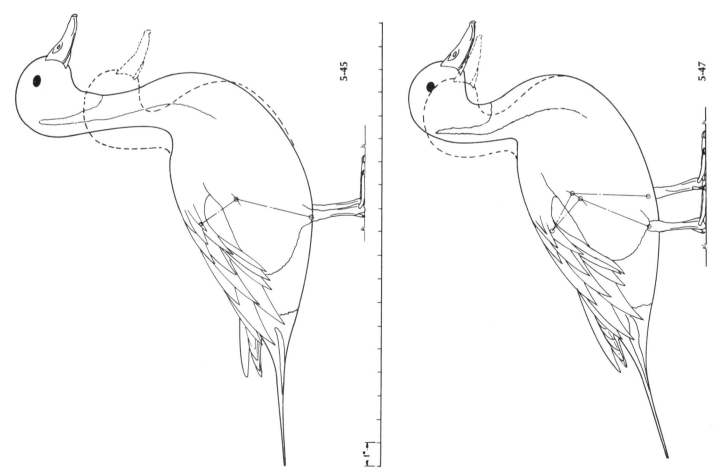

5-45

5-47

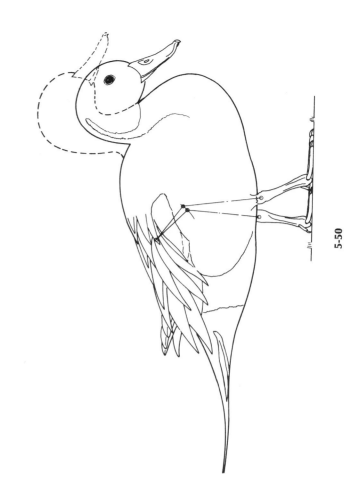

5-49

5-50

5-51 *Striding pintail drake about to enter water.*

5-52 *Pintail drake in a relaxed, striding pose.*

5-53 *Nice profile of a female pintail.*

5-54 *Front view—female pintail.*

5-55 *Rear view—female pintail.*

5-56 *Rare top view of a standing pintail hen.*

5-57 *Mallard drake about to land.*

DRAWING WINGS AND FLYING BIRDS

Before starting the drawing for a carving with extended wings, first decide on the general overall configuration desired. How the carving is to be supported for display will influence this decision. Flying-bird carvings are extremely difficult to display in a realistic manner without sacrificing some authenticity of the bird's overall shape and position.

The wall mount is one method of supporting flying carvings. For a mount of this type, the bracket supporting the carving is attached so that it is hidden by either a wing or the body. Birds landing or taking off are often depicted with their feet touching the mount and actually supporting the carving. In other cases, flying carvings are supported by some extrinsic means, such as a rod or piece of metal carved to represent marsh grass, or some other type of support. Many methods have been used to support flying carvings, but only a few of them display the ingenuity and artistry necessary to create the all-important illusion of free flight.

The complicated up-and-down, fore-and-aft, and rotational movements of the bird's wing in flight are accompanied by changes in the wing planform shape. The complexity of the wing's movements and shapes cannot be fully appreciated until the flight of a bird is seen in slow motion or in individual photographs taken with a high-speed camera. The late Edgar M. Queeny's superb book, *Prairie Wings*, contains many excellent pictures showing waterfowl in flight.

Most carvers attempt to duplicate only the simpler, classic wing positions: the standing bird stretching or preening (Fig. 5-58); gliding with fixed wings (Figures 5-59, 60); or in the take-off position (Fig. 5-61); or in the landing position (Fig. 5-63). There are an infinite number of graceful and artistic wing positions, and the carver can find unlimited possibilities in depicting some of these seldom, if ever, copied wing attitudes.

Before attempting to draw or carve a bird's wing, first study thoroughly the wing's skeletal structure (including the points and limits of articulation) and the feather patterns (See Chapter 3.) Next, make an accurate, full-size drawing of the plan view of the wing in the desired position. If a specimen is available, lay the actual wing on a piece of paper, stretch and pin in the proper position, and trace the overall planform shape and the location of the tips of the primaries, secondaries, and tertial feathers directly onto the paper. See Figures 5-65 and 66. By taking measurements from the specimen, all of the feathers can be located and accurately drawn in. When the upper surface has been completed, make a tracing of the wing outline on another piece of paper and add the feather pattern of the lower surface. Also, draw at least one cross-sectional view, taken near the wing's root (Fig. 5-62).

Next, determine the shape of the wing in the front view, including the spanwise curvature. The spanwise curvature of the wing, especially in the area of the primaries, largely depends on the amount of wing extension and the airload exerted upon the wing. It follows that the upward spanwise curvature will be much greater during the downstroke than at any other time. When there is no airload, for instance when the bird is stretching or preening, considerable curvature still exists in the primary feathers, but in the opposite direction. This is because the bird's primaries are curved downward, probably not only to fit its body when the wings are folded but also to reduce the amount of upward deflection during the downstroke. Flying upland game birds are often portrayed with their wings in a fixed, gliding position. In this configuration, their primaries have a very definite downward curvature.

5-59 *Mallard drake gliding in for landing.*

5-60 *Gliding mallard drake—side view.*

5-61 *Mallard hen taking off.*

5-58 *Male wood duck stretching his wing and leg.*

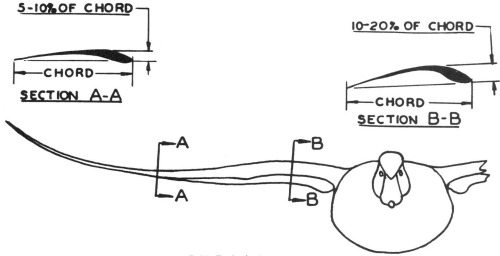

5-62 *Typical wing cross sections.*

The thickness of the wing in the front view is determined by the chordwise (fore-and-aft) curvature, often referred to a camber. Most of the camber of a bird's wing occurs in the area of the secondary and tertial feathers, as this part acts very much like the wing on an airplane to provide lift and stabilization. The thickness of the wing in the direct front view decreases rapidly outboard of the wrist joint and reduces to the thickness of one feather at the extreme tip.

The bird's body during straight and level flight has smoothly flowing lines and is fairly easy to draw, especially if a specimen is available. In this configuration, the body cross section becomes somewhat flatter and conforms quite closely to the shape of an ellipse. When drawing the planview, the fore-and-aft location of the wings is one of the more important details to consider. The approximate wing location for the different game bird families is given in Chapter 11.

Drawing the bird in the landing or take-off position is considerably more difficult. Tremendous power, which is reflected in every part of the bird's body, is required for these maneuvers. The body position sometimes approaches the vertical, and extreme head and neck positions are required in order to maintain balance and gain visibility. The wings move in a much larger arc, almost 180 degrees. The tail extension and position and the tarsi and feet positions are very distinctive. There are many good photographs available showing birds in the landing and take-off configurations; they should be carefully studied before attempting these modes of flight.

The bird's head usually remains level (an imaginary line drawn through the center of both eyes is almost always parallel to the horizon), and is generally pointed in the general direction of flight.

If the carver can afford the expenditure, a bird expertly mounted in the approximate desired flight position is the most valuable reference source. The use of a good mount is almost a necessity for producing a realistic, professional carving of this type.

5-63 *Canada "honker" about to touch down.*

5-64 *Mallard drake climbing shortly after take-off.*

5-65 *Wing of a male pintail pinned in position.*

5-66 *Wing of a pintail drake pinned in a partially extended position.*

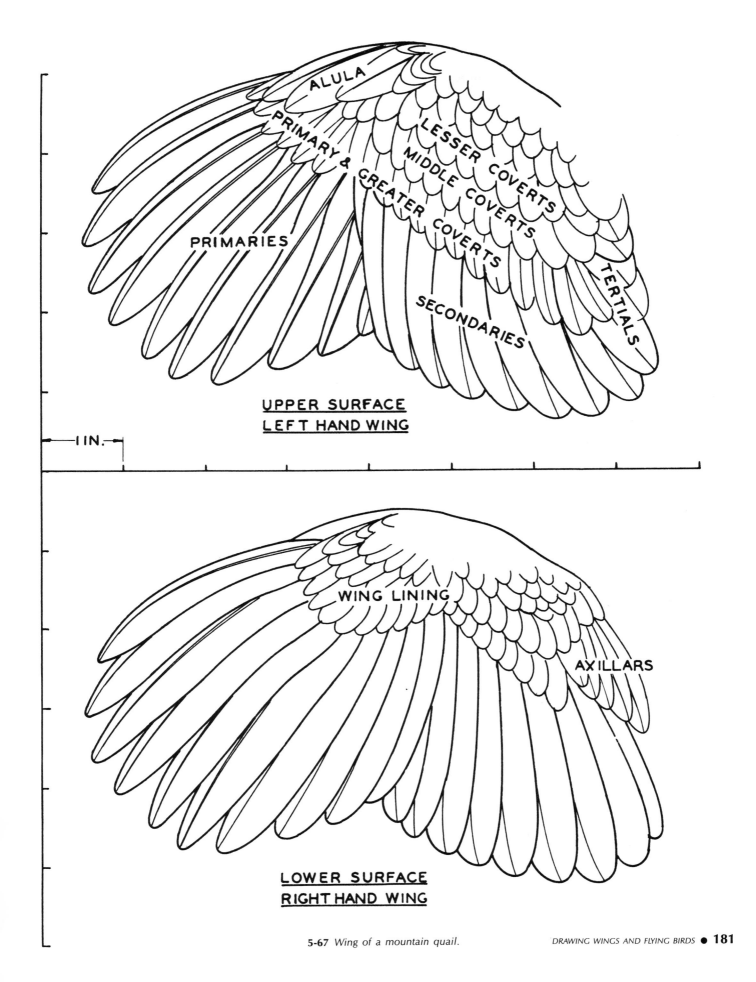

UPPER SURFACE
LEFT HAND WING

ALULA

PRIMARY & GREATER COVERTS

LESSER COVERTS

MIDDLE COVERTS

PRIMARIES

TERTIALS

SECONDARIES

1 IN.

LOWER SURFACE
RIGHT HAND WING

WING LINING

AXILLARS

5-67 *Wing of a mountain quail.*

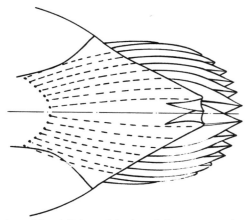

5-68 *Straight and level flight, tail feathers fully compressed.*

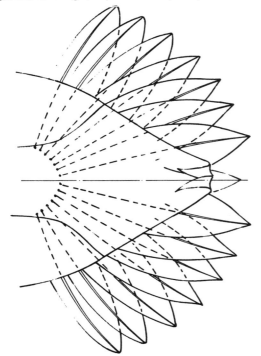

5-69 *Tail feathers fully extended.*

5-70 *Take-off.*

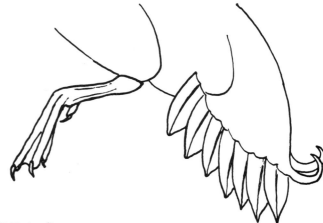

5-71 *Landing.*

5-72 *Turning.*

The position and the extension of the tail is another very important detail to be considered when drawing the bird in its various flight forms. Some of the more common tail configuations are:

Straight and level flight: tail is fully compressed (Fig. 5-68).

Take-off: tail is fully fanned out; it is also convex and raised (Fig. 5-70).

Landing: tail is fully fanned out; it is also concave and lowered (Fig. 5-71).

Turning: tail is fully fanned out; it is also twisted so that one side is much higher than the other side and acts as a rudder (Fig. 5-72).

6

The Clay Model—A Planning and Carving Aid

A growing number of serious amateur and successful professional carvers are now using models to aid them in the planning and execution of their carvings. Many fine pieces today are so involved and represent so much time that it has become necessary for the carver-artist to take whatever steps he can to insure that the finished product will be artistically composed, anatomically accurate, and dynamic if the piece was designed to portray action.

Models can be used in two different ways: one, to work out form, position, and anatomical detail; the other, to help establish good composition, especially where more than one bird is involved and when habitat depiction is used to complement the carving. However, the making of a model prior to doing the carving does not eliminate the need of having accurate structural information. Although the model can be used to an advantage working out position and the resulting form required to attain the position, certain overall dimensions and characteristic shapes must be known before an accurate and meaningful model can materialize. In other words, the model cannot replace the planning procedure covered in the preceding chapter—it can only supplement it. Before the carver attempts to make the model, he should first assemble all the information he has on the bird to be depicted and then work out overall shapes on paper in the form of a drawing. When he has gone as far as he can by this means, he should then resort to the model for working out details that are difficult to visualize or to delineate on paper.

Although models are constructed in a number of different ways and from a variety of materials, molding the model from clay is the most popular method. Clay has a number of advantages over most other materials but by far the most important one is that it can be removed from, or added to, the model with equal ease. Clay is also very flexible—it is easily formed, bent, or twisted. If it does crack, the break can be quickly repaired and smoothed over. Clay can be used in conjunction with wood, styrofoam, sheet metal, and metal rods or wires and will adhere well to them. Some varieties of the clay compounds can be easily baked hard, making the model durable and permanent.

Some carvers model clay in considerable detail while others use this medium only to define the overall character of the piece. A few carvers work clay similarly to a piece of wood, i. e., as a subtractive process, starting with a block and removing clay down to the final shape. Most carvers, however, use the additive process whereby the clay model is gradually built up on an *armature* (a skeletal structure for supporting the clay). In actual practice, both methods are probably used in most cases as corrections usually involve both the removal and addition of clay.

Clay is quite heavy and does not have sufficient strength to support itself when used to duplicate slender parts; therefore, in these cases it is necessary to reinforce the clay with wire or some other material to provide the required strength. Outstretched wings and extended tails should be supported by soft aluminum or lead sheet. The use of copper is not recommended as there is an electrolytic action between the two materials, causing the clay to turn black. In some cases, it is simpler to duplicate delicate parts with wood—the long bill on some shorebirds would be a good example.

Although there are a number of clays available for modeling, probably the best ones are the non-hardening, reusable clay substitutes called Plasticene which have been used for many years by school children. ROMA ITALINA PLASTILINA is one brand name and is available in four different hardnesses. POLYFORM MODELING COMPOUND is another. PLASTELINE is still another similar product which is somewhat cheaper to buy. For those who want a more permanent and durable model, a product called SCULPEY may be used. This material sculpts equally as well as the materials mentioned above and has the advantage that it can be baked hard in the home oven (300 degrees F. for about 30 minutes). Excess material from the hardened model can be removed fairly easily or areas can be built up by adding more of the compound and hardened by baking again. These materials and oth-

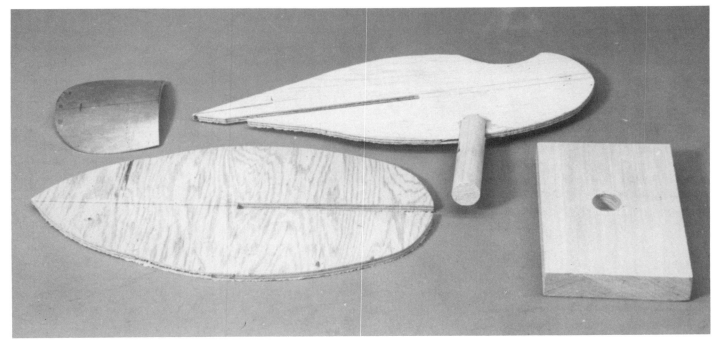

6-1 *Unassembled template-type armature for a duck's body.*

ers are available at most of the better art supply stores.

The clay model, like the carving, must also be planned. How is the model to be supported? Will an armature be required? If it is, what is the easiest way to construct it? Can styrofoam be used to reduce the amount of clay required? Can templates be used as part of the armature to help establish accurate contours? How will the contours and dimensions from the clay model be translated to the carving?

In most cases, unless the model is very small and simple, an armature is required for support. Armatures are constructed in many different ways using a variety of materials. Metal pipe and wire are often used, especially on the larger models.

As was pointed out earlier, a useful and meaningful model cannot be made without the benefit of fairly accurate structural information. Incorporating this information into the model presents problems. Basic dimensions and contours are often transferred to the model by means of simple measurements and the use of outside templates— time consuming methods which are often difficult to implement.

Although the author has had little experience sculpting clay, it occurred to him why not embody known dimensions and contours in the form of templates and use them as the actual armature? The basic profile and planform shape of the model could then be easily and accurately established by simply modeling the clay down to the edges of the templates (see Figure 6-1).

To complete the three-dimensional model, clay must be added and molded to establish accurate cross-sectional shapes. Again, some basic knowledge of these shapes must be known before an accurate model can emerge. Knowing the basic cross-sectional shapes, the clay can be modeled with the hands until they are duplicated on the

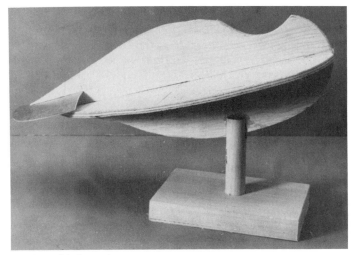

6-2 *Assembled template-type armature.*

model; or, if the basic cross-sectional shape is known with a fair degree of accuracy, a cross-sectional template, located at the maximum cross-section could also be incorporated into the armature (Fig. 6-4, 5).

The use of templates as the actual armature has other advantages. One, the profile template establishes, and retains, the fore-and-aft centerline of the model. Two, the profile and planform contours, which first were established on the original drawing and then transferred to the templates are "known" quantities. Any alteration to these contours on the model can be easily translated to the drawing. For example, suppose the profile contour needs to be fuller in a certain area. More clay can be added in this area and blended into the existing contour. The amount of clay that was added to correct the contour can be ascertained by means of a probe inserted through the clay, at known intervals, down to the template. These known depths of clay can then be transferred to the drawing and the contour corrected. Suppose the profile contour template is too full in a particular area. The clay can then be temporarily removed from around the template, the new contour marked with pencil, and the excess material from the template removed with a rasp or rotary tool, (after the new contour information was transferred to the original drawing). The clay can then be replaced and blended into the adjacent contours.

The accompanying photographs show one of the ways the template-type armature can be constructed. In the examples shown, the resulting models are relatively simple. On more complex models it may be somewhat more difficult to establish both profile and planform shapes with any degree of accuracy; however, usually at least the profile shape can be duplicated by the template. Note also, that in the examples shown, the head was made separately so that it could be moved to the desired position.

In many cases, styrofoam can be added to the armature to reduce the amount of clay required. Also, the addition of styrofoam can substantially reduce the weight of the model. The styrofoam fillers can be attached to the wood templates by means of white glue and can then be roughly shaped with a sharp knife used with a sawing motion (Fig. 6-5).

Plasticene clay is worked more easily when warm. The clay block, usually weighing two pounds, can be warmed in the kitchen oven. It can also be quickly warmed in about one minute if a microwave oven is available (if warmed for much longer, the material in the center of the block will melt). Melting does not appear to adversely affect the material. Actually, when covering aluminum or lead sheet, as required for wings, the melted Plasticene can be easily spread over the surface with a knife. Better results can be obtained if the knife and the metal sheet are first warmed with a hair dryer.

The modeling of clay requires few tools—most of the shaping and smoothing operations can be accomplished with the fingers. Sculpting tools can be purchased from art supply stores. It is suggested that the beginning clay sculpturer first try some clay modeling and then decide whether he wants to buy some tools or make them himself.

6-4 *Wood duck's head armature assembled.*

6-5 *Template-type armature for the forward part of a wood duck's body. Note styrofoam filler.*

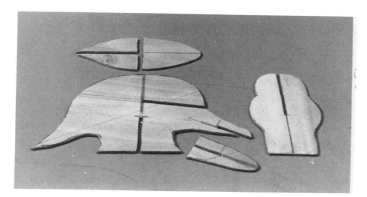

6-3 *Unassembled template-type armature for a wood duck's head.*

6-6 *Armature being covered with clay.*

6-7 *The molded head has been located on the body.*

6-8 *Head-body intersection and chest detail have been defined.*

6-9 *Unassembled template-type armature for a flying snipe. The wings have been cut from sheet lead.*

6-10 *Assembled armature for the flying snipe. Head has been temporarily attached to body.*

6-11 *Head has been tentatively located on the body. Several locations and positions were tried before the final selection was made.*

6-12 *Completed model. The wings have been coated with clay. The shape of the wing in the front view can still be altered if desired.*

PART III

Advanced Game Bird Carving

The projects and text in Part I took the beginner from his first carving and painting attempts to slightly more complicated carvings. Parts II, III, and IV will help the serious carver to achieve advanced amateur and professional work. Here, in Part III, the carver will not only progress into more complex carvings, he will also be introduced to some of the carving and finishing techniques used by professional bird carvers to add realism to their carvings.

Canada geese move into an echelon formation shortly after taking off.

7

Advanced Carving Techniques

In addition to the all-important position (or pose) selection, some of the distinctive qualities that separate a professional bird carving from an amateur bird carving are:

1. The accurate and painstaking detailed duplication of such important features as the overall body shape, the head and bill, tarsi and feet, wings, feather groups, and individual feathers.
2. The addition of realistic texture.
3. The creation of the illusion of softness.
4. The accurate reproduction of color.
5. The artistic manner in which the carving is displayed.

Accurately duplicating the bird and its parts· will be covered in detail in this chapter. The other distinctive qualities listed above will be handled in Chapter 8 "Advanced Finishing Techniques" and Chapter 9 "Displaying The Carving".

POWER TOOLS

Several power tools are almost a necessity for life-size, or nearly life-size, advanced and professional carvings. The carver of small or miniature birds will also find these tools useful, but considerably less important owing to the much smaller amount of wood removal involved.

Without much doubt, the band saw is the most useful labor-saving power tool for the bird carver. There are a number of band saws available. In selecting a bandsaw, an important consideration is the capacity of the machine, i. e., maximum depth and—of lesser importance—width of cut (the distance from the band saw frame to the blade). Most home workshop band saws have a maximum depth of cut of six inches or less, completely inadequate for cutting out the body blocks of life-size geese and some of the large ducks. If the carver can afford the expenditure, the Delta 14-inch wood cutting band saw is the best available (Fig. 7-1). For a relatively small additional cost, a height attachment for this saw can be obtained that increases the depth of cut from 6½ inches to 12¼ inches, a capacity of cut found only on the very large industrial band saws.

Although most of the operations performed by this tool can be done by hand without great expenditures of energy, the Foredome flexible shaft machine is probably the most popular power tool used by amateurs and professionals alike (Fig. 7-2). It not only can be used for rough carving but also for fine, detailed work, an operation for which it is best suited.

A new type of tool, well adapted for precision detail work, is rapidly gaining popularity among bird carvers (Fig. 7-3). Called "The Power Carver", it was originally developed by Gesswein for delicate die and mold finishing and is extremely well suited for feather carving, texturing, and many other detail wood and metal operations. Unlike the Foredom which utilizes a bulky, restrictive, and hard-to-maneuver flexible shaft to transmit rotational power to the handpiece, the motor of The Power Carver is located in the handpiece itself. A marvel of modern technology, the handpiece is only ¾ inch in diameter in the grip area, 1 inch in diameter in the motor section, 5 ⅜ inches long, and weighs only 7 ounces. The handpiece features a quick-release collet-type chuck. Both ³/₃₂-inch and ⅛-inch diameter collets are included as standard accessories.

The transistorized power control unit, which supplies direct current to the handpiece motor, has two power outlets, selected by a switch. One delivers controllable speeds up to 50,000 rpm; the other, the same but with more available torque. Both outlets permit motor reversing, a very important feature which can eliminate rough surfaces caused by cutting against the grain of the wood.

7-1 *The bandsaw is the carver's most useful power tool.*

7-2 *The popular Foredom flexible shaft tool.*

7-3 *The Gesswein "Power Carver".*

The handpiece is incredibly smooth and quiet and runs very cool. If the cutter being used is well-balanced, there is absolutely no vibration, even at 50,000 rmp.

For those who can afford the additional expenditure, having two handpieces would constitute an ideal arrangement. One handpiece could be set up with the ³/₃₂ collet and the other with the ¹/₈ collet, thereby eliminating the necessity of changing collets from time to time; or, for operations requiring two different cutters, considerable time could be saved by not having to stop to change tools.

Not a 'hobby-type' tool, the Gesswein Power Carver is a well-designed, beautifully constructed, industrial-type tool which will give many hours of trouble free operation. For the serious amateur and professional carver who spend a great deal of time power carving feathers and texturing, it is well worth the selling price.

For rough carving and other heavy work, the author prefers to use the heavier duty die grinder (Fig. 7-4). It is used exclusively with rotary files, or rasps, and burrs (up to about 1 inch in diameter) and is very effective for removing wood especially in hard-to-get-at places. Practically all carving of the brass legs and feet is done with this kind of tool. A large and powerful tool, the die grinder usually requires the use of both hands. To gain the necessary confidence for using it on a carving, a certain amount of practice is necessary. There are several manufacturers of this type of tool—Milwaukee, Dumore, Makita, Sears, to name a few.

Many carvers find that the ordinary electric hand drill is a most useful tool for bird carving. In addition to drilling holes for eyes and legs, it is suitable for disc sanding, wire brushing, and many other operations (Figs. 7-5, 6).

Power sanders utilizing sanding belts, contour wheels,

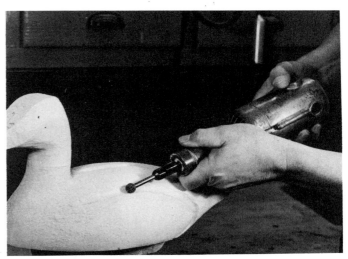

7-4 *The heavier duty die grinder.*

pneumatic drums, discs, and flap sanding wheels can be very useful for shaping and smoothing operations.

There are other power tools that many serious carvers and professionals find almost indispensable. The jointer is a must for accurately joining the individual pieces required for laminated body and wing blocks and for squaring the blocks (Fig. 7-9). A disc sander is most useful for accurately sanding head-body joints and for many other applications (Fig. 7-8). The drill press is used by many for hollowing decoy bodies, drilling holes for eyes, for sanding with drum sanders and flap sanding wheels. For making bases, both the wood lathe and the router are indispensable. Also, the use of the router can save considerable time when insetting the bottom plate of a hollowed decoy-type carving.

Most bird carvers today use power tools not only for roughing-out the piece but also for detail carving and for sanding. Besides making some chips, many of these tools create a great deal of fine wood dust. This dust not only makes a mess, it creates a real health and fire hazard. In addition quite a number of people are allergic in varying

7-5 *Disc sanders are available in several sizes.*

7-6 *The wire brush is useful for removing extraneous material from bases.*

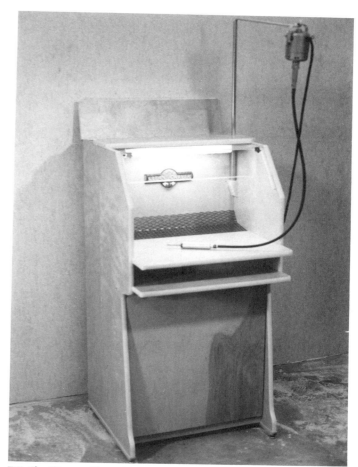

7-7 *The Weaver Clean Carver*

7-8 *The disc sander is a most useful power tool*

degrees to wood dust. Smoke caused by burning in feather detail can also cause health and allergy problems. A very large per cent of these undesirable bird carving by-products can be eliminated when a dust collecting and air cleaning devise called "THE WEAVER CLEAN CARVER" is used (Fig. 7-7). This unit is designed in the form of a not unattractive console, which is available either in a natural or painted finish. Its amazingly quiet, variable speed, twin electric powered fans draw up to 550 cubic feet per minute of air through a large, table height opening in the console and channel it into the collection chamber where heavy, industrial-type filters remove the dust.

Although skeptical of its practicability at first, when given a demonstration the author was pleasantly surprised at its neat appearance and very quiet efficiency. In his opinion, the unit is ideal for those carvers who hand hold their work while power carving—especially for those who must use some of their living quarters for their carving activities.

GLUING UP THE BLOCK

In many cases, the size of the carving and the thickness of the wood available make it necessary to laminate two or more pieces of wood in order to obtain a block of

7-9 *Accurate joints are easy to make on the power jointer.*

7-10 *Hand-joining requires careful removal of wood.*

7-11 *Check the block with a straightedge every few cuts.*

sufficient size. If possible, machine the pieces flat and true on a power jointer (Fig. 7-9). If a jointer is not readily available, have them joined for a nominal charge at a lumberyard or a cabinet shop. If this cannot be done, the only alternative is to join them by hand.

Accurate hand-joining is not easy. It can be facilitated considerably, however, by the use of a joiner plane or any plane with a long planing surface (Fig. 7-10). Check the block in both directions with a straightedge and start removing the high spots (Fig. 7-11). Take plenty of time, and after every few cuts check the block along its full length and width with a straightedge. As the block becomes flat, reduce the depth of cut on the plane and work even more carefully until an accurate surface is obtained. Small inaccuracies can be corrected by moving the block back and forth on a piece of sandpaper attached to a perfectly flat surface. Sanding is not normally recommended if the glue joint is to develop its maximum strength; however, if fairly coarse sandpaper is used, sanding causes less trouble than a thick glue line. Try to remove all of the sanding dust prior to applying the glue.

If an accurate joint has been made, one of the best glues to use is Weldwood's plastic resin glue. This glue comes in powder form and is easily mixed with cold water. Carefully read and follow the directions on the can, especially those regarding temperature and curing time. Brush on the glue evenly to both mating surfaces and allow the glue to set for approximately five minutes before closing the joint (Fig. 7-12). Toenail the blocks together on the ends to prevent slippage and apply sufficient pressure with clamps to squeeze out the excess glue and bring the parts closely together, forming a thin glue line (Fig. 7-13).

If an accurate joint between the two parts has not been made, it is much better to use an epoxy adhesive, which gives a strong joint even if the glue line is thick.

The importance of this procedure should not be minimized for nothing is more discouraging than to spend many hours on a good carving and then find that a poor glue joint was originally made on the block. Usually a bad glue joint is apparent after the glued-up block has been sawed to shape. If the glue joint is open for an appreciable length, it is much better to saw the block in two at the glue line, rejoin, and reglue. If the open joint is not extensive, it can be repaired without too much effort. Proceed with the carving until the bird is near its final shape. Then, make a saw cut into the glue line, cutting into the carving until the area of the bad joint is completely opened and the glue has been removed, leaving clean wood. Completely fill the saw cut with epoxy adhesive and cover the area with masking tape to prevent the adhesive from running out.

INSERTS

To provide sufficient strength for parts of certain carvings it is sometimes necessary to insert a separate piece of

7-12 *Brush on the glue evenly to both mating surfaces.*

7-14 *Add an insert to provide strength for the green-winged teal's crest feathers.*

wood whose grain runs at an angle to the grain of the body or head block. The crested head of a green-winged teal or a wood duck requires inserts of this type (Fig. 7-14). An insert of a stronger, and usually harder, wood may be required in some cases. The long and delicate tail feathers on male pintails (Figs. 7-15, 16) and old squaw ducks are good examples of features requiring hardwood inserts. For certain parts, such as the fanned-out tail of most birds, it is desirable to make the insert of two or more pieces with the grain of each piece running at an angle to the other, paralleling the feathers as closely as possible (Figs. 7-17, 18).

Sometimes it is simpler to make the whole part of hardwood rather than to make a separate insert. In Figure 7-20 the entire head of the mountain quail is made of alder instead of making a hardwood insert for the bill. Woodcock and snipe are other examples of where it may be easier to make the whole head and bill of hardwood. For

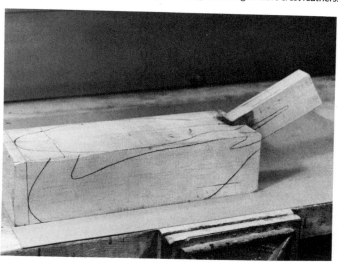
7-15 *A hardwood insert has been added to supply strength for the pintail's long tail feathers.*

7-13 *Apply sufficient pressure with clamps to squeeze out excess glue.*

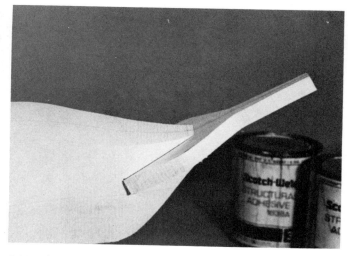
7-16 *A better method for making the tail insert for a male pintail.*

7-17 *Inserts have been installed for the band-tailed pigeon's tail.*

7-20 *In some cases, it is simpler to make the whole part of hardwood.*

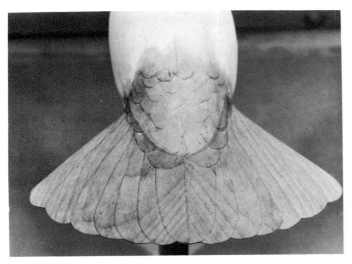

7-18 *The band-tailed pigeon's tail insert has been made from two pieces.*

the feeding mountail quail shown in Figure 7-19, a hardwood insert was used for the bill only, instead of making the entire head of hardwood. This was done because a separate head would have necessitated a glue joint between the head and the end grain of the body block: end-grain gluing should be avoided where possible.

An insert should be made for any fairly thin section where the grain of the wood runs at an angle of 20 degrees or more across the section. On extremely thin sections, the acceptable angle of the grain across the section would be much smaller than 20 degrees.

For some parts—the topknot feathers on valley, Gambel's, and mountain quail, for instance—even hardwood does not provide sufficient strength. When duplicating these and other delicate, vulnerable parts, brass or some other fairly easily worked metal should be used (Figs. 7-20, 21).

7-19 *A hardwood insert was added for the bill of this mountain quail carving.*

7-21 *For some parts, it is necessary to use metal for the insert.*

7-22 *Making cutout for tail insert on a wood duck carving.*

If the band saw is available, it is always easier to make the cut out for the insert before the block has been sawed to shape (Fig. 7-22). If the carver does not have access to a band saw, it is probably easier to make the cut out after the body block has been sawed, as the removal of considerably less wood is involved. In this case, two parallel cuts are made with a stiff-backed saw, such as a dovetail saw, and the wood in between is removed with a chisel.

The making of an insertion requires careful workmanship. It is very important that the inserted part fit tightly and that the thickness of the glue lines are kept to a minimum as they are always difficult to hide even with texturing. It is usually easier to make the insert fit its slot rather than vice versa.

REPAIRS

Sometimes, after the block has been sawed out or after the rough shaping has been partially accomplished, a check in the wood is uncovered (Fig. 7-23). If the check is not extensive, the wood can be quite easily salvaged. Proceed with the rough carving until the bird is near its final shape in the area of the check. Then, make a single saw cut into the check, cutting into the carving until the

check is no longer visible (Fig. 7-24). Completely fill the saw cut with epoxy adhesive and cover the area with masking tape to prevent the adhesive from running out (Fig. 7-25).

If the check is quite wide, it may be desirable to remove the checked area by making a wedged-shaped cut. Then, fit a wedge of the same material and with the grain in the same direction in place and secure with epoxy.

Quite often, some of the more fragile parts of the carving (bills, wing primaries, tail feathers, etc.) are broken accidently. If the broken-off piece can be found, it usually can be easily cemented back in place with 5-minute epoxy. When the epoxy has set, sand off the excess cement and retouch the area with matching paint. The wet adhesive force of the epoxy often will hold the broken-off piece in place until it has set. If some support is required

7-23 *A check has been uncovered in the tail area.*

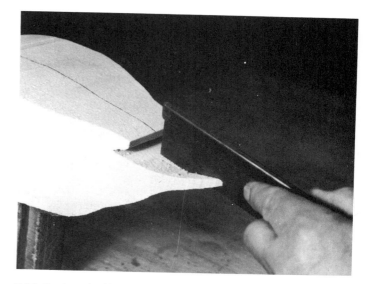

7-24 *Cut into the block until the check is no longer visible.*

7-25 *Completely fill the saw cut with epoxy.*

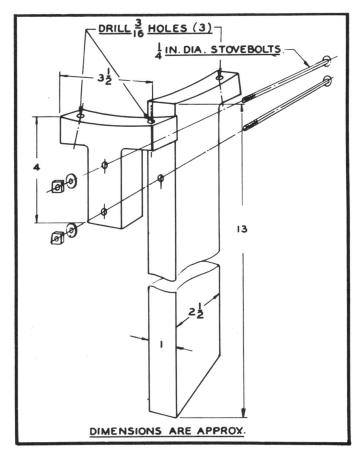

7-26 *A holding fixture capable of supporting large carvings.*

to maintain alignment, cover the area with waxed paper and apply a clamp. Another easy way to hold parts together is to wrap masking tape around the joint.

If the broken-off piece cannot be found, cut off the broken area on a bevel, and fit and epoxy a new piece of wood, cut to the same bevel, in place. Here again, masking tape will usually hold the parts in place until the epoxy sets.

MORE HOLDING FIXTURES

The importance of holding fixtures in reducing carving time and effort, and improving the quality of the carving by permitting the use of both hands to guide the wood-removing tool, has already been discussed in Chapter 1. Figure 7-26 shows how to construct a holding fixture capable of supporting larger, life-size carvings. Additional holding fixtures are shown in Figure 7-30.

A fixture, similar in design to the ones already covered, can be attached on the upper side of the carving to provide access to the underside of the carving. For some operations it is very practical to use both fixtures at the same time (Fig. 7-28). Where it is necessary to attach the holding fixture after detailed feather carving has been done, insert a piece of heavy felt between the fixture and the carving to protect the work (Fig. 7-29).

Although many carvers prefer to hand-hold the work while carving the head and bill, the author always uses a simple holding fixture so that he has complete use of both hands for the various wood removal operations. Fig. 1-149, pg. 55 shows an easily made fixture to which the head is attached by means of two small screws.

Other simple holding fixtures can facilitate the execution of the carving. For example, a block of wood can be temporarily glued to the wing block during the carving operations (Fig. 7-31).

7-27 *Attach the holding fixture by means of three woodscrews.*

7-28 *It is often practical to use both holding fixtures simultaneously.*

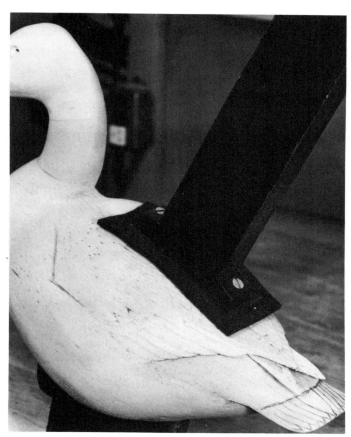

7-29 *Use heavy felt to protect carving details.*

7-30 *Various holding fixtures used by the author.*

CUTTING OUT THE BODY FROM ONE PIECE

The extent to which the wings, legs, and certain feather groups modify the bird's exterior shape depends on the actual position of the wings and legs and also upon muscular control of the feathers. This can only be learned by careful study of photographs and live birds. As the serious carver progresses to more complicated, professional carvings, he must devote more time and give additional consideration not only to these fine details of body form but also to faithfully duplicating other equally important details such as the crossed primaries, feather groups and individual feathers, head and bill details, tail details, and others.

7-31 *A piece has been glued to the wing block for support during carving.*

7-32 *The head of this coot carving is an integral part of the body.*

When the drawing has been transferred to the block, the body is normally sawed out in the manner described in Chapter 1. One exception to this procedure occurs when sawing blocks for birds in the flight position (or any other position where the neck and head are extended forward and turned to one side) and it is desired to make the head and neck part of the body block.

In a situation of this kind, the sequence of sawing out the block becomes important and the plan view should always be cut out first. After the plan view has been sawed, attach the two loose pieces in the usual manner and make the profile cut, extending it only to the point where the neck starts to curve in the lateral direction. Remove all the loose pieces at this point, and retransfer the profile head and neck layout to the actual curved surface. Then, lay the neck and head part of the body block flat on the saw table (holding the body up off the

table) and saw to shape. With this procedure, the head and neck layout will be true, and the saw cuts in this area will be made perpendicular to these parts (Fig. 7-32).

CARVING A PINTAIL HEN DECOY

A pintail hen decoy has been selected for the first advanced carving project. The drawing, or pattern, for this decorative decoy was developed in Chapter 5. See Figure 5-21. Actually, two decoys were made for this exercise. The first decoy features inserted crossed primaries, compressed tail (typical of a female pintail), and a hollow body. The crossed primaries were carved as part of the body block and the tail was expanded on the second decoy.

Most carvers now insert the crossed primaries. Besides eliminating a considerable amount of rather difficult carving, the most important advantage inserted primaries have over carved primaries, is that the rump and upper tail covert areas can be more easily carved, detailed, and painted before they are inserted permanently. However, the aspiring bird carver should at least know how to go about carving the primaries from the body block. See page 214.

CUTTING OUT THE HEAD AND BODY

The procedure involving the transfer of the pattern to the body block and head block and the cutting of these parts on the bandsaw has been covered in Chapter 1. If the crossed primaries are to be carved as an integral part of the body, sufficient material obviously must be provided on the body block for them.

HEAD-BODY JOINT

After the body and head have been sawed to shape on the bandsaw, the mating surfaces for the head-body joint should be prepared. This is the most important joint on the carving and, if it is not properly made, will always show even if the surface is textured, burned, and painted. If possible, sand these surfaces true on a disc sander (Figures 7-8 and 7-33A). When a disc sander is not available (or if the body joint is recessed to the extent that it is impossible to sand with a disc sander) it will be necessary to prepare these surfaces by careful hand sanding. Better results can usually be obtained if the sandpaper is glued to the sanding block. See Figure 1-135, page 52.

After an accurate joint has been made, locate the head on the body block and outline the desired position with a pencil (Fig. 7-34). Wood can then be safely removed up to these lines during the roughing-out of the body.

7-33 Cutting out the rough planform shape of the head.

7-33A A disc sander is excellent for making accurate head-body joints.

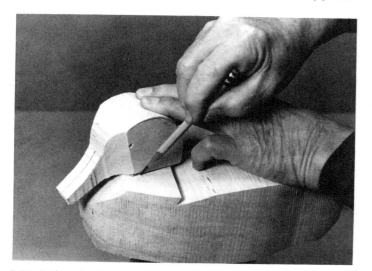

7-34 Outline the desired position of the head on the body.

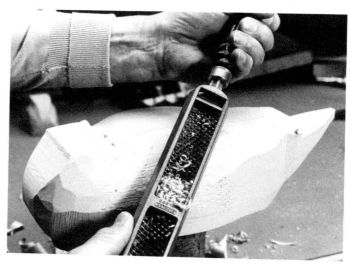

7-35 The half-round Surform rasp is an efficient, inexpensive tool for roughing-out the carving.

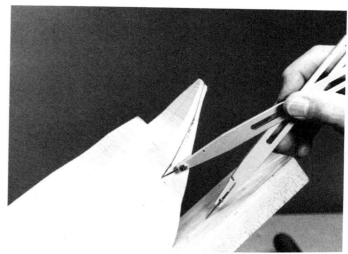

7-36 Establish the outermost edge of the tail.

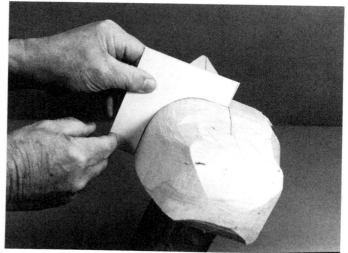

7-37 Check cross-sectional shape of the body with a template.

ROUGH-CARVING THE BODY

Although most carvers nowadays use power tools to rough-out the body, the author still prefers to remove most of the excess wood by hand, using a small Knotts drawknife and Surform rasps. In his opinion, the job can be done faster and more accurately and without a great deal of physical effort. Also, and of primary importance, little dust is involved in wood removal using hand tools. For the same reasons, he prefers to sand the roughly shaped body by hand, too.

Determine the vertical height of the forward part of the tail on the drawing and transfer this dimension to both sides of the body; then, pencil in the outermost edge of the tail (Fig. 7-36). As soon as the body has been carved to the approximate cross-sectional shape (as checked by a template—see Fig. 7-37), transfer the outline of the side feather group from the drawing to the body block (Fig. 7-38). Remove wood from the area of intersection between

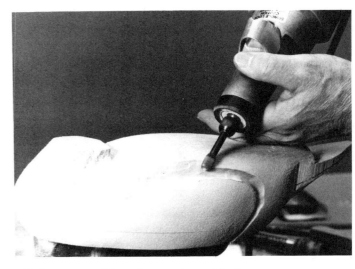

7-40 *Remove wood from the scapular and flank areas.*

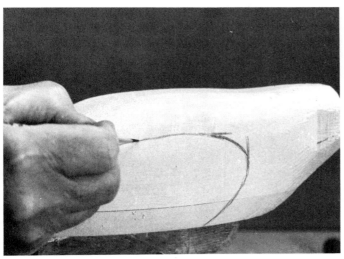

7-38 *Outline the side feather group.*

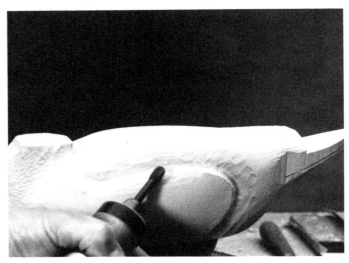

7-41 *Continue by shaping the side feather group.*

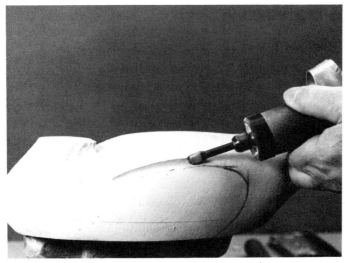

7-39 *Define the side feather group with a rotary tool.*

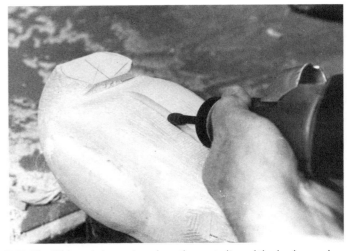

7-42 *The V-shaped depression along the centerline of the back can also be established with a rotary tool.*

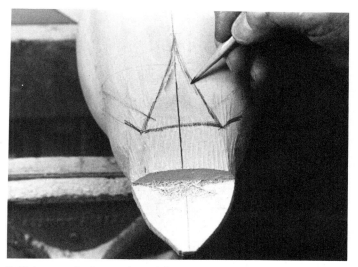

7-43 *Lay out the inner edges of the tertial groups.*

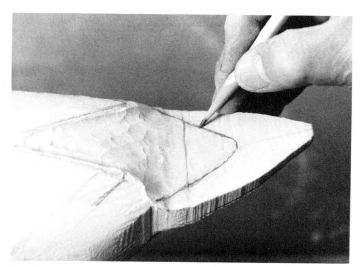

7-44 *Remove wood from between the tertials and lay out the extent of the upper tail coverts.*

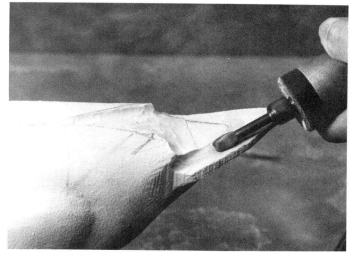

7-45 *Establish the upper surface of the tail.*

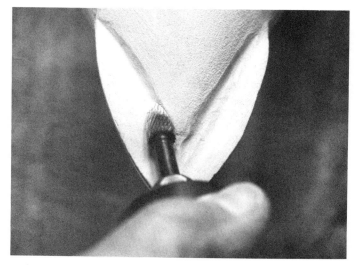

7-46 *Establish the lower surface of the tail.*

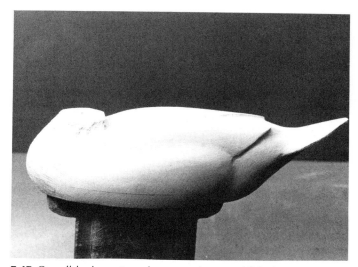

7-47 *Overall body contours have now been established.*

the side feathers and the scapulars by means of a burr driven by a die grinder or a Foredom (Figs. 7-39, 40, 41) and modify the cross-sectional shape to that of the bird's (Fig. 5-22). The V-shaped depression along the centerline of the back can also be created with a burr (Fig. 7-42) and smoothed by hand with a gouge and sandpaper. Next, lay out the tertial groups and remove wood in this area (Fig. 7-43). Continue by outlining the upper tail coverts (Fig. 7-44) and delineate the tail by removing wood down to the upper surface of the tail feathers (Fig. 7-45). Lay out the undertail coverts and remove wood in this area to the lower surface of the tail feathers (Fig. 7-46). Smooth out the established contours with course sandpaper (Fig. 7-47).

CARVING HEAD AND BILL

It is almost always desirable to finish-carve the bill and at least rough-carve the head prior to attaching it permanently to the body. The author follows this procedure except in the few cases where the head was an integral part of the body. He also always attaches the head to a holding fixture so that both hands are free for the carving operations. In an effort to obtain better pictures, the head was removed from the holding fixture in the accompanying step photographs.

The head and bill constitute two of the more conspicuous parts of the bird; their accurate duplication is essential for an advanced or professional carving. The head, more than any other part, determines the bird's character and its activity.

On most game birds, the size and shape of the feathered head for a particular bird remain fairly constant. Ducks are one exception; the size and shape of their heads can vary considerably, especially on the heads of the long-crested male ducks (wood duck, green-winged teal, hooded merganser, red-breasted merganser, American and Barrow's goldeneyes, and bufflehead). This variation in head size is due primarily to exquisite muscular control of the long, narrow head and neck feathers, although some puffiness in the cheek area possibly is due to direct muscular control, or air inflation, in addition to the enlargement caused by feather erection. For better or worse, most carvers exaggerate the width of the head primarily to establish more character. More realistic head widths can usually be obtained from photographs taken directly overhead.

The bill is one of the few parts of a bird's exterior with a fixed size and shape; there is no acceptable reason for the use of artistic license in depicting it. As was mentioned previously, once the bird is dead its bill not only loses its natural color, it also dries, causing changes primarily in its cross-sectional dimensions. Study bills, cast from fresh specimens, are now available for many of the game birds (Fig. 7-48). Unfortunately, bills like other parts of the bird, vary in size. When the carver uses a cast study bill for reference, he usually has no way of knowing whether it was cast from a small or large specimen. Whenever the carver has a fresh specimen, he should not only measure the length of the bill, but also measure the overall length of the bird. He can then compare this overall length with those given in Chapter 13 which were taken from Kortright's *Ducks, Geese, and Swans of North America* and can be considered authoritative. If the specimen is approximately average in length, the carver can assume the length of the bill as measured is average. Using this information, he can then determine if the length of the study bill is approximately correct for his particular carving.

When carving the head and bill on the pintail hen decoy, first reduce the thickness of the head above the eyes to the crown width (Fig. 7-50). Approximate crown widths for waterfowl are given in Figure 7-49. The actual crown width and shape can be determined from front or rear view photographs (see Fig. 5-23). After roughly carving the cheek areas, lay out the intersection of the bill and cheek.

Note: It is assumed that either a study bill or a fresh

7-48 *Cast study bills are a most useful reference.*

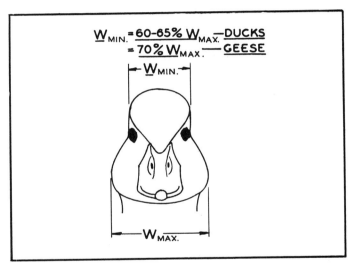

$$W_{MIN.} = 60\text{-}65\% \ W_{MAX.} \text{---DUCKS}$$
$$= 70\% \ W_{MAX.} \text{---GEESE}$$

7-49 *Crown width compared to overall head width.*

7-50 *Remove wood above the eyes and establish the crown width.*

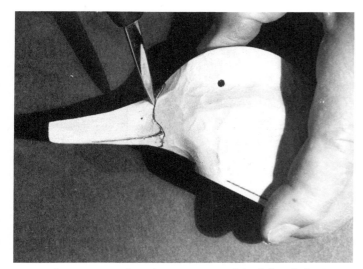

7-51 *Make a stop cut along the intersection of the bill and cheek.*

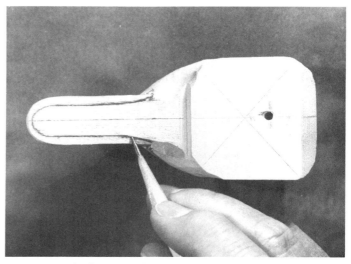

7-54 *Lay out the lower mandible.*

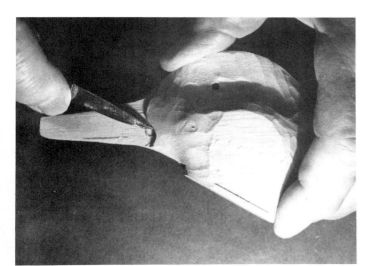

7-52 *Carve the bill down to its proper width.*

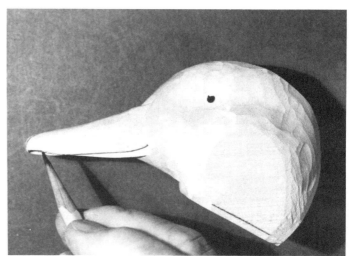

7-55 *Lay out the edge of the upper mandible.*

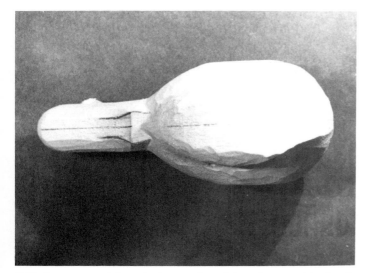

7-53 *Remove wood from the intersection of the culmen and forehead.*

specimen is available. If they are not, the dried bills of all game birds are shown life-size in Chapter 13. In the case of the female pintail, the dried bill is fairly accurate with the exceptions that approximately $1/16$ inch should be added to the width and the lower mandible should be opened slightly.

After the bill-cheek intersection is drawn on the carving, make a stop cut along this line (Fig. 7-51) and carve the bill down to its proper width in that area (Fig. 7-52). Continue by removing excess wood in the cheek area; laying out the culmen (the upper ridge of the bill); removing wood from the intersection of the culmen and the forehead; shaping the forehead; and rounding the front part of the bill to its correct planform shape (Fig. 7-53). Turn the head upside down and lay out the planform shape of the lower mandible (Fig. 7-54). Continue by sketching the lower edge of the upper mandible (Fig. 7-

55). Make a stop cut along this line and remove wood below this line until the proper width of the lower mandible is established (Fig. 7-56).

Now, lay out the intersection of the throat and bill, the long V-shaped depression area on the lower mandible, and the lower nail (Fig. 7-57). Using the study bill as a model, carve these details, also the grooves on the forward part of the lower mandible, with either a small gouge or with a small cone-shaped ruby cutter (Fig. 7-58). Complete the lower side by removing wood on the inner, lower edges of the upper mandible so that the lamellae can be burned in later. See Figure 7-59.

Now, draw in the nail on the upper mandible and the ridges along the sides of the upper mandible and carve these details with a knife or a small, pointed ruby cutter (Figs. 7-60, 61).

After further shaping of the culmen, locate the nostrils in both the plan and profile views (Fig. 7-62). Burn the nostril holes with a Detail Master 6A tip (writing type) or a heated ice pick (Fig. 7-63). Carve the raised detail around the nostrils with a small gouge (Fig. 7-64).

Duplicate the lamellae on both the upper and lower mandibles by carefully burning short, equally spaced lines using a small skew-type burning tip (Figs. 7-65, 66). Now, sand the bill smooth with fine sandpaper. Further detail in the form of lines, wrinkles, and indentations can be added with a smooth, rounded tool—the rounded point of a pencil can suffice.

The head is now ready to be attached to the body. Coat both mating surfaces with warmed (to make it thin) 5-minute epoxy. Permit the epoxy to soak into the wood for about one minute. Then place the head in its proper position and apply as much pressure downward with the palm of the hand as possible to force out the excess epoxy (Fig. 7-67). If the mating surfaces were true, a very thin glue line will result—one that will be practically invisible after the neck is textured, burned, and painted. If the mating surfaces were not accurately made, a thick glue line will result. In this case, a V-shaped groove

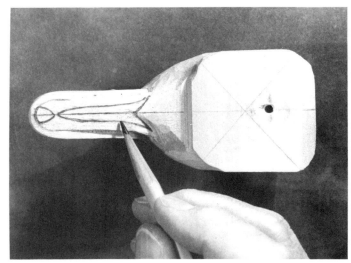

7-57 Lay out the lower mandible detail.

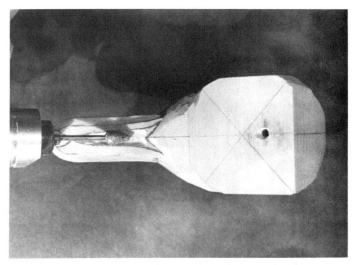

7-58 Some of the lower mandible detail can be carved with a rotary tool.

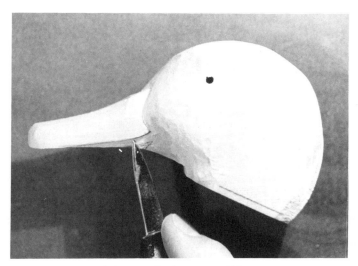

7-56 Remove wood down to the lower mandible.

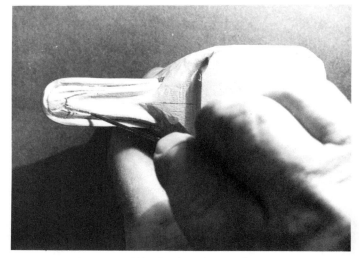

7-59 Carving lower mandible details with a small gouge.

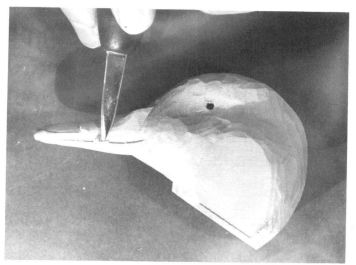

7-60 Carve the ridges on the sides of the upper mandible.

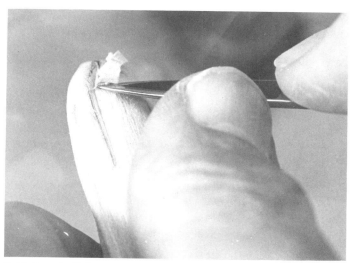

7-61 Round off the upper mandible in the area of the forward ridge.

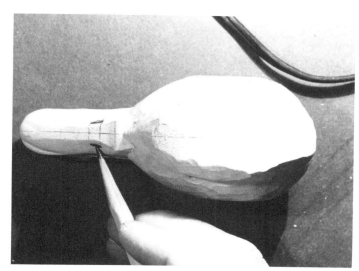

7-62 Locate the nostrils.

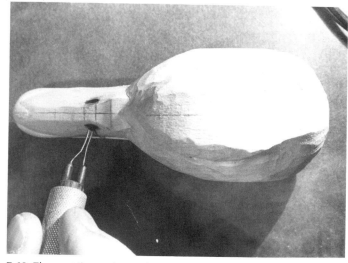

7-63 The nostrils can be made with a writing-type burning tip.

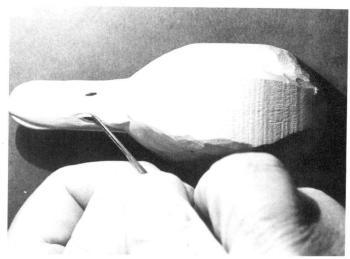

7-64 Carve the raised details around the nostril with a small gouge.

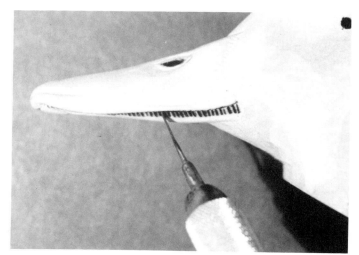

7-65 Create the lamellae on the lower mandible by burning with a small skew-type tip.

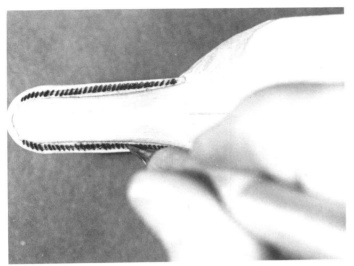

7-66 *Add the simulated lamellae on the upper mandible.*

7-67 *When attaching the head, apply as much pressure as possible to force out excess epoxy.*

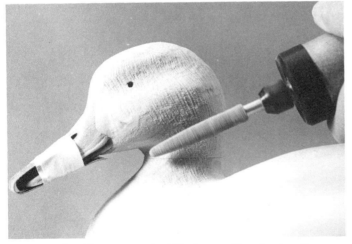

7-68 *It is advisable to protect the bill when working closely with power tools.*

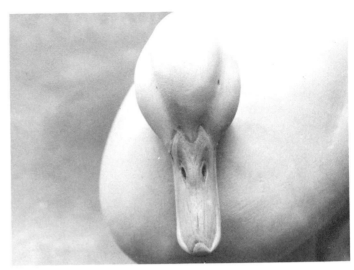

7-69 *Showing the finish carved head and bill.*

should be cut into the glue line after the carving of the neck is complete, and filled with plastic wood or some other similar type of filler. Kulis Karvit, a two-part resin seems to work quite well. It can be shaped and smoothed with a wet finger and, when dry, will accept burning detail (low temperature) as well as, or better, than most fillers (see Appendix for availability). After the epoxy has set, finish shaping the head and neck. A long carbide Kutzall rotary rasp, powered by a die grinder or the Foredom, works well in removing wood in the throat area and other parts of the head (Fig. 7-68). It is advisable to protect the finished bill by a piece of sheet metal, bent around the bill and taped in place, when using powered tools in adjacent areas. The finished head and bill is shown in Figure 7-69.

CARVING BODY DETAIL

After the body has been carved to its basic overall shape, the next step is to carve some of the main feather groups. The tertial feather groups are of first order importance due to the fact that the primary feather groups must originate from under them. The tertials, as a group, should now be outlined on both sides of the body and some of the surrounding wood removed. The carver must decide which primary group will lie on top of the other. In this exercise, the left primary group will lie over the right group; therefore, the left tertial group will remain high and the right tertial group will of necessity be carved much lower so that the primary groups, emanating from under them, can cross.

The primary inserts should be made next. These can be carved from a single piece of wood (see Fig. 7-203, page 240) or they can be made by gluing individual feathers together.

The individual feather method will be used here.

The primary inserts on many carvings appear to have been stuck on as an afterthought. Careful planning and workmanship are required to make and install crossed primaries that realistically duplicate those on the actual bird. These feather groups must be bent to match the curvature of the bird's primaries and properly fitted and inserted so that they appear to have originated from along the side of the bird, as is actually the case when the bird's wings are folded and are covered by the side feathers and the tertials.

The crossed primaries of the female pintail shown in Fig. 5-22 are rather hard to discern; however, they show quite well in Fig. 5-43 which pictures the rear view of a pintail drake.

The primary group, in this case, will consist only of the six outermost feathers. The size, shape, and location of these feathers should be determined from an actual wing. For this exercise, this information can be approximated from the drawing, Figure 5-21.

Cut the individual feathers from strips of thin wood (Fig. 7-70). Veneer can be purchased from some carving supply stores or it can be cut on the table saw or bandsaw.

Feather detail may be burned either before or after the individual feathers are assembled. In most cases, the author prefers to burn the feather detail after the group is assembled. Each feather should be bent (using moisture and heat) to the approximate curvature prior to their being assembled. See section entitled "Individual Feathering Technique", Fig. 7-191, page 237 for one method of bending feathers. In addition to bending each feather, a form cut from a scrap piece of wood to the proper curvature and covered with waxed paper, should be used when gluing up the group (Fig. 7-71).

Proceed with the primary insertion process by carving the left tertials as a group (Fig. 7-72). Next, establish the location of the left primary group and undercut the tertials to a depth of about ¼ inch matching the thickness of the primary group insert, and maintaining the correct angle as seen in the rear view (Fig. 7-73). Trim the primary insert to fit. Now, remove wood inboard of the right tertial group in the rump area so that the right primary group

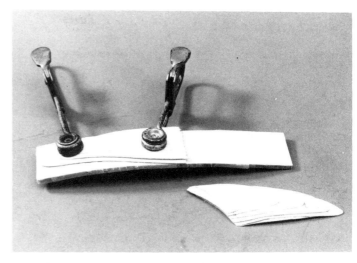

7-71 *Glue-up the feathers on a curved form.*

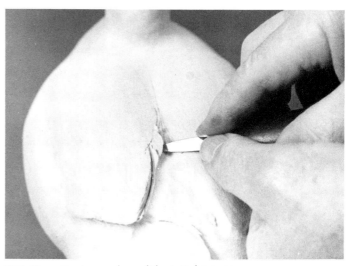

7-72 *Carve the inner edges of the tertial groups.*

7-70 *Cut out the six outer primary feathers.*

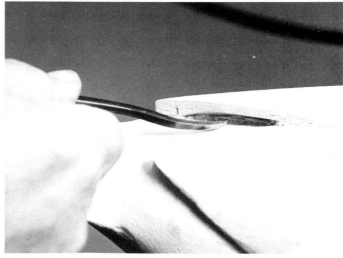

7-73 *Undercut the tertials to receive the primary group insert.*

can lie under the already inserted (temporarily) inserted left group at the proper angle and undercut these tertials in a similar manner. Proceed slowly when making undercuts for the primary insertions as errors are difficult to correct. Fig. 7-74 shows the primary inserts temporarily in place. When the insertion and fitting of the right primary group is completed to the carver's satisfaction, carve the right tertial group down to its proper height (Fig. 7-75).

Proceed by drawing in the individual tertial feathers on the left side (Fig. 7-76) by referring to the drawing Fig. 5-21; photographs Figs. 5-15, 18 and 21 and painting Fig. 7-260, page 257. When this layout is completed, trace it on a piece of vellum (Fig. 7-77) and transfer the layout to the right side (Fig. 7-78). Remove wood to the rear of the scapulars (Fig. 7-79). Carve the individual tertial feathers using the procedure described previously (Figs. 7-80, 81). Remember, feathers are convexly shaped, not only in cross-section but also lengthwise.

Next, redefine the side feather group and lay out the

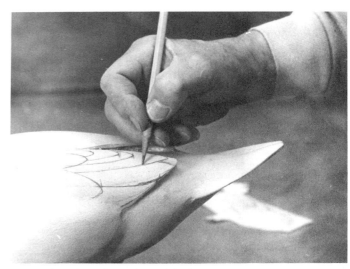

7-76 *Outline the individual tertial feathers.*

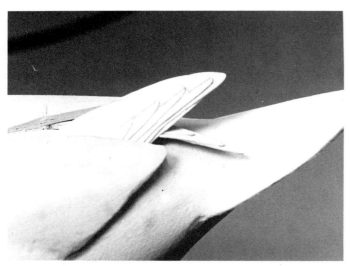

7-74 *Showing the inserted primaries.*

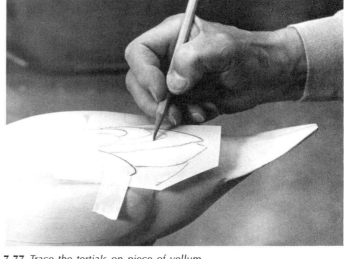

7-77 *Trace the tertials on piece of vellum.*

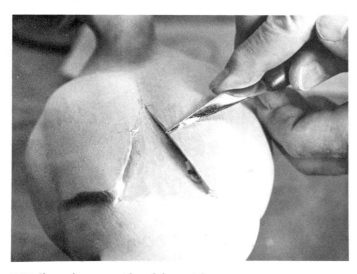

7-75 *Shape the upper sides of the tertials.*

7-78 *Transfer the tracing to the right side.*

outline of the back feather group (Fig. 7-82). Again, referring to Figures 5-21, 5-15, and 5-18 and 7-260, sketch in individual scapular feathers on the left side. When the layout of these feathers is satisfactorily accomplished, trace them and transfer the layout to the right side. Carve the individual feathers with a knife or with a ruby cutter, or both (Fig. 7-83). The author prefers to carve prominent feathers with a knife; however, the cut that outlines each feather should not be too deep and should be completely removed when the feather is carved and sanded. It may be necessary to cut the outline of the individual feathers more than once in order to make the carved feather stand out realistically. The outline cut also can also be eliminated by redefining the feather with a pointed, conical-shaped ruby or diamond cutter after the feather has been carved with the knife.

Next, lay out the individual back feathers (using the above referenced photographs and painting). First, remove wood around the outside to make the feather group

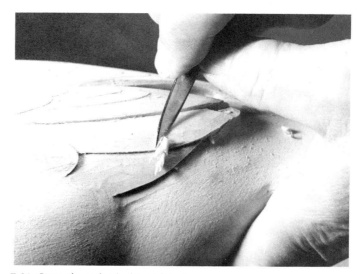

7-81 Carve the individual tertial feathers.

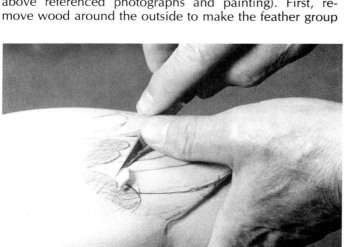

7-79 Establish the tertials as a group.

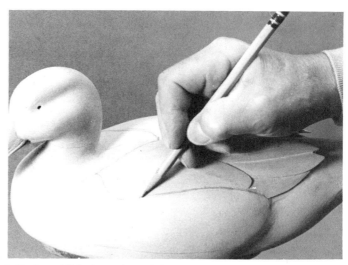

7-82 Reestablish the outline of the side feather groups, also the back feather group.

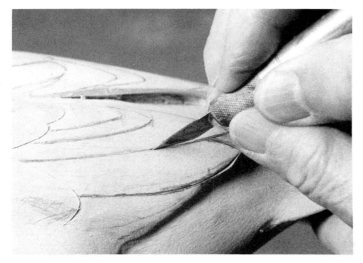

7-80 Outline the individual tertials with a sharp knife.

7-83 Sketch in and individually carve the scapulars.

prominent (Fig. 7-84) and then carve the feathers individually with a ruby cutter (Fig. 7-85).

Continue with detail work on the body by drawing the upper tail coverts (Fig. 7-86) and remove wood down to the upper surface of the tail feathers (Fig. 7-87). Lay out and carve the individual tail feathers next (Fig. 7-88). In a similar manner, lay out the undertail coverts and outline and carve the tail feathers on their lower side (Fig. 7-89).

Although it was not done in this example, it is usually advisable (especially on expanded tails) to lay out the outlines of each complete tail feather on the upper surface of the tail (Fig. 7-90). When this layout is satisfactorily completed, the outer edges of the tail can be cut accurately and the layout for the lower surface can be transferred to the underside. The making of an original accurate layout of the tail necessitates having access to a specimen.

Carved tail feathers, if they are to be realistic, must be quite thin. Considerable care must be exercised when

7-86 Lay out the upper tail coverts.

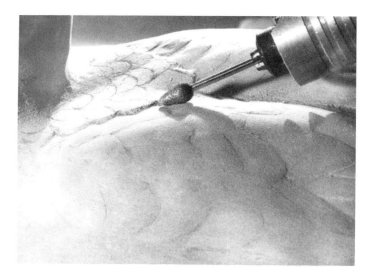

7-84 Outlining the back feather group with a diamond cutter.

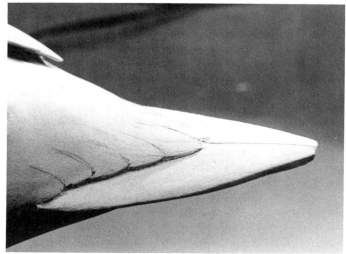

7-87 Carve the outer edges of the coverts down to the tail surface.

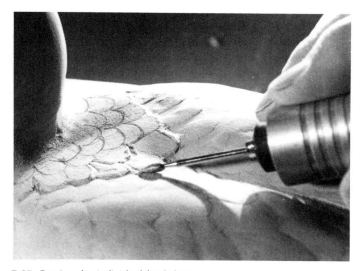

7-85 Carving the individual back feathers.

7-88 Lay out and individually carve the tail feathers.

outlining the individual feathers with a knife on both the upper and lower sides. The outline, if cut too deeply, can either drastically weaken the feather, or cut clear through it. If desired, the tail feathers in the tip area, can be effectively separated by very careful burning (Fig. 7-91). Fig. 7-92 shows the carved and sanded tail and the upper tail coverts.

Continue with body detail carving by laying out the flank, rump, and undertail feathers (Fig. 7-93). These feathers are not as prominently defined as most of the other feathers and can be realistically carved with a ruby cutter (Fig. 7-94).

Next, lay out the side and chest feathers using the aforementioned references (Fig. 7-95). After the individual feathers of the side group have been drawn, delineate this group by removing wood in the scapular, tertial, and flank areas (Fig. 7-96). The side feathers are large and prominent and can be carved effectively with a knife or chisel, although some carvers prefer using ruby or dia-

7-91 *Tail feathers can be separated by careful burning.*

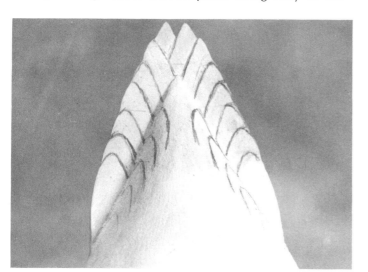

7-89 *Lay out the underside of the tail group.*

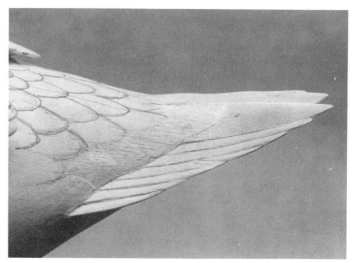

7-92 *Showing carved tail and upper covert feathers.*

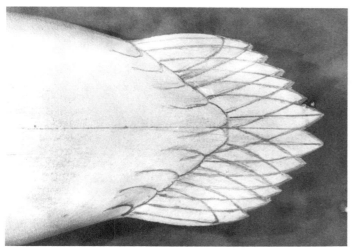

7-90 *When making the tail lay out, it is usually advisable to show each complete feather.*

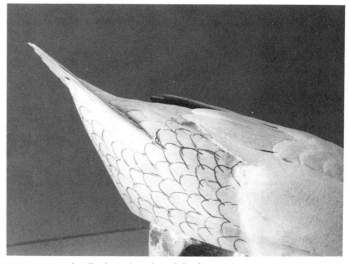

7-93 *Lay out the flank and undertail feathers.*

mond cutters. Realistic detail can be attained by first carving some of these feathers, when they lie in a row, as a group (Fig. 7-97). Redefine these feathers and carve them individually, rounding them both cross-sectionwise and lengthwise (Fig. 7-98). Carefully carve the wood down until all the outline cuts are removed. Sand these feathers, and all other carved feathers, smooth, using a small, folded piece of sandpaper held in the fingers (Fig. 7-100).

Texture may be added to the relatively undefined flank feathers with a small, cylindrical-shaped ruby or diamond cutter (Fig. 7-101).

The chest feathers can be duplicated realistically in a number of ways. One quite effective way is to lightly outline each feather with the small cylindrical-shaped cutter, followed by burning (Fig. 7-102). Some carvers prefer to texture this area by burning only. Figure 7-103 shows the finshed carved and sanded decoy.

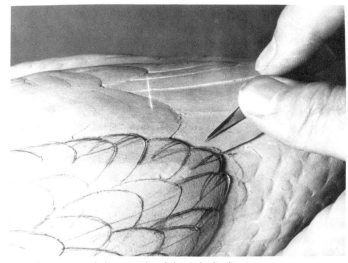

7-96 *Carve around the outside of the side feather group.*

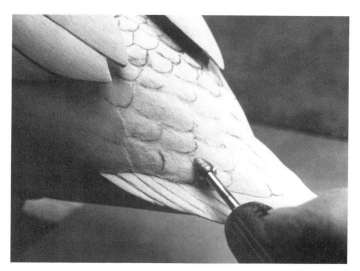

7-94 *Carving the rump feathers with a diamond cutter.*

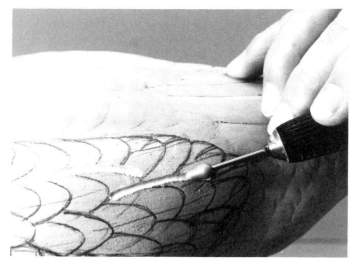

7-97 *Some side feathers can first be carved as a group.*

7-95 *Lay out the individual side and chest feathers.*

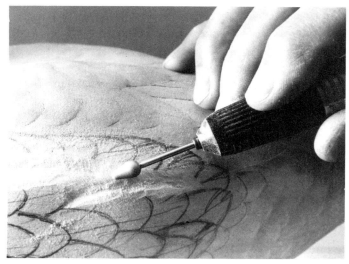

7-98 *Round off these feather groups with the Gesswein.*

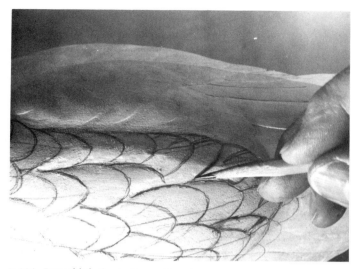

7-98A *Reestablish the feather pattern layout.*

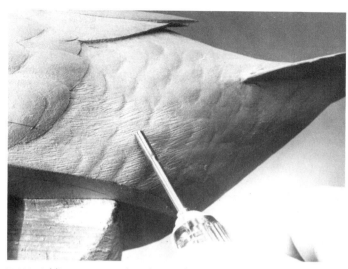

7-101 *Adding texture with a diamond cutter.*

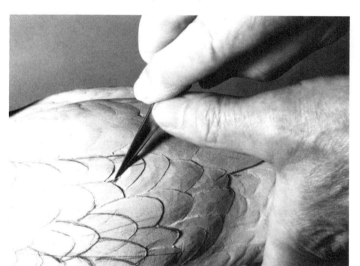

7-99 *Carving the individual side feathers with a knife.*

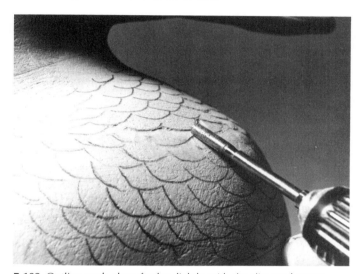

7-102 *Outline each chest feather lightly with the diamond cutter.*

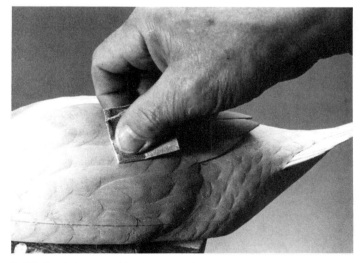

7-100 *Sand the carved feathers smooth.*

7-103 *Showing the finished carved pintail hen.*

CARVING CROSSED PRIMARIES

Almost all carvers of decorative decoys and full-body carvings now insert the primary feather groups. The advantages of using this procedure have already been covered. However, a few carvers not only carve the crossed primaries from the body block, they also carve the entire bird (including head and bill) from one block of wood. Crossed primaries which are not raised from the body are often carved on working decoys. The aspiring bird carver should at least know how to go about carving the crossed primary group when they are an integral part of the body.

The carving of primaries from the body block is not easy and requires a considerable amount of planning and careful workmanship. There is some ingenuity and also a variety of gouges and chisels required to remove wood from some of the tight places.

Obviously, sufficient wood must be left on the body to accommodate the extended crossed primaries. Furthermore, it is usually advisable to have more wood available for these parts than would appear necessary.

Start by rough-carving the body in the manner described earlier in this chapter but remove very little wood in tip area of the primary groups. Next, lay out the rearmost extent of the scapular groups and remove wood down to the upper surface of the tertials (Fig. 7-104). Proceed by sketching both sets of primaries on the body and lay out the individual feathers of the left tertial group (Fig. 7-104). Next, remove the wood forming the V behind the crossed primaries but only to a depth corresponding to the rump contour. This can be accomplished by making deep cuts with a sharp knife along the outlines of the primaries and removing wood in steps by means of a chisel. Continue by making cuts around the outline of the left tertials and removing wood adjacent to these cuts to establish the tertials as a group (Fig. 7-105). Re-define the left primary group.

Note: Remember that the primaries are curved and conform neatly to the contour of the bird's body in the flank area. This, in turn, means that the two groups of primaries, at their points of intersection, do not rest flatly one upon the other, but are actually slightly on edge.

The upper side of the left-wing primary group, which protrudes from under the tertials, can now be carved to its final depth and shape, taking into account the curvature of the primaries and the angle at which they lie (Fig. 7-106). It is much easier to visualize the curvature of the upper primary group than the lower. The individual feathers of the left tertial group can also be carved at this time.

Continue by carving the upper side of the right primary group, where it protrudes from under the left group. Remove very little wood at the point of intersection between the leading edge of the right group with the trailing edge of the left group (Fig. 7-106).

Outline the tertial group on the right side and remove wood from around this group down to the approximate upper surface of the right wing primaries (Fig. 7-107).

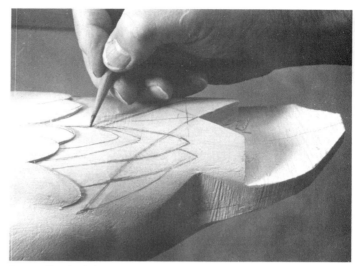

7-104 *Sketch in the tertial and primary feather groups.*

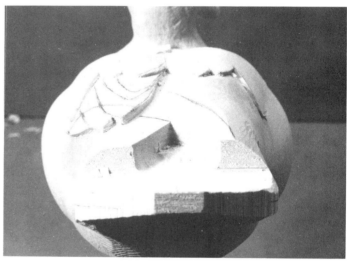

7-105 *Carve around the left tertials and remove the V-shaped piece of wood between the outer primaries.*

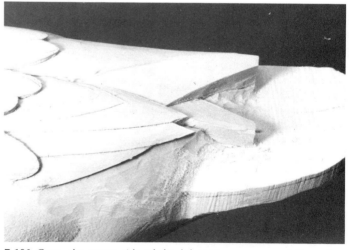

7-106 *Carve the upper side of the left primary group and the outer portion of the right group.*

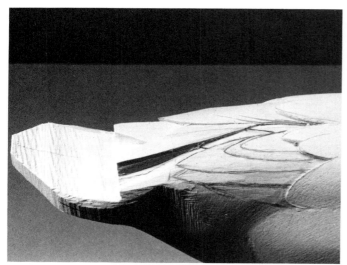

7-107 *Lay out the right tertial group.*

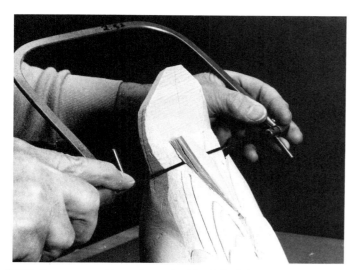

7-108 *Remove wood from the underside of the left primary group.*

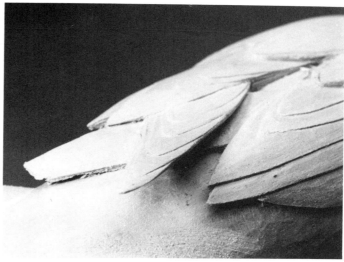

7-110 *Lay out the individual left primaries.*

Outline the primaries of the right wing again in the area between the tertials and the left wing primaries and remove wood from both its front and rear edges. Work slowly and carefully, keeping in mind the curvature of the primary feathers and the fore-and-aft angle at which they lie. Remove the wedge-shaped piece of wood from under the tip of the left wing primaries with a coping saw (Fig. 7-108) and remove wood along the trailing edge of the right primary group, under the left primaries, until the planform shape of the right primary group has been established (Fig. 7-109). Remove more wood in the rump area, adjacent to the trailing edge of the right primary group until the desired curvature of these primaries is obtained. Now, remove wood from the upper side of the right primaries until this group is about ¹⁄₁₆ to ³⁄₃₂ inch thick. Also remove wood from the underside of the right group in the tip area maintaining this thickness. Continue by removing wood from the underside of the left primary group until

7-109 *Individually carve the left primary feathers.*

7-111 *Lay out the individual right primary feathers.*

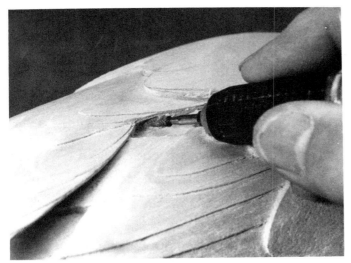

7-112 *Small cutters are useful for removing wood under the tertials and primaries.*

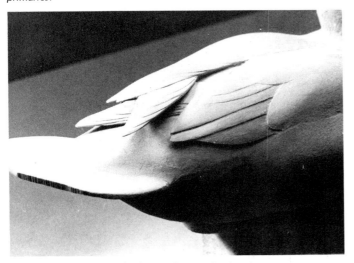

7-113 *Showing the finished carved crossed primaries.*

the desired thickness is reached. The individual feathers of the right tertial group can now be carved.

Now, lay out the individual primary feathers of the left group (Fig. 7-109) and carve them, starting from the uppermost feather and working down. Lay out and carve the individual feathers of the right tertial group (Fig. 7-110). Next, lay out and carve the individual right primaries (Fig. 7-111). Continue by carving the rump and upper tail covert areas and establish the upper surface of the tail feathers. Finish by defining and carving the rump area ahead of the crossed primaries (Fig. 7-112). The finished crossed primaries are shown in Fig. 7-113.

HOLLOWING THE BODY

Practically all competition floating decorative decoys have hollowed bodies. Fig. 1-126, page 49, shows six different ways of constructing and hollowing a decoy

body. Because of the problems involving the successful hiding of glue lines, most decorative decoy carvers prefer to use either the method shown in Figure 1-126A or 1-126B.

The method shown in Fig. 1-126A, where the decoy bottom is made from a separate piece rabbeted into the body, will be used for the hollowing of the pintail hen decoy. This method of construction requires rather careful workmanship when done with hand tools, but when accomplished with a router, the job is relatively simple.

The author prefers to hollow the body after it is carved to its final shape and usually after the detail work has been completed—a procedure that almost always necessitates the need of a holding fixture of some sort. Fig. 7-114 shows a simple fixture made from two boards which have been hollowed to roughly fit the decoy's body. The scooped out areas have been covered with thick felt to protect the decoy. In this photograph, a woodworker's vise supplies the necessary clamping pressure to hold the decoy firmly. In Fig. 7-123, a clamp has been substituted.

A template tip guide is available as an accessory for most routers (Fig. 7-115). This collar-like part rides against a template which accurately guides the router to whatever shape the template is made. The router bit will always cut a small distance out from the template. This distance equals one-half of the difference between the outer diameter of the template guide and the diameter of the router bit; or, this distance can be determined by making a sample cut.

In this case, the distance the router cuts out from the template is approximately 1/16 inch.

Start by drawing a centerline on a piece of 1/4-inch plywood approximately 12 inches by 16 inches. Place the decoy on the plywood so that the centerline of the bottom of the decoy aligns with the drawn centerline on the plywood.

Trace around the base of the decoy and establish the contour identified as "Carving Base" in Figure 7-116. By

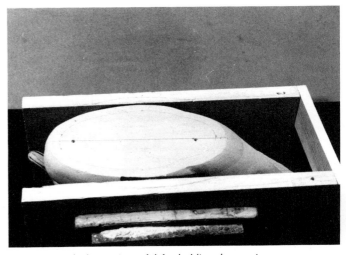

7-114 *A simple fixture is useful for holding the carving.*

7-115 *Showing the installed template tip guide.*

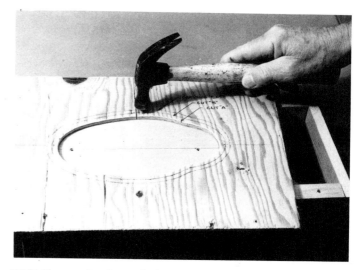

7-117 *The template is attached with small brads.*

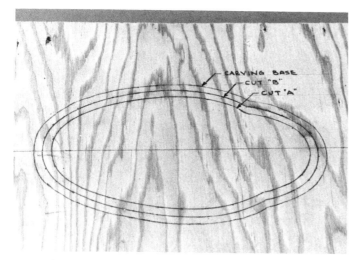

7-116 *The router template is made from a piece of ¼-inch plywood.*

7-118 *Starting cut "A" with the router.*

measuring ¼ inch (this dimension could be more or less, depending on the width of lip desired on the bottom of the carving) at regular intervals, establish the contour identified as Cut "B". Repeat this operation by measuring ¼ inch from this new contour establish the contour identified as Cut "A". Now, using a bandsaw or a jigsaw, cut out the plywood along the Cut "A" line and sand smooth. Locate the template on the decoy base so that the centerline of the template aligns with the centerline on the base of the decoy and is properly located fore-and-aft (Fig. 7-117) and secure it in place with small brads. Adjust the depth of cut on the router to about ½ inch (plus the thickness of the plywood template) and rout the wood to this depth around the inside of the template (Figs. 7-118, 119). Remove the template and cut out the plywood along the Cut "B" line. Place the template on the decoy again, locate it properly, and attach it with brads. Readjust the depth of cut on the router so that it will make a cut ⅜ inch in depth (the thickness of the bottom board of

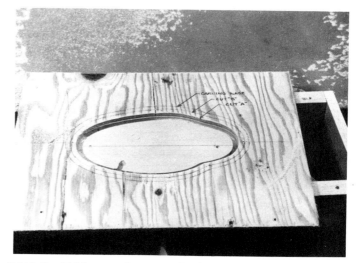

7-119 *Cut "A" has now been completed.*

the decoy). This cut establishes the bottom of the rabbet (Figs. 7-121, 122).

Now, remove the fixture and the decoy from the vise and add a clamp to hold the decoy securely in the fixture and move it to the drill press. Using a 1-inch diameter Forstner-type bit, remove as much wood as possible (Fig. 7-123). Be very careful that the cuts are not made too deeply (the amount of material left beneath the cut can be fairly accurately determined by placing the forefinger in the cut hole and extend the thumb of the same hand around to the decoy's upper side. When no more wood can be safely removed by the Forstner bit, place the decoy and fixture into the vise again and chisel out most of the remaining wood (Fig. 7-124). Remove even more wood and smooth the interior of the decoy with a large, spherical-shaped burr (Fig. 7-125).

Continue by placing a piece of vellum, or other thin paper, over the bottom of the decoy and rub the side of a pencil point on the outer edge of the router cut (Fig. 7-

7-122 *Showing cut "B" with the template removed.*

7-120 *Showing cut "A" with template removed.*

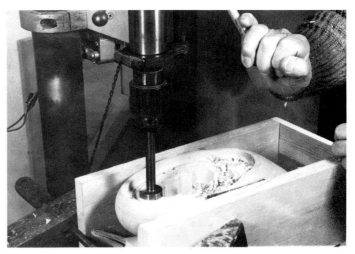

7-123 *Removing wood from the body with a Forstner bit.*

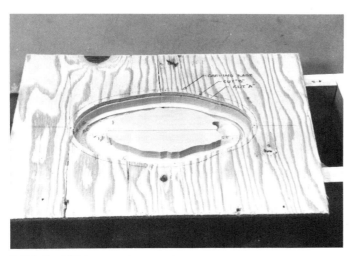

7-121 *Cut "B" has now been made.*

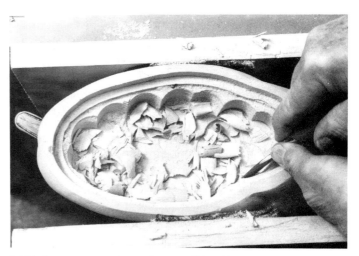

7-124 *Remove as much wood as possible with a gouge.*

7-125 *A large spherical-shaped burr is effective for removing the remaining wood and smoothing the interior.*

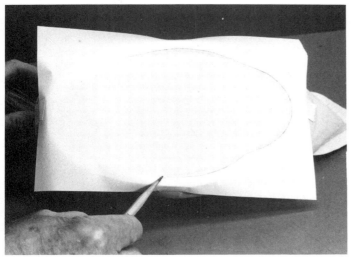

7-126 *Trace off the outline of cut "A" and transfer this tracing to the bottom board.*

7-127 *Float the decoy to determine ballast requirements.*

7-128 *Showing bottom board with lead ballast weights attached.*

7-129 *Install bottom board using automotive filler as an adhesive.*

126). Transfer this contour to the decoy's bottom board and cut it out to this line. If the cut is carefully made, the bottom board should fit nicely.

Next, thoroughly seal the interior of the decoy and bottom board with thinned lacquer sealer.

The decoy must be floated at this point. A floating decorative decoy does not need to be self-righting; however, it must float properly, i. e., it must not list; the body must be at the correct fore-and-aft angle to the water; and the proper amount of profile must be exposed.

Install the bottom board temporarily, cover the decoy with Saran wrap, or a similar material, and place it in the water (Fig. 7-127). The amount of ballast, and its location, to meet the above criteria must be determined by trial and error. When the proper amount of ballast has been placed correctly, attach it permanently to the bottom board with screws or nails (Fig. 7-128). The bottom board can now be cemented in place. Automotive filler, available at auto parts stores, is a surprisingly good, waterproof adhesive (the author has had two test joints soaking continuously in water for over one year without any sign of separation). If it is used, mix plenty and work quickly as it sets up in a relatively short time (Fig. 7-129). After the body filler has set-up hard, sand the bottom of the decoy smooth.

INSTALLING EYES

The character of the bird carving can be affected greatly by the location and positioning of the eyes. They must be accurately and symmetrically located in the plan, front, and profile views. Even a slight asymmetry in their location is very noticeable on a carving.

First, ascertain the correct fore-and-aft location of the eye in the profile view. There are two ways of accurately determining the distance from the tip of the bill to the center of the eye. The easier way of the two is to obtain this dimension from a fresh specimen. The other way is to calculate it from a true profile photograph. This last procedure has been covered in Chapter 5—see page 164. If proportional dividers are available, they can be used to determine this distance in a similar, but strictly mechanical manner (See Chapter 1, page 34). When this dimension has been established by one of the above methods, transfer it to the carving and describe a small arc, maintaining the dimension as a radius (Fig. 7-130): (The original reference location of the eye represented by the small hole appears to have been slightly off).

It is now necessary to locate the eye vertically. A rather arbitrary means of determining the vertical location of the eye is sometimes used. First, a line is drawn tangent to the lower edge of the upper mandible. A second line, drawn parallel to the first, is extended back from the upper, most rearward point on the upper mandible. The eye is purported to lie on this line. Part of the arbitrary eye location method just described can be used to an advantage in accurately determining the vertical location of the eye from a photograph. A line is drawn on a true profile view of the head as before, tangent to the lower edge of the upper mandible. See Figure 7-131. The distance the eye is above this line can be then calculated using the method described on page 164. In this particular case, the arbitrary method was fairly accurate; however, in many cases, the eye lies either above or below this prescribed line.

7-131 *The eye can be accurately located from a photograph.*

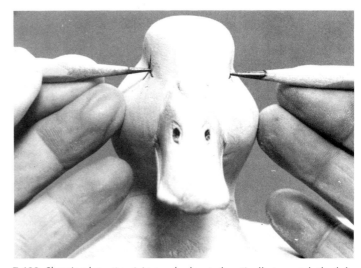

7-132 *Showing how the right can be located vertically to match the left eye.*

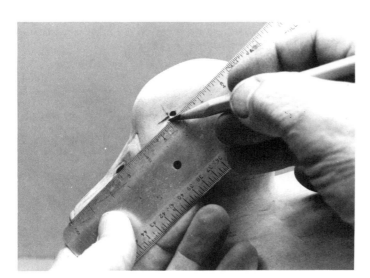

7-130 *Accurately locate eyes from end of bill.*

7-133 *Locating the right eye fore-and-aft.*

Invariably, there are exceptions to all of these so-called axiomatic rules of establishing the salient features of a bird. The carver should use them only if no accurate source for this information is available.

Once the eye has been located correctly on one side of the carving, it is an easy matter to locate the other eye symmetrically with two pencils as shown in Figures 7-132 and 7-133. The holes for the eyes can now be made. This can be accomplished in a number of ways. One fairly easy one is to cut out the eye socket with a small, spherical-shaped burr (Fig. 7-134). The eye sockets should be made slightly larger than the glass eye, which is 9-mm in diameter, and cut approximately 1/8 inch deeper than required to accommodate the eye. Several different fillers are used by carvers for setting eyes—plastic wood, wood dough, plumber's putty, to name some. Kulis Karvit (see Appendix for availability), a two-part resin filler was used in this exercise. One of its advantages is that it can be easily shaped and smoothed with a wet, or damp finger. It also carves and burns reasonably well. Apply a sufficient amount of the filler into the eye socket so that when the eye is inserted excess material will be forced out. A plane through the eye should be canted slightly downward and forward toward the tip of the bill. The eye normally extends out from the head contour approximately 1/16 inch. Front and rear view photographs are useful in determining the lateral location of the eyes. When the eye has been inserted to the proper depth, dampen the forefinger with water and shape and smooth the excess material around and over the periphery of the glass eye.

After the filler has set, open and shape the eye with a pointed blade—an Exacto #11 works well (Fig. 1-135). Many carvers carve the eyelid after the eye is shaped. Carving filler materials, which are usually brittle, is not easy and pieces of the eyelid often break off during the carving procedure. A simple and effective way of duplicating the eyelids is to take a small amount of mixed Kulis Karvit and roll it on a flat surface with the forefinger, dampened with water, until the roll is about 1/32 inch in diameter. Then, cut off a piece about 3/8 inch long and

transfer it by means of small sable brush, dampened with water, to the lower portion of the eye (Fig. 7-136) and carefully position it. If the piece is too long, trim it with an Exacto blade. Repeat the process for the upper lid. Smooth and shape both eyelids with a damp brush (Fig. 7-137).

7-135 *Shape the eye with the point of a sharp knife.*

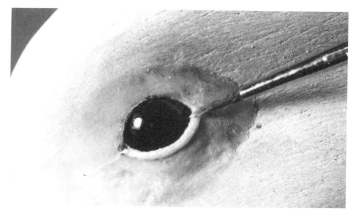

7-136 *Locate lower lid material with a small brush.*

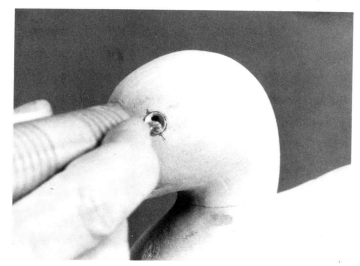

7-134 *The eye hole can be easily made with a spherical-shaped burr.*

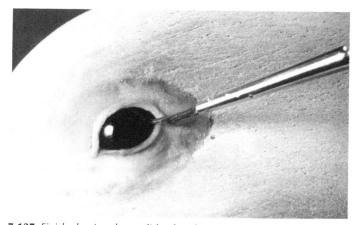

7-137 *Finish shaping the eyelids after the upper is in place.*

OPEN BILL CARVING (see Fig. 5-12, pg. 155)

To duplicate a bird in an aggressive or feeding position or to make the bird appear to be calling or talking, it is necessary to carve the bill in the open position. Carving the upper and lower mandibles and the tongue in detail is very difficult to accomplish accurately due to their very limited accessibility. It can be done in a relatively easy manner, however, if the head is cut in two on a line roughly bisecting the angle formed by the upper and lower mandibles.

First, make an accurate drawing of the head profile with the lower mandible opened the desired amount and with the tongue in its correct position. (See Figure 8-47.) Draw in the cut-off line, located as mentioned above. Now, make a new drawing with the upper part of the head raised 1/8 inch as shown. (Adding the 1/8 inch will provide extra material, so that when the two parts are cut and are accurately sanded and glued together, the head will conform to the original profile drawing.) Although the tongue can be carved as an integral part of the lower mandible, it is easier to carve it as a separate piece and attach it with epoxy.

Proceed with the carving of the upper mandible in the usual manner, roughly shaping the forward part of the head at the same time. Do not attempt to carve the lower mandible at this point. When the upper mandible (Fig. 7-138) is completed, saw the head in two along the line shown (Fig. 7-139). Clamp the upper part of the head in a vise and hollow out the inside of the bill and continue the hollowing into the throat area. To accurately duplicate the inner sides of the mandibles and the tongue most carvers need to refer to a fresh or thawed specimen.

Next, cut the lower mandible to its proper width and shape and carve the side and underside details. Hollow out the inside to receive the tongue. The lamellae (the comblike serrations on the inside of the upper mandible

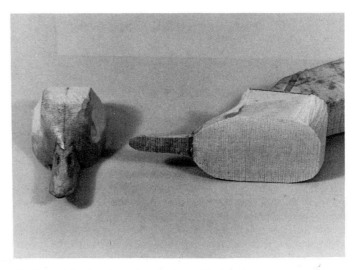

7-139 *Cut the head into two parts on the band saw.*

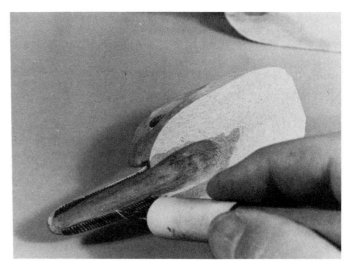

7-140 *After hollowing the bill, burn in the lamellae.*

7-138 *Carve the upper mandible and draw in the cut-off line.*

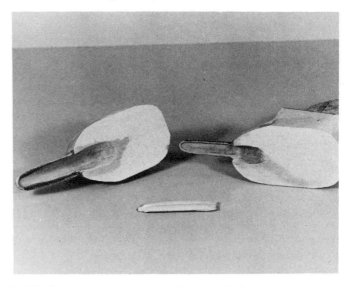

7-141 *The parts are now ready to be assembled.*

and the outside of the lower mandible are duplicated by burning in short parallel lines with the feather-detail burning tool described in Chapter 7 (Fig. 7-140). Cut out the tongue from a small piece of wood and carve it to shape, making it fit the inside of the lower mandible (Fig. 7-141). Attach it with epoxy.

Now, sand the mating surfaces of the two head parts accurately. Apply epoxy to these surfaces and accurately position them so that the mandibles are in proper alignment (Fig. 7-142). After the epoxy has set, the head can be attached to the body, or neck, and carved to its final shape (Fig. 7-143).

7-142 *Epoxy the parts together. Be sure mandibles are properly aligned.*

7-143 *Finished widgeon head.*

WING CARVING

Prior to actual carving, make an accurate full-size drawing showing the planform shape and feather detail on both the upper and lower surfaces; a front view; and usually at least one cross-sectional view (see Chapter 5).

After the drawing has been completed, ascertain the size of the rough wing block. The plan view provides the length and width dimensions. The thickness of the block must be sufficient to accommodate both the curvature of the wing as seen in the front view and the maximum cross-sectional thickness, which occurs at the wing's root. When the overall wing block size has been established, consideration must be given to grain direction so that adequate strength of the entire finished wing is assured.

The bird's wings become very thin (actually one feather thick) in the areas where the primaries, secondaries, and tertials are not overlapped by the wing covert feathers. To duplicate the wing with any degree of realism, these thin areas must be approximated.

When the wing is fully extended, the angle between the outermost primary feather and the secondary feathers (also the tertials) approaches 90 degrees. As the amount of wing extension decreases, this angle also decreases and approaches zero degrees when the wing is folded or almost folded. In duplicating most wing positions, therefore, it is necessary to make the wing block from two or more pieces in order to obtain the proper grain direction for maximum strength. If the carved wing in the areas of the primaries, secondaries, and tertials is to be quite thin (approaching the thickness of the actual wing), it is also advisable to make the wing block in the manner described above but from a stronger wood. The author uses alder, a hardwood species that carves quite well, for all wing carvings.

As shown in Figure 7-144, the block for the outstretched wings of a band-tailed pigeon was made from three pieces, whereas in Figure 7-145 the partially extended wing of a wood duck was made from one piece.

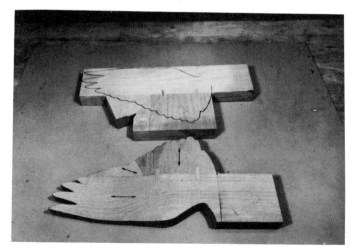

7-144 *Each wing for the band-tailed pigeon was made from three pieces.*

Figure 7-146 shows still another situation, where the wing for a preening mallard was in an intermediate position and two pieces of wood were required for the wing block.

When duplicating a fully extended wing, it is necessary to glue the end grain of the block that forms the secondaries and tertial to the main spanwise block. End grain gluing is generally considered unacceptable; however, the advent of epoxy adhesives makes possible a much stronger end grain joint. It is still advisable to add splines, with their grain running in a fore-and-aft direction, to reinforce the end grain joint (Fig. 7-147). On wings with considerable camber, or chordwise curvature (the wings of a band-tailed pigeon are excellent examples), the block forming the secondaries and tertials should be cut at an angle so that the resulting grain direction will be more or less parallel to these feathers (Fig. 7-147).

Some means of holding the wing block during the shaping and carving operations must be provided. In most cases, sufficient material can be left on the inboard section of the wing to permit clamping in a vise. In the case of the block for the preening wood duck wing, the board from which the block was cut was not of sufficient width to provide a holding point, so it was necessary to attach by means of epoxy a temporary scrap piece of wood for holding purposes (Fig. 7-148).

After the wing block has been assembled and the adhesive cured, transfer the plan-view layout of the wing to the block and cut to shape (Fig. 7-144). It is usually possible, especially on outstretched wings, to approximate some of the spanwise wing curvature (as seen from the frontview) by removing wood with the band saw in a manner similar to that of sawing out the body block.

When as much wood as possible has been removed with the band saw, start shaping the upper side of the wing (Figs. 7-149 through 152). Most of the chordwise curvature exists in the inboard section of the bird's wing, with maximum curvature near the root of the wing and practically none near the tip. Completely shape the upper surface and sand smooth.

7-146 *The wing for a preening mallard was made from two pieces.*

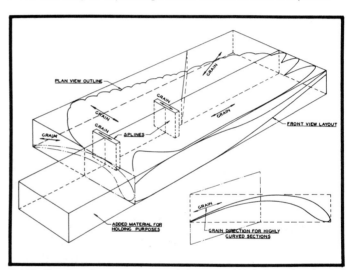

7-147 *Showing the construction of the wing block for a band-tailed pigeon.*

7-145 *The wing for a preening wood duck was made from one piece.*

7-148 *This wing was attached to a scrap piece of wood for support while being carved.*

7-149 *Remove wood from the top side of the wing with a Surform rasp*

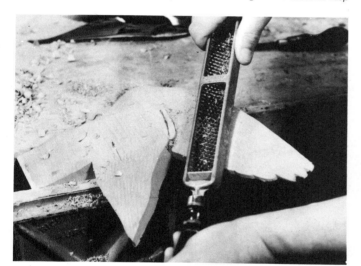

7-150 *The Surform rasp is being pulled to remove the wood from the primaries.*

7-151 *The round Surform rasp is also useful for shaping the upper surface.*

7-152 *Further shaping of the upper surface with a Surform rasp.*

7-153 *Removing wood from the lower wing surface with a gouge.*

7-154 *Wood can be removed from concave areas with a large rotary file.*

Now, turn the wing over and start removing wood on the lower surface. Figures 7-153, 154 and 155 show some of the ways to accomplish this wood removal.

After the wing has been shaped to its final thickness (except in the root area, where wood is retained for holding or attaching purposes), transfer the feather-pattern layout to both the upper and lower surfaces (Fig. 7-156). Proceed with individual feather carving as described earlier (Fig. 7-157). The primary feathers have heavy, prominent shafts. Considerable realism can be obtained by carving in these feather members (Fig. 7-158). Burning in feather detail (see Chapter 8) is accomplished much easier before the wing is attached to the body (Fig. 7-159).

When all carving and other detail work has been completed, cut off the excess wood at the root, leaving enough material to make the wing-body joint—usually one half inch is sufficient—and shape the wing in this area. Locate the wing (or wings) accurately and gouge out

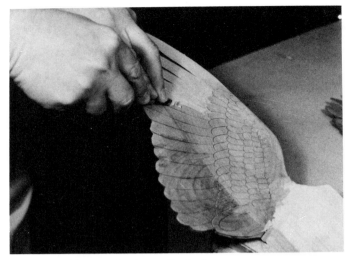

7-157 Carve the wing feathers individually.

7-155 The disc sander is useful for removing wood from the under surface.

7-158 The shaft of each primary feather has been carved in on this wing.

7-156 Lay out the feather pattern on both surfaces of the wing.

7-159 Feather detail burning is easier to do before rather than after the wing is attached to the body.

the body to receive the wing stub (Fig. 7-160). Now, attach the wing with epoxy adhesive and hold in place with one or more nails until the epoxy cures. When the epoxy has cured, complete the wing joint by filling all openings around the wing butt with Plastic Wood or wood dough and sand smooth. The remaining feather carving in this area can now be completed.

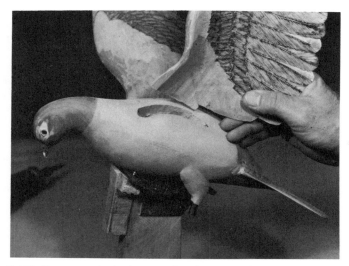

7-160 *Gouge out the body to receive the wing stubs.*

7-161 *Showing completed wing installation (band-tailed pigeon.)*

CARVING LEGS AND FEET

Contemporary bird carvers use more different methods in duplicating the legs (tarsi) and feet than on any other part of the carving. These techniques vary from legs and feet carved from wood to complicated castings of metal, or plastic with metal inserts, made from molds of the actual foot and leg of a bird. Some of the more popular ways of constructing these parts will be covered here. The carver can then select the method or combination of methods that appeals to him. In most cases, his decision will be based not only on his mechanical ability but also on the available tools. Like all other phases of bird carving, there are many ways to get the job done; possibly some of the best ways are yet to be discovered. Regardless of which method of duplicating legs and feet is used, in order to obtain professional results it is essential that actual parts or commercially cast feet whose molds were made from actual parts, be used for reference.

The author has not used castings for legs and feet for two reasons. The first is the large number of patterns and molds required to duplicate not only the many game bird species, but also the different leg and foot positions of each species. The second is the difficulty involved, using the limited materials that lend themselves to home foundry work, in obtaining the strength required for shipping life-size birds. However, carvers should not be discouraged from experimenting with this fabrication process and taking advantage of its possible savings in time.

Because of the difficulty in obtaining the very high temperatures required to melt most stronger metals, home castings usually are done with lead or a lead alloy that can be melted fairly easily. For larger carvings, cast lead legs do not provide sufficient strength, and it is usually necessary to cast around a reinforcing steel or brass rod. Because the strength requirements of feet are less, they lend themselves to the casting method of fabrication better than legs. However, there are problems in casting the toe nails (if they are duplicated realistically) as it is often difficult to make the molten metal flow into these parts.

Molds can be made from several materials. One of the more popular mold materials is hardwood, such as maple, which will resist the melted lead for some time. Plaster is also used but its life is short. Flexible molds made from silicon rubber (RTV) are best but are rather expensive to make.

Commercially produced legs and feet are now available (see Appendix) for those who are unable to make their own or wish to save time and effort. These legs are usually cast from molds that were made using actual bird parts as patterns. The use of commercial legs and feet, or homemade ones, made in this manner is discouraged in most competitive shows. Points may be lost and an otherwise winning carving may lose because of this. The author is definitely opposed to using actual bird parts as patterns for molds for he believes this practice violates the ethics of realistic bird carving. There is nothing unethical about using cast parts provided the patterns and molds are made by the carver himself. Carving feet and legs, like other parts of the bird, is a challenge—the serious carver should face this challenge rather than take the easy way out.

Probably the simplest way to depict the legs and webbed feet (and the method requiring fewest tools) is to carve them from wood (Fig. 7-162). The legs of some birds, however, are so small that wood does not supply sufficient strength for normal handling. If wood is used, make the tarsi from hardwood; maple dowel stock is readily available and a good choice. The feet for waterfowl carvings can be made from a small flat piece of the same kind of wood used for the body of the carving; but, again, making them from hardwood will help reduce the possibility of accidental breakage. The detailed carving on both tarsi and feet can be performed with a knife and small gouges, although small rotary files, powered by the Foredom flexible shaft tool, or small hand grinders are very useful in carving the rather complicated details. Make the small hind toe from an individual piece of wood and cement it into a hole after the leg is carved to shape. When constructing the legs completely from wood, locate both legs at approximately the same angle so that they can be inserted into the holes drilled in the body and also in the mounting base.

A variation of this method is shown in Figure 7-163. Greater strength and the necessary flexibility for different leg positions are provided by the use of a small metal rod or wire running through the wood leg. The leg rod must extend sufficiently above and below the leg to provide attachment to the body and to the mounting base. Drill

the holes for the legs in the body in the manner described on page 234. Where the rods extend below the feet, bend them at angles to make them parallel to each other and at approximate right angles to the mounting surface. Then, drill holes in the base to match the leg rods. After the leg rods have been fitted by temporarily installing them in the body and mounting base, the drilled wood dowel, which will be carved to the leg's shape, can be slipped on and attached by means of epoxy adhesive. If drilling the dowel presents a problem, make the wood part of the leg from two pieces, gouge it out to receive the metal rod, assemble on the rod, and attach with epoxy. Relieve the wood foot at the proper angle to fit the leg and then affix with epoxy.

Unfortunately, wood does not provide sufficient strength for the legs and feet of professional bird carvings which will be handled by others and those that must be transported. The toes and claws are especially vulnerable to breakage when the carving is handled or dusted. Also, it is difficult to make wooden feet conform accurately to an irregular shaped mounting base, such as a piece of driftwood. As soon as the beginner acquires some experience shaping legs and feet, he should start experimenting with the use of metal.

One of the more popular methods of simulating the feet of waterfowl is to make the legs and toes from small brass or copper rods and solder them together (Fig. 7-165). This so-called armature is then built up to the approximate final shape of the tarsus and toes with epoxy-type putty—ribbon epoxy made by Duro is one of the popular ones. Automotive body filler, plumber's putty, and other are also used. Some of the detail can be incorporated into the epoxy before it hardens, the rest can be carved with hand tools or rotary tools powered by the Foredom.

Note: If the carver does not have an actual specimen from which to work, he should purchase a commercially cast foot and use it for reference in a similar manner as a study bill. It must be remembered, however, that although the pattern for the casting was made from an actual foot, the position of the toes and the resulting overall shape of the foot, may not necessarily be correct.

The webs of waterfowl feet can be made from any soft material that can be formed in two directions to fit the toes.

Start by cutting the main leg rod to the proper length as determined by the specimen or cast foot. Bend it to the proper angles in the manner described for the wood-covered metal leg. Bend and taper a smaller rod to form the middle toe. Then, make the inner and outer toes from a common rod bent in a rough V-shape and notch it at the point where it contacts the main leg rod. Notch the main leg rod at this point, too.

It is desirable to file the claws to their final shape at this point. Lay the toe on its side and flatten the rod in the claw area with a hammer. If sufficient height for the claw cannot be obtained by hammering, build up this area with solder. Referring to the cast foot, or specimen, shape the claw with a half-round needle file. After the claws

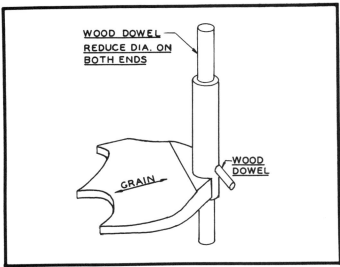

7-162 *Simple wood leg and foot.*

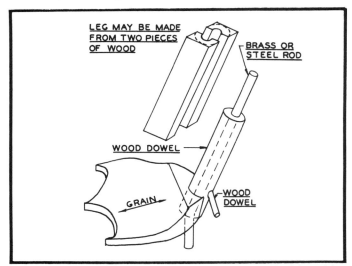

7-163 *The use of a brass or steel rod permits greater flexibility of leg positions.*

7-164 *A simple fixture for holding the parts while soldering.*

7-165 *Showing assembled foot.*

7-166 *Showing finished foot.*

have been shaped, solder the three parts together. Fig. 7-164 shows a simple holding fixture made from a piece of aluminum sheet. Inasmuch as considerable heat is required to bring these parts up to the solder's melting point, the use of a small propane or Presto-Lite torch is advisable. If the parts are to be joined with silver solder instead of lead solder, the use of an oxy-acetylene (or propane-acetylene) torch is almost mandatory.

Now, temporarily install the legs in the carving and locate the feet on the mounting base. Drill holes for the leg tangs and stand the carving on its base. The toes can now be bent to conform to the mount. Whenever it becomes necessary to bend the metal toes, make bends only at the joint locations. As previously mentioned in Chapter 3, the outer toe has four joints, the middle toe has three, and the outer toe has two joints (the number of joints include the attachment joint). To bend down the toe, make a V-shaped cut with a file or other tool on the bottom of the toe at the joint location. This cut will permit the toe to bend in a realistic manner. Close joints with soft solder after all of the bends have been made.

After the toes have been bent to their final positions, remove the legs from the base and from the carving and thoroughly clean these parts down to bright, clean metal. Now, using ribbon epoxy, start building-up the toes and tarsus to their approximate final shapes as determined by referring to the cast foot. Keep fingers and tools moistened with water to prevent the epoxy from sticking to them. If the epoxy does not adhere readily, warm the epoxy and the metal feet. It is sometimes advisable to roll the epoxy into a flat sheet and wrap it around the metal. Do as much shaping as possible while the epoxy is still pliable.

After the tarsus and toes have been shaped and carved to their final form, hammer a piece of lead sheet until it is approximately 1/32 inch thick and sand it smooth, removing all of the dark-colored oxidation. Notch it to fit around the leg tang and locate it under the toes. Trace the outline of the toes on the lead sheet and cut the web to shape with a pair of scissors. Clean the underside of the toes and the web with acetone. Apply 5-minute epoxy to the underside of the toes, place the foot on the web, and hold the web in place with wood clothes pins (see Figure 7-178).

Now, make the small hind toe from a piece of rod and file the claw to shape. Drill a hole into the epoxy at the proper location and angle and attach the hind toe with epoxy. Build up this toe in a similar manner to the other toes Fig. 7-166.

The writer prefers to carve the legs and feet from solid brass. This method provides excellent strength and durability but is not simple and requires tools and equipment that may not be available to some carvers. The legs (tarsii) are carved from brass rod and the toes from heavy brass sheet. The procedure normally followed by the author is described below.

The diameter of the leg rod is determined from an actual specimen. If a specimen is not available, this dimension, as well as the length of the leg, or tarsus, and the size and shape of the foot, can be approximated from the data given in Chapters 11 and 12. The length of the rod is determined by the length of the tarsus plus the length of the tang (the part of the rod that inserts into the body). The length of the tang should be at least four times its diameter, and it is turned on a metal lathe to the diameter of the hole drilled in the body block. When the lower part of the tibia (drumstick) is exposed and is at a pronounced angle to the tarsus, the upper tang is made from a separate brass rod, silver soldered in place (Fig. 7-167). The attachment of the lower tang, by which the standing carving is secured to the mounting base, is somewhat more difficult to make. It is very important that the lower tangs of the two feet be parallel to each other and, to facilitate drilling the mounting holes in the base, perpendicular to the ground.

Set the miter gauge on a disc sander to match the angle of the leg as seen in the profile view, and tilt the sander table to match the camber angle of the leg as seen from the front view. The bottom of the leg rod is then sanded off at this compound angle. The body, with the legs inserted, is now placed on a flat surface. If the above procedure has been properly carried out, the legs can be rotated until both of their bottoms are flat against the surface and the angle of the body relative to the ground, as seen in the profile view, will be correct. The centerlines of the leg rods, as seen from the front, are now marked.

The lower tangs are cut from a brass rod (their length, again, should be at least four times their diameter). These rods are located on the leg centerlines, as far forward as possible, and are silver soldered in place (Fig. 7-168).

After the lower tangs are silver soldered, the legs are again inserted into the body and are rotated until the bottom of each tang rests against a flat surface. The front centerlines are remarked, using a felt tip pen. The rough shape of the tarsi, as seen from the front, is drawn on the rods and as much excess material as possible is removed using a band saw with a metal cutting blade.

In the past the author cut out the foot as one piece from brass sheet. But now he usually cuts the toes out separately because this requires less material, makes the cutting out and carving easier, and permits a more realistic placement of the toes relative to the tarsi. Silver soldering the individual toes to the leg rod, however, is more difficult than attaching an entire foot and requires a holding fixture of some sort (Fig. 7-174).

Whenever possible, the author mechanically attaches the lower tang prior to silver soldering it to the leg (Fig. 7-167). If the lower tang is not mechanically attached, this most important joint will very likely be lost when the toes are silver soldered in place. When a mechanical joint is not used, the alignment of the two parts must somehow be maintained. The author drills a hole in a concrete block of the proper diameter and to such a depth that the tang will just hit bottom. The leg rod is then restrained by a holding fixture to prevent movement. Although the tang leg joint will probably melt during the soldering of the toes, its alignment will remain unaffected after the joint has cooled (Fig. 7-173).

Practically all the carving of the legs and toes is done with rotary files (there are many shapes and sizes from which to choose) used in a high-speed grinder (Fig. 7-

170). The Foredom flexible shaft tool with small, rotary files is also useful for some of the fine detail. Almost all the shaping of the claws is done by hand, using diemaker's files (Fig. 7-172). The final smoothing is also done by hand, using riffler files. The claws are polished smooth on a buffing wheel.

The procedure involved in carving a part from brass is not unlike that in carving a part from wood, although removal of metal is, of course, more difficult and slower. The harder brass is, the easier it is machined. Because soft brass tends to clog the teeth of the rotary files, they will require frequent and rather difficult cleaning. The overall shape of the leg is first established and then the details—tendons, joints, and wrinkles—are carved in. If too much material is removed, the part can be built up with either

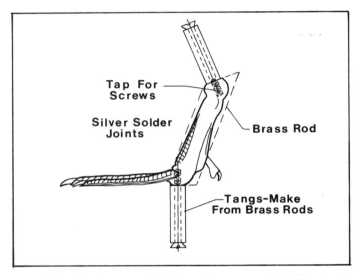

7-167 *It is advisable to attach the lower leg tang mechanically prior to soldering.*

7-168 *The lower tang is silver soldered to the leg rod.*

7-169 *Uncarved leg and carved toes for a wood duck.*

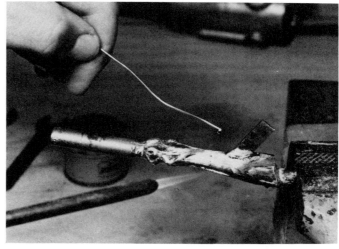

7-171 *Soft soldering small hind toe to leg.*

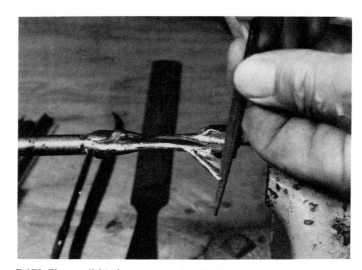

7-172 *The small hind toe is carved with diemaker's files.*

soft solder or silver solder. If silver solder is used, care must be exercised to prevent melting and losing some, or all, of the previously made joints. For example, silver solder can be added to the upper part of the leg provided the lower part and toes are wrapped with a wet cloth. The part may also be built up with ribbon epoxy or automotive body filler.

The hind toe is made from a separate piece of brass sheet or a rod sanded flat on both sides. The leg is drilled at the proper location and the toe is soft soldered (to prevent melting the other joints) in place and is then carved to shape (Figs. 7-171, 7-172).

Because the heel of the rear foot of a striding bird is usually off the ground, the lower mounting tang can not be attached to the leg rod. In this case, a small tang can

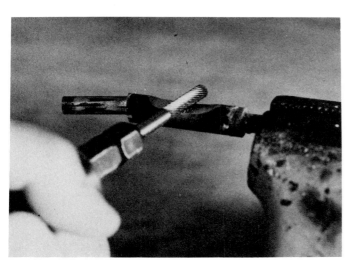

7-170 *Removing metal from side of leg with a rotary file.*

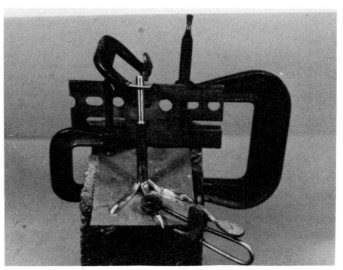

7-173 *Jury rig for soldering when lower leg tang is not mechanically attached.*

be silver soldered to the middle toe (Figs. 7-175, 7-176).

The author uses lead sheet, hammered thin and sanded clean, for the web of the feet of waterfowl (Fig. 7-177, 7-178). After cutting a hole in the lead sheet, slip the lead over the tang and form the web to the bottom of the foot. Once the lead sheet is in its proper place, draw lines around the toes and between the toes. Then remove the sheet and cut it to shape with a pair of scissors. Scale detail is added with a thin, dull instrument, and the small V-shaped notches on the front edge of the web are either cut or filed. The smaller webs on upland game birds, including the pectinations (the comblike membranes along the edges of the toes), can also be duplicated in this manner.

After all the detailing is finished, the mating surfaces are sanded clean and wiped with acetone or some other grease remover. 5-minute epoxy is applied on the underside of the toes. The web is clamped in place using wood clothespins (Fig. 7-178).

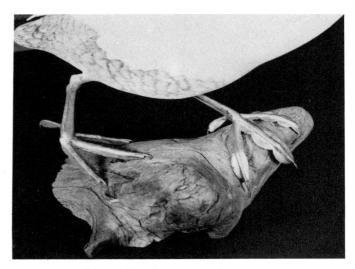

7-176 *Completed feet and legs for a coot carving.*

7-174 *Simple fixture for holding parts while attaching toes.*

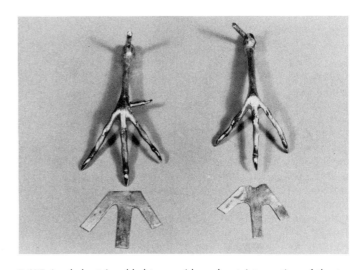

7-177 *Lead sheet is added to provide webs at intersection of the toes and to built up toe pads on upland game birds.*

7-175 *Note small tang on center toe (coot feet).*

7-178 *Lead web is held in place by wood clothespins.*

7-179 *Finished leg and foot for wood duck.*

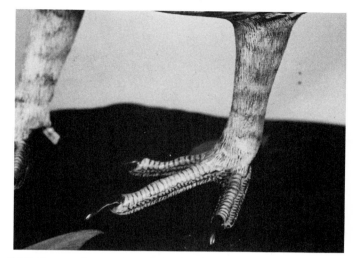

7-181 *Carve to shape and burn in feather detail*

On some upland game birds (prairie chickens, grouse, and ptarmigans) the tarsi are covered with feathers. This can be duplicated by drilling two pieces of wood clamped together to fit the leg rod (Fig. 7-180). The lower ends of the wood pieces are carved to fit the toes and are then assembled to the leg with epoxy. After the epoxy has set, the feathered leg is then carved to shape (Fig. 7-181).

The feet of full-bodied birds that are resting or crouching are not attached to the base. The carved bird is attached by means of a dowel extending from the base into the body of the carving. The legs and feet are made in the normal manner except the lower mounting tangs are eliminated.

Complete the feet and legs by spraying them with primer.

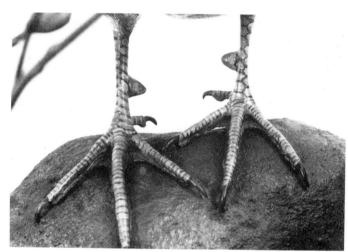

7-182 *Finished feet on a chukar partridge.*

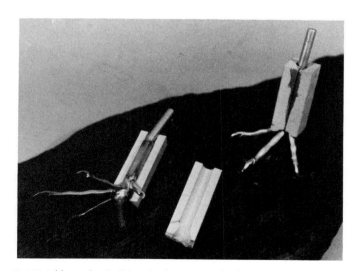

7-180 *Add wood to build up leg for some upland game birds.*

7-183 *Finished feet and legs on a white-fronted goose carving.*

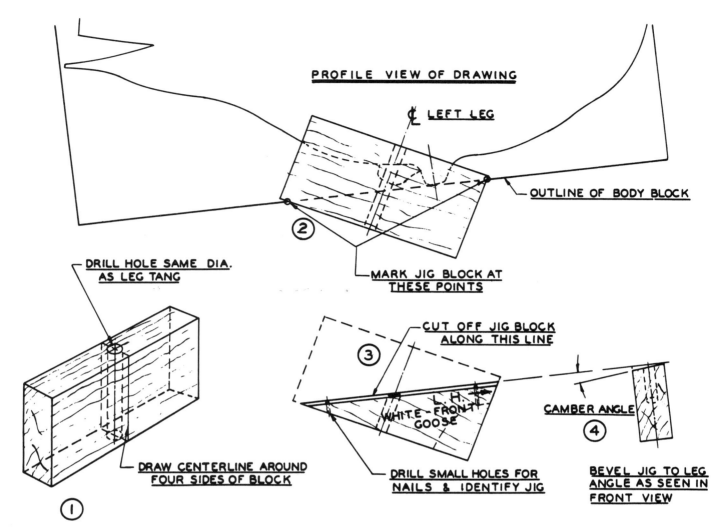

PROFILE VIEW OF DRAWING

₵ LEFT LEG

② OUTLINE OF BODY BLOCK

MARK JIG BLOCK AT THESE POINTS

DRILL HOLE SAME DIA. AS LEG TANG

CUT OFF JIG BLOCK ALONG THIS LINE

③

WHITE FRONT GOOSE
L. H.

CAMBER ANGLE

④

DRAW CENTERLINE AROUND FOUR SIDES OF BLOCK

①

DRILL SMALL HOLES FOR NAILS & IDENTIFY JIG

BEVEL JIG TO LEG ANGLE AS SEEN IN FRONT VIEW

7-184 *Simple jig for drilling leg hole.*

DRILLING FOR LEGS

Although not required for small standing carvings whose leg tangs can be easily bent, simple jigs for drilling the leg tang holes in the body block are a necessity for the larger standing carvings requiring strong, stiff legs. If the desired leg positions which were determined on the drawing are to be duplicated, the leg holes must be drilled at the correct compound angle. (Fig. 7-184).

These jigs are quite easy to construct from scrap pieces of wood (preferably hardwood) approximately 1 inch thick, 2 to 3 inches wide, and 6 inches long. First, near the midpoint of each block, locate the hole centerline and drill holes of the proper diameter through the blocks at this point. By means of a square, continue this centerline around on all four sides of the block. Add the outline of the body block to the profile view of the drawing, lay the jig block on one of the leg centerlines, and make a mark at each end so that the jig block can be cut off at the proper angle. Cut the jig block along this line and bevel the edge to an angle equal to the camber angle of the leg (the leg angle as seen in the front view). Make the drill jig for the other leg in the same manner. Identify the left and

7-185 *Drilling the leg holes.*

right jigs, show the direction they are to be installed by an arrow, and further identify these for future use.

Transfer the leg centerlines to the body block at the same time the profile view is transferred. Using a square, extend the intersections of the leg centerlines with the edge of the body block on across the bottom of the body block. Locate the legs symmetrically on either side of the body block centerline. Nail the drill jigs in place at these locations (be sure that they are parallel to the body block centerline) and drill holes to the proper depth (Fig. 7-185).

INDIVIDUAL FEATHERING TECHNIQUE

Great improvements in the carving and painting of birds were made during the 1960's, primarily as a result of formal and informal competitions. In a continual effort to more closely duplicate the actual bird, carvers added more detail, refined existing methods, and originated new techniques.

Probably the most dramatic change in the art of bird carving was brought about by the introduction of the individual feathering technique, which basically consists of making many of the feathers (primaries, secondaries, coverts, tail feathers, and others) individually and assembling them to the wing and body structures in a manner very similar to that of the real bird's. Although used to a very limited degree much earlier, this technique became prominent in the early 1970's when a number of super carvings were displayed that not only featured this method of construction to its fullest extent but also incorporated positions and actions that had rarely been attempted before.

Since then, many beautiful carvings have been planned and completed. However, like all good things, the use of individually made feathers have, in some cases, been carried to extremes. Rather than limit their use to the effective duplication of prominent feathers such as wing primaries, secondaries, tertials, some wing coverts, and tail feathers, a few carvers have also included many body contour feathers and almost all wing and tail covert feathers resulting invariably with a very rough and shingled appearing carving. The bird's feathers are extremely thin. The feather thickness in the barb area of a duck's primary is approximately $5/1000$ inch thick. Body contour feathers are even thinner—about $3/1000$ inch thick. In addition to being very thin, they are also very flexible and overlap each other perfectly. It is, therefore, almost physically impossible to simulate many of the bird's feathers by making them individually. The carver should limit their use to areas where they can be realistically and effectively used.

Although many carvers may not have the ability to conceive a super-carving or the energy, skill, and patience to execute such a complicated project, they can learn much from this relatively new technique that can be applied directly to simpler types of carvings.

About the only way to accurately determine the shape, contour, and location of individual feathers and their attachment to the basic structure is by reference to an ac-

tual bird. Therefore, a fresh or thawed specimen is almost a necessity if individually made feathers are to be used to any great extent.

To make individual feathers, the carver must have thin wood strips, of even thickness, approximately $1/32$ inch thick and of sufficient width to accommodate the widest feather he plans to make. Basswood is generally preferred, although other woods can be substituted successfully. The author has used alder (a wood similar to maple, but softer), which is stronger than basswood, with good results. If precut veneer is not available, probably the easiest way to make your own is to rip the thin strips on a table saw. A smooth-cutting, hollow ground blade works well and leaves few saw marks. If a table saw is not available, a band saw can be used, although it will not produce strips as thin or even as those possible with a table saw. A portable belt sander is useful for reducing the thickness and/or removing saw marks (Fig. 7-186).

Although making individual feathers is tedious and very time-consuming, the procedure is quite simple. First, a drawing of the feather that is to be reproduced, showing its shape and shaft location, must be transferred to the thin piece of material. The feather is then cut out using a sharp knife; if the material is quite thin, a pair of sharp scissors may be used. The edges are reduced in thickness by further sanding.

Shaft detail can be added in three different ways. Except on strongly shafted feathers, such as the primaries on most birds and the tail feathers on large birds, the shaft is usually burned in by making two accurately converging lines with the burning tool (Fig. 8-13). When the shaft is quite prominent, it can either be carved as part of the feather (a very difficult and time-consuming job) or added as two separate pieces. When individual pieces are used, a tapered piece of material whose length is equal to that of the shaft and whose thickness on one end is equal to slightly more than one half of the total shaft thickness and tapered to practically nothing on the other end must be

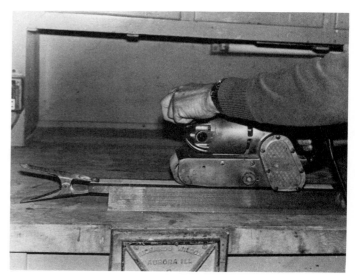

7-186 *The portable belt sander quickly reduces the thickness and smooths the thin feather material.*

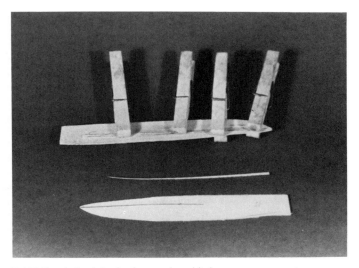

7-187 *The shaft of the feather can be added as two separate pieces.*

Individual feathers can be constructed in another manner—one that provides considerably more strength than those cut from a veneer. Feathers constructed by this method are ideal for the long, outer primaries when they are completely, or almost completely, separated and, especially if vane splits are contemplated. This unique method of feather construction was originated by Harry Seiler of Valders, Wisconsin.

The feather is made of three parts; the hardwood shaft, whose grain runs parallel to the length of the feather; and the softer individual vanes whose grain runs at approximately 45 degrees to the shaft. In this example, the shaft was made from alder (a wood similiar to maple but less dense) and the vane pieces were made of basswood.

First, make an accurate drawing of the feather which is to be simulated. Next, transfer the shaft outline to the piece of hardwood and cut along the convex side of the drawn shaft with a bandsaw. Accurately sand to the cut-off line with a disc or a belt sander. Now, take a piece of basswood whose width is about equal to the length of the

made. This can be done by hand, or more easily with a portable belt sander. A strip whose width equals the maximum width of the shaft on one end and tapers to practically nothing on the other end is then cut off this piece with a straight edge and a very sharp knife or razor blade. This small, tapered strip is then dragged through some epoxy spread thinly on a flat surface (care must be taken that the epoxy is applied evenly to the entire length of the shaft piece). The shaft is then laid on the feather shaft line and is held in place by small clamps, such as clothespins (Fig. 7-187). After the epoxy has set fairly well, the same procedure is followed on the other side of the feather.

When the epoxy has hardened, the surplus can be removed quite easily by lightly scraping the area with the tip of the burning tool set at a fairly low temperature. The shaft should be sanded to its final cross-sectional shape, which is oval or elliptical on the upper side and rectangular with the edges rounded over on the lower side.

7-189 *Attach right vane.*

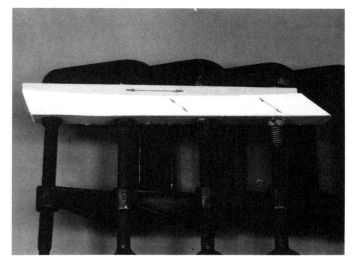

7-188 *Attach partially cut out shaft to left vane.*

7-190 *Showing glued-up blank, cut off feather, and finished feather.*

feather and cut off two pieces at 45 degrees to the grain. The width of each piece should be somewhat more than the individual vane widths. Transfer the outline of the edge of the sanded shaft piece to the edge of its corresponding vane; cut along this line with the bandsaw; and sand accurately to this line using the roller end of a belt sander or a drum sander. Check the two parts, and if they fit accurately, they are ready to be glued together (Fig. 7-188). If there are inaccuracies, correct one or the other, or both until a good joint is obtained. Apply one-hour type epoxy on both parts, allow to stand for a few minutes, and then clamp the two parts firmly together.

When the epoxy has cured, cut along the other side of the shaft, sand carefully to this line, and transfer this contour to the other vane piece, cut, and sand. When an accurate joint has been made, epoxy the two parts together in the manner described previously (Fig. 7-189). After the epoxy has thoroughly cured, cut off the individual feathers with a bandsaw or jigsaw. These feathers can now be cut to their planform configuration and carved to their correct cross-sectional shape (Fig. 7-190).

In many cases, several of the primary feathers have similar shaft sizes and curvatures. If this occurs, ascertain the number of feathers that can be made from the same blank and make the blank of sufficient thickness to accommodate them.

The carver must be careful when burning in barb detail to make sure that the tip of the iron, though placed next to the shaft, is not so close as to burn into it. See Chapter 8 for instructions on feather-detail burning.

It is most important that all burned surfaces be cleaned thoroughly before they are painted. The products of combustion and other particles can be removed or loosened quite effectively and easily by brushing lightly with a soft stainless steel brush. If compressed air is available, the loose particles can be removed with a high velocity stream of air; if not, brushing with a soft bristle brush while blowing with the mouth will usually do the job. Rubbing the surface with a tack rag (an impregnated cloth obtainable at a paint store) also helps to remove loose particles.

As was mentioned previously, many carvers accentuate the parting of barbs, which causes the v-shaped gaps in feather vanes. Although this practice can be carried to an extreme, a certain amount of barb parting adds realism and texture. Separation of barbs can be duplicated easily and effectively with a burning tool, such as The Detailer whose tip can be made very hot. The barb lines are burned in a normal manner up to where the part in the barb lines is desired. The V-shaped piece is removed by making two deep burns. The barb lines are then continued but are made parallel to the other side of the V-cut (Fig. 7-193). See Fig. 8-28.

Because feathers are not flat, but are curved along their length and cross-section, some means of forming the simulated feather must be used to duplicate the natural curve. One of the easiest ways to permanently bend wood is to apply heat, water, and pressure. This can be done in many ways: holding the feather in the steam from a tea kettle or applying a household steam iron directly,

7-191 *Bending a feather lengthwise using a soldering iron.*

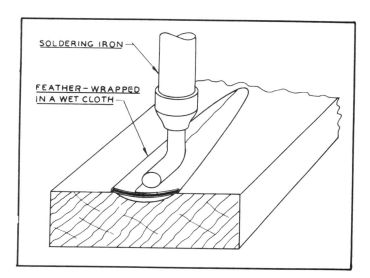

7-192 *One way that feathers can be bent along their cross section.*

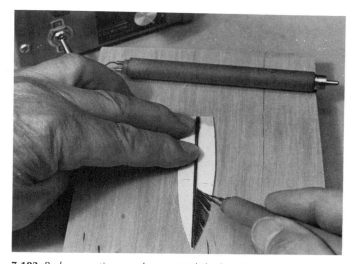

7-193 *Barb separation can be accomplished with a hot burning tool.*

for example. The author uses a large, old-fashioned electric soldering iron as the heat source and lays a wet rag on the tip to provide steam. The feather is then placed directly on the wet rag and pressure is applied to both sides to obtain simple lengthwise curvature (Fig. 7-191). To obtain curvature in both the lengthwise and crosswise directions, a female form (made from a piece of scrap wood gouged to the proper shape) is used. The simulated feather is wrapped in a wet cloth and placed over the form. Heat and pressure are then supplied with the tip of a hot soldering iron (Fig. 7-192).

Several ways in which the individual feathering technique can be applied to improve conventional carvings are described in the following sections.

Crest Feathers

Duplicating the raised crest feathers on such birds as the prairie chicken (Figs. 7-194, 195), ruffed grouse, sharp-tailed grouse, scaled quail, and others is one of the simplest applications of the individual feathering technique.

If a specimen is available, either remove one of the crest feathers or lift one up with a needle or the point of a knife. Note the length, width, and shape of the feather. When it is not possible to check a real feather, try to determine its length from a photograph (since the length of the bill is known, the feather length can be estimated by ratio and proportion). The width of these feathers is usually about one fifth or one sixth of their length, and

7-196 *Place the feathers on the layout to determine their overlaps.*

7-197 *Attach the tail feathers to each other in their proper sequence and position.*

7-194, 195 *Crest feathers on a prairie chicken carving.*

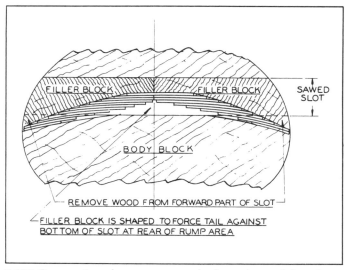

FILLER BLOCK   FILLER BLOCK   SAWED SLOT

BODY BLOCK

— REMOVE WOOD FROM FORWARD PART OF SLOT —

FILLER BLOCK IS SHAPED TO FORCE TAIL AGAINST BOTTOM OF SLOT AT REAR OF RUMP AREA

7-198 *Cross section of rump area near the forward part of the tail.*

they are generally tapered with rounded ends. Lay out seven or eight feathers, making them somewhat longer than the actual feather, on one of the thin strips of wood. Because crest feathers are small and hard to hold, it is easier to burn in the shaft and barbs before cutting out the feathers. Next, using one of the methods described earlier, bend each of the feathers until their curved shape (lengthwise) corresponds to the real thing.

Now, hold the feathers individually on the head of the carving and determine their locations. Cut the feathers to their proper length and trace around each of them so that the wood can be mortised out to receive them. Attach the feathers with epoxy, starting with the rearmost and working forward. Tiny pins, the type used for attaching sequins, are useful for holding the feathers in place while the epoxy is setting.

Tail Feathers

The making of an accurate layout of the shape and the arrangement of the tail feathers is the most important phase of this procedure. Changes are infinitely easier to make on paper than on the final tail; therefore, do not attempt any shortcuts or minimize the importance of this step.

The tail of a bird is divided into a right group and a left group, each group often acting separately (Fig. 5-69). The hooded merganser's tail used here as an example has twenty feathers (Fig. 7-196). Most birds have fewer tail feathers, usually from twelve to eighteen. Except when viewed from below, all of the feathers can be seen only when the tail is fanned out.

After the layout is completed, trace off the individual feathers onto the thin material, numbering them so that their proper location can be easily determined later. Now, cut them out and place them, two adjacent feathers at a time, on the layout and mark their upper and lower overlaps. This is done to define the area which is to be burned as it is usually not necessary to burn barb detail over the entire feather on both sides (Fig. 7-196).

The tail feathers are quite strongly shafted. However, only the shafts on the lower side of the two outermost feathers and the upper side of one center feather are exposed along most of their lengths. At the carver's discretion, the shafts on these three feathers may be added as separate pieces (Fig. 7-187) or burned in along with the rest of the tail feather shafts.

After the barb detail is burned, steam the feathers and bend them, so they are slightly convex along their cross section (Fig. 7-192). Attach the finished feathers together with epoxy, starting with the outermost and working toward the center (Fig. 7-197). Use epoxy sparingly so as to avoid forcing any onto the exposed part of the feather. If this does occur, the excess epoxy can be removed later by carefully placing the tip of the hot burning tool in the previously burned barb lines. After the epoxy has set, accurately trim or sand the forward edge of the assembly.

The tail feather assembly must now be attached to the body. The slot to receive the tail should be made before cutting out the original body block and can be accom-

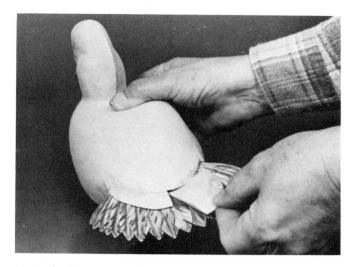
7-199 *The filler is made from two pieces of wood.*

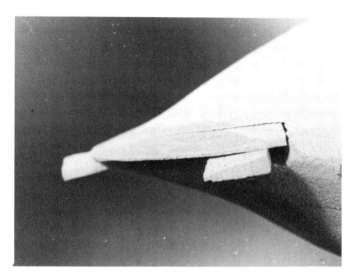
7-200 *Hold the filler blocks in place with wedges.*

7-201 *Install the tail and carve and burn the upper tail coverts.*

plished with a band saw or, more accurately, by making a series of cuts on a table saw. The tail used in this example was for a stretching (wing and leg) hooded merganser. In this case, the tail would be convex (as viewed from above). In other instances, such as when the bird is taking off, the tail would be concave.

The forward part of the slot's lower surface is now shaped to conform to the convex shape (Fig. 7-198). A filler block, or blocks, must be carved next to fill the void between the tail feathers and the body. In the example shown, the filler was made from two pieces (Figs. 7-198, 199). It is most important that these filler blocks be made to fit accurately and tightly. After they have been fitted, remove the tail assembly and replace the filler blocks, holding them securely in place with temporary wedges (Fig. 7-200). The upper and lower tail covert area and the rump can now be carved to their final shapes without damaging the fragile tail feathers. When this is finished, install the tail and filler blocks with epoxy. After the epoxy has set, carefully carve and burn the individual tail covert feathers (Fig. 7-201).

Insertion of Crossed Primaries and Tertials

The advantages of inserting the primary feather groups, rather than carving them from the body block, was discussed previously on page 198. A somewhat different procedure whereby not only the primaries, but also the tertials feathers, are inserted will be covered here. In the next section, entitled "Standing Carvings", this procedure will be carried one step further by constructing a partially exposed wing in a similar manner.

To describe and illustrate this procedure, the carving of a green-winged teal decorative decoy is used as an example. This general method, with slight variations can be applied to other waterfowl species.

The body block is cut out and carved in the normal manner except no wood is left from which to carve the crossed primaries and the tertials. The tail feathers, upper

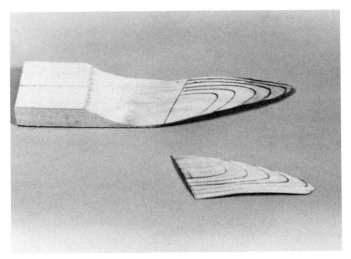

7-203 *The primary groups are carved to match the template.*

7-204 *Relieve the body block to receive the primary groups.*

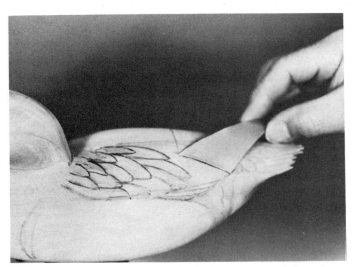

7-202 *Use a metal template to check the curvature of the primary groups.*

7-205 *Remove wood from the rear of the scapular groups.*

tail coverts, and rump feathers are drawn in and carved. The primary groups are located next and the exposed secondaries, tertials, and scapular feathers are sketched on one side of the carved surface and are transferred to the other side as previously described. A drawing of one set of the folded primaries is made and is traced on to a piece of soft metal. Lead sheet works very well, but if it is not available soft aluminum or galvanized sheet can be used. At this point, the carver must decide where to terminate the primary group. In this example, it was terminated just above the wing secondary group. The metal template representing the primary group is cut off at that point and bent to match the curvature and twist of an actual duck's wing. It is formed to match the curvature of the body where the folded primary group will attach to the body block (Fig. 7-202). This template is now used as a form for checking the shape of the carved primary group (Fig. 7-203).

Additional realism can be obtained with very little more work by making the folded primary groups from individual feathers as was shown on page 207. The method described above is followed except that instead of carving the folded primary group from a single piece, the feathers are made and bent individually. It is usually necessary to make only the outermost six or seven feathers as the secondaries and tertials cover the others. Also, as only the tips and the trailing edges of these feathers are exposed, it is not necessary to burn barb detail over the entire feather. Except for the lower side of the outermost primary, very little of the shafts are exposed; therefore, they may be effectively burned in rather than added as separate pieces.

The body block is now relieved to receive the folded primary groups (Fig. 7-204). Before attaching the primary groups to the body block, barb detail is burned in on the tail, coverts, and rump.

Wood is removed from the body block at the rear of the scapular group (Fig. 7-205) to a depth that will allow for the installation of the individual tertial feathers, which are

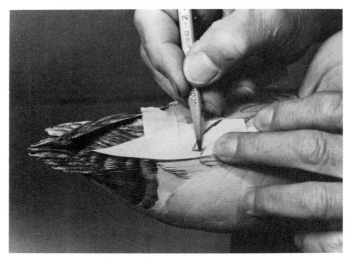

7-207 *A paper template is used to mark the feather cut off.*

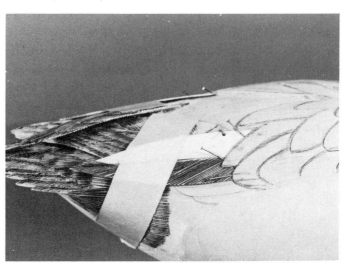

7-208 *The feather is held in place by means of masking tape and small pins.*

7-206 *Tertial feathers for a green-winged teal carving.*

7-209 *The individual tertials have all been installed.*

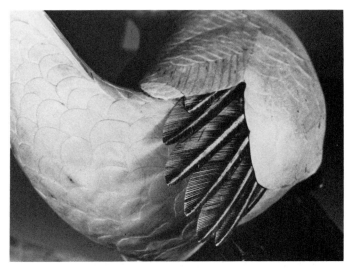

7-210 *The inserted primaries are epoxied in place.*

made at this time (Fig. 7-206). The outline of the lower-most tertial feather is traced on a piece of transparent paper and is cut out. This paper template is then placed in its proper position on the carving and its cut-off line is marked and carefully trimmed (Fig. 7-207). If the paper template does not fit perfectly, the procedure is repeated until an accurately fitting template is obtained. The paper template is then placed on the back side of the simulated tertial feather, the cut-off line is transferred to the wood, and the excess wood is trimmed off cleanly with a sharp knife.

An alternative method for installing the tertials, which probably gives more consistent results with no more effort, is to undercut the scapulars to a depth of 1/32 to 1/16 inch and then slip the tertial into this slot. Undercutting can be performed with a hook-bladed knife (Fig. 7-219), with a small pointed saw (such as made by Exacto), or with a small cutting wheel used in the Foredom.

After a little epoxy is applied to the underside of the feather, it is placed on the carving and held in its proper place by means of masking tape and tiny pins (Fig. 7-209). After the epoxy has set, the thickness of the unex-posed part of the feather is reduced to practically nothing in order to keep the overlap areas from becoming too thick. Repeat this process for the remaining tertials (Fig. 7-204). After the tertials are all in place, the individual scapular feathers are carved.

The extended primaries of displaying upland game birds can be made individually and inserted. After the individual feathers are made and detailed, they are joined together with epoxy, as previously described for the tail group. Figure 7-210 shows the inserted primaries of a displaying prairie chicken.

The Complete Wing

Besides being unbelievably light, splendidly functional, and extremely durable, a bird's wing is beautiful and complex almost beyond description—it is certainly one of nature's masterpieces. Although man can never come

close to duplicating the superb construction of a wing, the individual feathering technique makes it possible to attain a delicate realism that is almost impossible to achieve by carving from a solid block. Also, the use of very thin, but strong, and completely separated flight feathers greatly enhances the feeling of motion. The individual feathering technique is definitely shown to its very best advantage when used on wings, especially those in the flight config-uration.

Before attempting to duplicate the wing of a bird in great detail, the serious carver should do as much re-search as he possibly can and study live birds at every opportunity. Some wing movements are too fast to be discerned by the unaided eye, but fortunately many fine photographs are available for close study. Edgar Queeny's fine book, *Prairie Wings*, for example, contains an excel-lent collection of photographs of waterfowl in flight.

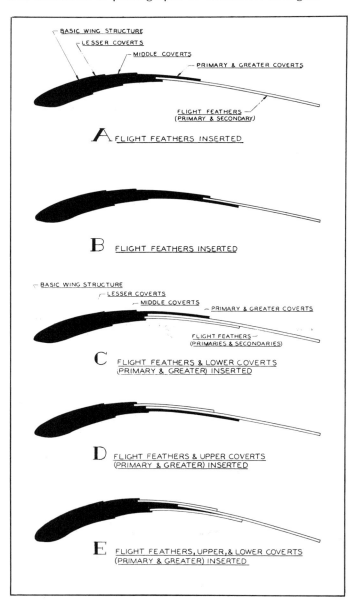

7-211 *The wing can be constructed in at least four different ways.*

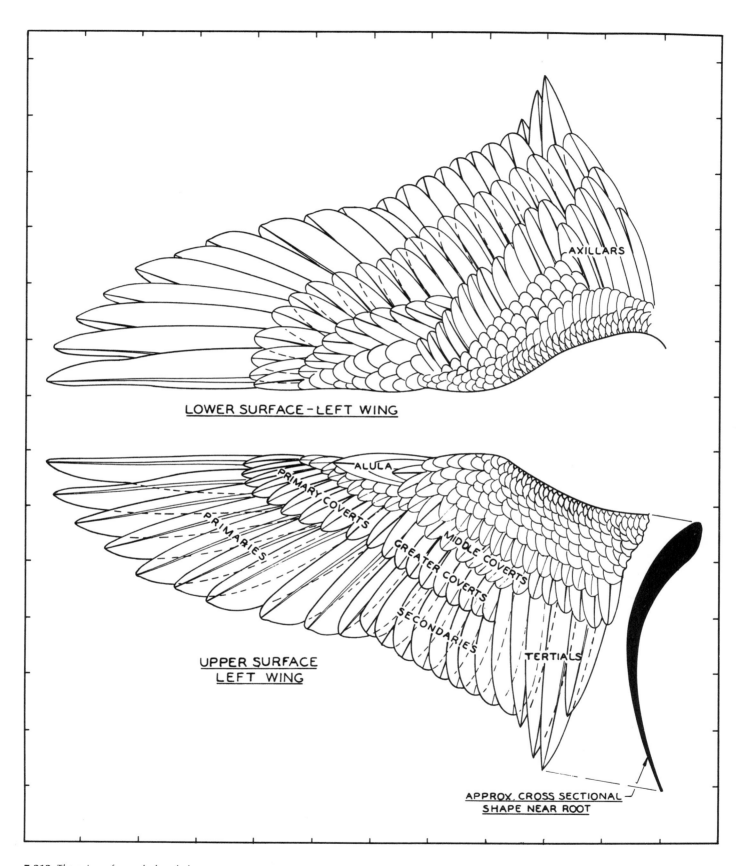

LOWER SURFACE-LEFT WING

AXILLARS

UPPER SURFACE
LEFT WING

ALULA

PRIMARY COVERTS

PRIMARIES

MIDDLE COVERTS

GREATER COVERTS

SECONDARIES

TERTIALS

APPROX. CROSS SECTIONAL
SHAPE NEAR ROOT

7-212 *The wing of a male hooded merganser.*

The wing is capable of assuming many positions and shapes. The very flexible flight feathers dramatically reflect the air loads imposed on them which in turn help impart the feeling of movement. During the downstroke and in gliding flight, the flight feathers are pressed closely together. In these conditions, the pressure on the lower side is positive, causing the covert feathers on the underside to conform smoothly to the wing's surface, while the coverts on the upper side lie more loosely, being subjected to a negative pressure. During the upstroke, the flight feathers are separated to permit the flow of air between them. When there is no air load, such as when the bird is stretching its wing, the lower coverts lie quite loosely and extend from the surface of the wing. These are but a few of the details that a carver who wishes to attain realism must consider.

The individual feathering technique can be used in at least four different ways in the construction of a wing.

1. Both the upper and lower coverts are carved on the basic wing structure and the flight feathers are individually made and inserted (Fig. 7-211 A and B)
2. The upper coverts are carved on the basic wing structure and the flight feathers and lower coverts are individually made and inserted (Fig. 7-211 C)
3. The lower coverts are carved on the basic wing structure and the flight feathers and upper coverts are individually made and inserted (Fig. 7-211 D).
4. The flight feathers are attached to a tang carved from the basic wing structure and both the upper and lower coverts are individually made and inserted (Fig. 7-211 E).

Usually the insertion of individual feathers on a wing is limited to the flight feathers, tertials, and the upper and lower primary and greater coverts. The upper and lower middle coverts may also be inserted individually. However, if feather insertion is carried too far, an artificial, shingled effect often results. When birds are portrayed in flight, a good effect is obtained by individually making and inserting the alula feathers and the axillars.

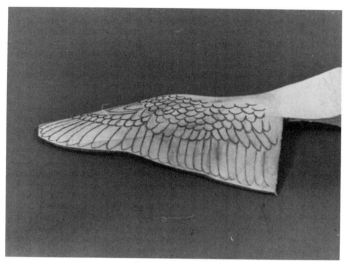

7-214 *Transfer the layout of the wing's upper surface from the drawing to the basic wing structure.*

7-215 *Carve the upper primary and greater coverts.*

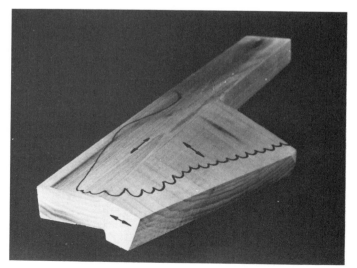

7-213 *Showing the build-up and grain direction of the basic wing structure.*

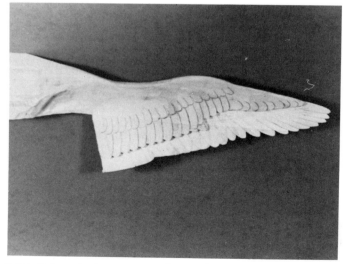

7-216 *Relieve the lower wing surface to the rear of the coverts.*

7-217 Showing the wing drawing, the basic wing structure, and the individual flight feathers.

As before, an accurate drawing of the upper and lower surfaces of the wing is *mandatory*. Mistakes on the actual wing are very difficult to correct. It is, therefore, most important that the drawing show the exact location of each feather that is to be inserted and also the ones that are to be carved (Fig. 7-212).

First, the shape and grain direction of the basic wing structure must be determined. It is essential that at least some of this structure have grain running in the spanwise direction. If either the upper or lower coverts are to be carved from the wing structure, the grain in this area should be generally fore and aft. Figure 7-213 shows one way this can be achieved. When end-grain gluing is involved, as shown in Figure 7-213, epoxy should be used.

In this example of a male hooded merganser stretching his wing, carving the upper coverts and inserting the lower ones works best because the lower coverts lie loosely in this configuration—a condition ideal for feather insertion.

After the epoxy has set, the basic wing structure is carved to its final shape, as described earlier in this chapter. The upper covert feather layout is then transferred from the drawing to the wing (Fig. 7-214), and these feathers are individually carved on the upper surface (Fig. 7-215). Note how the coverts in the tertial area are carved quite deeply (about $3/32$ inch) in order to receive the inserted tertials.

Now, transfer the lower covert layout to the lower surface and carefully remove wood aft of this area to a depth of approximately $3/32$ inch at the rear of the lower coverts tapering to approximately $1/32$ inch thick at the trailing edge of the upper coverts. After this has been accomplished, lay out the lower side of the upper coverts and individually carve them. It is necessary to carve only about the rear one third of each covert as they will be covered by the flight feathers (Fig. 7-216).

Make the individual flight feathers (Fig. 7-217), as described previously. In order to seal effectively on the downstroke, the flight feathers have the cross-sectional

7-219 *Undercut the coverts to receive the inserted tertials.*

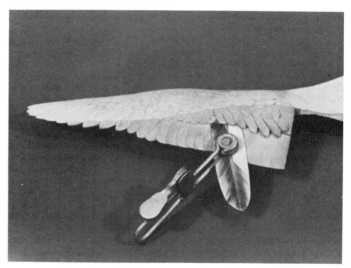

7-220 *Install the outermost tertial.*

7-221 *Reduce the thickness of the inserted feather in the unexposed area.*

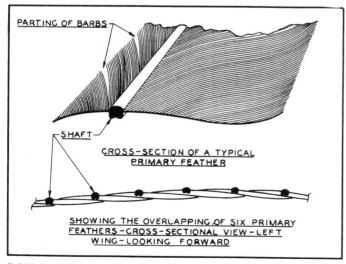

PARTING OF BARBS

SHAFT

CROSS-SECTION OF A TYPICAL PRIMARY FEATHER

SHOWING THE OVERLAPPING OF SIX PRIMARY FEATHERS - CROSS-SECTIONAL VIEW - LEFT WING - LOOKING FORWARD

7-218 *Typical cross-sectional shape of the flight feathers.*

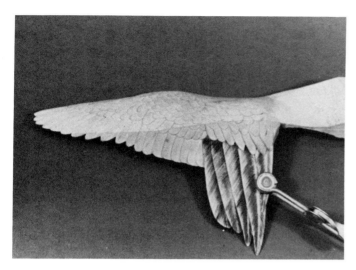

7-222 *Showing the last tertial clamped in place.*

shape shown in Figure 7-218. If the carved feathers are to nest realistically, this S-shaped bend must be duplicated as closely as possible, using the bending methods described earlier. The secondary feathers are further "cupped" on their tips, which also should be duplicated. After this bending, or forming, is accomplished, the flight feathers must also be bent along their length. Under conditions of no load, these feathers have a permanent downward bend to offset deflections from air loads and also, possibly, to conform to the shape of the body when they are folded. This amount of downward bend can be determined from a specimen. For wings in the flight configuration, the lengthwise bend of the flight feathers can be determined from photographs.

The actual feather insertion is started with the outermost tertial. As described earlier, a paper template of the feather is made to determine the cut-off line, and then the deeply carved covert feathers are undercut to receive the

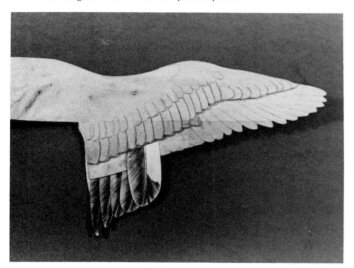

7-223 *First secondary feather is epoxied in place.*

7-225 *Continue inserting the primaries, proceeding outward.*

7-224 *All of the secondaries have now been inserted.*

7-226 *All of the primaries have now been inserted.*

tertials (Fig. 7-219). Apply epoxy sparingly and clamp the tertial in place (Fig. 7-220). Before the epoxy sets, double check to be sure the feather is in its proper location. After the epoxy has set, reduce the thickness of the feather in the unexposed area to practically nothing so that an excessive build-up will not occur, especially in the primary area (Fig. 7-221). Now, undercut the coverts for the second tertial and continue this procedure for the remaining tertials (Fig. 7-222). Although not shown in this example, it is a good practice to burn the coverts before inserting any feathers. This eliminates the possibility of getting burn marks on the already detailed feathers.

Now, turn the wing over and insert the flight feathers, starting with the innermost secondary feather (Fig. 7-223) and continuing outward until all the flight feathers have been installed (Figs. 7-224, 225, 226).

Make the individual lower covert feathers next and insert them, starting with the innermost and proceeding on out (Figs. 7-227, 228). In the example shown, some of the middle coverts were also inserted. The insertion of these feathers is optional.

After all the feathers have been inserted, individually carve the remaining coverts and burn them (Fig. 7-229). On the wing shown in Figure 7-229, the alula feathers were carved, not inserted, which also is optional. However, on wings depicting a flight configuration, it is easier and more effective to insert the alula feathers. Because they would have been completely hidden, the axillars were not made, but in most flight configurations, they would be visible and should be individually made and inserted.

Other Uses

Although the individual feathering techniques also may be used for body feathers, it generally produces an artificial, shingled effect because of the difficulty in making body feathers thin enough to lay as flat as they do on the

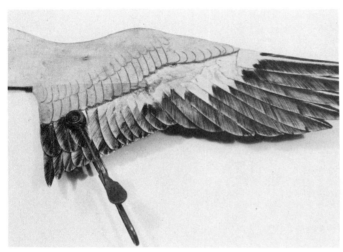

7-227 *Start inserting the lower greater coverts and proceed outward.*

7-228 *A few of the middle coverts were inserted on this wing.*

7-229 *Complete the wing by carving and burning the rest of the under and upper coverts.*

7-230 *The finished wing of a male hooded merganser carving (Collection of Dr. and Mrs. J. L. Silagi, Texas).*

7-231 *Male wood duck in an interesting pose.*

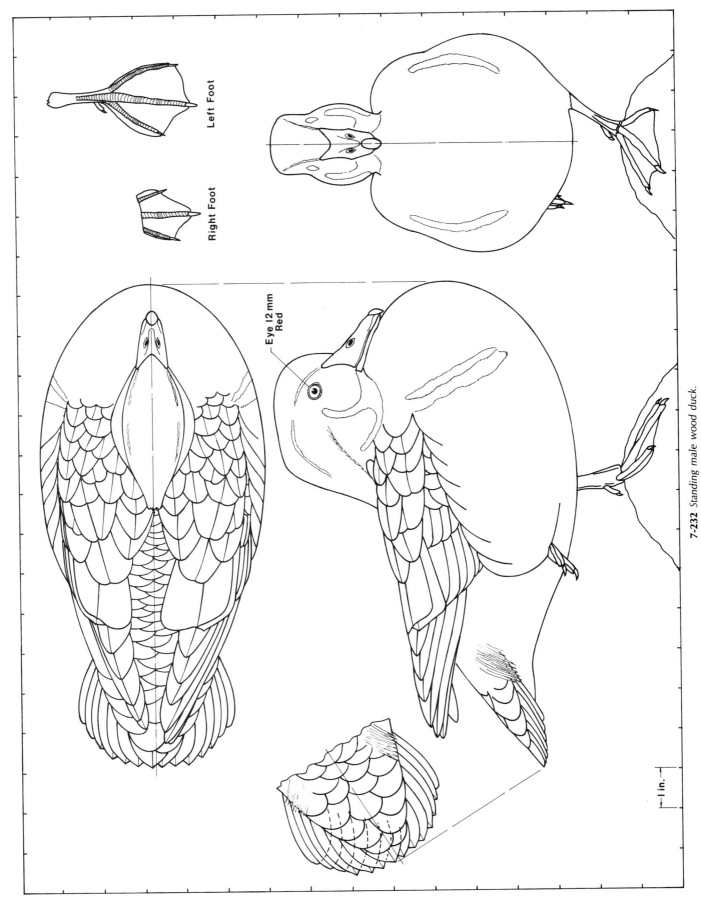

Left Foot

Right Foot

Eye 12 mm
Red

1 in.

7-232 *Standing male wood duck.*

real bird. In some instances, as when the scapulars or other body feathers are raised, individually inserted feathers add realism and produce results that would be extremely difficult to obtain with feathers carved from a solid block. Leg coverts on long-shinned birds such as hawks can also be effectively inserted.

STANDING CARVINGS

With the exception of added complications brought about by the necessity of constructing feet and legs, carving a standing bird is not much more difficult than carving a decoy. In the opinion of the author, a great deal more satisfaction can be realized by producing a carving of this type for many more interesting poses can be incorporated into a standing carving than with floating bird depictions.

In addition, standing carvings offer infinitely more opportunity for their artistic display. After the beginner has acquired experience carving decoys, he should move forward to carving a full-body bird.

Provisions for the location and installation of the legs must be made early in the planning stages of life-size waterfowl or other fairly large bird carvings. The legs of these carvings must of necessity be strong to withstand normal handling and, in many cases, shipping. It is often difficult (and usually not practicable) to attempt to bend these parts to accommodate corrections or changes. Therefore, it is essential that the legs and their geometry be well planned and constructed accordingly. As in the case of all carvings, the important details should be worked out in the planning stages on the drawing. The location of the legs (tarsii) and their positions should be determined before the body is cut out from the block. Before attempting a standing carving, it is strongly suggested that the beginner review the section entitled "Drawings For Standing Birds", page 171, and the skeletal structure of the legs and their movements as shown on page 138. Figure 7-184 shows one method of drilling leg holes and three different methods of constructing legs and feet are covered in the section entitled "Carving Legs and Feet", page 227.

A resting male wood duck in an interesting pose has been chosen for this standing carving project (Fig. 7-232). The one-legged stance eliminates one problem—that of making the tangs of two legs parallel (so they can be inserted into the base).

Start the project by gluing-up a block 6 inches wide, 5¾ inches high, and 13 inches long (see page 192). Transfer the profile and plan views to the block in the usual manner. Before cutting out the body, locate and drill the hole for the leg tang (Fig. 7-233). Cut the head out next and completely carve the bill and forward part of the head. Locate the head on the body block and outline its position. Now, rough carve the body and establish overall contours using a template to check cross-sectional shape. After the chest shape has been established, epoxy the head permanently in place (Fig. 7-234). Next, lay out the left tertials and the scapular feathers. Carve the tertials as

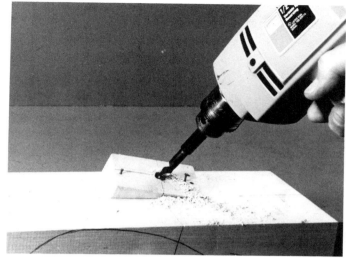

7-233 *Drill leg hole prior to cutting out body.*

7-234 *Showing rough carved bird on holding fixture.*

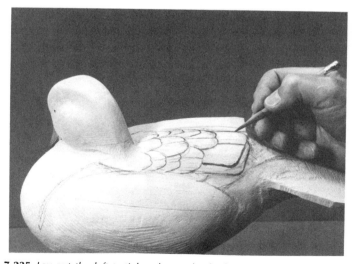

7-235 *Lay out the left tertial and scapular feathers.*

7-236 *Actual left primaries of a male wood duck.*

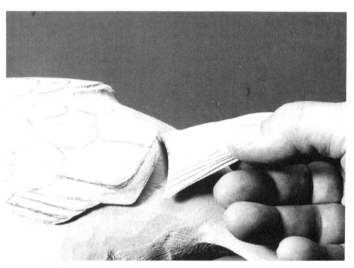

7-237 *Undercut tertials for left primary group assembly.*

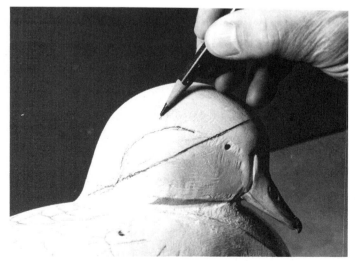

7-238 *An excessive amount of wood was inadvertently removed from the sides of the crest.*

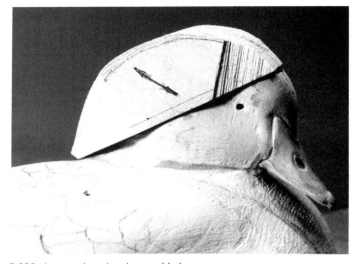

7-239 *A new piece has been added.*

7-240 *Rough-carved head after new piece was attached.*

a group and undercut them for the insertion of the folded primary group. Cut six of the outer primary feathers from thin veneer, bend them, and assemble them in the manner already described on page 207. Trim this assembly so that it will fit properly under the tertials (Fig. 7-237). Continue by finish carving the head. In this example, the author found that he had inadvertently removed too much wood from the sides of the crest (Fig. 7-238). Rather than remove the head and carve a new one, he decided to remove the incorrectly carved area and add a new piece (Figs. 7-239, 240).

Note: Every carver makes mistakes, some more than others. The author has made his share and he invariably spends valuable time trying to justify the error, or worrying about it, or hoping it will never be noticed. Instead of doing all of these things, he should say, "I have made a stupid mistake which must be corrected and I will not feel right until I do. Now, what is the easiest and best way to go about making this correction?" In

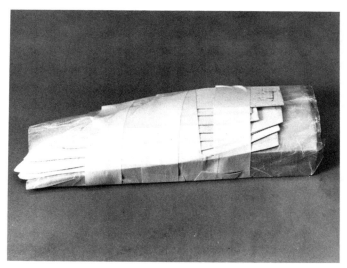

7-241 *Assemble the right primaries on a block curved in two directions.*

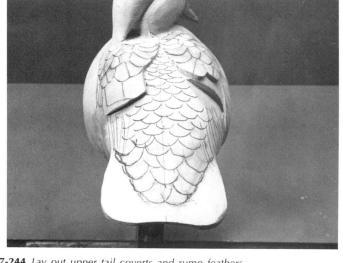

7-244 *Lay out upper tail coverts and rump feathers.*

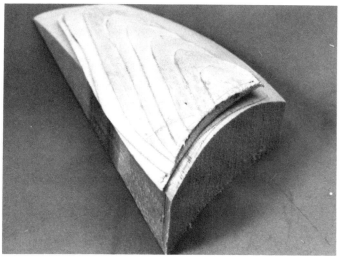

7-242 *Showing epoxied primaries on form block.*

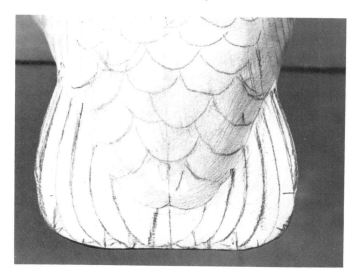

7-245 *Lay out individual tail feathers.*

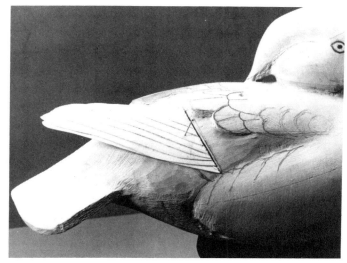

7-243 *Recess body to receive primaries.*

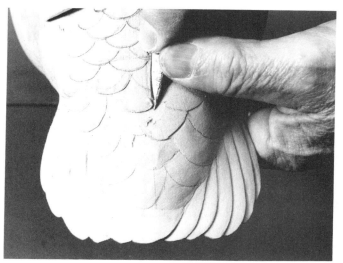

7-246 *Carve upper tail coverts and rump feathers.*

7-247 *Sand carved feathers smooth.*

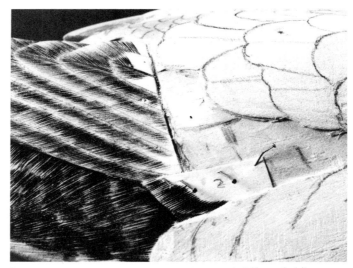

7-249 *Undercut side feathers to receive inserted secondary feathers.*

7-248 *Showing burned right primaries permanently attached.*

almost all cases, the author has found that once a positive course of action had been determined, the correction required much less time and effort than he had already wasted. In this case, he had two options: one, to remove the head and make a new one; the other, to remove the portion of the head that was incorrectly carved and attach a new piece.

Make the primaries for the right wing next. Cut out eight of the outer primaries from veneer and bend them to their proper lengthwise curvature. Place them one on top of the other in their proper locations and mark these positions with a pencil. Now, make a block that is curved in one direction to conform with the lengthwise curvature of the primary feathers and the cross-sectional curvature of the wing in the other direction and cover it with waxed paper. Apply 5-minute epoxy sparingly and assemble the primary feathers on this form. Hold them in place and apply pressure by means of wrapped masking tape (Figs. 7-241, 242). Trim this assembly and relieve the body to accommodate it (Fig. 7-243).

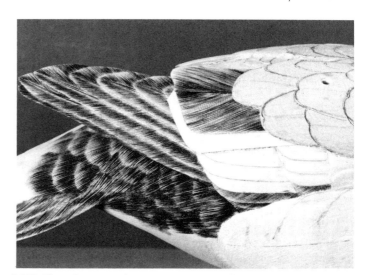

7-250 *The wing secondary, wing coverts, and tertials have now been inserted.*

7-251 *Lay out crest feathers and flow lines.*

254 ● *ADVANCED CARVING TECHNIQUES*

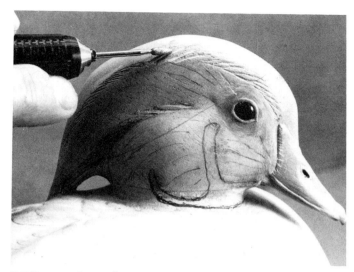

7-252 *Carve the small crest feathers with small diamond or ruby cutter used in the high speed Gesswein.*

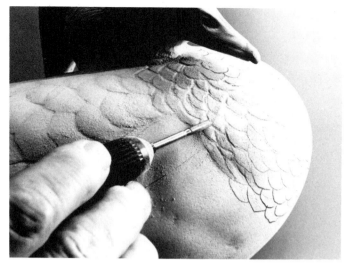

7-255 *Lightly outline the chest feathers.*

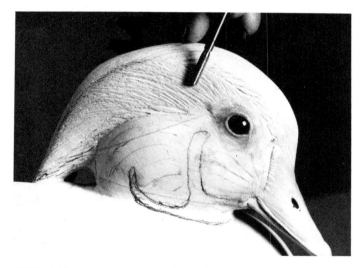

7-253 *Add texture to the crest sides with a cylindrical-shaped cutter.*

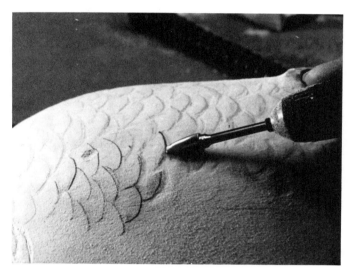

7-256 *The breast feathers can be carved with a cone-shaped tungsten burr.*

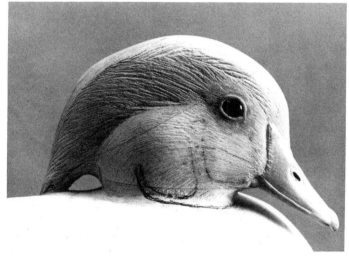

7-254 *Showing textured head.*

7-257 *Partially exposed toot. Bend web downward and compress toes together.*

Continue by sketching in the upper tail coverts and rump feathers (Fig. 7-244). Carve the upper tail coverts as a group and lay out the individual tail feathers—both upper and lower sides (Fig. 7-245). Carve the tail feathers before continuing with the covert and rump feathers (Fig. 7-246). Carve and sand these feathers until the original outlining cuts no longer exist (Fig. 7-247).

Carve the upper outline of the upper side feathers in the exposed wing area and undercut them to receive the inserted secondary and wing covert feathers (Fig. 7-249). Cut out and install these feathers in the manner previously described on page 241. After the secondary and wing covert feathers are epoxied in place, cut out and install the two large tertial feathers (Fig. 7-250).

Complete the upper side of the bird by carving the individual tertial (left side), scapulars, and back feathers.

Install the eyes next and form the eye lids (Fig. 7-251) and texture the head (Figs. 7-252, 253, 254).

Draw in the chest feathers and outline them lightly with a small, cylindrical-shaped diamond cutter (Fig. 7-255). Carve the belly feathers with a cone-shaped tungsten cutter (Fig. 7-256). The side feathers on a male wood duck are quite smooth and, except for their upper edges do not need to be carved. A few undulations can be added to soften the area prior to burning.

Establish the location of the barely exposed right foot (Fig. 7-257) and cut a rectangular-shaped hole to receive it. Attach the foot with epoxy and fill the voids around it with plastic wood. Permanently attach the left leg with epoxy and contour the body around the leg area (Fig. 7-258). Complete the carving by burning feather detail over the rest of the body and head (Fig. 7-259).

7-258 *Contour body in the leg area.*

7-259 *Wood duck carving ready to be painted.*

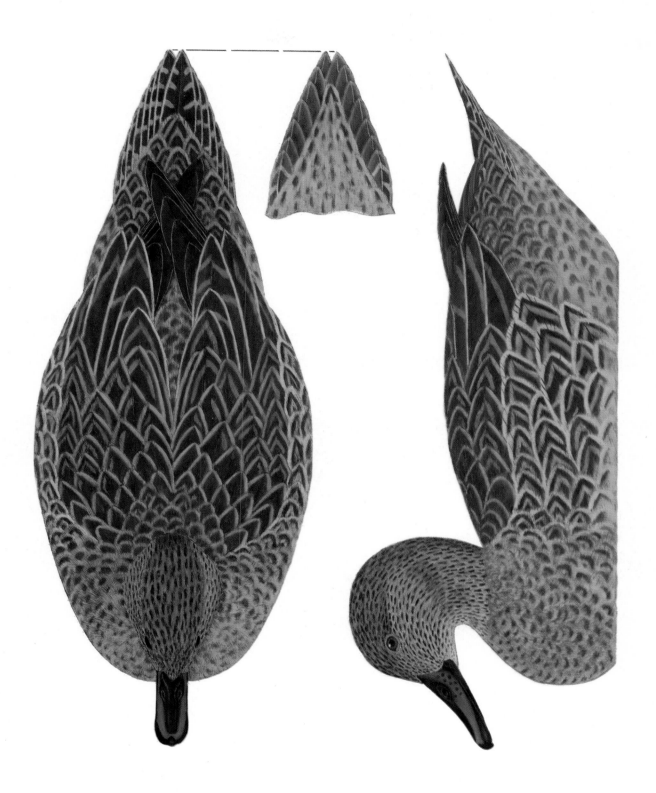

7-260 *Female Pintail*

7-261 *Female Pintails*

7-262

7-263 *Wood duck drake.*

7-264 *Wood duck drakes.*

7-265

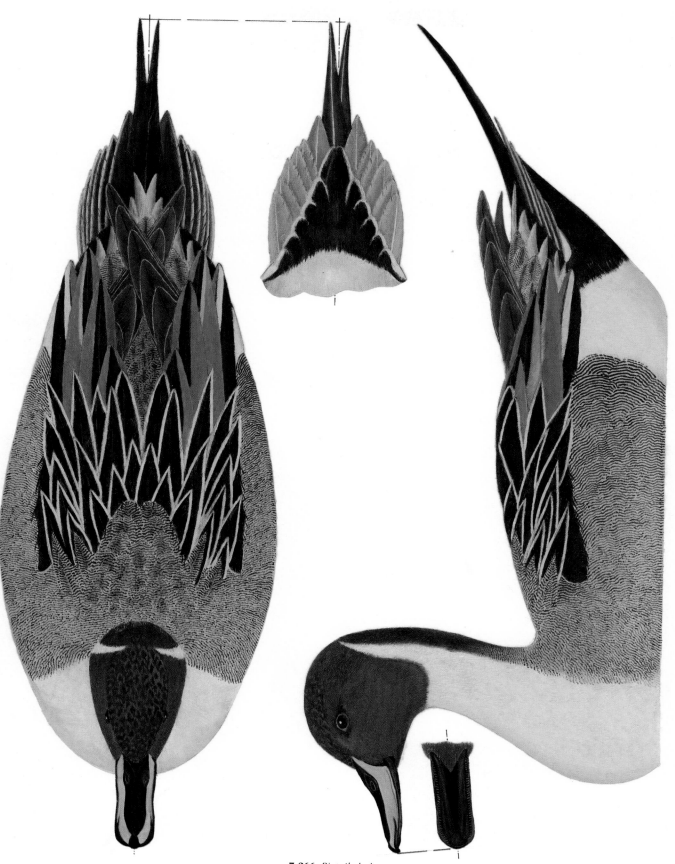

7-266 *Pintail drake.*

7-267 *Pintail drakes.*

7-268

7-269 *American widgeon drake.*

7-270 *American widgeon drakes.*
7-271

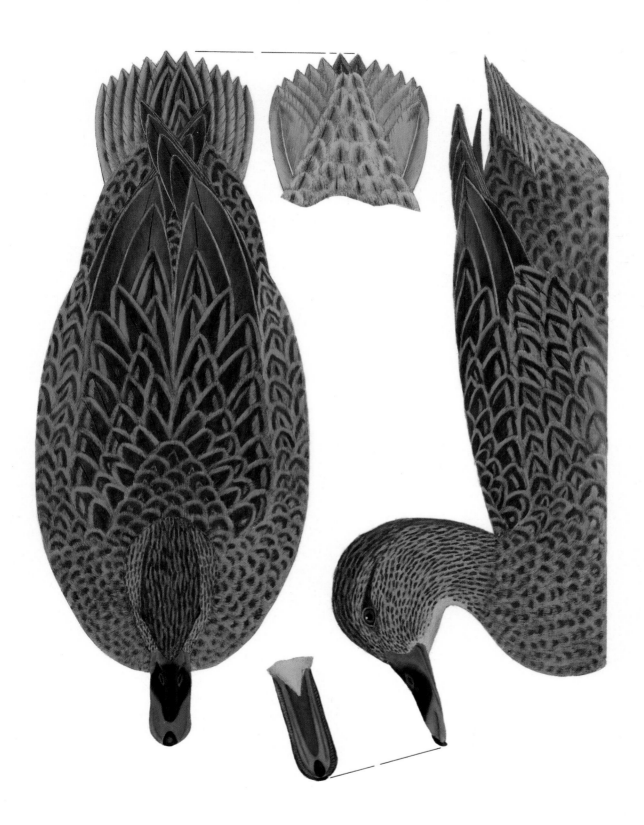

7-272 *Common mallard, female.*

7-273 *Common mallard, female.*

7-274

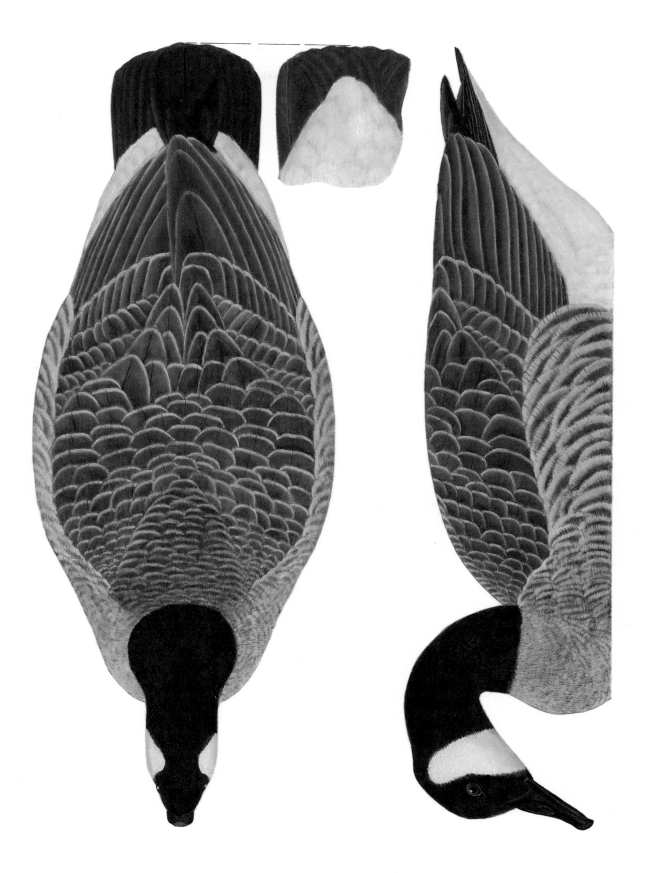

7-275 Common Canada goose.

7-276 *Common Canada goose.*

7-277 *Blue goose.*

7-278 *Black brant.*

7-279 *American brant.*

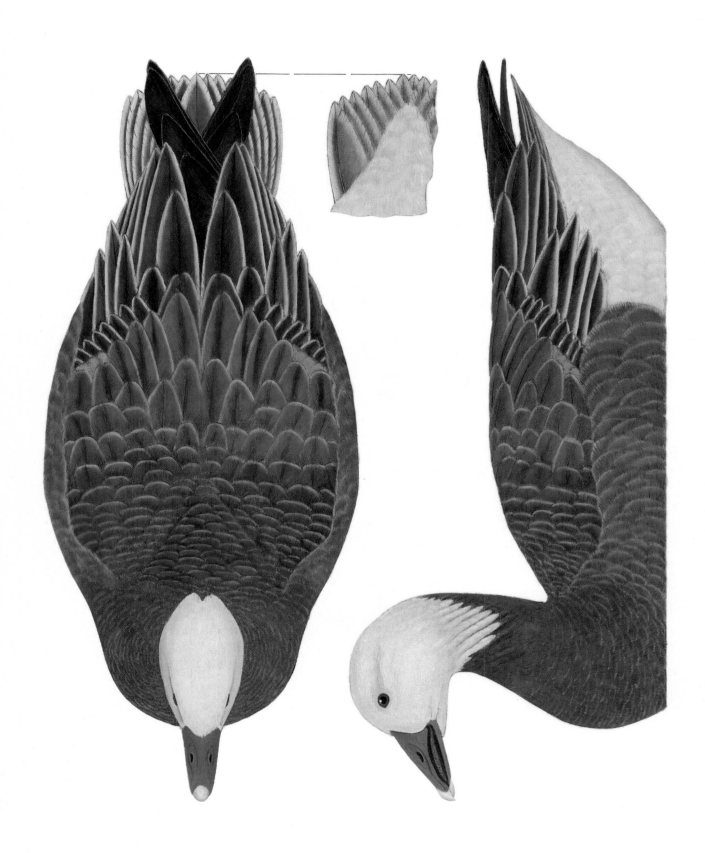

7-280 *Blue goose.*

7-281 *Mountain quail.*

7-282 *California quail (male)*

7-283 *California quail (female).*

7-284 *Hooded merganser, male.*

8

Advanced Finishing Techniques

During the past 18 years, many advances have been made in the lifelike simulation of the bird's texture and color, especially the former. Prior to this period, the carver-artist was limited to the use of brushmarks to simulate feather texture; also, many feathers were delineated with the brush only, rather than being carved or shaped individually. A few carvers of this earlier period, who were also excellent painters, improved their painting techniques until they were able to achieve quite remarkable results. Today, with the exception of actual working and service decoy carvers, only a handful of successful bird carvers rely on paint alone to create texture.

In 1969, carvers began using the heated tip of a modified soldering iron to burn-in the shaft and barb detail of feathers and gradually perfected the most effective means available at the present of reproducing feather detail. In more recent years, some carvers began adding more texture, prior to burning, with rotary tools. A few of them have become so adept with the use of these tools that they prefer to add feather detail in this manner instead of burning.

The bird's feathers are extremely thin, flexible, and soft and the barb detail is incredibly fine. Their feathers overlap each other neatly and the overall effect of the bird's plumage is generally quite smooth. All attempts by man to duplicate feathers result in exaggeration; therefore, considerable restraint must be exercised when adding texture. Power texturing, in some areas can be used effectively to help create the feeling of softness, but it also can, and often is, carried to extremes. In addition to heavy texturing, the use of barb separations, or ''splits'' as they are called, also can be used excessively. A dry, well-groomed, healthy bird normally has few feather splits. When the feathers become wet, splits are more apt to form.

The plumage of even the drabbest bird is unbelievably complex and beautiful. No one appreciates this more than the carver-artist who tries to simulate the infinitely detailed texture and coloring of these winged marvels. Chapter 2, ''Painting for Beginners'', dealt mainly with mixing and matching colors and the novice's first attempts at applying these colors to the carving. This chapter will be devoted primarily to some of the ways the carver-artist can more closely duplicate the texture, detail, and color of the bird's plumage.

There are four important goals to strive for in the finishing of a bird carving, namely:
1. The accurate delineation of the bird's prominent feather groups and individual feathers.
2. The accurate simulation (within practical limits) of the texture and detail of the individual feathers.
3. The accurate reproduction of color.
4. The creation of the illusion of softness.

Of the above goals, the fourth is the most difficult to achieve. Although the elusive quality of softness in the finished carving is somewhat easier to obtain on birds with distinctive feather markings than on birds of the one color, or with areas of the same color, it is certainly not a simple accomplishment in either case. The techniques described below will help produce a soft-appearing, realistic carving.

CARVING FEATHERS

Feather carving has already been covered in considerable detail in Chapters 1 and 7. The two most important points to remember are: one, the overall feather group

8-1 *Clumps of feathers have been outlined on the canvasback's side feather group.*

must first be made prominent; two, the individual feathers should have curvature in both directions.

Although the manner in which all feathers on a carving are depicted help create the feeling of softness, the contour feather groups contribute the most to this illusion. The side feathers, being the largest and most visible, is the most important of these groups.

It is much harder to duplicate and make the side feathers of many male ducks, which are basically one color (and without markings, except for vermiculations), to appear soft. However, it is usually possible to carve feather clusters within the feather group, rather than individual feathers (Fig. 8-1). When this is effectively accomplished, the relatively hard-appearing side feather areas on these carvings are broken up into softly undulating contours, which can be further softened by texturing and burning. The all important painting of this type of side feathers will be discussed later in this chapter under the heading "Painting Feathers with Burned In Detail".

8-4 *Chest feathers and markings on a wood duck drake.*

8-2 *Showing the fine chest feathers on a canvasback drake.*

8-5 *Flanks on waterfowl are heavily feathered.*

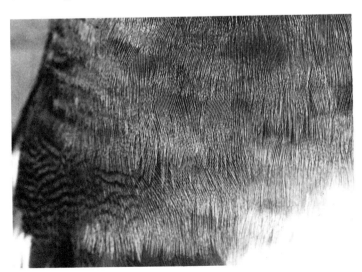

8-3 *Chest feathers on a widgeon drake.*

8-6 *The compound curvature of the scapulars and tertial feathers on a wood duck show clearly here.*

The carving of feathers clusters also can be effective on birds with distinctively marked side feathers such as on most female ducks (see Fig. 7-97). In this case, individual feathers are carved in addition to carving feather clumps.

Chest feathers on birds are generally quite smooth, bumps and undulations should be used here only in a restrained manner. Softness must be obtained mainly by the use of either very fine texturing, or burning, or both. Unlike most other feathers, the barbs in the exposed tip area do not fan out. Chest feathers are very delicate and can be discerned as individual feathers only by color variations; therefore, any outlining must be subtle. These feathers get progressively larger from the neck down to the breast feathers and usually lie in rather irregular patterns (Figs. 8-2, 3, 4).

The breast and belly of waterfowl are very heavily covered with feathers which are of a fairly uniform size. They tend to mat and bunch; softness can be obtained by the use of bumps and undulations supplemented by texturing

and burning. Random differences in angularity of barb direction also can be effective in helping to create softness.

The coloration of the breast and belly of most waterfowl is white. Because of the difficulty in achieving depth of color when applying white paint over burned surfaces, some carvers feel it is better to texture these areas only.

The flanks of waterfowl are also heavily covered with feathers, larger than those on the breast. Their markings are usually not prominent except in the case of most female ducks. Softness can be simulated with the use of surface irregularities in conjunction with individual feather carving, texturing, and burning with variations in barb directions (Fig. 8-5).

The scapular areas are not heavily or thickly feathered but constitute a most visible group. A limited amount of softness can be gotten by making the compound curvature of each feather prominent, by fine burning, and by the restrained use of small splits (Fig. 8-6).

The tertials also are very prominent feathers and softness, to a degree, can be suggested again by curvature. Some tertial feathers, especially those on geese, are rippled along their edges and, when duplicated, the ripples tend to soften them (Fig. 8-7). The heavy shafted primaries also can be softened by carving ripples on their trailing edges and by the judicious use of small splits.

The head and neck can be made to appear soft by very fine texturing and burning with short strokes and varying angles (Fig. 8-8).

Some of the ways the hard, wood surface can be made to appear soft and yielding have been discussed here. Very likely, the best ways are yet to be discovered. Modifying the wood surface can only complement the expert application of paint. As was mentioned previously, there have been some carver-artists who did a creditable job of creating the illusion of softness with paint alone.

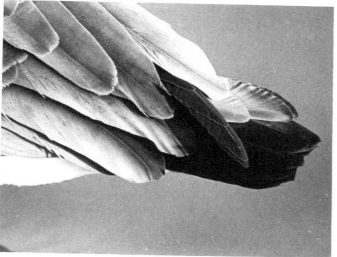

8-7 *Note the ripples on the edges of the primary and tertial feathers—Canada goose.*

8-8 *The neck feathers are more like hairs—green-winged teal hen.*

POWER CARVING AND TEXTURING

Several different types of rotary cutters are now available in many different sizes and shapes. Three types of cutters are used primarily for the fast removal of wood—Kutzsall structured carbide rasps, carbide burrs, and rotary rasps. Although small carbide burrs can be used effectively for feather carving, most carvers use ruby and diamond cutters and texturing stones for this purpose. There are four general shapes of rotary type cutters (with the exception of the rotary rasps which are available in a cylindrical shape only)—cylindrical, conical, spherical, and wheel-shaped, plus variations of these forms. (See Appendix for availability). The larger diameter cutters for fast wood removal are available in 1/4-inch diameter shanks while the smaller carbide burrs, ruby and diamond cutters, and texturing stones are available in both 1/8- and 3/32-inch diameter shanks. To be effectively used, the larger fast wood removal cutters should be powered with the die-type grinder, although many carvers use them in their Foredoms. The smaller cutters and texturing stones are also used in the Foredom and the higher speed Dremel flexible shaft machines. Previously covered in Chapter 7, the Gesswein Power Carver type of grinder eliminates the restrictions of a flexible shaft and supplies a respectable amount of rotary power up to speeds of 50,000 rpm. Although much smoother and faster cuts can be made by running most cutters at high rotational speeds, caution should be exercised, especially on the larger diameter tools, as some of them may not be capable of withstanding the centrifugal forces involved or may not be properly balanced. Their limitations should be ascertained from the manufacturer before attempting high speed use. Also, when first using any cutter, check its balance by starting with low rotational speeds and then increase rpms gradually.

Power carving and texturing involves so many different types of cutters and techniques that further discussions on the subject will be brief and generalized. Most carvers have their own ideas and have developed their own ways of getting the job done to their satisfaction. Generally speaking, cone-shaped cutters are used for carving and cylindrical and wheel-shaped cutters are used for grooving (texturing) and adding splits. The author is not a great proponent of power carving although he does some roughing and the carving of certain relatively undefined feathers in this manner. For most roughing-out operations and the carving of well defined feathers, he feels that a better and a faster job can be done usually by means of hand tools, with probably no more effort, and with considerably less mess and cleaner air. However, for those carvers who hand hold their carvings during all wood removal operations, rotational power tools have their advantages.

BURNING IN FEATHER DETAIL

Although very time consuming and tedious, burning is the most effective way to add texture, feather detail, and to help create the feeling of softness. Cloth appears to be "soft", not only because of its folds and wrinkles, but mainly due to the fact light is reflected at many different angles from individual, roughly surfaced threads which are in turn woven into detailed patterns causing further breaking up of the reflected light. Similarily, when barb detail is burned into the carved feather, the many surfaces made by the burning tool tip reflect light at different angles tending to soften the "hard" appearance of the wood surface.

The equipment used for burning feather detail has improved tremendously since carvers first attempted this technique in 1969. The tips of the old soldering-type burning pens required constant sharpening and cleaning and the carver's fingers usually received more heat than the simulated feather. One of the modern woodburning tools, the exceptionally well designed and constructed Detail Master "Excalibre" Model, is shown in Figure 8-9. This unit features 130 watts of controllable heat, two selectable outlets, and over 20 differently shaped and read-

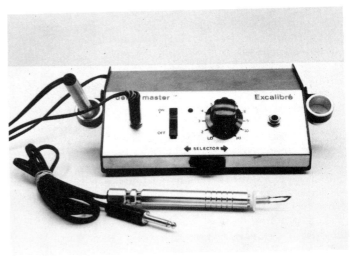

8-9 A modern woodburning tool—The Detail Master "Excalibre" model.

ily interchangeable handpieces (see Appendix for availability).

The metal tip of the old soldering-type burning pen was heated by an element inside it. The tip of the modern burning tool handpiece, such as the Detail Master's, is made from a special hard alloy bent and/or welded to the desired shape, ground flat, and sharpened. It is heated within a few seconds by its own resistance to the voltage controlled electric current that passes through it. The tip can be used for long periods before requiring light honing, or stropping, to bring back its sharp knife-like edge (Fig. 8-10). The aluminum handpiece stays remarkably cool even when using higher tip temperatures. Unlike the old burning tools, there is little build up on the tip. Three models of the Detail Master are available, the Excalibre being the top of the line.

8-10 The sharp edge of the burning tip can be maintained by an occasional stropping.

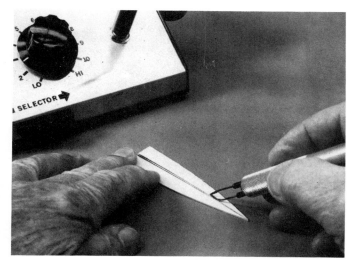

8-11 *Duplicate the feather shaft by burning two converging lines.*

8-12 *Practicing burning feather detail.*

The wood burning handpiece is held like a pencil, and the feather shaft is first burned as two converging lines (Fig. 8-11) and the barbs, which radiate from the shaft, are burned with parallel strokes. If the barbs are short, they can be burned by finger movement only. On longer barbs, arms movement is required. Fine, accurate burning requires good eyesight, a steady hand, and practice. The barbs of most feathers are not straight and often have a gentle "S"-shaped curvature. The beginner should acquire some feathers and study the barb lines first hand. He then should draw the outline of some feathers on a piece of wood and practice until a relaxed, rhythmic movement is developed which will produce burned lines uniformly and closely spaced (Fig. 8-12).

How finely should one attempt to burn? This is a question that often is asked. First, the individual has physical limitations in regard to eyesight, steadiness, and deftness.

Second, he also has practical limitations such as available time and patience—extremely fine wood burning is

very time consuming and it certainly requires a great deal of patience. While the quality and fineness of burning barb lines can be increased with practice, the physical and practical limits mentioned are the deciding factors on just how fine and accurate a particular person can and will burn.

Although there is a least one carver who claims he can burn over 200 lines per inch, the author finds that about 60 to 70 lines per inch is about the best he can do and he normally burns fewer lines per inch than that. To duplicate the barbs on a feather realistically, is it necessary to burn upwards to 200 lines per inch? Barb counts were made on the primary feathers of several birds. The results are listed below.

	Barbs per inch (Approx.)		Barbs per inch (Approx.)
Mallard	80	Canada goose	110
Cinnamon Teal	110	California quail	110
Pintail	90	Western Tanager	90
Canvasback	105	Prairie chicken	90
Greater Scaup	110	Turkey	40

From the above and from checking a few other feathers (side, tertials, and secondaries) which had a slightly higher count in some cases, it would appear that the barb count on most feathers would not exceed 100 per inch by a substantial amount. Also, except in the case of the turkey, it appears that the size of the bird does not have any direct bearing on the barb count.

On larger, more prominent feathers such as the primaries, tertials, some scapulars, and tail, greater realism is attained by raising their shafts, in addition to burning their outlines. This can be accomplished in two different ways. The easiest way is to lay the tip of the burning tool flat and against the side of the burned shaft and move it away in a wiping motion (Fig. 8-13). The other way is to first burn in the shaft outline and then carefully remove wood adjacent to the shaft with a knife or a chisel (Fig. 8-14). In this case, wood removal must be blended until all tool marks are removed and the feather vanes should be sanded smooth. In addition to adding realism, raised shafts are much easier to paint.

When burning detail on carved feathers, start from the rear of the group and work forward. The tip of the burning tool being hotter at the start of the stroke will burn somewhat deeper than at the finish of the stroke, giving the feather a soft, lacy effect. On feathers such as those on the chest, head, and neck that are not carved, or outlined with a power texturing tool, the reverse procedure is used, i. e., start from the front of the group and work towards the rear (after the outline of each feather is drawn with a pencil). The heavier burning at the start of the stroke will tend to make the edge of the preceding feather more noticeable (Fig. 8-15).

The burning tool tip can be used effectively to outline some uncarved feathers like those mentioned above. This is accomplished by laying a small skew-type burning tool tip almost flat against the surface and dragging it around the drawn outline of the feather (Fig. 8-16). The feather

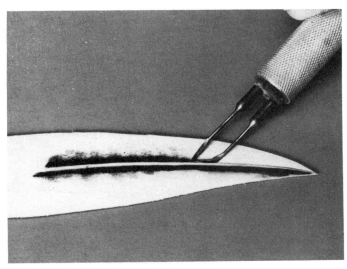

8-13 *Raising the shaft with the burning tip.*

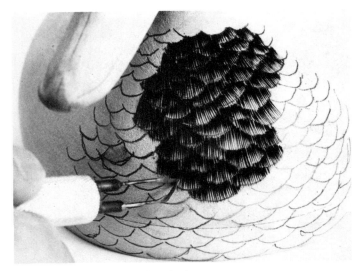

8-15 *Burning un-outlined chest feathers.*

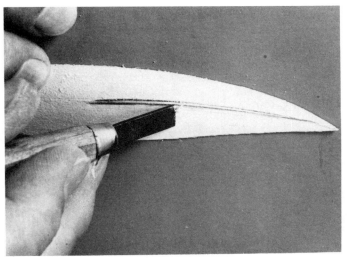

8-14 *Raising the shaft by removing wood with a chisel.*

8-16 *These chest feathers have been outlined lightly with the burning tip.*

edges can be made more prominent by burning the feather group from front to rear. If it is desired to make their edges less pronounced, the feather group can be burned from rear to front.

When burning detail on a carving, start with the lower tail surface and continue with the lower tail coverts on forward into the belly area (Fig. 8-17). Then, burn the upper tail surface, upper tail coverts, rump, and flanks. The primaries and tertials are burned next, followed by the scapulars and the back area (Fig. 8-18). Burn the side feathers next on up to the chest (Fig. 8-19). If the individual chest feathers have not been carved, or delineated in some other manner, establish feather flow lines and lay out each feather. Starting from the neck, burn downwards and rearwards (Fig. 8-15). All of the burning thus far can be accomplished with the standard size skew-type tip such as Detail Master #1C. For burning around the neck-body intersection (and some parts of the chin and throat), it will be necessary to use a rounded tip like Detail Mas-

ter #2C, or 2D (Fig. 8-20).

Continue by establishing feather flow lines on the head and neck and outline each feather (Figs. 8-21, 22, 23, 24). Then, using a small skew-type tip (Detail Master #1B), start burning from the frontal parts of the head and proceed rearwards (Fig. 8-25). Texture the neck, where the feathers are more like hairs, by burning short strokes at varying angles to the flow lines (Fig. 8-8). If desired, additional texture can be added in this area by means of a diamond or ruby cutter (Fig. 8-26).

As was previously mentioned, many carvers utilize splits in the feather vanes in an attempt to add realism and to create the feeling of softness. There is more involved in the accurate duplication of a feather vane split than just removing a V-shaped piece of wood. Three different types of vane splits are shown in Fig. 8-27. Figure 8-28 shows the mechanics entailed in the proper making of a split.

The construction of an actual feather was covered in

8-17 *The author burns the lower side first.*

8-18 *Showing the burned primaries, tertials, and scapulars on the wood duck.*

8-19 *Burned side feathers on the pintail hen decoy.*

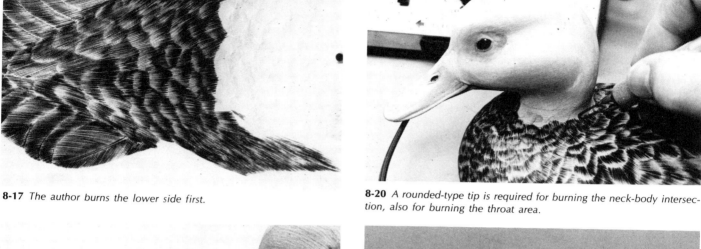

8-20 *A rounded-type tip is required for burning the neck-body intersection, also for burning the throat area.*

8-21 *Sketch the feather flow lines on the head and neck.*

8-22 *Outline the crown feathers.*

Chapter 3, page 132. The barbules and barbicels hold the individual barbs together in a manner somewhat similar to the holding action of "Velcro" tape. Although the barbules and barbicels permit some expansion (or contraction) of the space between the barbs, the barbs remain parallel to each other. When the connection between two barbs is broken, the vane opens and the section nearest the quill rotates out and away from the part closest to the feather tip. When this occurs, the shape of the feather is altered (the amount of change depends on the width of the split). On individually made, or carved, feathers, this change in the basic feather shape must be anticipated prior to making the split.

The vane is weakened considerably when splits are cut in individual feathers made from one piece of wood. If splits are to be used on this type of feather, it should be constructed in the manner covered in Figs. 7-188, 189, 190. Very little strength is sacrificed when the grain of the vane runs parallel to the split.

8-25 *Use the small skew-type tip for burning the small head feathers.*

8-23 *Burn the crown feather from front to rear.*

8-26 *Texture can be added to the neck area with a cylindrical diamond cutter.*

8-24 *Outline the individual cheek feathers.*

8-27 *Showing three different types of feather splits.*

Figure 8-29 shows the small triangular piece being removed from the vane with a small, pointed Exacto knife. This also can be accomplished with the burning tip if the control is set to a higher temperature. The wood can be removed from carved feathers by means of an Exacto knife. Cuts are made on both sides of the split, and with the knife held almost parallel to the surface of the feather, the sliver is carefully removed from one side of the split. The knife is then reversed and the remaining piece is cut from the other side (Fig. 8-31).

When the burning is completed, remove all loose products of combustion from the carving by lightly brushing the surface with a soft, metal brush (Fig. 8-32). Further clean the carving with compressed air, if available.

8-30 *The splits have been removed from this feather.*

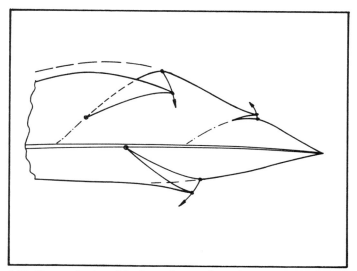

8-28 *The mechanics of feather splits are shown here.*

8-31 *Removing wood from splits in side feathers.*

8-29 *Carefully remove the "split" with an Exacto knife.*

8-32 *Burned particles can be removed by brushing.*

PAINTING FEATHERS WITH BURNED-IN DETAIL

The accurate reproduction of the bird's plumage color-wise is of prime importance. Regardless of how well the bird is carved, textured, and burned, if the paint does not portray the color of the bird's plumage truly and if it is ineptly applied, the carving will be forever relegated to the novice class. Stated another way, good painting can improve a poor carving to a degree, but not vice versa.

The texturing and burning of feather detail have simplified the application of the paint. The carver-artist can now concentrate on applying and blending colors without being concerned greatly with the duplication of feather detail by the use of brush strokes. Prior to the advent of texturing, a considerable amount of paint had to be used so that the lines made by the brush bristles would simulate visibly the feather barb lines. When the carving is textured and/or burned, a minimum amount of paint is used—just enough to accurately establish the desired color without filling the burned grooves.

Although painting on a textured and burned surface has made the painting procedure easier, the faithful duplication of the bird's coloring is not a simple process by any means as there are very subtle and hard-to-duplicate nuances involved. In addition, the carver-artist at times, in order to create the illusion of softness, must resort to shading (changes in color values) to establish depth. In some cases, the bird's coloring is complicated further by the existence of structural colors (iridescence) that are impossible to duplicate accurately with pigmented colors. Painting a bird, whether on a carving or on a flat surface, is an unending learning process—the carver-artist should never be satisfied with his work as there will always be room for improvement.

While the author feels that oil paints have a number of advantages over acrylics, the two most important ones are: one, oils provide plenty of time for color blending; two, with oils the final color can be mixed, matched, and applied immediately without the use of intermediate coats. For the beginner, especially, it is much more straightforward to mix and apply the final coat in one operation than to gradually work up to this color with a number of mixtures. When two or more colors are used on the same feather, the determination and application of the intermediate wash coats is even more confusing. In the author's opinion, it is also much easier to obtain the slight variations and subtleties in color and changes in value mentioned above when using oils as compared to using acrylics. Some easy ways by which some of the popular objections to the use of oil paints can be overcome were covered in Chapter 2. Again, it is recommended that the aspiring carver-artist use oil paints until at least he has acquired some proficiency in the handling of colors.

As has been stated a number of times in this book, the only way painting, or carving, can be learned is by doing. Reading books, talking to others, attending classes and seminars, and viewing video tapes obviously can assist and speed up the process of learning but these instructional sources cannot begin to replace one's own initiative and hard work. When working with one's hands, most of the learning must be acquired through their actual use.

PAINTING THE FEMALE PINTAIL DECORATIVE DECOY

Prior to painting the actual carving, it is suggested that the progressing bird carver first practice painting on a burned surface. The following two exercises also will give him some practice burning in feather detail.

Start by sketching three of the female pintail's tertial feathers on a flat, smooth piece of wood. Outline the feathers with the tip of the burning tool and burn shaft and barb detail in the manner already described (Fig. 8-33). Clean the burned surface with a soft, metal brush (a brush sold for cleaning suede leather can be used).

Mix a small amount of raw umber into white (W,•RU), add medium and outline each feather using a size 2 round sable brush (Fig. 8-34). Next, mix W,RS,•RU,•BS (see page 85 for abbreviations and explanation of the color formula) and paint the markings on these feathers (Fig. 8-35).

Note: The size, shape, and location of these markings vary from bird to bird. In fact, some female pintails have no markings on their tertial feathers (See Fig. 7-261, page 258).

Work this paint into the burned lines smoothly with a size 1 or 2 flat sable brush (Fig. 8-36). Continue by painting the rest of the feather with BU,••RS,••W (Fig. 8-37). Brush out this paint smoothly, just up to the lighter colored markings and the feather edgings (Fig. 8-38). Now, using a dry size 2 flat sable brush, blend the light and the dark paints by *very* light stippling around the periphery of

8-33 *Outline the pintail hen's tertials on a flat piece of wood.*

the markings. Keeping the brush dry and clean, lightly and carefully drag the light colored paint just barely into the dark paint (Fig. 8-39) and reverse the process. If necessary, touch-up either of these paints until the two colors are distinctly separated but the line of demarcation is subtle with just a hint of blending between the two colors. If one color or the other gets muddied in the process, either wipe the area clean and start again or wait until the paint is dry and touch-up the areas.

Proceed by blending the light colored edges of the feathers into the dark paint and vice versa. The transition between the two colors is slightly more pronounced in these areas. The whitish edge will probably get muddied during this blending. Lightly repaint the extreme feather edge to restore the original color being careful to blend this paint lightly into the already blended area (Fig. 8-40). Further blending can be accomplished by going over each feather *very, very* lightly with a soft fan blender brush.

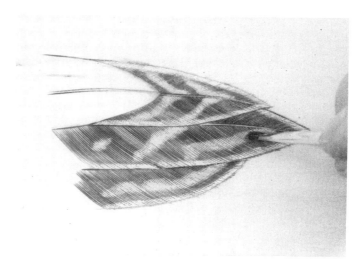

8-36 *Work the paint smoothly into the burned grooves.*

8-34 *Outline the feathers with the light-colored paint.*

8-37 *Add the dark paint over the rest of the feather.*

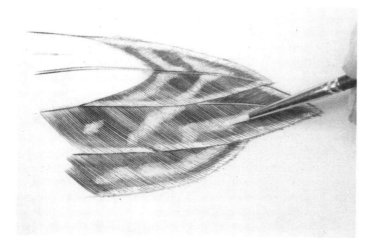

8-35 *Paint the feather markings next.*

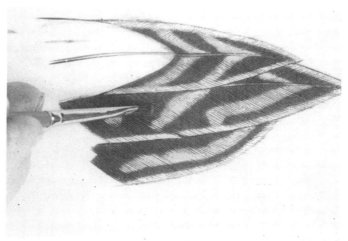

8-38 *Smooth out the dark paint.*

Tertial feathers often are darker in the shaft areas. Additional depth and softness can be gotten by adding more BU on either side of the shafts and by blending this paint smoothly into the existing dark paint only. Inspect these feathers when the paint is dry and touch-up or re-define any area whose color has been improperly modified. The painting of these feathers is now complete except for the shafts.

The shafts of feathers are hard and shiny; therefore, a painting medium which will produce a high gloss should be used. The author uses a 50-50 mixture of Grumbacher's Copal Painting Medium and turpentine for almost all of his painting. Copal medium is a synthetic hard resin oil which dries to a fairly high gloss when undiluted. It is used straight from the bottle as a medium by the author for painting feather shafts, claws, and the nails on the upper mandibles.

The shafts of the female pintail's tertials are a glossy black. Mix B,•BU and add undiluted copal medium until the mixture is fairly thin and manageable. Apply this to the shaft with a size 000 round sable brush, one that points well (Fig. 8-41). If any of this black paint inadvertently gets on the feather paint, carefully remove the unwanted paint with a size 1 or 2 flat sable brush moistened with turpentine (Fig. 8-42). Wipe the brush clean after each stroke. Even though the shaft has been painted in a rather sloppy manner, which is easy to do, the excess paint can be removed easily, leaving a sharply painted shaft. Additional realism can be gotten by adding a very fine highlight (W,•RU plus copal medium) to the shaft and carefully blending it into the black paint (Fig. 8-43). If the shaft dries on the dull side, re-paint the shaft with undiluted copal painting medium.

The painting of the female's side feathers can provide additional burning and painting practice. In a manner similar to the previous painting exercise, sketch and burn a single side feather. Mix W,•RU,•RS and medium. Using this mixture further thinned with turpentine and a size 1 or 2 round sable brush, lightly sketch or delineate the

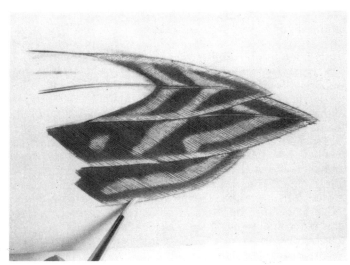

8-40 *After the paint has been blended, carefully touch up the feather edges.*

8-41 *When the feather has dried, paint the shaft.*

8-39 *Carefully blend the edges.*

8-42 *Excess paint from the shaft can be removed with a flat brush moistened with turpentine.*

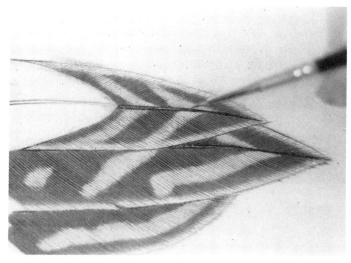

8-43 *If desired, the shaft can be highlighted.*

8-44 *Sketch the feather markings with a brush.*

feather markings. When this has been satisfactorily accomplished, paint the feather edges and markings with the above mixture (Fig. 8-44). Brush-in and smooth this paint with a flat sable brush. Now, mix BU,•• + RS,•• + W and paint the rest of the feather. The color value of the dark area of these side feathers decreases going forward; therefore, a small amount of BU should be added to the dark rear markings and a small amount of white to the forward brown markings and blend until the value of the brown areas has gradually decreased toward the front of the feather (Fig. 8-45).

Note: If desired, the brown paint can be added and modified prior to painting the light colored feather markings.

Now, smoothly blend the edges of the two different colors as was done on the tertials (Fig. 8-46). Also as on the tertials, the area of color transition between the brown and the light colored rear edgings is more pronounced. Carefully blend colors in this area (Fig. 8-47) and retouch the feather edgings, if necessary. Again, further blending can be accomplished using extremely light strokes with a soft fan blender.

The vanes of side feathers often have splits. If splits are used on the actual carving, paint them using the color of the portion of the feather which theoretically lies directly beneath. It may be necessary to paint one part of split with the light color and other part with the dark color.

The exposed portion of the side feather shafts are very fine and is darker than the lowest value on the feather. If desired, this fine shaft can be carefully painted after the feather is dry using BU plus undiluted copal medium as was described for the tertial feather.

The carver-artist should now proceed with the painting of the actual decoy. See full color illustration, Fig. 7-260, page 257 for general coloring and feather detail. The finished carving is shown in color on page 2. The live pintail hen is shown in color in Figs. 7-261, 262.

8-45 *Reducing the value of the dark area.*

8-46 *Carefully blend the edges of the different colored paints.*

8-47 *Blend the paint near the feather's edge.*

The author uses about the same sequence in painting the different areas on a carving as he did when burning them. The various steps involved in painting a tertial feather and a side feather have already been covered. These same steps are followed in a general manner when painting the other feathers on the carving, with the exception of the head and neck.

When painting the head and neck, the author first applies the basic color, W,••RS,•BU, to the cheeks and sides of the neck. The throat and chin are painted somewhat lighter, W,•RS,•-RU. The crown and forehead are painted with W,RS,•BU. He then allows this paint to dry.

When the paint is dry, the fine markings (BU,RS) are then painted on the cheeks and neck, following the same flow lines that were used when burning feather detail. Using a size 000 round sable brush, he then carefully adds paint of the same basic color between the fine markings (Fig. 8-52). If, after the fine marks were added, the area did not appear to be the correct value, the basic color would be altered accordingly. The dark markings and the basic color are then blended, ever so lightly with a soft fan blender (Fig. 8-53).

The crown is painted in a similar manner. The dark centers of the feathers are first painted and the lighter basic color is then applied for the second time and the area is lightly blended.

PAINT MIXING INSTRUCTIONS

Head and Neck
Upper mandible: W,••B,•TB. Darker (add black) along culmen.
Lower mandible: B,•BU,•W.
Crown, forehead, and back of neck: BU,••RS. Small feathers edged with W,RS,•BU.
Cheeks and sides of neck: W,••RS,•BU; streaked with BU,RS.
Chin and throat: W,•RS,•RU; finely streaked with BU,RS.

Body
Back and scapulars: BU,••RS. V-shaped markings: W,RS, •RU,•BS. Feathers edged with W,•RS,•RU.
Rump: BU,••RS. V-shaped markings: W,•RS. Feathers edged with W,•RU.
Sides: BU,••RS,••W. V-shaped markings: W,•RS,•RU. Feathers broadly edged with W,•RS,•RU.
Chest: BU,••RS,•W. V-shaped markings: W,•RS,•RU. Feathers broadly edged W,•RU. Feathers become smaller with edgings about the same width, giving an overall lighter effect.
Flanks: BU,W,RS. Feathers broadly edged with W,•RU.
Upper tail coverts: BU,••RS,•W. V-shaped markings: W,RS,•RU,•BS. Feathers edged with W,•RU.
Lower Tail Coverts: BU,RS,W; edged with W,•RU.

Tail
Upper side: BU,RS,••W; barred with W,RS,•RU,•BS; lightly edged with W,•RU.
Lower Side: W,••RU; edged and barred with W,RS,•RU.

Wing
Primaries: BU,RU,••W; faintly edged with W,•RU.
Secondaries (speculum): BS,BU,Y,W: double edged with W,•RU and B,•BU.
Greater coverts: BU,••RS,••W; edged on rear with RS,•W.
Tertials: BU,••RS,••W; barred with W,RS,•RU,•BS; edged with W,•RU.

PAINTING SOLID COLORED SIDE AND CHEST FEATHERS

As was mentioned earlier, and also in Chapter 2, it is difficult to make the side feathers of most male ducks, which are basically one color, to appear soft. The carving of feather clusters, or clumps, and individual feathers helped break up these hard appearing surfaces into soft

8-48 *Paint the underside first.*

8-49 *Painting has progressed to the tertials and scapulars.*

8-50 *The edging and marking have been applied to the scapulars.*

8-51 *Showing the painted side feathers prior to blending.*

8-52 *Repaint the light-colored areas between the fine markings.*

8-53 *Blend very lightly with a fan blender.*

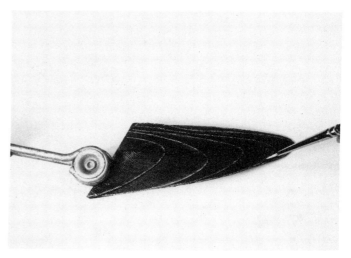

8-54 *After the paint has dried, add the fine edging to the primary group feathers.*

8-55 *The finished pintail hen decoy.*

undulations that were further softened by texturing and burning. Although these carving and texturing techniques helped establish the illusion of softness, the skillful use of paint can contribute even more to the desired overall effect.

There is normally a change of value in the coloring of these feathers. The value on light-colored feathers usually increases moving rearward along the length of the individual feather. On dark-colored feathers, the reverse is often true. When the color value is changed on these feathers, highlights and shadows result and the feeling of softness is accentuated.

The side feathers on the ringed-neck duck working decoy, which were neither carved nor textured, were painted using the change-of-value technique. See page 112.

PAINTING THE STANDING WOOD DUCK DRAKE

Before attempting to paint the standing wood duck drake, the carver-artist should read the section in this chapter entitled ''Duplicating Iridescence'', as many of the drake wood duck's colors on his upper side and head are iridescent. Depending on the angle of reflected light,

8-56 *The finished wood duck drake.*

these upper parts can appear to be black, or they can burst into a rainbow of colors. Some of these colors can be approximated by using the paint mixing formulas given on page 120. Painting the wood duck drake can be a real challenge to the budding artist and, if his attempts at duplicating iridescence are reasonably successful, also can be also most satisfying.

Refer to the full color illustration, Figure 7-263, page 259, for general colors and feather details. See Figures 2-10, page 96 and 2-20, page 99 for painting the wood duck's head. Actual photographs in color are shown in Figures 1-230, 231, page 80 and Figures 7-264, 265, page 260. The finished carving is shown in color on page 3. Paint mixing instructions, except for the breast, belly, wing coverts, and feet are included on page 120.

Breast; W,•RU.
Belly: W,•RU.

Feet
Tarsi and toes: YO,•RU. Toe joints are somewhat darker—
    add more RU.
Webs: BU, ••Y1.
Claws: BU,RS,••W.

Wing
Greater coverts: W,B,••AC,•TB. Edged with B,•BU.
Middle coverts: BU,W,••RS. Rear rows glossed with
    W,B,••AC,•TB.

ADDING VERMICULATIONS

Many male ducks and, to a lesser degree, female canvasbacks and scaups have fine, irregular, wavy lines called vermiculations on at least some of their feathers. Vermiculations vary from the bold markings on the back of scaups (Fig. 1-176, page 62) to the very fine markings on the male canvasback, mallard, and ring-necked ducks. These feather markings, probably incorrectly classified as texture, are a very important plumage detail. For realism, the vermiculations on these ducks must somehow be duplicated.

Vermiculations are formed by elongated dark markings on each barb of the feather. On bolder vermiculations, the lengths of the individual markings on the barbs are rather consistent; on fine vermiculations, the barb markings are more likely to vary in length; on very fine vermiculations, the markings appear to be more like a series of irregular dots. The individual bold vermiculation is often continuous across the feather vane while individual fine vermiculations usually are short in length and start and stop in a very irregular pattern.

The vermiculations often become progressively finer towards the tip of the feather; however, on the rearmost side feathers of such species as the male pintail, greenwinged teal, wood duck, and hooded merganser, the vermiculations actually become heavier moving rearward.

When the overlapping feathers on a bird are arranged in normal manner, the vermiculations on the upper feathers align quite closely with the vermiculations on the feathers lying under them and also with adjacent feathers (Fig. 8-57). However, feathers, being very thin, are also transparent to a degree (especially the lighter colored ones) and sometimes the vermiculation pattern of an underlying feather can be discerned. This usually happens when the upper feather has been moved from its normal location (Fig. 8-58).

In the past, many different techniques have been employed to copy these difficult feather markings with varying degrees of success. While some of these methods produced results adequate for decoys, none of them simulated actual vermiculations realistically. The only way vermiculations can be depicted accurately is to do them one at a time—an operation not only very time consuming but also extremely tedious. One way this can be accomplished is to paint each of these lines with a small, pointed brush. When oil paint is used, the small brush

8-57 *Vermiculation detail on a green-winged teal drake.*

8-58 *The vermiculation pattern on several underlying feathers can be seen in this photograph—green-winged teal drake.*

must be loaded many, many times and the paint must be applied smoothly.

Instead of paint, India ink can be used for vermiculations. Brownish-gray, gray, brownish-black, and black covers the colors of vermiculations on most ducks. These colors can be duplicated by mixing white and/or brown inks with black ink; they also can be duplicated with inks supplied in photo retouch kits. Ink has two advantages over oil paint when used for vermiculations: one, it goes on smoothly and requires no brushing to eliminate ridges; two, it flows well from the brush which permits more painting between brush loadings (also, larger, watercolor type brushes that point well can be used to an advantage).

Ink not only can be brushed on, it can be also applied with a Rapidograph-type pen. These pens come with different tip sizes and are available at most art and drafting supply stores. When ink is applied with a brush, the width of the vermiculation can be varied easier than with a pen—an important feature when the vermiculations on the feather to be duplicated become finer toward the tip. When adding heavy vermiculation with varying widths, such as those on the backs of scaups, the brush works much better than the pen.

The painted oil surface sometimes does not receive ink well. If this occurs, rub the surface with a soft eraser (Eberhard Faber's Pink Pearl works well). The mild abrasive action of the eraser modifies the painted surface so that ink will adhere readily.

Ink has one disadvantage—it is not completely waterproof. Therefore, inked vermiculations should be covered with a protective coating. Krylon Satin Finish Varnish #7002 can be used with good results. This varnish is supplied in spray cans and dries quickly with only a slight sheen.

Ink also works well when adding vermiculations on carvings painted with acrylics. Ink has much better covering power than acrylic paint and the final vermiculations can be applied in one operation.

The beginner should practice making these very detailed feather markings with a pen and with a brush. He can then decide for himself which method produces the better results.

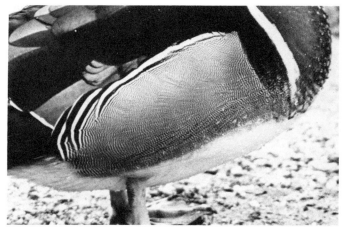

8-60 *Side feather group on a wood duck drake.*

8-61 *Vermiculations on a male hooded merganser.*

8-59 *Vermiculations on a pintail drake.*

8-62 *Showing the very fine vermiculations on a mallard drake.*

8-63 *Practicing the vermiculations of a wood duck drake with a pen.*

8-64 *Practicing adding vermiculations with a brush.*

DUPLICATING IRIDESCENCE

Of all the problems involved in painting a carving, duplicating iridescence is the most difficult and frustrating. The coloring of bird feathers is of two types: pigmentary and structural. The blue in a tie or the red in a shirt are pigmentary colors; the colors in a rainbow or a drop of oil on water are structural colors. The brilliant iridescent colors seen on parts of certain birds are structural. Some of a bird's colors are structural but not iridescent; however, the carver-artist should consider all feather colors, except the iridescent colors, as pigmentary.

Iridescent colors on bird feathers result from the interference of light waves by the thousands of overlapping and twisted barbules in conjunction with pigment granules located just under the surface of the barbules. Under certain conditions the light waves are refracted so that a particular color of the spectrum is seen; all other colors are absorbed by the pigment granules. A mallard drake's head is a good example. Under many light conditions only the pigmented color, a dark blackish-blue, is seen. When the direct light comes from behind the observer, a very brilliant iridescent green highlights parts of the head. As the bird moves his head, or the observer his position, the areas of iridescence will move to different locations or disappear completely.

This brief discussion of iridescence on bird feathers is oversimplified, but it does point out some of the problems facing the carver-artist when trying to duplicate iridescence on a three-dimensional object usually illuminated from a variable light source. It is much simpler to achieve the effect of iridescence on canvas than on a carving, because the light source is always from a fixed point.

Most carvers attempt to duplicate iridescence by one of two methods, or a combination of the two. Both techniques involve duplicating the iridescence that would normally be seen when the light source is from a predetermined location relative to the carving. Here, again, there is no substitute for an actual specimen, preferably a mounted bird, from which to determine not only the iridescent colors but also their location.

The first method utilizes different colors or shades of pigmented paint to duplicate the iridescence. Some carver-artists apply all the colors wet on wet; others allow one color to dry before adding additional colors; still other carver-artists apply the different colors in the form of washes (colors thinned with medium until they are translucent).

The other popular method of duplicating iridescence is to utilize bronze powders, metallic flakes, or other materials iridescent in themselves. Bronze powders are generally mixed into a vehicle such as varnish, painting medium, or some other liquid, which allows the metal flakes to float to the surface. This mixture, applied over a pigmented surface, creates a metallic effect that can be somewhat iridescent. The most popular objection to the use of these metallic materials is their apparent lack of color permanence when exposed to sunlight. However, if the carving is always located in areas with only subdued indirect light, the bronze powders will retain their color over fairly long periods. The author has two carvings done more than twenty-five years ago on which the bronze powder used still retain their colors.

The author's biggest objection to the use of bronze powders and other similar materials is the difficulty of floating the flakes without creating the effect of a hard-appearing, metallic-like surface. He completely discarded their use some years ago and uses only oil paints in attempting to duplicate iridescent colors. This change was made after he had gained considerable experience in locating, mixing, and applying the colors seen as iridescent on the actual bird under given lighting conditions.

When attempting to duplicate the bird's iridescent areas and colors, it is essential that the carver have access to a study skin or a mount.

The first step is to locate the iridescent areas. These areas move depending on the angle of reflected light; therefore, a fixed theoretical light source must be established. Inasmuch as a carving can be viewed from either side, it is actually necessary to locate two theoretical light sources, one from the left and one from the right. Once the location of the light source has been determined, the study skin or mount can be held in its proper position relative to the light and the iridescent areas can be located accurately.

The next step is to locate the affected areas on the carving and to make notes regarding the different colors. All iridescent colors seen on birds are brilliant and they often delicately blend into different iridescent shades or into non-iridescent adjacent colors. The duplication of these iridescent shades, and their blending, and the blending into the non-iridescent areas are of equal importance to the duplication of the main iridescent color. It is very difficult to apply a bright, sparkling color on the carving without making it appear out of place and gaudy. The trick is in the blending—making very subtle changes while still retaining the brilliance of color in the desired area. It is usually necessary to go over the painted iridescent feathers more than once and to carefully highlight the brilliant areas and to refine the blending.

All methods of simulating iridescence with which the author is familiar leave much to be desired. There is probably more room for improvement in this phase of the finishing of realistic bird carvings than in any other area. The carver-artist should use all of his ingenuity to try to improve upon existing methods or, better still, to develop a new technique of simulating this beautiful marvel of plumage coloring.

PAINTING LEGS AND FEET

Feet and legs (tarsi) are two of the most difficult parts of the bird to paint, largely because they are covered with small, intricate scales that are extremely hard to duplicate. While some of the scale detail can be carved on legs and feet made from wood, it is difficult to do this when these parts are made of metal. The web is one exception, however, if it is made from lead the scale detail can be scratched into the soft metal quite easily and fairly realistically.

The author recently initiated a method of painting these detailed parts that works fairly well and can give realistic results, depending on how carefully the carver-artist wishes to work.

The foot and tarsus are first painted to their approximate final color and the paint is allowed to dry (a small amount of Cobalt Drier can speed up the process). Scale detail is then drawn in a relatively short time on the toes and the tarsus with a sharp, soft lead pencil (Fig. 8-68). The individual scales are then painted, between the penciled lines, with a 00 or 000 round sable brush, using paint of the approximate final color (Fig. 8-69). Minor corrections to the penciled lines can be made at this time and the lines can be made finer by brushing with paint, if desired.

After all of the scales have been painted individually, the paint can be lightly stippled. After this paint is dry, a wash coat of the final color is then applied over the toes and tarsus, which covers, tones down, and fills over the penciled lines to some extent. Additional washes can be added, if desired, until the proper color is obtained and the prominence of the scale markings have been subdued (Fig. 8-70).

When the wash coats have dried, the prominent scales (those on the upper side of the toes and on the front of the tarsus) should be highlighted (Fig. 8-71). These scales have some gloss, so either copal or linseed oil should be used as the painting medium. The claws should also be painted to their proper color using the glossy medium.

The web adjacent to the toes on the feet of most ducks is a lighter color than the rest of the web. Also, the joints of the toes usually are slightly darker than the toes themselves. Making the entire web on ducks one color is one of the more common errors in painting feet.

Finding a reference for the actual color of feet is very difficult. Probably the best reference for waterfowl is F. H. Kortright's *The Ducks, Geese, and Swan of North America*. True colors can be observed only on the live bird as the feet (and bills) lose their natural color rapidly once the bird is dead. Anyone having access to fresh specimens should make color sketches of these parts before the colors start to change.

8-65 The webs of some ducks, such as the pintail drake, are a lighter color near the toes. Note the darker toe joints.

8-66 Mallard's partially dried foot.

Canvasback   Mallard

8-67 *Comparison of dabbling and diving ducks' feet. Note large lobe on the hind toe of the canvasback's foot.*

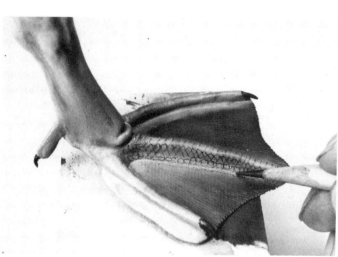

8-68 *Drawing scale detail with a pencil.*

8-70 *The painted foot before light stippling.*

8-69 *The scales are painted individually.*

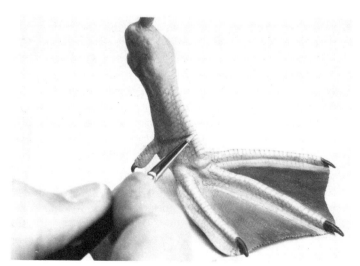

8-71 *The wash coats have been added and the prominent scales highlighted.*

9

Displaying the Carving

As stated in Part II, the success of a realistic bird carving primarily depends on four factors, the last—but by no means the least important—being the artistry shown in selecting the mount or support to display the finished carving. To the casual observer, it may seem that some carvers have an inherent artistic sense in designing or picking out a mount for a particular carving, while others, although capable of turning out top-quality carvings, lack the ability to display their work effectively. A certain amount of visual sense is necessary, of course, but this writer maintains that tasteful display of a carving results more from study, planning, and concerted effort than from innate artistic ability. When mounts made from natural materials enhance the aesthetic quality of a carving, it is not by happy accident. Undoubtedly, a great deal of patient, diligent searching had to be done before material of the size, shape, and color to complement the carving was found.

It is important to consider the method of mounting and displaying while the carving is in the planning stage. Furthermore, it is usually desirable to select the actual mount at this time. The pose of the carving can then be altered if necessary to conform with the mount, and the chances of obtaining unity between carving and mount will be greatly enhanced.

In some instances, an interesting piece of driftwood or similar material may inspire the creation of a carving or alter not only the species but also the pose of one already conceived. Seeing a certain natural form, the carver may immediately envision a particular bird perched upon its surface in a specific pose.

For instance, the author was given an unusual piece of rootstock. He had planned to carve a pair of wood ducks for some time and when he saw this interesting formation, he immediately visualized the two ducks (and their poses) perched on this piece (Fig. 9-1).

Although these inspirations do occur, more often the carver first visualizes the bird and pose, and then happens upon a mount that seems formed by nature especially for his carving.

It is difficult, if not impossible, to set down any hard-and-fast rules for selecting the mount for a carving. Some

of the more obvious generalizations include the following:

1. The mount should reflect, if possible, the natural habitat of the bird.
2. The base or mount should be proportionate to the carving. It should not be so large as to overpower the carving, nor so small that the carving is inadequately or precariously supported.
3. Avoid selecting mounts that appear unstable. For example, it is possible to mount a carving on a branch extending from a piece of driftwood that has sufficient weight so that it will not tip over under normal conditions; however, the undesirable feeling of top-heaviness and instability can still persist.
4. Any fresh-appearing, man-made alterations to mounts made from natural materials should be avoided whenever possible. If it becomes necessary to cut or rework the natural surface, the cuts should be artificially aged by burning, wire-brushing, staining, or other means. The more formal bases described later in this chapter are exceptions.

SHADOW BOXES, PLAQUES, AND DIORAMAS

Half decoy carvings, such as those covered in Chapter 1, are usually mounted either on a fabric covered surface or mat stock and displayed in a frame or shadow box. See page 1 and Figure 1-108.

Another effective means of displaying half-body decoys is to mount them directly on a weathered or antiqued board.

Flying carvings can also be attractively mounted within a frame or shadow box, although a great deal of skill and artistry is required, both in the carving and the mounting, to produce a realistic and pleasing effect. For a mount of this type, a painted natural habitat scene is generally used as the background. The background can also include three-dimensional objects such as branches and leaves, cattails, or others. These props can be natural materials or can be carvings made to depict natural materials.

9-1 *Wood ducks. (Collection of author)*

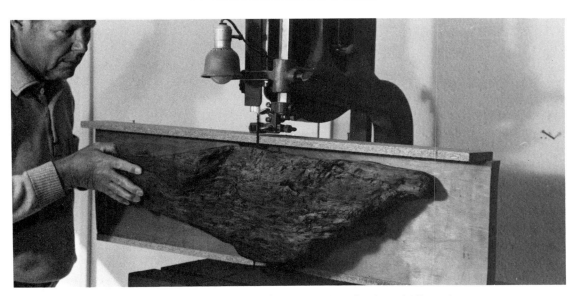

9-2 *One method of making straight cuts on an irregular piece of driftwood. Driftwood is attached to jig with wood screws. Movable upper board serves as a cutting guide.*

Miniature carvings can be effectively displayed by creating a three-dimensional scene or diorama. Here again, considerable skill is needed, especially in realistically blending the three-dimensional foreground with the curved, painted background. A great deal of ingenuity is also involved in faithfully duplicating plants, trees, and other natural objects, so necessary for completing a true-to-life scene.

DRIFTWOOD

The most popular way of displaying a realistic bird carving is to mount the bird on an attractive piece of driftwood (Fig. 9-3). The term driftwood is very loosely applied to almost any piece of wood, usually (but not always) in its natural form, that has been weathered and sometimes shaped by the elements. Interesting pieces of weathered wood, in an infinite number of shapes and sizes, can be found almost anywhere: on the seashore, along streams or lakes, on the desert, in the mountains, under the ground (roots of dead trees can make very attractive mounts), or sometimes in the backyard.

In most instances, driftwood, after dirt and other extraneous materials are removed, is used in its natural state; however, some carvers prefer to coat the exposed surface with flat or low-luster varnish or similar finish. Quite often, especially when the driftwood has been in contact with the ground over an extended period, the wood is infested with termites or other wood-eating insects. These insect holes usually add to the rustic charm of the piece, but when it becomes a mount, any further wood eating must be prevented. The surest way to kill all of the wood-eating insects is to have the piece of driftwood fumigated by an authorized termite-control service. Another satisfactory method is to soak the piece in chlordane.

Whenever possible, the driftwood selected should be self-standing or able to be made self-standing in the desired position by a flat saw cut. In some cases, it may be necessary to attach the driftwood piece to a separate base in order to make it stand. This should be avoided whenever possible, according to some collectors. Other collectors prefer the piece of driftwood to be mounted on a more formal base. Burls, sliced from the trunks of dead trees, make excellent mounts, especially for the smaller bird carvings. The saw cut should be trued so that the base will rest accurately against a flat surface. In all cases, the support surfaces should be covered with felt or another soft material to prevent the possible scratching of fine furniture.

A piece of driftwood often can be cut in many different ways, creating just as many different effects. Before making any cuts, the carver should study the piece carefully, bearing in mind how he intends to mount the carving and determining how it will appear relative to the base. It is often necessary to remove certain parts of the piece, leaving an exposed, fresh-appearing cut. If the undesirable protuberances are small, it may be better to break them off rather than to cut them. In either event, the exposed, unweathered wood should be made to match the rest of the mount as closely as possible. Various methods can be used to accomplish this. Some of the more common ways are burning, wire brushing, gouging, staining or some other antiquing means, or a combination of two or more of these methods.

Some present day carvers are of the opinion that all components of the mount should be manmade and they simulate driftwood and other natural forms by carving them from blocks of wood.

SEMIFORMAL BASES

Some carvers prefer to mount at least some of their carvings on bases a little less rustic than driftwood. In the past, the author has mounted quite a few of his standing birds on semiformal bases composed of a single cross-sectional slice cut from the trunk, burl, or roots of beautifully grained trees. The sides of the base are left in their natural state but the top is given a furniture finish. Almost any thoroughly cured, beautifully textured and colored wood can be used for a base of this kind. Burls—walnut, redwood, and others—are especially desirable.

In making this type of base, slice the wood to the approximate thickness desired on a band saw. Machine both the upper and lower surfaces of the slice with a planer-type cutter in conjunction with a drill press (Fig. 9-

9-3 *Coot mounted on driftwood with a walnut base. 1971 (Collection of Dave Hagerbaumer, Washington)*

9-4 *Horned grebe mounted on small burl. 1970*

9-5 *Machine the slice flat with a drill press-driven planer.*

9-6 *Fill all checks and imperfections with casting resin dyed black.*

becomes necessary to shape the base on the back side, make all cuts on a bevel and sand smooth. Then, texture these cuts by vigorous wire brushing and stain, if necessary, to match the natural surfaces.

The base is now ready to be finished. A fine finish can be obtained by filling the minute low spots and sanding down the high spots until the finished surface is uniformly smooth. The author uses lacquer sanding sealer applied with a spray gun, although brushing lacquer (such as Deft) can be used with good results. After the first coat is applied and thoroughly dry, sand down the surface almost to the bare wood, using 400 wet or dry sandpaper, and smooth further with 3/0 steel wool. This sanding removes the high spots and prevents the sealer from building up. Apply another coat of sealer. Repeat this procedure until the desired finish is obtained. Sanding sealer produces a satin finish. If a glossy finish is desired, a coat or two of high-gloss finish lacquer, thinned about

5). Fill all checks and other defects with casting resin, dyed opaque black (Fig. 9-6). After the casting resin has completely cured, sand smooth the top side of the base—do final sanding with 6/0 paper. Remove all loose matter such as dirt and bark from the sides of the base with a rotary wire brush powered by an electric drill motor. If it

9-8 *Carvings can be used to decorate desk sets.*

9-7 *Typical functional mount — lesser Canada goose lamp.*

50 per cent with lacquer thinner, is applied with a spray gun.

Other semiformal bases can be cut from boards of different wood species, carved and sanded, or gouge carved to the desired shape, finished with a coat or two of lacquer sanding sealer, and rubbed smooth with 3/0 steel wool. Bases of this type, and those molded from clay or plaster, can be effectively painted with oil or acrylics to represent natural materials such as sand, mud, or rock.

FUNCTIONAL MOUNTS

Game bird carvings are often attractively used to decorate functional objects. Some of the more popular decorative items include table lamps, wall lamps, desk sets, paperweights, and bookends (Figs. 9-7, 8, 9).

9-9 Half-body decoys can be displayed on attractive wall lamps.

9-10 Pair of California quail (Collection of Ward Bros. Foundation Museum, Salisbury, Maryland).

Very unusual and beautiful lamp bases can be made from cross-sectional pieces made as described in the preceding section. Decoy carvings are normally used to decorate lamps of this type, although standing and flying bird carvings can be used just as effectively.

Designs for handsome functional mounts are limited only by the imagination and ingenuity of the carver.

FORMAL BASES

During the past ten years or so, when fine, realistic bird carving came into its own as a legitimate American art form, mounting bases have become more elaborate and formal. Many top artists now go to extremes in attempting to create aesthetic bases that reflect the natural habitat of the bird being depicted.

The bases on most fine carvings are made from beautifully grained hardwoods, black walnut being probably the most popular. Some bases are assembled using molding stock; however, most are made from solid material with the edge detail either added by means of a router/shaper or, in the case of round bases, turned on a wood lathe.

The easiest way to add edge detail is with the router using a piloted cutter. During recent years, routers have

become less expensive, and there now are many differently shaped cutters from which to choose. The base is first cut to shape and sanded smooth. The router is then moved around the periphery of the base with the pilot riding against the outside edge. The cutting of the final edge should not be attempted in one pass—three or more passes, increasing the depth of cut each time, produces smoother results. After the final cut has been made, the edge must be sanded perfectly smooth. The base can then be finished with a brushing lacquer sealer, such as Deft, or regular lacquer sanding sealer can be sprayed on to attain a more professional appearance. A number of applications of the lacquer sealer, sanded or steel-wooled between coats, is required to obtain a good finish.

If a simulated ground effect is desired, the top of the base should be undercut before cutting it out from the flat stock. This can be done by making an inside template from ¼-inch plywood approximately ¼ inch smaller (around the periphery) than the finished top detail of the base. The top can then be undercut using a straight cutter in conjunction with a template guide on the router.

Ground can be simulated with water putty. First, fill the undercut area with putty mixed with sufficient water so that it will pour. Then, mix more putty with very little water, permitting the formation of lumps or small clods, and add this lumpy material while the putty on the base is still wet (Figure 9-13). Spray water on the lumps, which makes them adhere to the wet putty. After the putty has thoroughly dried, paint it the desired color with either acrylics or oils.

Elliptically shaped bases are often more pleasing to the eye and blend with the carving better than round ones. Figure 9-15 shows a simple way of laying out a true ellipse. First, the length and width of the ellipse must be determined. It is much simpler, and cheaper, to determine the desired size by making trial bases from scrap, such as plywood or heavy corrugated paper. The carving can then be placed on these makeshift bases and the overall effect appraised. When the final dimensions have been chosen, lay out two lines at right angles to each other, representing the major and minor axes of the ellipse, on paper or cardboard. Next, make two marks on the edge of a strip of cardboard or thin wood whose distance between is equal to exactly one half of the length of the ellipse. Add a third mark at a distance equal to one half of the width of the ellipse as measured from the mark on the right-hand end of the strip. By keeping the mark at the extreme left-hand end of the strip on the minor axis and the mark just to the right on the major axis, as many points on the ellipse as desired can be marked off.

The use of natural materials, such as leaves, plants, grass, or other actual plant or animal life (and those commercially made) on carving bases, is generally considered taboo, especially on carvings that are entered into competition. The duplication of these natural materials with wood, paper, metal, plastics, etc., is limited only by the imagination, ingenuity, and resourcefulness of the individual carver.

The leaves shown in Fig. 9-17 and 9-20 were made from thin brass shimstock (available at automotive parts stores) and the leaf stalks and the twigs were made from small brass rods, soldered together.

The leaves pictured in Fig. 9-11 were made from heavy 60# Kraft wrapping paper and are more realistic and

9-12 *Protect edge of base with masking tape.*

9-13 *After water putty is poured, lumpy putty is added to the wet surface.*

9-11 *Finished base for standing wood duck drake.*

9-14 *Some of the pebbles were carved from wood; the others were molded from water putty.*

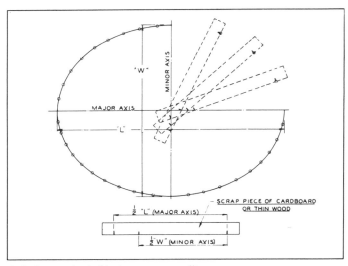

9-15 *One method of laying out a true ellipse.*

9-18 *The bracket fungi added to this piece of driftwood were made from thin lead sheets.*

9-16 *Base for a quail carving is being turned on a wood lathe.*

9-19 *Base for Canada goose carving (see Figure 8-158). The corn stalks were carved from wood, the leaves were made from lead sheet.*

9-17 *Finished base for quail carving (see Figure 9-10).*

9-20 *Base for California quail carving (see Figure 8-103). The ivy leaves were made from thin brass sheet.*

much easier to make than those made of metal.

First, obtain an actual leaf of the desired species and trace its outline on the Kraft paper. Cut the leaf to shape with scissors. Next, saturate the leaf with thinned lacquer sanding sealer and, when dry, paint it with acrylics using brownish color that matches the leaf's veins. Draw the vein pattern on the underside with a pencil.

Now, paint the upper side of the leaf to its final color with oil paints. Duplicating fall colors and realistically blending them with a brush is very difficult. An air brush is ideal for the delicate blending involved. However, very realistic results can be easily gotten by applying the different colors on the leaf with a brush and by blending them with a paper towel used in a wiping motion.

After the oil paint is dry (or almost dry), lay the leaf painted side down, on a resilient surface—a paper tablet works well. Emboss the veins using a smooth, rounded stylus-type tool (one can be fashioned from an awl or an ice pick). Considerable pressure must be exerted and the embossing may have to be done more than one time (Fig. 9-21).

If the embossing has been accomplished properly, most of the oil paint on the vein will be transferred to the paper tablet making the raised vein prominent and about the same color as was first applied on the paper leaf with the acrylic paint.

The leaf's stalk can be duplicated with a small wire or a sliver of bamboo, attached to the underside of the leaf with epoxy. The enlargement at the end of the stalk, where it attaches to the twig, can be simulated with a drop of epoxy (Fig. 9-22).

The small-variety hardstem bullrushes (pictured in Fig. 9-23) were made from 1/8-inch diameter wood dowels. Tapering was accomplished by means of an electric drill which rotated the dowel while it was being held against a moving disc sander.

The lichen clump shown in Fig. 9-24 and Fig. 9-25, was made from end-grain jelutang. The individual shoots

9-22 *The finished leaves.*

9-23 *Simulated hardstem bullrushes.*

9-21 *Embossing the veins on a paper leaf.*

9-24 *Base for snipe carving (see Fig. 10-48) is ready for the water putty simulated ground.*

were formed with a homemade tool similar to a nail set. The entire clump was painted and then each shoot was highlighted.

The individual blades of grass shown in Fig. 9-25 were cut from a Manila folder which was painted the proper color prior to the cutting. The blades were then epoxied to a piece of cardboard. A simple jig for holding the blades upright while the epoxy hardens is shown in Fig. 9-26.

The marsh-type grass blades shown in 9-28 were also cut from a Manila folder. The cross-sectional V-shape of the blades was formed by forcing the individual blade into a V-shaped groove with the hot tip of a burning tool. The blades were then assembled in clumps with epoxy.

The acorns pictured in Fig. 9-11 were turned from wood in lathe. The detail on their bases was carved.

The dried weed shown in Fig. 9-29 was made from brass rods soldered together. The dried seed pods were turned from wood on a lath and then carved.

9-27 *Marsh-type grass made from paper.*

9-25 *Clump of grass made from paper. Note lichens in background.*

9-28 *Close-up of simulated grass. The rocks shown were carved from wood blocks.*

9-26 *Simple jig for holding grass blades while epoxy hardens.*

9-29 *Chukars. 1983. The dried weed was made from brass rods—the seed pods from wood.*

CHAPTER *10*

Advanced Carving Projects

Several projects have been included in this chapter to provide an incentive for the serious amateur bird carver to progress. As we have stressed before, and covered in detail in Chapter 5, the carver should seriously attempt to introduce changes to the drawings and pictured carvings rather than copy them directly.

THE PINTAIL DRAKE DECOY
(See Fig. 5-1, page 152, full-color illustration Fig. 7-266, page 261, and color photos, Figs. 7-267, 268, page 262).

The pintail drake, with his long graceful neck and tail and his strikingly marked scapulars and tertials, is an interesting and beautiful subject for carving. Also, this carving can be a companion piece for the female pintail decoy covered in Chapters 7 and 8.

To obtain sufficient strength for the long and delicate tail feathers, make a hardwood insert and attach it with epoxy. See Figures 7-15, 16, page 193.

The primaries can be carved, or assembled from individual pieces, and inserted under the carved tertials (as was done on the pintail hen decoy) or they can be attached and covered by inserted tertials and scapulars (Figs. 10-5, 6).

10-2 *Front view of pintail drake showing head and neck shape.*

10-3 *Rear view shows body shape and tail detail.*

10-1 *Good profile view of the pintail drake.*

10-4 *Decorative pintail drake decoy. c. 1968.*

Head and Neck
Bill culmen and lower mandible: B,••BU.
Bill sides: W,••B,•TB
Forehead, crown, chin, throat, and cheeks: BU,RS,W.
Back of head: BU,B.
Iridescent area on rear upper part of cheeks, near white stripe: AC
Hindneck: BU,B, shading gradually the body color at base of neck; vermiculated with B,BU near base.
Foreneck: W,•RU; extending into sides of neck.

Body
Back, forward scapulars, and sides: W,••B,•RU; vermiculated with B,BU.
Outer and rear scapulars: B,••BU,•TB; edged with W, •RS,•B. Outer webs of some outer scapulars: B, ••BU,•TB, forming a black patch.
Rump: W,•RU,•BU; edged with W,•RU; streaked with B,BU,••W; finely vermiculated with W,••RS,•BU.
Upper tail coverts: B,••BU,••TB. Inner web: W,•B, •BU; edged with W,•RS.
Lower tail coverts: B,••BU. Outer webs edged with W,•RU.
Flanks: W,•RS.
Breast and chest: W,•RU.

Tail
Two center upper feathers: B,••BU,••TB.
Outer upper feathers: B,•BU,•W; edged with W,•RU.
Lower side: W,•RU,•BU; edged with W,•RS,•RU.

Wing
Primaries: BU,RU,••W; faintly edged with W,•RU.
Secondaries (speculum): BU,••Y,••AC; double edged on rear with W,•RU and B,•BU.
Tertials: W,•RU,•B,•RS. Center stripe: B,••BU,••TB.

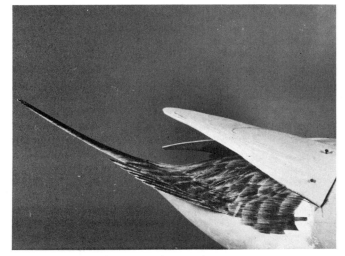

10-5 *Body is mortised to receive the carved primary groups.*

10-6 *Scapulars are inserted next, covering the forward ends of the tertials.*

10-7 *American widgeon drake. Photos of standing birds can be useful in planning a decoy carving. Note added imaginary waterline.*

AMERICAN WIDGEON DRAKE DECOY
(See color photographs, Figs. 7-270, 271, page 264 and full-color illustration, Fig. 7-269, page 263.)

The colorful and graceful American widgeon drake makes a fine carving subject. This saucy and feisty character is best represented in an aggressive position, a pose that will give the amateur carver a chance to try his hand at open bill carving. The carving of the open bill is described and illustrated in Chapter 7, pages 222 and 223.

Figure 10-7 shows how a photo of a standing bird can be used in the planning of a decoy carving. Although not absolutely necessary, a tail insert was used for added strength (Fig. 10-8).

PAINT MIXING INSTRUCTIONS

Head and Neck
Bill: W,••B,•CB.
Lower mandible, tip, and base of bill: B,••BU.
Forehead and crown: W,•RU,•RS.
Eye patch: Y,•TB. Darker around eye and hindneck (add black).
Rest of head: W,•RU,•RS; speckled with B,BU.

Body
Back, scapulars, and side feathers: W,BS,••BU,•B. Feathers edged with W,••BU,••BS,••B.
Chest: W,BS,••BU,•B. Feathers edged with W••BU, ••BS,••B.
Rump: W,•B,•RU; vermiculated with BU,•W,•RS.
Flank: W,•RU.
Upper tail coverts: B,••BU. Inner edges bordered with W,•RU.

Lower tail coverts: B,••BU. Rearmost feathers edged on outer side with W,•RU.

Tail
Upper side: Middle feathers: BU,•B,•W. Others: W,••BU, ••RU; faintly edged with W,•RU,•RS.
Lower side: W,•BU,•B. Feathers edged on outer webs ands tips with W,•RU.

Wing
Primaries: BU,RU,••W; faintly edged with W,•RU.

10-8 *A tail insert is used for added strength.*

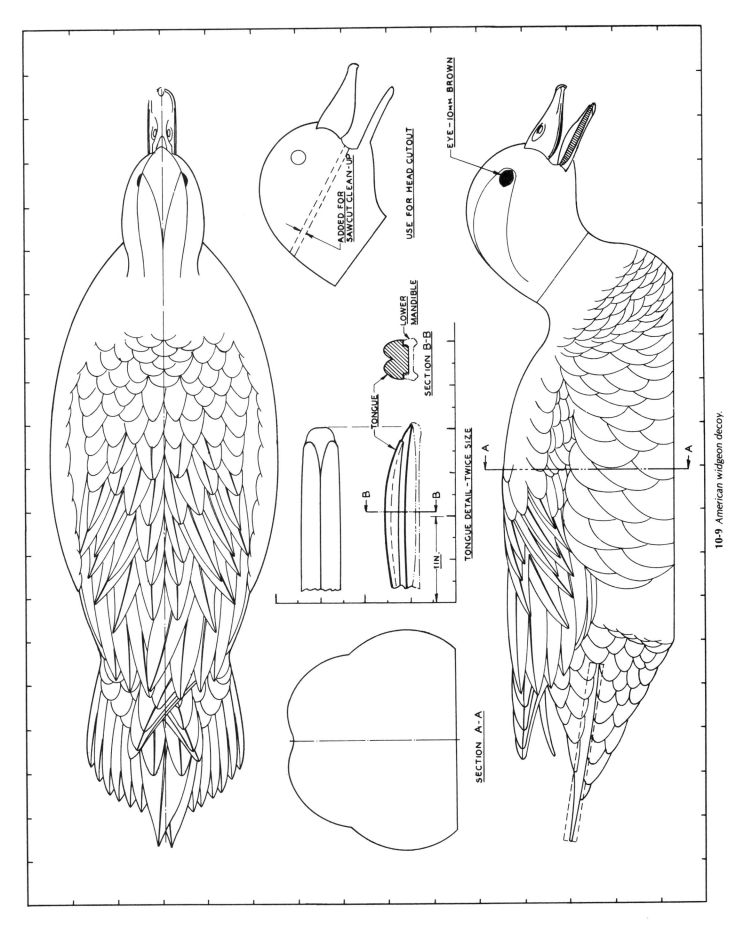

EYE - 10mm BROWN

ADDED FOR SAWCUT CLEAN-UP

USE FOR HEAD CUTOUT

LOWER MANDIBLE

TONGUE

SECTION B-B

TONGUE DETAIL - TWICE SIZE

1 IN.

SECTION A-A

10-9 *American widgeon decoy.*

10-10 *Showing carved tail feathers and coverts.*

10-12 *Inserted and carved feathers have been painted.*

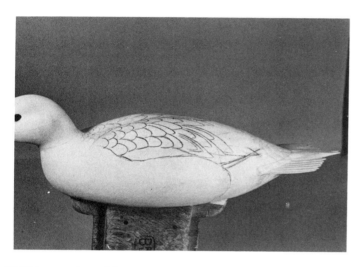

10-11 *Lay out the tertials, scapulars, and the location of the primaries.*

10-13 *Rear view of finished widgeon drake decoy.*

10-14 *Finished American widgeon decorative decoy (Collection of Doug Miller, Colorado.)*

10-15 *The mallard hen. Note large tertials and scapulars.*

Secondaries (speculum): B,••BU,•TB; shading into Y,•TB on forward part of feathers.

Tertials: Outer webs: B,••BU,•TB; edged with W,•RU. Inner webs: BU,••W. Outermost tertials: W,•B,•RU; edged with W,•RU.

Exposed greater and middle coverts: W,•RU.

FEMALE MALLARD DECOY

(See full-color illustration, Fig. 7-272, page 265, and color photos, Fig. 273, 274, page 266.)

Although female ducks are less popular with most carvers than their male counterparts, they certainly have a subdued beauty of their own. Due largely to their feather markings, it is easier to capture the feeling of softness on female duck carvings—a few of us actually prefer to paint them. In any case, painting a female duck provides excellent experience for the carver-artist who wants to progress.

Head and Neck
Upper mandible: O,••BU. Variable dark area: BU,B,W. Nail: B,••BU.

Lower mandible: O,••BU.

Crown, forehead, and back of neck: B,BU. Small feathers edged with RS,W,•RU.

Chin and throat: W,••RS; finely streaked with B,BU,RS,W.

Body
Back and scapulars: B,BU,RS,•W; broadly edged with W,RS,•BU.

Sides, flanks, chest, and rump: BU,RS,•W; broadly edged with W,RS,•BU.

Upper tail coverts: BU,RS,•W; broadly edged with W, RS,•BU.

Lower tail coverts: W,•BU,•RS; broadly edged with W,•RS,•RU.

Tail
Upper side, center feathers: BU,RS,•W; marked and broadly edged with W,RS,•BU. Outer feathers become increasingly lighter in color.

Lower side: W,•RS,•RU. Inner edges: W,•RU. Marked with W,••RU.

10-16 *Rear view of mallard hen shows body shape.*

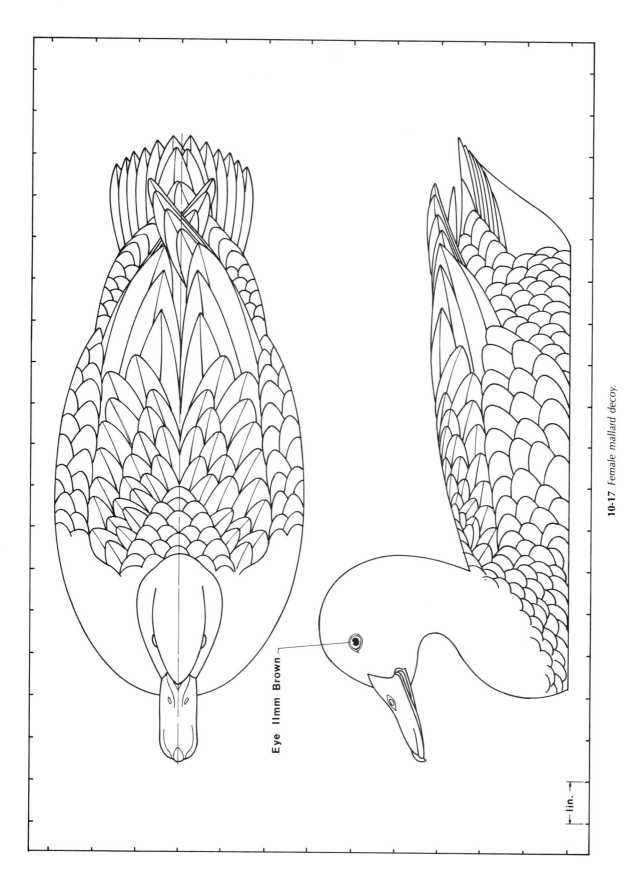

Eye 11mm Brown

10-17 *Female mallard decoy.*

10-18 *Western Canada goose.*

Wing
Primaries: BU,RU,••W; faintly edged with W,•RU.
Secondaries (speculum): W,AC,••TB; double edged with
    W,•RU and B,••BU.
Tertials: BU,RU,W. Outer webs of large tertials: BU,•RS.

COMMON CANADA GOOSE DECOY

*(See full-color illustration, Fig. 7-275, page 267, and color
photograph, Fig. 7-276, page 268).*

The Canada goose is without a doubt the most widely
known of all waterfowl and perhaps is more American
than the bald eagle. Their intelligence, strength, and fidel-
ity are probably unsurpassed by an other bird. Although
they vary from 2½ pounds (cackling goose) to over 20
pounds (giant Canada goose), their general physical characteristics, markings, and coloration are quite similar. The
common Canada goose is next only to the giant Canada
in size and is one of several strains that weigh on the
average approximately 9 pounds. Similar markings and
coloration for both sexes. A block 7 × 9½ × 22 inches
long is required for the body of a life-size carving.

Head
Bill: B,••BU (black Hyplar works well).
Cheek patch: W,•RU.
Rest of head and neck: B,••BU,•TB.

Body
Back and scapulars: BU,RS,W; feathers edged with W,
    •RS,•BU.
Sides: BU,RS,W; feathers shading to a lighter color to-
    wards the rear; feathers edged with W,•RS,•BU.
    Feathers become progressively smaller going forward.
    Lighter edges become closer together, producing a
    lighter over-all effect.
Rump: B,••BU,•TB.
Upper and lower tail coverts, flanks and belly: W,•RU.
Breast: RU,W,••RS; feathers edged with W,•RS,•BU.
Chest: same as breast.

Tail
Upper side: B,••BU,•TB.
Lower side: BU,W,•B.

Wing
Primaries: BU. Slightly lighter (•W) near inner edge of
    feathers. Shafts—B.

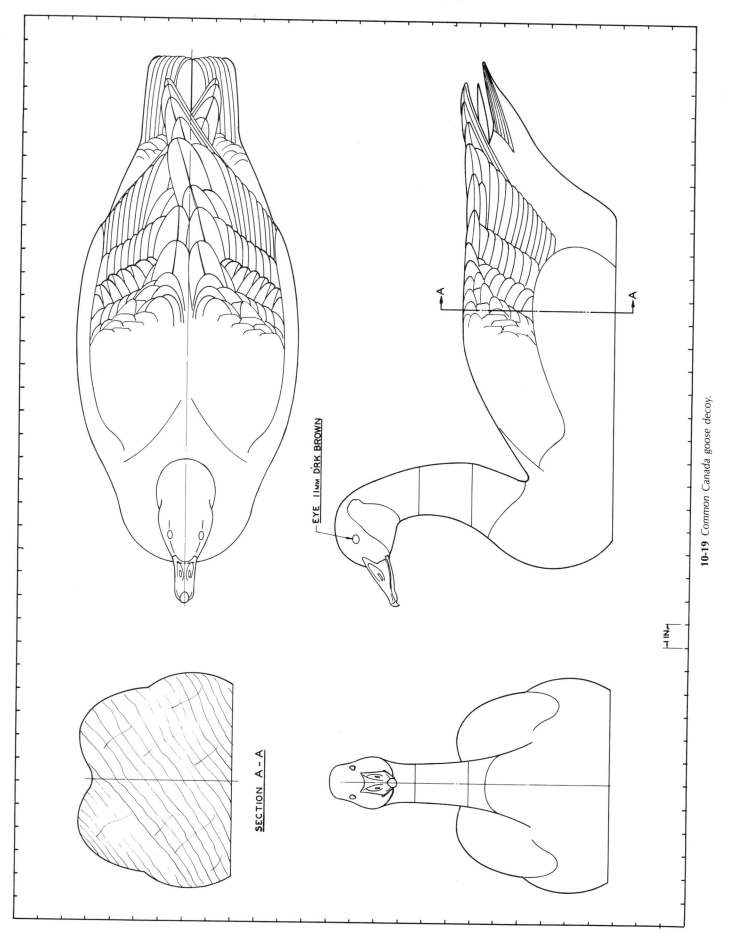

EYE 11mm DRK BROWN

SECTION A - A

A ── A

⊢ I IN ⊣

10-19 *Common Canada goose decoy.*

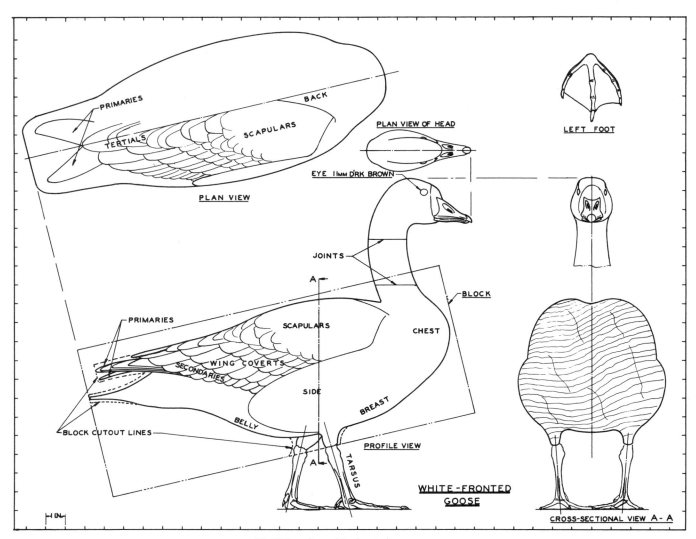

10-20 *Standing white-fronted goose.*

Tertials: W,••RU,•BU. Inner webs and area near shaft—
    W,••RU,••BU. Shafts—B.
Secondaries and wing coverts: same as back and scapu-
    lars.

STANDING WHITE-FRONTED GOOSE

Although rare in the eastern half of the continent, the
whitefronted goose is fairly common in the West. The
adult birds, with their reddish bills, white area at the front
of their heads, strikingly marked breasts, and yellowish
feet, are beautiful medium-size geese.

A block 7¼ × 8 × 19 inches is required for the body
of a life-size carving. In almost all cases, it will be necessary to make not only the body block but also the head
and neck from more than one piece of wood (See Chapter
7, ''Gluing up the Block'', page 191). Special attention
should be paid to the shaping of the body cross section
and the exposed part of the tibia.

Head
Bill base: W,•TB,•Rd.
Bill culmen and sides: W,Rd. Blend into base.
Bill, area around nostrils: Rl,••B.
Bill nail: W,•Rm.

Bill, underside of lower mandible: Rl,•B.
Forehead, front of cheeks, around base of lower mandi-
    ble: W,•RU.
Rest of head and neck: RS,RU,•W. Areas just behind
    white on head—add more RU.

Body
Back and scapulars: RS,RU. Feathers edged with
    RS,RU,••W.
Sides: RS,RU. Feathers edged with RS,RU,••W. Upper
    edges of large feathers broadly bordered with W,•RU,
    forming a white line along the side.
Rump: RS,RU.
Upper tail coverts: W,•RS. Shafts—W,•RU,•BU.
Lower tail coverts: W,•RU.
Flanks and belly: W,•RU.
Breast: W,RU. Irregularly splashed with B,••BU and
    RS,RU,•W.
Chest, lower: RU,W. Feathers edged with W,•RU.
Chest, upper: RS,••RU,••W. Feathers edged with W,
    ••RU.

Tail
Upper side: RS,RU. Feathers edged with W,•RU. Shafts—
    BU,B,W.
Lower side: RU,W. Feathers edged with W,•RU. Shafts—
    W,•BU.

10-21 *White-fronted goose family. 1978. (Collection of Carroll L. Wainwright, Jr. New York.)*

10-22, 22A *Adult white-fronted goose.*

Wing

Primaries: BU. Shafts—W,•RS.

Secondaries: BU.

Tertials: RS,RU. Feathers edged with W,•RS,•RU. Shafts—BU.

Coverts, greater: W,••BU,•RS,•B.

Other coverts: same as tertials: inner coverts edged with W,•RU.

Tarsi and Feet

Tarsi and toes: O,•RU. Toe joints—lighter (add more Y).

Webs: Y,•RU.

Claws: W,••AC,•TB; use glossy medium.

STANDING BRANT

(See color photographs, Figures 7-278, 279, page 269).

The brant are true sea geese and seldom found away from salt water. Two species are native to North America: the black brant of the Pacific, and the American brant of the Atlantic. These two species, slightly larger than a mallard duck, are very similar except for the extent of their white neck collars and coloration differences in their side and breast feathers. The two sexes have similar markings and coloration.

BLACK BRANT

Head

Bill: B,••BU (black Hyplar works well).

Entire head and neck, except for neck collar: B,••BU.

Neck collar, incomplete behind: W,•RU; neck delicately barred with B,••BU on upper part of collar.

Body

Back and scapulars: BU,W,••B; feathers edged with W,RS,•BU,•B.

Sides: BU,RS,••W,•B, shading lighter towards rear of feather: feathers edged with W,•RU; edgings becoming broader on upper edges of long side feathers.

Rump: BU,B.

Flanks, upper and lower tail coverts, and rear part of belly: W,•RU.

Breast: BU,B,W; feathers broadly edged with W,••BU, ••B.

Chest: B,••BU; feathers near breast edged with BU,••B, ••W. Edging becomes smaller, feathers blend into back of neck.

Tail

Upper and lower surfaces: B,••BU.

Wing

Primaries and tertials: B,••BU.

Coverts: B,••BU; feathers faintly edged with B,BU,••W.

Tarsi and feet: B,••BU. Claws—same as feet, use glossy medium.

AMERICAN BRANT

(same as black brant except as noted)

Head: same as black brant, except neck collar is incomplete at front and back of neck.

10-23 *Black brant.*

10-24 *Black brant.*

10-25 *American brant.*

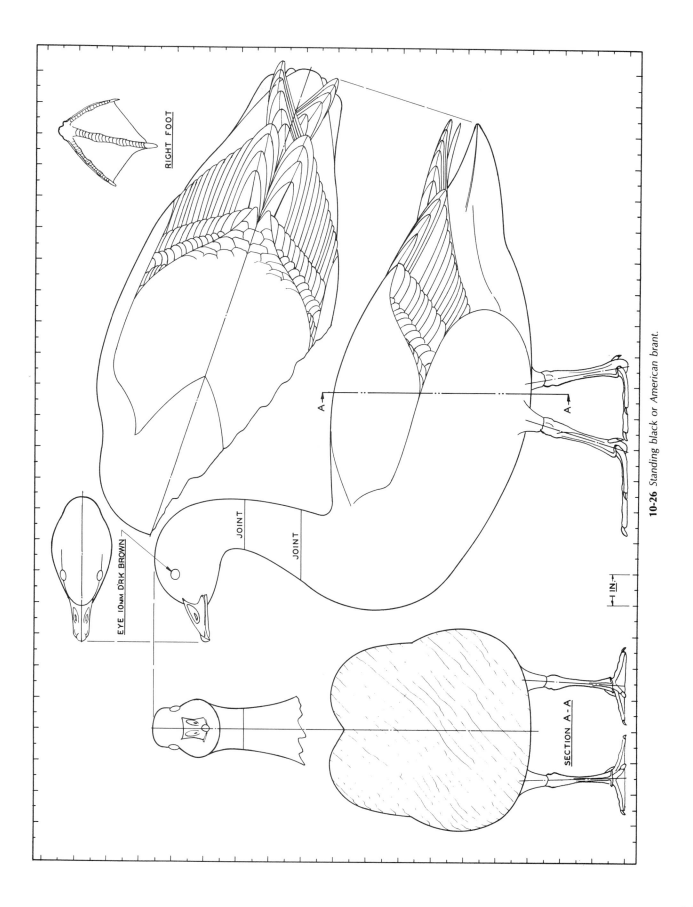

RIGHT FOOT

EYE 10mm DRK BROWN

JOINT

JOINT

A

A

SECTION A - A

1 IN.

10-26 *Standing black or American brant.*

10-27 *Finished black brant carving. c. 1970 (Collection of Dave Hagerbaumer, Washington).*

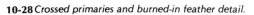

10-28 *Crossed primaries and burned-in feather detail.*

10-29 *Unpainted head of a brant carving.*

10-30 *Blue goose.*

10-31 *Snow goose.*

Body
Back and scapulars: BU,••RS,••W,•B; feathers edged with
  W,•BU,•RS.
Sides: BU,RS,W, shading lighter towards rear of feather;
  feathers edged with W,•RU.
Flanks, upper and lower tail coverts, and belly: W,•RU.
Breast: W,••RS,••BU,•B; feathers edged with W,•RU,•RS.

Wing
Tertials: B,BU; feathers edged with W,•RU.
Coverts: B,BU; feathers edged with W,•RU.

SNOW GOOSE AND BLUE GOOSE
(See full-color illustration Fig. 7-280, page 270)

Except for coloration, the blue goose is identical with
the snow goose and is generally believed to be a color
phase of the same species. They make most interesting
carving subjects. Sexes are similar in markings and coloration.

SNOW GOOSE

Head
Bill, except for tip and "grinning patch": W,••Rm.
Bill tip: W,•RU.
Edges of upper and lower mandibles: B,••BU. Serrated
  edges of mandibles—W,•RU.
Entire head and neck: W,•RU; forehead and forward
  cheeks often stained with W,•Rl,•BU.
Body: entire body, tail coverts, and tail: W,•RU.

Wing
Primaries: B,••BU.

Greater coverts: W,B.
Rest of wing: W,•RU.
Tarsi and feet: W,Rd,•RU. Claws—B,••BU; use glossy
  medium

BLUE GOOSE

Head and upper neck: same as snow goose.
Lower foreneck: BU,W,••RS,••B.

Body
Back, scapulars, and chest: BU,W,••RS,•B; feathers edged
  with W,••BU,•RS.
Sides: W,••BU,••RS,••B; feathers edged with W,••BU,
  •RS.
Rump: W,••B,••BU; feathers broadly edged with W,•RU.
Flanks: W,•RU.
Breast and belly: variable in coloration, some birds
  W,•RU, other birds same as side feathers.
Upper and lower tail coverts: W,•RU; mottled with
  W,••BU,••B.

Tail
Upper side: W,••BU,••B; feathers broadly edged with
  W,•RU.
Lower side: W,•+B,•+BU; feathers broadly edged with
  W,•RU.

Wing
Primaries: B,••BU; faintly edged with W,••BU,••B.
Secondaries: B,••BU; faintly edged with W,••B,••BU.
Tertials: W,BU; broadly streaked with B,BU,•W. Feathers
  edged with W,•BU.
Greater and some middle coverts: same as tertials.
Other coverts: W,•B,•BU.
Tarsi and feet: same as snow goose.

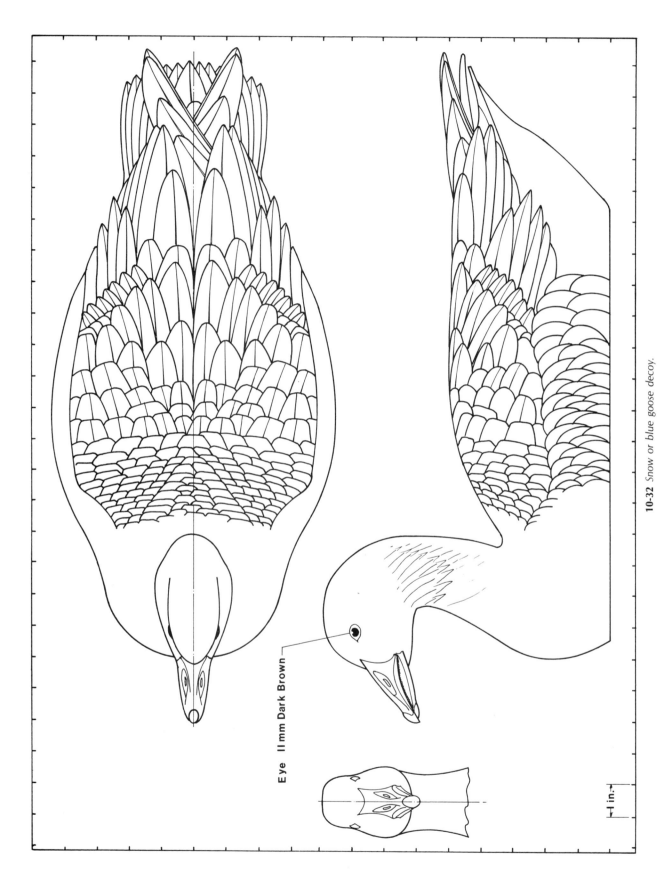

Eye 11mm Dark Brown

10-32 *Snow or blue goose decoy.*

⊢1 in.⊣

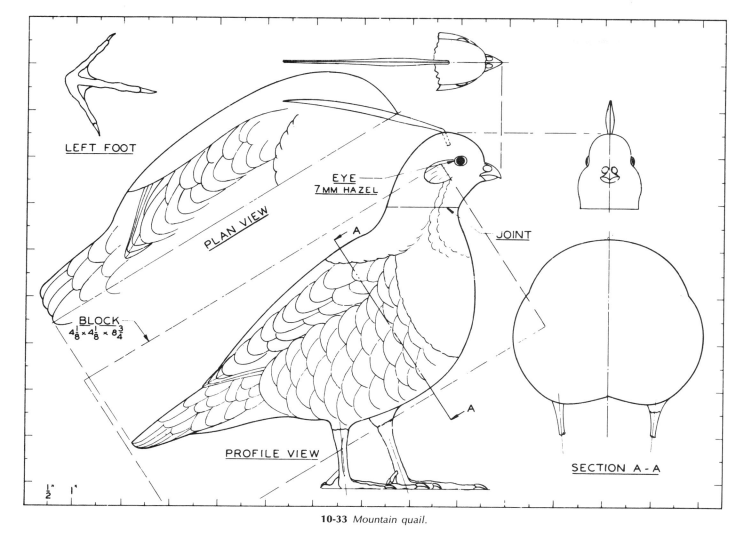

10-33 Mountain quail.

10-34, 35 Mountain quail carving (Collection of Doug Miller, Colorado).

MOUNTAIN QUAIL

(See full-color illustration Fig. 7-281, page 271).

The mountain quail a western game bird, is the largest and most beautiful of all the quails. With the exception of the long topknot feather, there are no unusual problems connected with carving this bird. For strength it is necessary to carve the long crest feather from metal. The two sexes have similar markings and coloration.

Head
Bill: BU,B, lighter at the tip.
Forehead: W,•RU.
Crown: W,••B,••BU,•CB.
Forward part of cheeks and chin: W,•RU.
Back of head: same as crown but highlighted with RS,W,••BU,•B.
Topknot feather: B,••BU,•TB.

Neck
Hindneck: same as back of head.
Sides: same as back of head.
Foreneck and throat: BS,YO,Rd,••B; outlined on sides with W,•RU.

Body
Back and scapulars: RS,W,••BU,•B.
Upper tail coverts: same as scapulars.
Sides: BS,YO, Rd,•B; feathers barred and edged on upper parts with W,•RU.
Rump: YO,•BS.
Lower tail coverts: B,••BU,•TB; rear covert feathers striped and forward covert feathers striped and edged with YO,•BS.
Belly: W,•RU.
Forward breast and chest: W,••B,•CB.
Rear part of chest: BS,YO,Rd,••B; feathers finely edged with W,•RU.

Tail
Upper and lower sides: BU,RS,W.

Wing
Primaries, inner webs: BU,RS,•W.
Primaries, outer webs: W,•BU,•B. Shafts—BU.
Secondaries, inner webs: same as primaries.
Secondaries, outer webs: same as scapulars.
Tertials: same as scapulars but broadly edged with W,•RU on inner webs.
Tarsi and feet: BU, RS,•W. Claws—BU,RS; use glossy medium.

CALIFORNIA QUAIL

(See color photographs, Figs. 7-282, 283, page 272)

The beautiful and jaunty California quails are widely distributed in the valleys and low mountains of the western states. They are fine birds in every respect and their life style and habits are exemplary.

Head
Bill: B,BU,•W.
Forehead: W,•RU; streaked with W,•YO,•B.
Crown, forward and sides: B,••BU.
Crown, rear: B,••BU; highlighted with BU,•YO,•W.
Chin, throat, and forward cheeks: B,••BU. Black area outlined with W,•RU.
Back of head and back and sides of neck: W,B,CB; feathers striped and edged with B,••BU; double tips of smaller feathers edged with W,•RU.
Ear coverts: B,••BU.

Body
Back, scapulars, and rump: B,W,•• + RS
Upper tail coverts and upper tail: W,B,RU,•CB.
Lower tail coverts, flanks, and belly: W,••RS,•RU; feathers striped with W,•RU,•RS,•BU.
Lower tail: W,RS,••B
Breast: BS,Y,•B, shading forward to W,••YO, •–BU. Feathers outlined and delicately striped with B,••BU.
Chest: same as upper tail coverts.
Sides: RS,RU; feathers striped with W,•RU.

Wing
Primaries: BU,•W.
Secondaries: same as scapulars; outer webs lightly edged with W,•RS.
Tertials: same as scapulars; inner webs broadly edged with W,•RS,•YO.
Tarsi and feet: B,BU,•W. Claws—B,•BU, use glossy medium.

10-36 *California quail—males and females.*

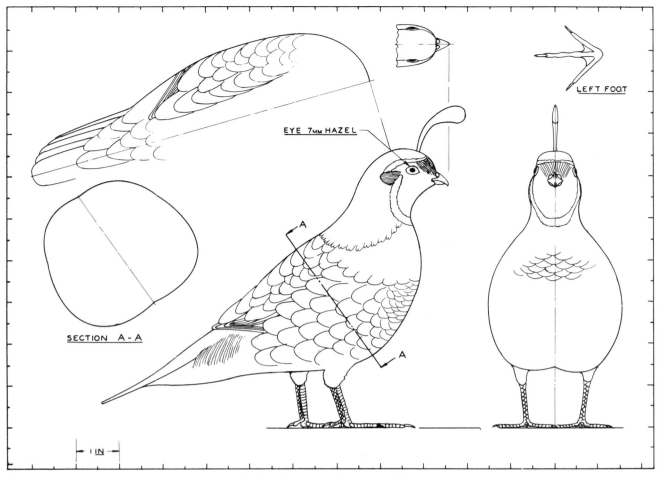

EYE 7MM HAZEL

LEFT FOOT

SECTION A - A

1 IN

10-37 *California quail—male and female.*

10-37A *California quail carving. 1981. (Collection of Diane Byrnes, California).*

10-38 *California quail carving. 1986.*

10-39 *Body profile of a California quail.*

10-40 *Front view—California quail. Note breast feather pattern and lower body shape.*

10-41 *A beautiful pair of California quail.*

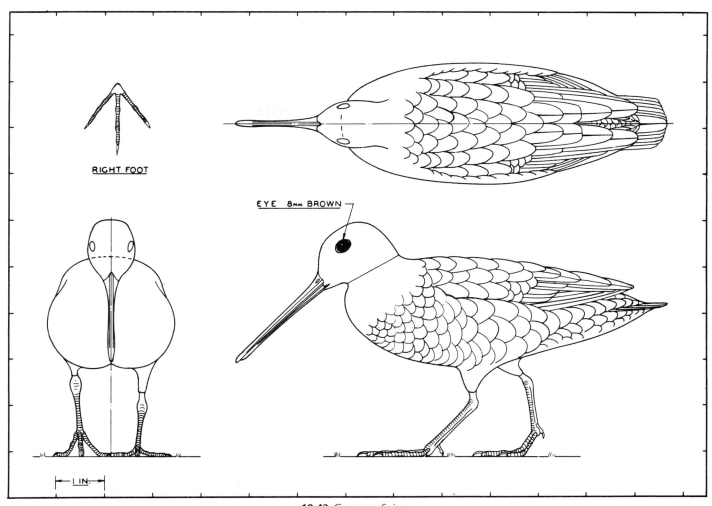

10-42 *Common Snipe.*

COMMON SNIPE

The common snipe is the smallest of our game birds. Its beautiful coloring and markings make it a most interesting carving subject. In the example illustrated in Figures 10-43 through 10-48, the primaries were carved as in integral part of the body block, and the tertials were inserted individually. Both sexes have similar markings and coloration.

Head
Upper mandible: Culmen—W,••BU,••BS. Sides—W,••B,•BS. Nail—B,BU.
Lower mandible: Sides and bottom—YO,•RU.
Throat: W,•RS,•RU.
Head and neck (except for stripes): W,••RS,•RU.
Stripes: BU,••B.

Body
Back: B,BU. Outer edges of feathers—W,••RS,•RU. Inner markings—RS,•BS,•RU,•W.

Scapulars: same as back.
Rump and upper tail coverts: B,BU. Feathers edged with W,••RS,•RU.
Lower tail coverts: same as upper but lighter (add W).
Flanks: same as rump.
Sides: W,•RU,•B. Barred with RU,W.
Breast and chest: similar to flanks.
Belly: W,•RU.

Tail
Upper side: W,••BU,•RU. Marked with B,••BU. Tips—W,RS.
Lower side: similar to upper side but lighter (add more W).

Wing
Primaries: B,••BU,•W.
Coverts: BU,••B. Edged with W,•RU,•RS.
Tarsi and feet: W,••YO,•RS,•–TB. Claws—B,BU,•W, use glossy medium.

10-43 *Carve the folded primaries from the body block.*

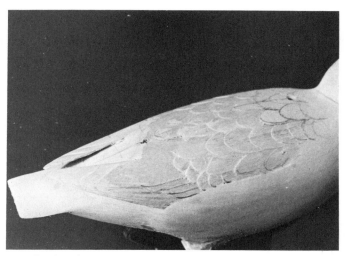

10-44 *Continue by carving the scapulars.*

10-45 *The first tertial has been inserted.*

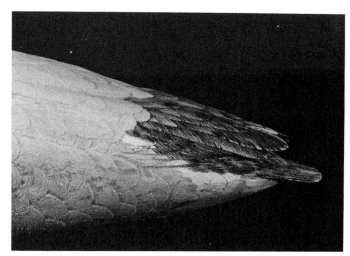

10-46 *The insertion of the tertials has been completed.*

10-47, 48 *Common snipe carving, two views. 1978. (Collection of Mary Halbert, California).*

CHUKAR PARTRIDGE

(See page 7)

Although not native to this country, chukar partridge, or chukar as they are commonly called, are well established in the semiarid high deserts and mountains of the western states. They are most often found in lonely, rugged, and inaccessible terrain and are fine game birds. The coloration and markings of both sexes are similar.

Head
Bill: W,••Rl,•Rd.
Forehead stripe: B,••BU.
Forehead above stripe: W,•RU,•CB.
Crown top: W,••RU,••BS
Crown sides: lighter than forehead (add W)
Chin and throat: W,••RS,•RU. Vestlike marking—B,••BU.
Back of head: same as top of crown.
Cheeks, lower: same as throat.
Ear coverts: YO,••BS.
Eyelid: Rl,•RU.

Neck
Hindneck and sides: W,••RU,••BS,•CB.

Body
Back: same as hindneck and sides of neck.
Scapulars: same as back; feathers highlighted with same color as sides of chest. Add some blue highlights which are the same color as the front and lower chest.
Sides: W,••RS, barred with B,••BU, followed with crescent-shaped edgings of Y,BS,••RU.
Rump, upper tail coverts, and flanks: W,••RU,••CB,•BS.
Lower tail coverts: W,RS,•BS,•B.
Belly: W,••RS,•BS,•B.
Chest sides: W,••RS,••BS,•CB.
Chest front and lower chest: W,•RU,•CB, blending into sides of chest.
Breast: same as front and lower chest.

Tail
Upper and lower sides: YO,BS,••W,•RU.

Wing
Primaries: BU,W,••RU. Shafts—W,••BU,•BS. Outer webs of the outer primaries marked near tip with W,••RS.
Secondaries: same as rump and upper tail coverts.
Tarsi and feet: same as bill. Claws—BU,B; use glossy medium.

10-49 *Chukar partridge.*

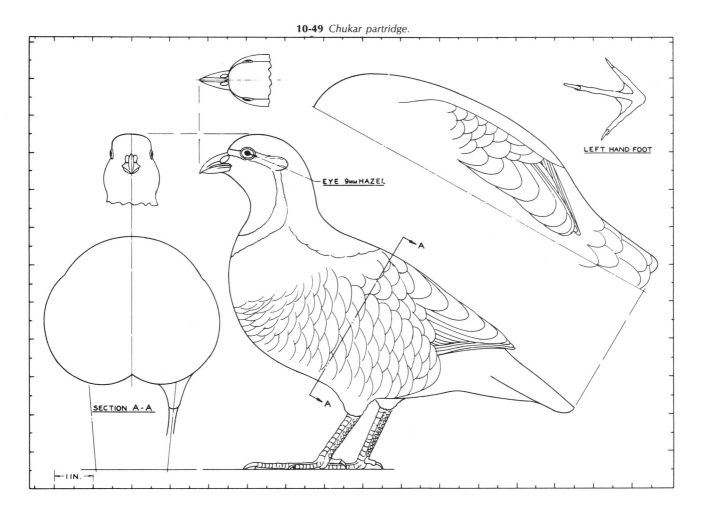

EYE 9MM HAZEL

LEFT HAND FOOT

SECTION A-A

A

1 IN.

10-50 *Chukar pair. 1983. (Collection of author).*

10-51, 52 *Chukar partridge.*

10-53 *Stretching hooded merganser drake.*

EYE 9mm YELLOW

10-54, 55 *Hooded merganser drake, two views.*

STRETCHING HOODED MERGANSER DRAKE
(See page 4 and color photograph, Fig. 7-284, Page 272)

The strikingly marked hood merganser drake, in a wing and leg stretching pose, is a good example of the extensive use of the individual feathering technique described in Chapter 7. In the carving illustrated, the tail feathers were inserted (see Figures 7-196 thru 7-201) and the wing was constructed using inserted feathers (see Figures 7-212 through 7-231).

Head
Forehead: BU,W,•B.
Crest: W,•RU. Edged with B,••BU,•TB.
Rest of head and neck: B,••BU,•TB.
Bill: B,••BU.
Comb (above eye): Y,•RU.
Bill: RS,••BU,W.

Body
Scapulars, exposed wing coverts, rump, and upper tail coverts: BS,RS,W. H-shaped markings—BU,•B. Broadly tipped with W,•RS,•RU.
Back: BS,RS,W. Barred with BU,•B. Feathers broadly tipped with W,•RU.
Sides, chest, breast, and belly: W,••RS,•RU. Feathers barred with BS,RS,W. Broadly tipped with W,•RS,•RU.

Under tail coverts: W,•RS,•RU. V-shaped markings—BU.

Tail
Upper side: BU,••RS,•W. Edged with BU,••RS,••W. Edged with BU,••RS,••W. Tipped with W,•RS, •RU.
Lower side: BU,••RS,•W. Tipped with W,•RU.

Wing
Primaries: W,••BU. Barred on outer webs with W,•RS,•RU.
Secondaries: W,•RS,•RU. Some triangular-shaped markings—BU. Other triangular-shaped markings—BS,RS,W.
Coverts: See scapulars.
Tarsi and Feet Tarsi covert feathers: W,•RS,•RU. Barred with W,•BU.
Toes: Y,•RU.
Claws: RS,••RU,•W; use glossy medium.

Body
Sides: RS,••YO.
Back, scapulars, and crescent-shaped markings on chest: B,••BU,•TB.
Rump and upper tail coverts: BU. Feathers edged with RS,•BU.
Chest, breast, and belly: W,•RU.
Undertail coverts: W,••RS,•RU. Vermiculated with RU,W.

10-56 *Mortise the body for the primaries.*

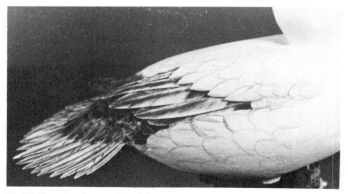

10-57 *Showing inserted tertials.*

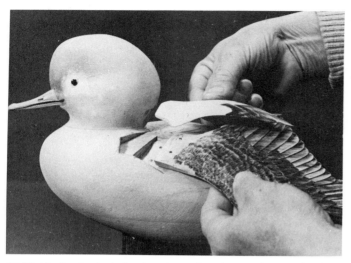

10-58 *Mortise the body for the wing stub and carve the scapulars from a separate piece.*

10-59 *Showing wing and scapulars attached to the body.*

10-60, 61, 62, 63 *Stretching hooded merganser drake carving 1981. (Collection of Dr. and Mrs. J. L. Silagi, Texas).*

10-64 *Greater prairie chicken carving 1980. (Collection of author).*

PRAIRIE CHICKEN

Although once very plentiful over much of the United States, the prairie chickens' range now is limited and their number are quite low. The lesser prairie chicken is very similar to the greater except that it is smaller and lighter in coloration. The air sacs on the greater male are yellowish, while those on the lesser male are reddish. The published overall length and weight of the greater male is 18 inches, 2 pounds and 3 ounces; of the lesser male, 16 inches, 1 pound and 12 ounces. See Figures 7-194 and 7-195 for insertion of crest feathers and 7-210 for insertion of wing primaries.

Head

Forehead, crown, back of head, and neck: BU,RS,W. Broadly edged with RS,W,•RU.

Chin, cheeks, and throat: W,•RS. Mark above and below eyes, auricular (ear coverts), and lower cheek—BU.

Pinnates (stiff, narrow neck feathers): W,•RS. Marked on outer edges with BU. Inner webs of smaller feathers—BS,RU,W. Edged with BU.

Air sacs (bare spots on neck): Greater—Y,••O,•RU. Lesser—Rl,O,•RU.

Comb (above eye): Y,•RU.

Bill: RS,••BU,W.

Body

Scapulars, exposed wing coverts, rump, and upper tail coverts: BS,RS,W. H-shaped markings—BU,•B. Broadly tipped with W,•RS,•RU.

Back: BS,RS,W. Barred with BU,•B. Feathers broadly tipped with W,•RU.

Sides, chest, breast, and belly: W,••RS,•RU. Feathers barred with BS,RS,W. Broadly tipped with W, •RS,•RU.

Under tail coverts: W,•RS,•RU. V-shaped markings—BU.

Tail

Upper side: BU,••RS,•W. Edged with BU,••RS,••W. Edged with BU,••RS,••W. Tipped with W,•RS, •RU.

Lower side: BU,••RS,•W. Tipped with W,•RU.

Wing

Primaries: W,••BU. Barred on outer webs with W, •RS,•RU.

Secondaries: W,•RS,•RU. Some triangular-shaped markings—BU. Other triangular-shaped markings—BS,RS,W.

Coverts: See scapulars.

Tarsi and Feet

Tarsi covert feathers: W,•RS,•RU. Barred with W,•BU.

Toes: Y,•RU.

Claws: RS,••RU,•W; use glossy medium.

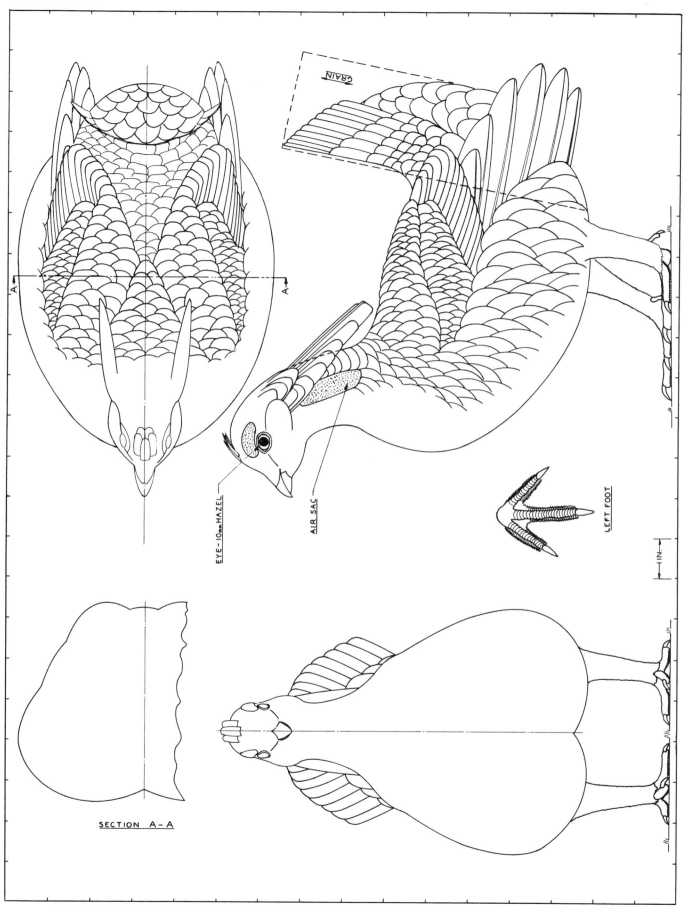

GRAIN

EYE - 10mm HAZEL

AIR SAC

LEFT FOOT

1 IN.

SECTION A-A

10-65 *Greater prairie chicken (male).*

10-66 *After the bird is roughly carved to shape, lay out the scapulars and secondary feathers.*

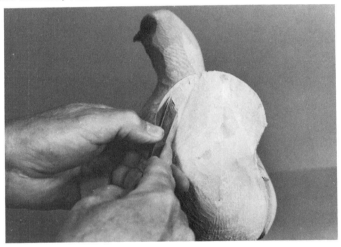

10-67 *Carefully carve the underside of the tail.*

10-68 *The underside of the tail and the lower tail coverts have been carved. Relieve side feathers to receive primaries.*

10-69, 70, 71 *Male lesser prairie chicken carving 1979. (Collection of Dr. Ray Zeigler, Texas).*

PART IV

Game Bird Carving Data

One of the greatest difficulties the realistic bird carver faces is obtaining accurate structural information on a particular bird. This scarcity of published information was one of the factors that prompted the writing of this book. Ideally, each carver should have access to actual specimens; since this is not possible for many, the author incorporated structural information on a number of game bird species in drawings presented in earlier chapters. In addition, photographs of those parts of most game birds pertinent to the carver and important dimensional information on all the game birds have been included in the remaining chapters.

11

Dimensional Data

The following dimensional information has been assembled as an aid to the carver without access to actual specimens. This information, at the very best, must be considered an approximate average. Scientific dimensional data for birds are normally limited to wingspan, overall length, and weight; they do not include the information most necessary to the carver—body length, width, and height; head and bill dimensions; and foot and tarsus dimensions. Whenever possible, these dimensions were obtained from actual specimens. In some cases, however, dimensions were approximated from photographs; in other cases, dimensions were ratioed from other similar species, using their overall lengths as the basis for comparison.

It must be remembered that the bird's dimensions vary for a particular species; also, some dimensions on an individual bird vary considerably due to muscular feather control. Check the dimensions included in this chapter whenever you have the opportunity and, if there are differences, note them.

Additional information that can be obtained from a fresh specimen was listed in Chapter 4, page 143. The progressive bird carver should conscientiously collect all first hand information he can, rather than rely on published data.

The average overall body widths, wing spans, and weights of waterfowl used in the following tables were taken from Kortright's *Ducks, Geese, and Swans of North America*. These figures can be considered authoritative as they are the mean derived from a considerable number of specimens. When comparing dimensions taken from a fresh specimen, its size (overall body length and weight) should be compared to the averages determined by Kortright. The carver can then ascertain whether his specimen is small or large and he then can revise any dimension taken off his specimen accordingly.

As a result of the availability of a number of overhead photographs, the body width of ducks has been revised in the following tables. In almost all cases, the body widths were found to be greater than those taken from fresh specimens.

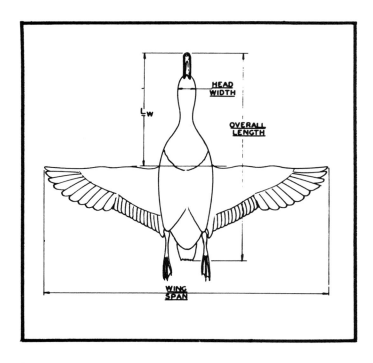

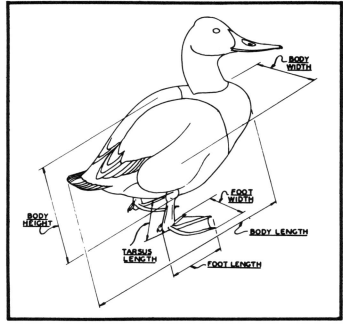

WATERFOWL

SPECIES	SEX	OVERALL LENGTH	WING-SPAN	WEIGHT (lb./oz.)	BODY			HEAD WIDTH	FOOT		TARSUS LENGTH	L_W
					LENGTH	WIDTH	HEIGHT		LENGTH	WIDTH		
Geese												
Common Canada goose	M	37.0	69.0	9/4	21.5	9.0	7.8	2.5	4.2	3.75	3.75	17.25
	F	35.0	64.0	7/14	20.0	8.5	7.25	2.4	4.0	3.6	3.7	16.5
Lesser Canada goose	M	29.0	58.0	5/0	18.0	8.0	6.75	2.0	3.25	3.0	3.5	13.25
	F	27.0	55.0	4/0	16.75	7.75	6.5	2.0	3.0	2.9	3.3	12.3
Cackling and Richardson's geese	M	25.0	52.0	3/8	16.0	6.4	5.8	1.9	2.75	2.5	3.0	10.75
	F	23.0	48.5	2/14	14.75	6.2	5.6	1.9	2.7	2.4	2.9	10.0
White-fronted goose	M	29.0	59.0	5/5	18.75	7.5	6.6	1.9	3.25	3.12	3.25	13.5
	F	26.75	55.5	4/13	17.12	6.9	6.45	1.85	3.12	3.0	3.2	12.5
Lesser snow and blue geese	M	29.0	58.0	5/5	19.0	7.5	6.75	2.2	3.25	3.12	3.75	13.5
	F	27.6	56.5	4/11	18.0	7.12	6.3	2.2	3.1	3.0	3.7	12.9
Ross's goose	M	24.5	51.0	2/15	16.0	6.5	6.0	1.9	2.75	2.5	3.12	10.5
	F	23.0	49.5	2/11	15.0	6.1	5.7	1.9	2.65	2.25	3.06	10.0
Black and American brant	M	25.0	47.0	3/5	16.0	6.6	6.0	1.9	2.75	2.5	3.0	10.75
	F	23.0	45.5	3/2	14.75	6.1	5.5	1.9	2.65	2.4	2.9	10.0
Barnacle goose	M	27.5	56.0	4/0	17.0	6.5	6.0	1.7	2.8	2.75	2.8	11.3
	F	23.5	52.0	3/9	15.37	6.0	5.6	1.65	2.7	2.65	2.75	10.3
Emperor goose	M	27.0	52.0	6/2	17.5	7.5	6.5	1.8	3.0	2.8	3.0	11.6
	F	26.5	51.0	6/0	17.12	7.25	6.37	1.8	3.0	2.8	3.0	11.4
River or Puddle Ducks												
Mallard and black	M	23.0	36.0	2/13	14.25	6.5	5.2	2.0	2.75	2.75	2.2	12.0
	F	21.5	35.0	2/6	13.25	5.8	5.0	2.0	2.7	2.7	2.1	10.0
Gadwall	M	21.0	35.0	2/0	12.75	6.0	4.9	1.8	2.4	2.3	1.75	9.7
	F	19.5	33.0	1/14	12.5	6.0	4.7	1.75	2.4	2.3	1.75	9.0
American widgeon	M	20.4	33.7	1/11	13.0	5.25	4.7	1.8	2.3	2.0	1.6	9.3
	F	18.5	31.0	1/9	12.0	5.75	4.5	1.75	2.3	2.0	1.6	8.7
Pintail	M	*26.0	35.0	2/2	*17.25	5.75	5.37	2.0	2.5	2.4	1.87	12.0
	F	21.6	33.0	1/13	13.0	5.75	5.0	2.0	2.4	2.3	1.87	10.0
Green-winged teal	M	14.6	23.9	0/13	9.5	4.25	3.7	1.8	1.6	1.6	1.37	7.6
	F	14.0	22.2	0/12	9.37	4.25	3.5	1.5	1.5	1.5	1.25	7.0
Blue-winged teal	M	15.8	24.6	0/14.5	9.75	4.75	4.0	1.6	1.75	1.75	1.37	7.8
	F	15.2	23.6	0/13.5	9.5	4.75	3.8	1.5	1.75	1.75	1.37	7.5
Cinnamon teal	M	16.0	25.0	0/13	10.0	4.6	4.0	1.6	1.75	1.75	1.37	8.0
	F	15.5	24.0	0/12	9.75	4.6	3.8	1.5	1.75	1.75	1.37	7.8
Shoveler	M	20.0	31.4	1/9	11.6	5.25	4.6	1.9	2.37	2.3	1.75	10.0
	F	18.6	29.8	1/4	10.75	5.25	4.2	1.75	2.25	2.2	1.75	9.75
Wood duck	M	18.6	28.3	1/9	12.5	5.4	4.5	2.0	2.25	2.1	1.70	9.5
	F	17.7	28.3	1/2	11.5	4.7	4.0	1.8	2.2	2.0	1.6	8.5

*Includes the 2.75-inch-long tail feathers.

Sea or Diving Ducks

SPECIES	SEX	OVERALL LENGTH	WING-SPAN	WEIGHT (lb./oz.)	BODY LENGTH	BODY WIDTH	BODY HEIGHT	HEAD WIDTH	FOOT LENGTH	FOOT WIDTH	TARSUS LENGTH	L_w
Redhead	M	20.0	33.0	2/8	11.5	6.0	4.6	2.0	3.0	3.6	1.87	9.7
	F	19.0	31.0	2/4	11.2	6.0	4.5	2.0	3.0	3.6	1.87	9.37
Canvasback	M	21.6	32.0	3/0	12.0	6.8	5.25	2.0	3.1	3.5	2.0	12.0
	F	20.8	30.5	2/13	11.8	6.8	5.2	2.0	3.1	3.5	2.0	11.3
Greater scaup	M	18.5	31.0	2/0	11.0	5.5	5.2	2.0	2.8	3.2	1.8	9.75
	F	17.5	30.0	1/15	10.8	5.5	5.0	1.9	2.8	3.2	1.8	9.0
Lesser scaup	M	17.0	28.75	1/14	10.25	5.25	4.75	1.9	2.8	3.18	1.75	8.75
	F	16.25	26.5	1/12	10.0	5.25	4.62	1.75	2.7	3.0	1.62	8.5
American golden-eye	M	19.2	30.7	2/2	12.5	5.5	5.2	2.0	3.0	3.3	1.75	10.0
	F	17.0	28.0	1/12	11.5	5.0	4.75	1.8	3.0	3.3	1.75	9.25
Barrow's golden-eye	M	19.2	31.4	2/2	12.5	5.5	5.25	2.0	3.0	3.25	1.75	10.75
	F	17.0	28.0	1/10	11.5	5.0	4.75	1.8	3.0	3.25	1.75	9.25
Ring-necked duck	M	17.0	27.7	1/11	10.5	5.2	4.75	1.7	2.75	3.0	1.6	9.75
	F	16.3	26.8	1/8	10.25	5.0	4.50	1.65	2.75	3.0	1.6	9.5
Bufflehead	M	14.75	23.5	1/0	10.0	4.8	4.0	2.0	2.25	2.5	1.37	6.37
	F	13.5	21.9	0/12	9.0	4.4	3.6	1.6	2.0	2.12	1.37	5.6
Old Squaw	M	*21.12	29.0	1/13	*16.37	5.3	4.75	1.75	2.4	2.6	1.56	9.5
	F	15.7	27.5	1/11	11.0	5.0	4.5	1.6	2.37	2.5	1.5	8.87
Harlequin	M	17.5	26.5	1/8	11.8	4.8	4.5	1.75	2.6	2.8	1.5	10.0
	F	15.9	24.0	1/3	10.75	4.5	4.1	1.6	2.5	2.6	1.5	9.0
Steller's eider	M	18.0	29.0	1/15	12.25	5.25	5.1	1.6	2.56	2.7	1.6	10.25
	F	17.5	28.75	1/15	11.87	5.12	5.1	1.6	2.5	2.68	1.6	10.0
American eider	M	24.0	40.0	4/6	14	7.5	6.56	2.5	3.35	3.54	2.37	11.7
	F	22.75	38.75	3/6	13.5	7.0	6.25	2.25	3.12	3.25	2.0	11.0
Pacific eider	M	25.75	43.0	5/12	15.0	8.0	7.0	2.5	3.6	3.7	2.4	12.56
	F	23.75	40.5	5/7	14.5	7.75	6.7	2.4	3.37	3.5	2.25	11.6
King eider	M	22.75	36.5	4/0	13.75	7.25	6.25	2.5	3.15	3.25	2.28	11.0
	F	21.0	36.4	3/10	13.5	7.25	6.0	2.25	2.84	3.09	2.12	10.25
Spectacled eider	M	21.75	36.25	3/10	13.5	7.25	6.0	2.25	2.75	2.83	1.8	10.6
	F	21.0	34.5	3/10	13.25	7.0	5.75	2.2	2.5	2.7	1.68	10.25
Hooded merganser	M	18.0	26.0	1/8	11.5	5.5	4.25	1.8	2.4	2.5	1.62	8.87
	F	17.0	24.5	1/4	11.0	4.9	4.0	1.6	2.37	2.4	1.5	8.37
American merganser	M	25.5	36.75	3/7	16.0	6.4	6.0	1.75	3.12	3.37	2.3	13.62
	F	22.9	34.3	2/6	14.75	5.4	4.8	1.6	3.0	3.0	2.12	12.5
Red-breasted merganser	M	23.0	33.25	2/10	14.37	5.5	5.2	1.75	3.0	3.25	2.25	12.25
	F	21.0	30.75	1/13	13.5	5.37	5.12	1.6	2.75	2.9	1.9	11.0
Ruddy duck	M	15.4	22.6	1/5	9.5	5.25	4.2	1.8	2.4	2.75	1.5	7.1
	F	15.1	22.4	1/2	9.25	5.0	3.8	1.7	2.4	2.75	1.5	6.75
White-winged scoter	M	21.5	38.0	3/8	14.5	6.5	5.9	2.0	3.54	3.75	2.5	10.5
	F	20.5	37.0	2/10	13.87	6.25	5.8	1.9	3.25	3.5	2.3	10.0
Surf scoter	M	19.6	33.0	2/3	13.6	5.6	5.4	2.0	3.25	3.5	2.0	9.4
	F	18.0	31.0	2/0	11.75	5.5	4.8	1.75	3.0	3.25	2.0	8.75
American scoter	M	19.75	33.0	2/8	13.0	60	5.8	2.0	3.25	3.5	2.0	9.5
	F	18.5	31.9	2/3	12.25	5.75	5.0	1.7	3.12	3.37	2.0	8.8

*Includes the 4.375-inch-long tail feathers.

UPLAND GAME BIRDS

SPECIES	SEX	OVERALL LENGTH	WING-SPAN	WEIGHT (lb./oz.)	BODY LENGTH	BODY WIDTH	BODY HEIGHT	HEAD WIDTH	FOOT LENGTH	FOOT WIDTH	TARSUS LENGTH	L_w
Ruffed grouse	M	18.0	24.0	1/6	13.1	4.5	3.9	1.62	2.36	2.5	2.1	6.8
	F	17.0	22.8	1/3.5	12.4	4.4	3.8	1.5	2.25	2.36	1.87	6.4
Sage grouse	M	30.0	36.0	5/5	21.9	8.5	7.35	1.87	2.87	2.8	2.4	11.5
	F	22.0	27.0	3/0	16.0	6.25	5.4	1.5	2.5	2.5	2.2	8.37
Sharp-tailed grouse	M	17.5	28.0	2/1	12.8	5.75	4.8	1.75	2.37	2.37	2.0	6.75
	F	17.5	28.0	1/13	12.8	5.5	4.5	1.56	2.37	2.37	2.0	6.75
Greater Prairie chicken	M	18.0	27.5	2/3	13.3	5.75	4.8	1.75	2.37	2.37	2.0	6.62
	F	18.0	27.5	1/13	13.3	5.62	4.7	1.56	2.25	2.25	1.9	6.62
Lesser Prairie chicken	M	16.0	24.4	1/15.5	11.8	5.7	4.7	1.5	2.25	2.25	1.9	5.9
	F	16.0	24.4	1/11.5	11.8	5.5	4.5	1.4	2.25	2.25	1.9	5.9
Blue grouse	M	22.0	31.0	2/13	15.37	5.87	5.25	1.4	2.5	2.31	2.2	7.8
	F	18.5	27.75	1/14	13.5	5.25	4.62	1.37	2.37	2.25	2.12	7.0
Spruce grouse	M	15.75	21.75	1/6	11.5	4.5	3.87	1.4	2.16	2.09	1.7	5.9
	F	15.5	21.0	1/5	11.3	4.4	3.8	1.3	2.16	2.89	1.7	5.87
Willow ptarmigan	M	17.0	26.5	1/12	11.25	5.0	4.6	1.5	2.04	1.9	1.5	6.4
	F	16.0	26.0	1/10	10.75	4.75	4.25	1.4	2.04	1.9	1.5	6.0
Rock ptarmigan	M	14.5	24.5	1/5	9.62	4.5	4.0	1.4	1.87	1.87	1.4	5.5
	F	13.5	23.75	1/4	9.0	4.6	4.0	1.3	1.87	1.87	1.4	5.2
White-tailed ptarmigan	M	12.0	19.5	1/1.5	8.0	4.2	3.8	1.25	1.7	1.7	1.2	4.5
	F	11.5	19.0	0/15	7.62	4.1	3.7	1.25	1.7	1.7	1.2	4.37
Bobwhite quail	M	10.0	15.0	0/9	7.5	3.5	3.25	1.25	1.56	1.56	1.5	3.0
	F	9.5	14.0	0/8.5	7.18	3.4	3.1	1.1	1.56	1.56	1.5	3.0
Scaled quail	M	11.0	15.0	0/8.7	8.25	3.5	3.25	1.25	1.5	1.5	1.4	3.1
	F	10.0	14.5	0/7.7	7.5	3.4	3.1	1.1	1.5	1.5	1.4	3.0
California quail	M	10.5	15.0	0/6.6	8.25	3.5	3.25	1.25	1.5	1.5	1.4	3.1
	F	9.5	14.0	0/6.5	7.5	3.25	3.0	1.1	1.5	1.5	1.4	3.0
Gambel's quail	M	11.0	15.0	0/7.3	8.25	3.5	3.25	1.25	1.5	1.5	1.4	3.1
	F	10.0	14.5	0/7.3	7.5	3.25	3.0	1.1	1.5	1.5	1.4	3.0
Mountain quail	M	10.5	17.0	0/10.3	8.5	4.0	3.5	1.3	1.75	1.75	1.56	4.0
	F	10.25	16.5	0/10	8.37	3.8	3.25	1.2	1.75	1.75	1.56	3.9
Harlequin quail	M	9.0	17.0	0/7.9	6.0	3.5	3.25	1.25	1.5	1.5	1.4	2.8
	F	8.5	16.5	0/7.1	5.75	3.25	3.0	1.12	1.5	1.5	1.4	2.7
Ring-necked pheasant	M	35.0	30.5	2/11	29.0	6.25	5.62	1.7	2.6	2.6	3.25	8.0
	F	24.0	28.0	2/2	19.0	6.0	5.25	1.6	2.5	2.5	3.12	6.87
Turkey	M	49.0	68.0	16/5	36.0	12.5	10.5	2.0	4.5	4.25	6.5	16.5
	F	36.0	48.0	9/5	26.5	9.25	8.0	1.9	3.75	3.50	5.75	12.0
Chukar partridge	M	13.5	22.4	1/4	10.0	4.5	3.87	1.4	2.12	2.0	1.9	5.0
	F	13.0	21.5	1/2	9.56	4.4	3.75	1.3	2.12	2.0	1.9	4.8
Gray partridge	M	13.0	21.5	1/0	9.6	4.3	3.75	1.4	2.0	2.0	1.8	4.8
	F	12.0	20.0	0/15.3	8.87	4.2	3.6	1.3	2.0	2.0	1.8	4.62

OTHER BIRDS

SPECIES	SEX	OVERALL LENGTH	WING-SPAN	WEIGHT (lb./oz.)	BODY LENGTH	BODY WIDTH	BODY HEIGHT	HEAD WIDTH	FOOT LENGTH	FOOT WIDTH	TARSUS LENGTH	L_w
Pigeons and Doves												
Mourning dove	M & F	11.87	17.25	0/4.5	9.75	2.7	2.5	.81	1.18 / *1.68	1.18	1.0	3.82
White-winged dove	M & F	11.75	18.87	0/5.7	8.62	2.7	2.5	.81	1.37 / *2.06	1.37	1.12	3.8
Band-tailed pigeon	M & F	15.5	26.25	0/13	12.0	4.37	3.5	1.2	1.8 / *2.43	1.8	1.25	5.0
Shore Birds												
Wilson's snipe	M & F	10.5	16.75	0/4.2	6.5	2.62	2.37	1.0	1.65	1.56	1.35	5.5
Woodcock	M	10.5	16.5	0/6.2	6.37	3.25	2.75	1.12	1.75	1.6	1.3	5.5
	F	11.5	17.5	0/7.7	7.0	3.37	2.87	1.12	1.75	1.6	1.3	6.0
Marsh Dwellers												
King rail	M	16.0	22.5	0/11	9.6	3.7	3.5	1.25	2.8	3.2	2.6	8.87
	F	15.0	21.0	0/10	9.0	3.6	3.4	1.25	2.8	3.2	2.6	8.25
Virginia rail	M & F	10.5	14.25	0/3.6	6.3	2.4	2.6	1.0	1.8	1.7	1.62	5.75
Clapper rail	M	15.0	21.0	0/12	9.0	3.8	4.0	1.25	2.75	3.15	2.56	8.25
	F	14.0	19.0	0/11	8.4	3.7	3.9	1.2	2.67	2.95	2.4	7.75
Sora rail	M & F	9.75	14.0	0/2	5.62	2.12	2.25	.8	1.75	1.96	1.28	4.5
Common gallinule	M & F	14.0	23.5	1/0	10.0	4.12	3.5	1.25	3.37 / *4.75	4.0	2.56	6.3
Coot	M & F	15.25	26.25	1/6	10.25	4.75	4.75	1.37	3.37 / *4.5	3.75	2.5	7.0

*Including length of hind toe.

CHAPTER 12

Game Bird
Feet and Tarsi

The proper location and position of the tarsi for a given pose or activity are very important considerations in planning a standing carving. Approximate tarsi locations, both profile and front view, for game birds in their normal, relaxed stance are given below. The bird's leg (tarsus) location in the profile view is extremely variable, inasmuch as its location and position are affected by three points of articulation. (The location of a man's leg relative to his body is affected by two points of articulation.) The location and position of the tarsus in the front view are not quite as variable since the femur (thigh) on a bird articulates fore and aft only. The carver should be thor-

oughly familiar with the bone structure and points of articulation of the bird's legs and tarsi. See Chapter 3, especially Figures 3-15 and 16.

Representative photographs (which can be scaled) of the tarsi and feet of the different game bird families are presented on the following pages. The tarsi and feet of birds in the same family (subfamily, in the case of waterfowl) are similar, except for size. Therefore, by using the dimensions given in Chapter 11 in conjunction with these pictures, the size and shape of the foot and tarsus for a particular game bird can be approximated with a fair amount of accuracy.

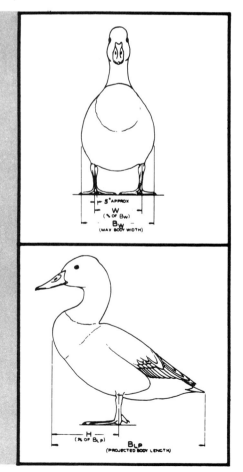

Family or Subfamily	H (%)	*W (%)
Waterfowl		
Geese	38–42	50
River or puddle ducks	45–50	54–58
Sea or diving ducks and mergansers	45–55	60–65
Ruddy duck	50	60–65
Tree duck	50	55
Upland game birds		
Quails	30–35	40–45
Partridges	35–45	40–45
Pheasant	25	40–45
Grouse	35–40	40–45
Turkey	35	40–45
Pigeons and doves	35	45
Shore birds	45	40–45
Marsh dwellers	35–40	40–45

*Considerably less when bird is striding, especially upland game birds.

Approximate Tarsi Location

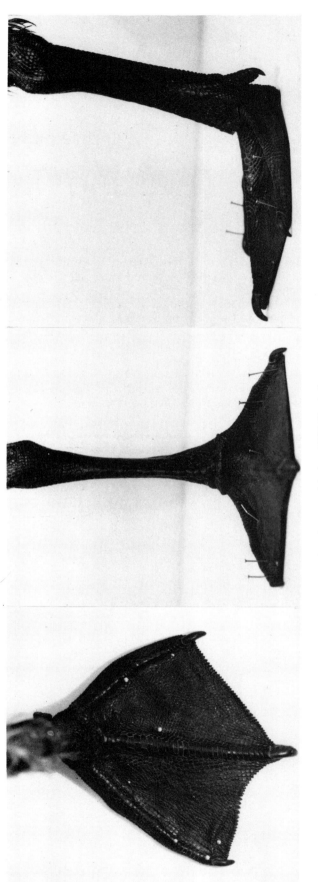

Lesser Canada goose, right foot (13/16 life-size).

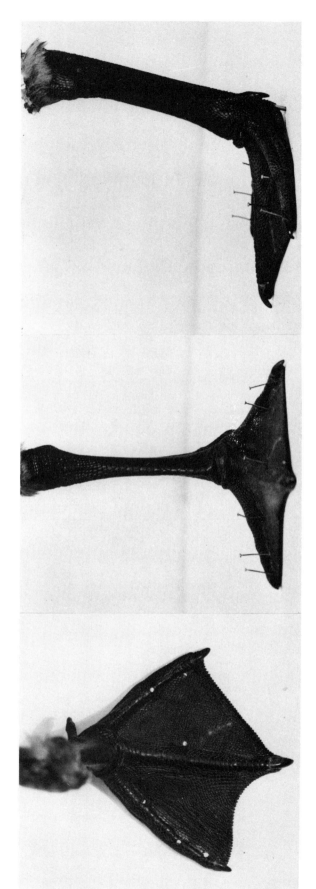

Cackling Canada goose, right foot (13/16 life-size).

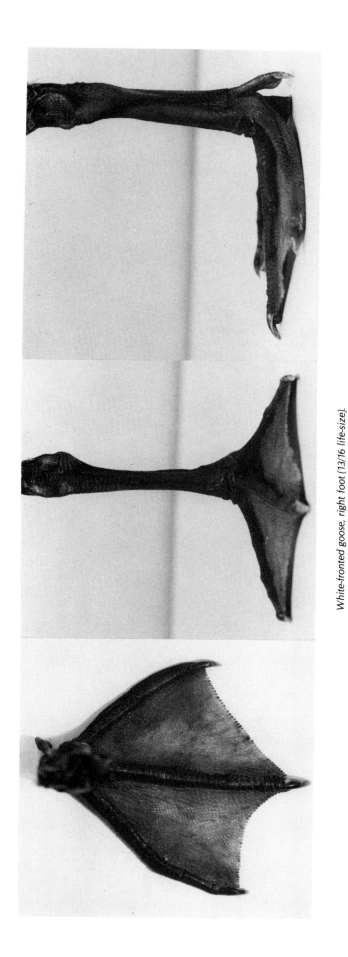

White-fronted goose, right foot (13/16 life-size).

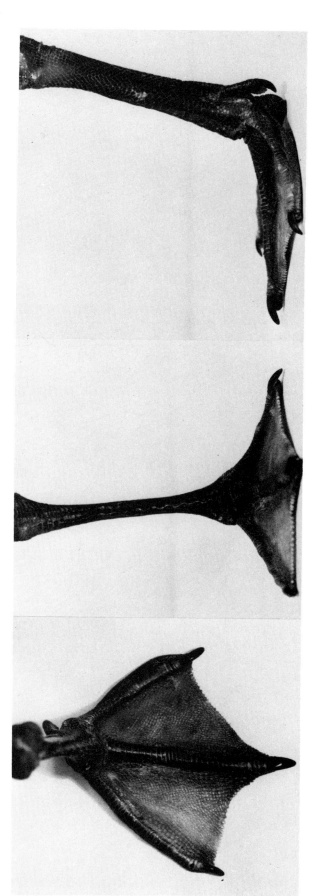

Lesser snow or blue goose, right foot (13/16 life-size).

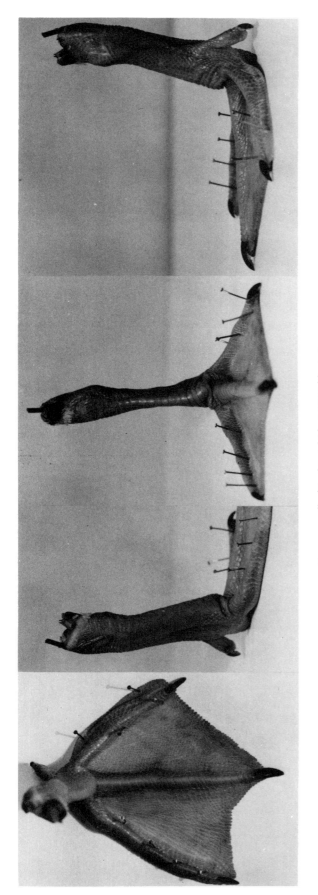

Common mallard (male), right foot (13/16 life-size).

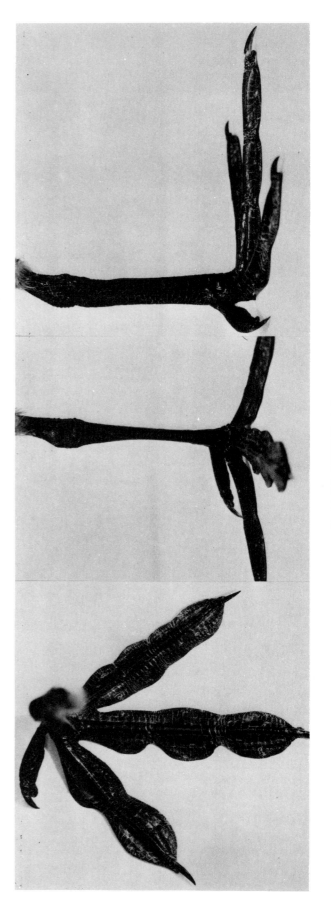

Coot, left foot (13/16 life-size).

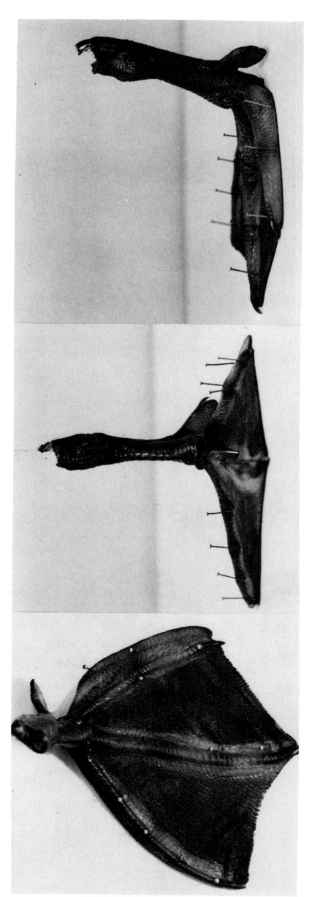

Canvasback (female), right foot (13/16 life-size).

White-winged scoter (male), right foot (13/16 life-size).

Top row: Pintail (male), right foot (life-size).

Center row: Shoveler (male), left foot (life-size).

Bottom row: Green-winged teal (male), right foot (life-size).

Top row: Ruddy duck (male), right foot (life-size).

Center row: Bufflehead (male), right foot (life-size).

Bottom row: Wilson's snipe (male), right foot (life-size).

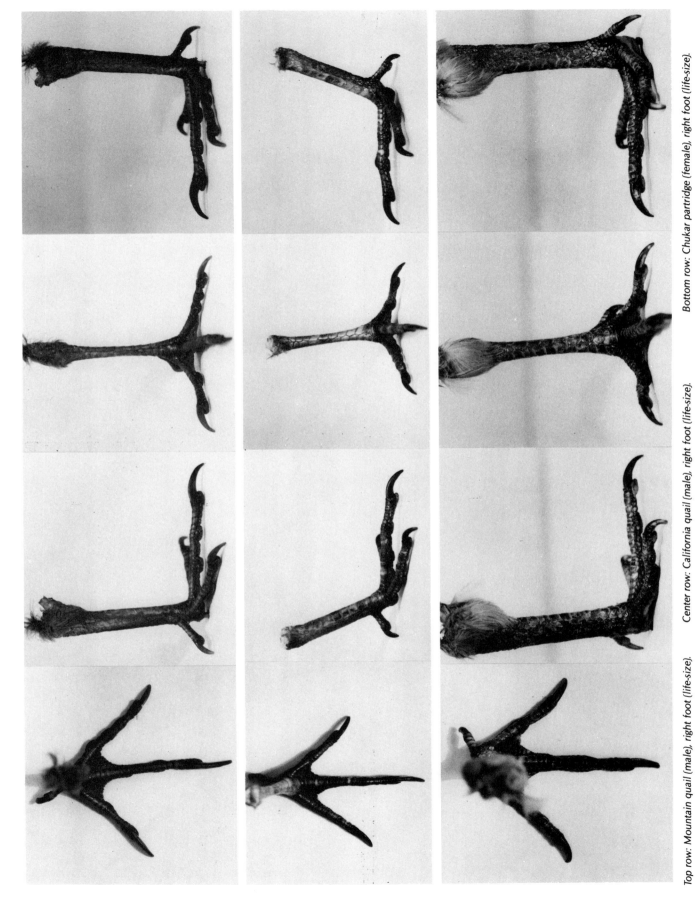

Top row: Mountain quail (male), right foot (life-size).   Center row: California quail (male), right foot (life-size).   Bottom row: Chukar partridge (female), right foot (life-size).

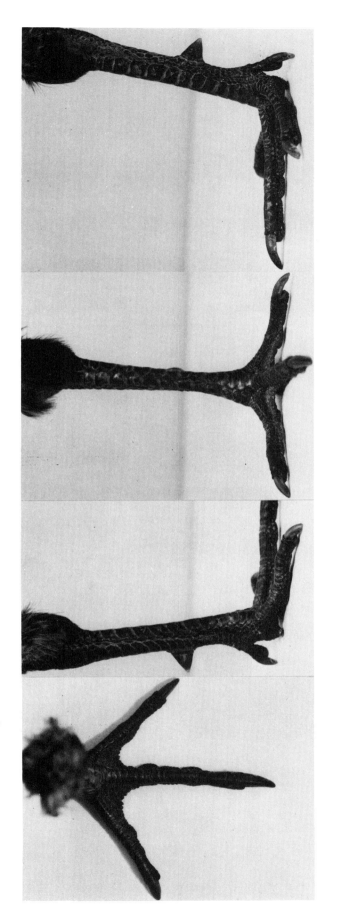

Ring-necked pheasant (male), right foot (13/16 life-size).

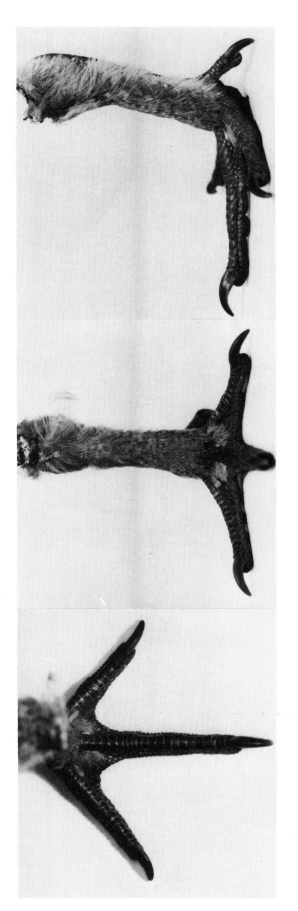

Blue grouse (male), right foot (life-size).

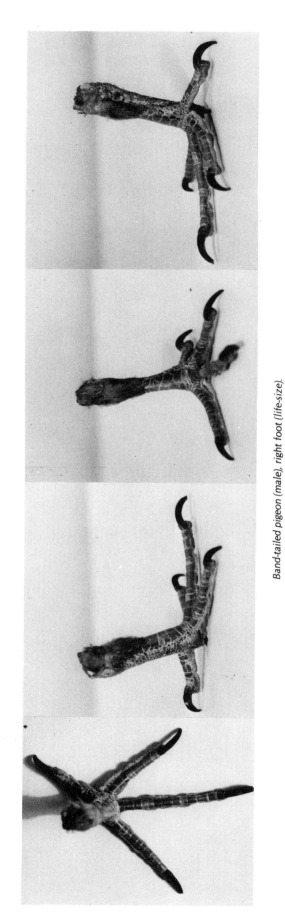

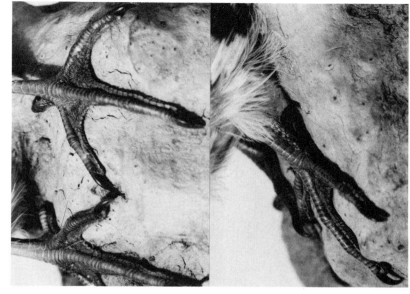

Ruffed grouse, left foot (life-size).

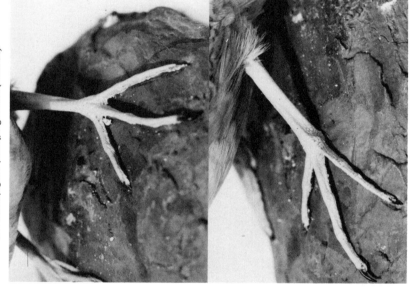

Band-tailed pigeon (male), right foot (life-size).

Woodcock, left foot (life-size).

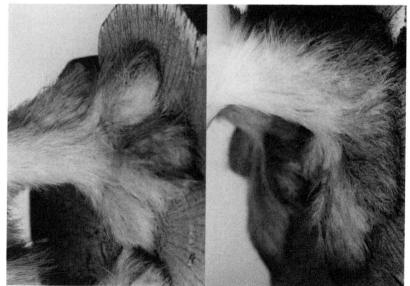

Willow ptarmigan, left foot (life-size).

13

Game Bird Bills

The bill on a particular bird is of a fixed shape and must be accurately duplicated to achieve an advanced or professional carving. Having a fresh specimen from which to work is ideal. However, bills dry (even in the freezer) so it is always advisable to record pertinent bill dimensions and a number of other important structural dimensions for future use (See page 143).

For those who do not have fresh specimens, plastic study bills, cast from fresh specimens, are available now for many game birds (see Appendix for availability). Unfortunately, the bill size varies considerably for a particu-

lar species and the carver, who strives for accurate detail, has no way of knowing if the study bill was cast from an average size, or a large, or a small specimen.

Life-size photographs of the profile, top, and bottom views of the dried bills of all game birds have been included in this chapter for the carver who has neither specimens or study bills. When bills dry, dimensional changes occur, primarily in the bill's cross-section which affects its width. An addition of approximately 5 to 10 percent should be made to the width of the dried bill to allow for the shrinkage due to drying.

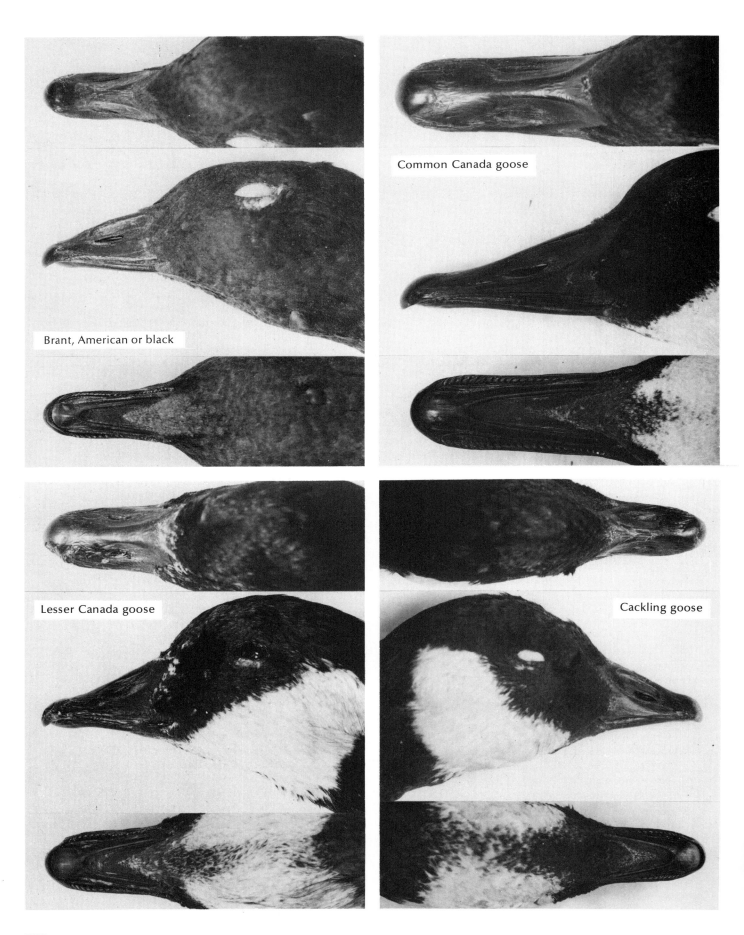

Common Canada goose

Brant, American or black

Lesser Canada goose

Cackling goose

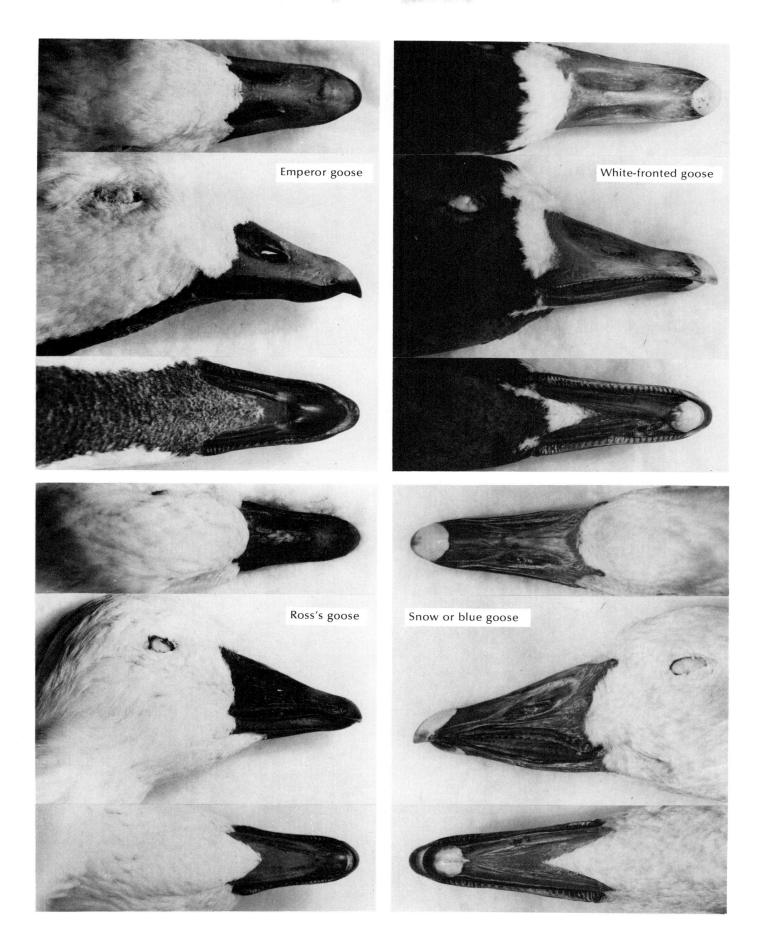

Emperor goose

White-fronted goose

Ross's goose

Snow or blue goose

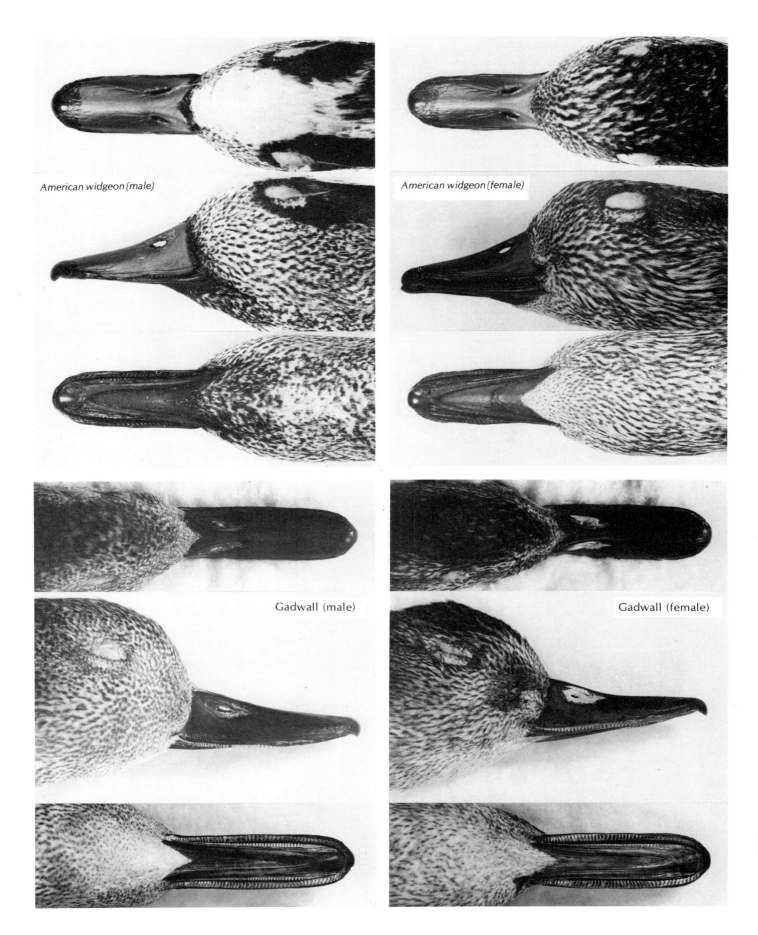

American widgeon (male)

American widgeon (female)

Gadwall (male)

Gadwall (female)

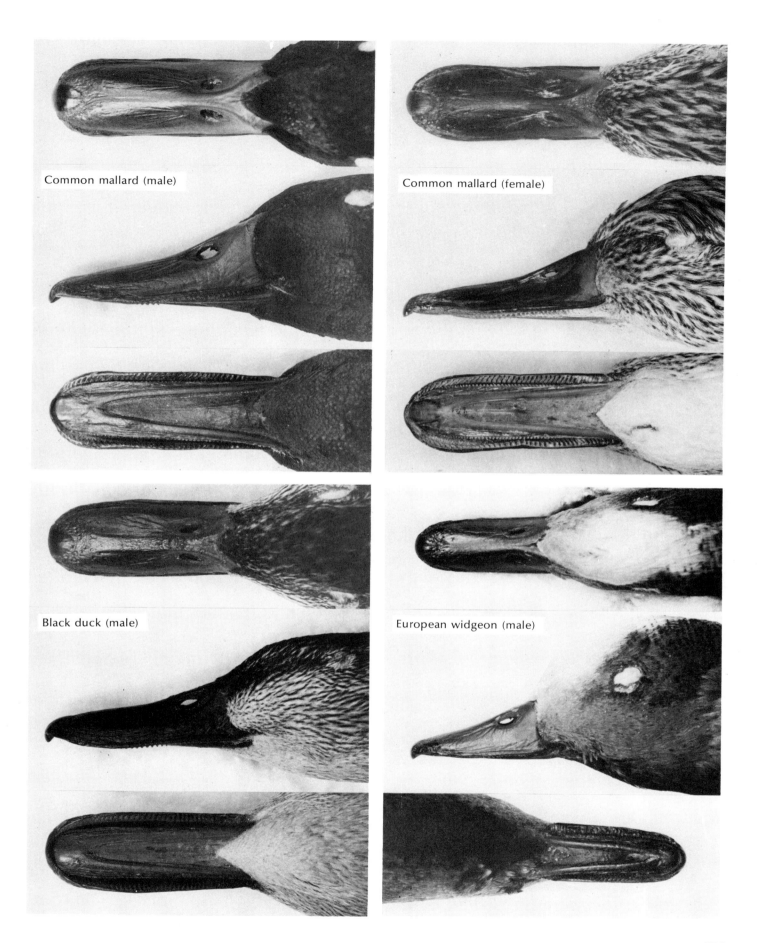

Common mallard (male)

Common mallard (female)

Black duck (male)

European widgeon (male)

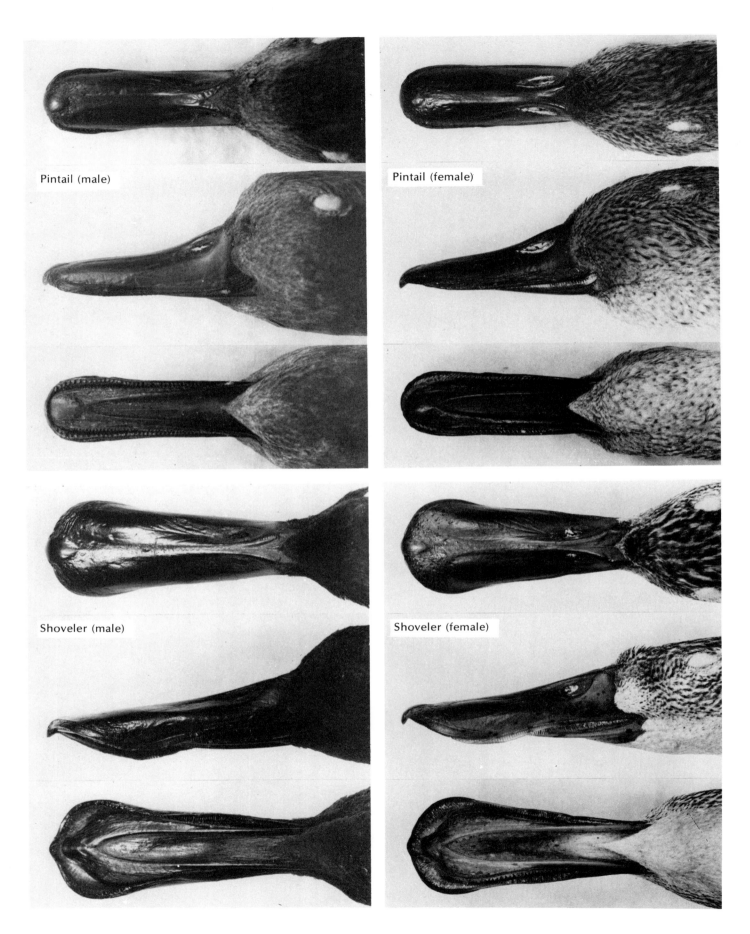

Pintail (male)

Pintail (female)

Shoveler (male)

Shoveler (female)

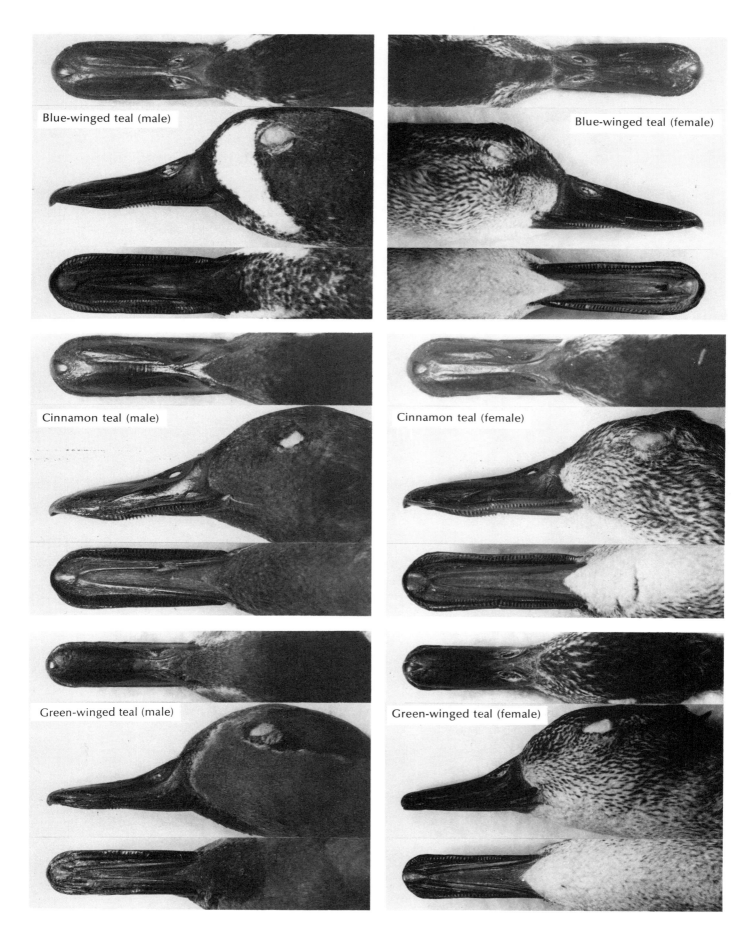

Blue-winged teal (male)

Blue-winged teal (female)

Cinnamon teal (male)

Cinnamon teal (female)

Green-winged teal (male)

Green-winged teal (female)

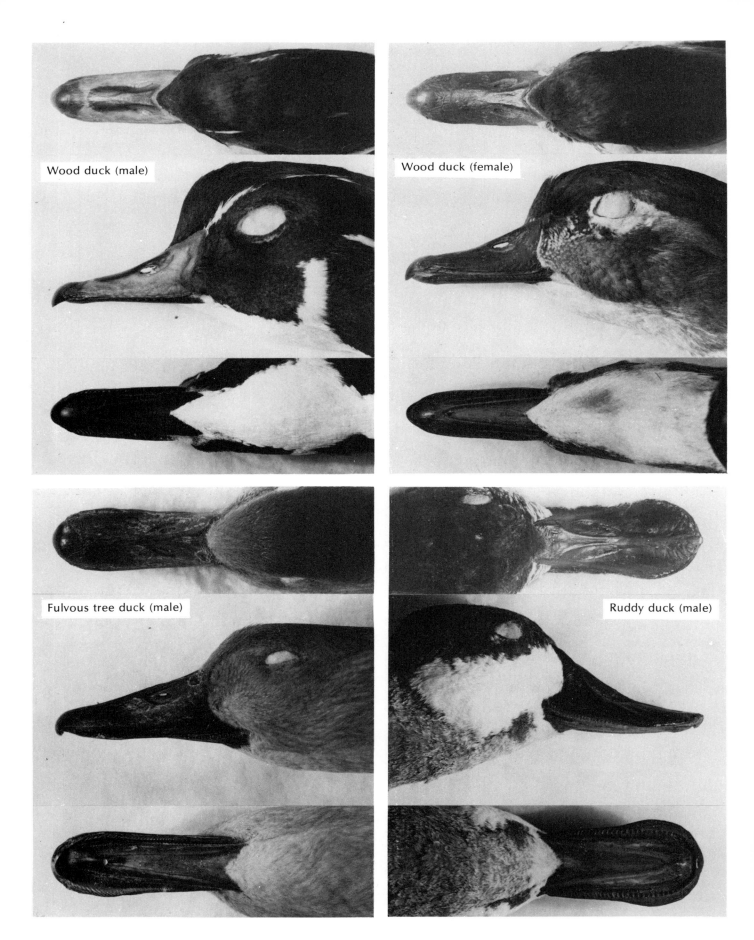

Wood duck (male)

Wood duck (female)

Fulvous tree duck (male)

Ruddy duck (male)

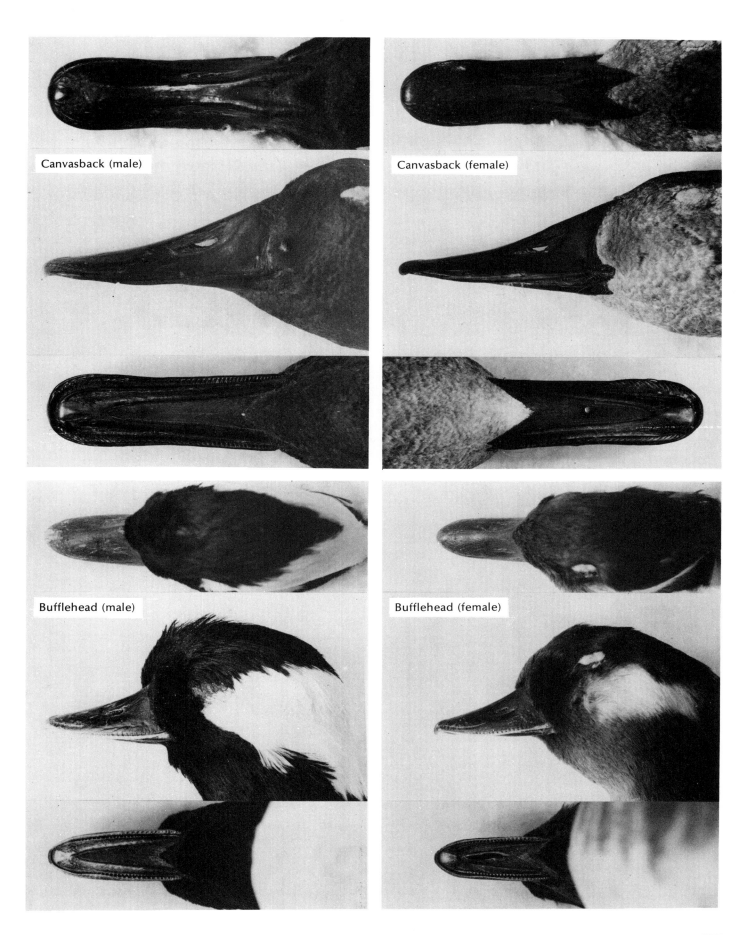

Canvasback (male)

Canvasback (female)

Bufflehead (male)

Bufflehead (female)

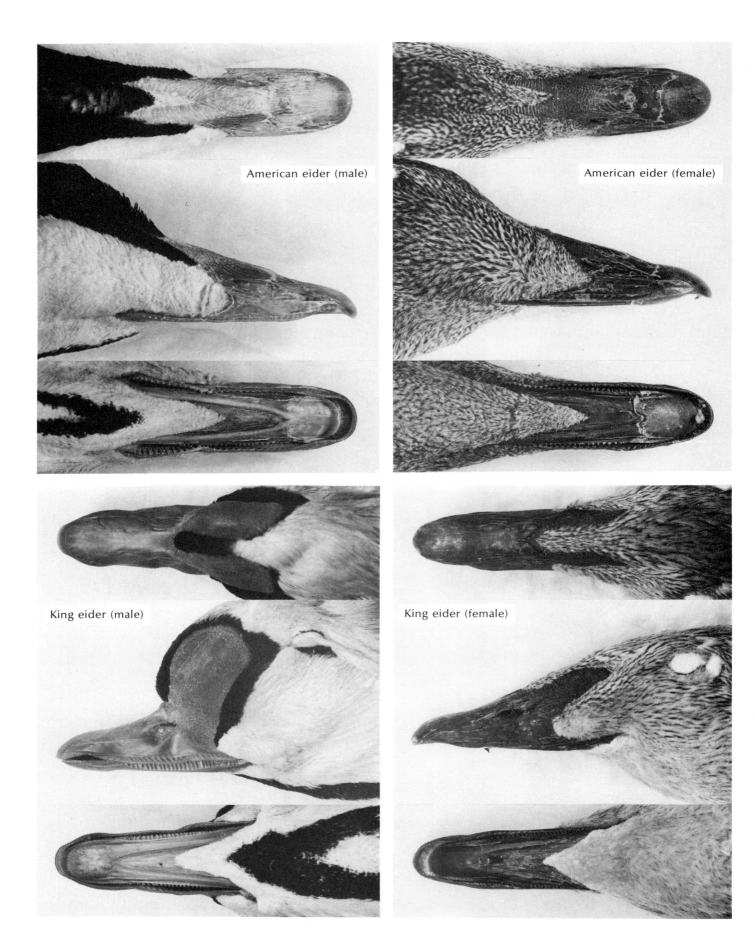

American eider (male)

American eider (female)

King eider (male)

King eider (female)

Spectacled eider (male)

Spectacled eider (female)

Steller's eider (male)

Steller's eider (female)

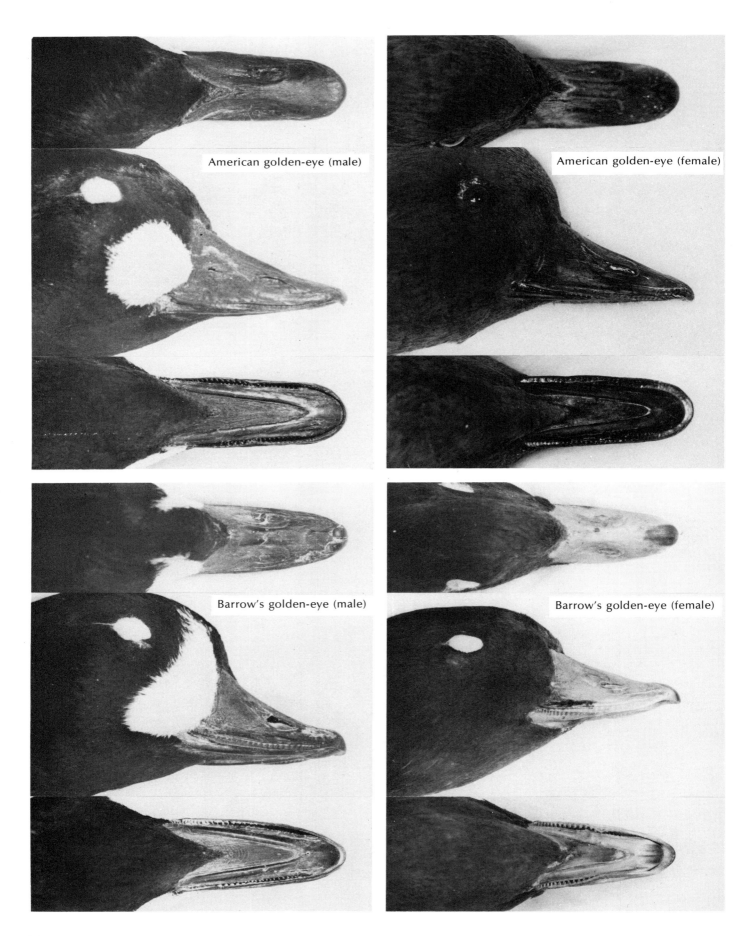

American golden-eye (male)

American golden-eye (female)

Barrow's golden-eye (male)

Barrow's golden-eye (female)

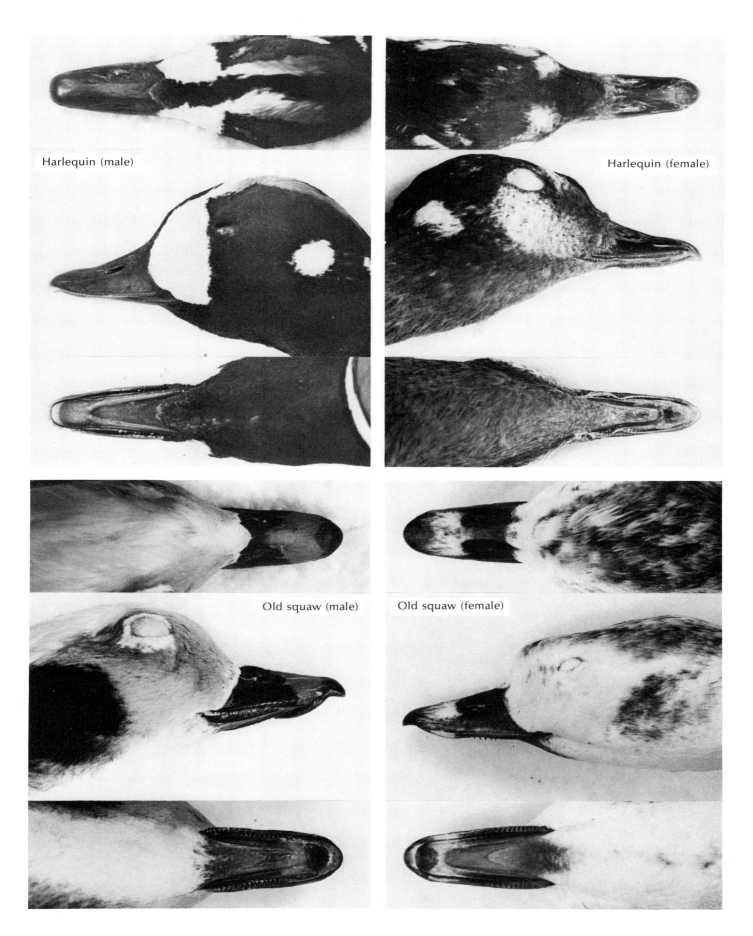

Harlequin (male)

Harlequin (female)

Old squaw (male)

Old squaw (female)

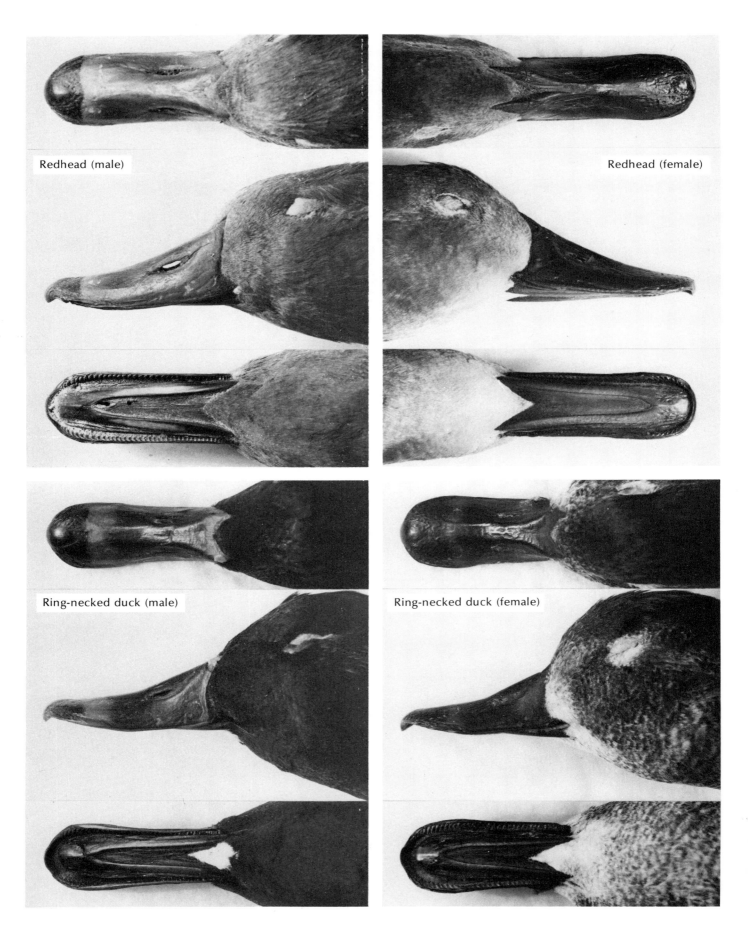

Redhead (male)

Redhead (female)

Ring-necked duck (male)

Ring-necked duck (female)

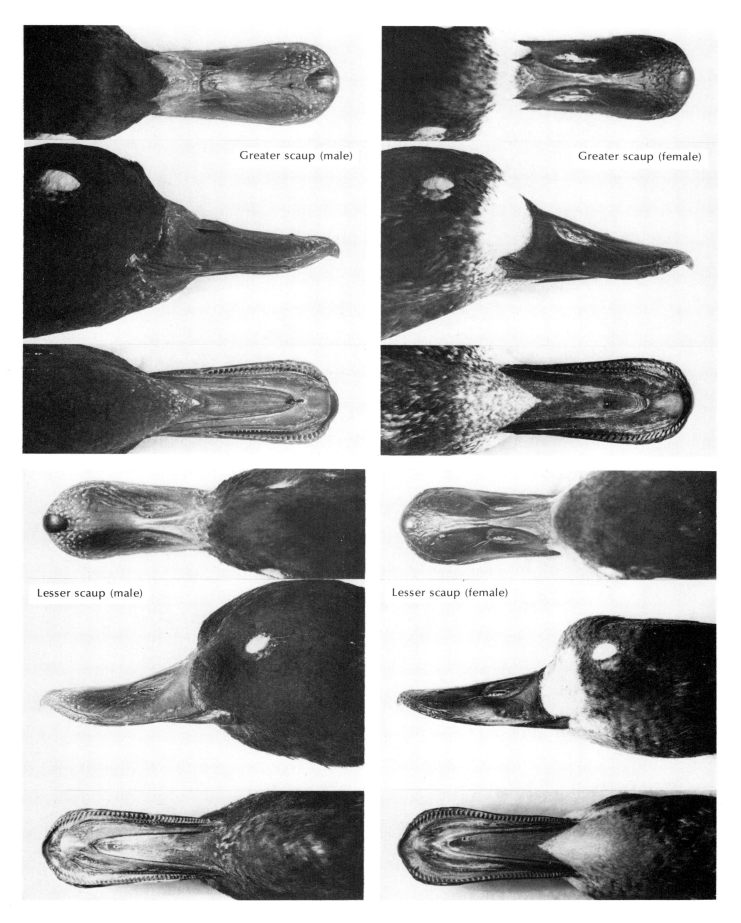

Greater scaup (male)

Greater scaup (female)

Lesser scaup (male)

Lesser scaup (female)

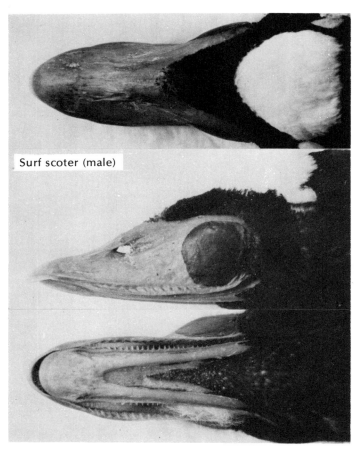

Surf scoter (male)

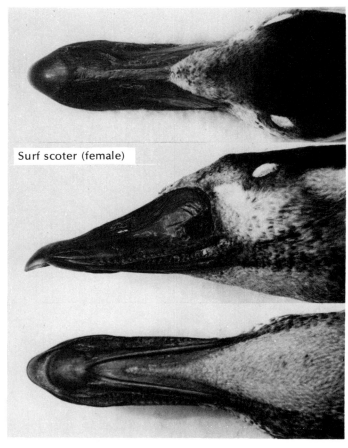

Surf scoter (female)

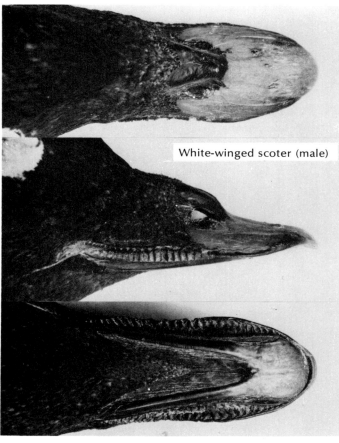

White-winged scoter (male)

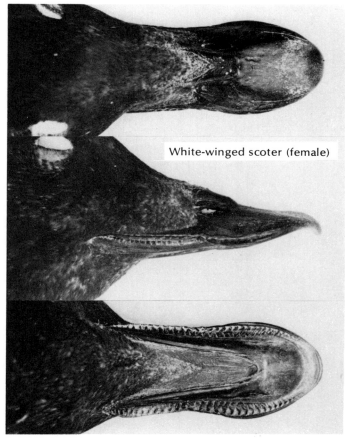

White-winged scoter (female)

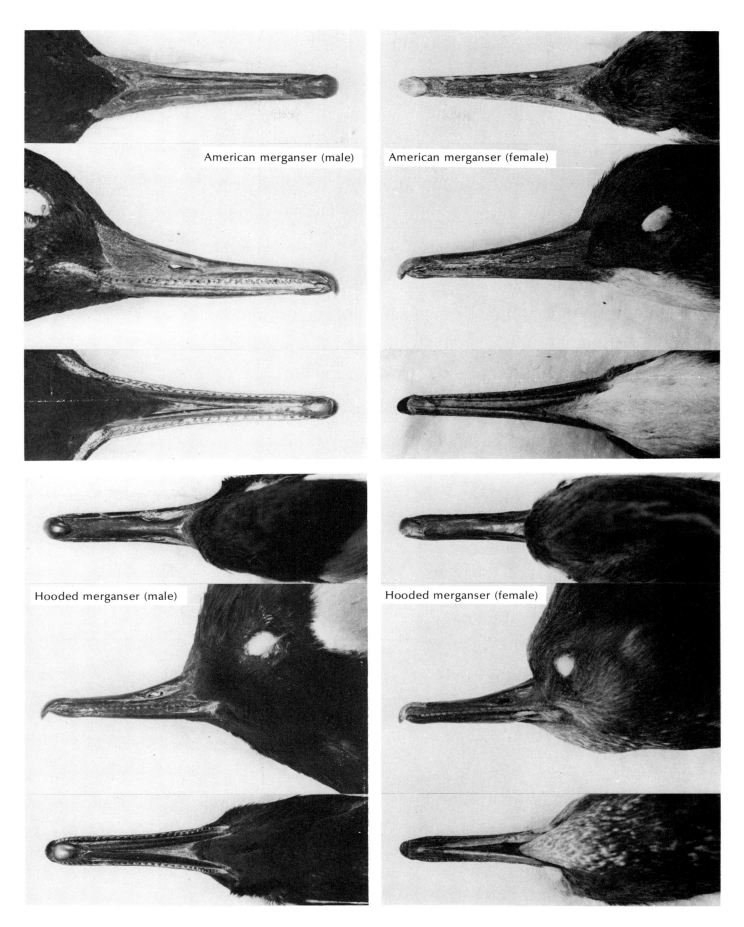

American merganser (male)

American merganser (female)

Hooded merganser (male)

Hooded merganser (female)

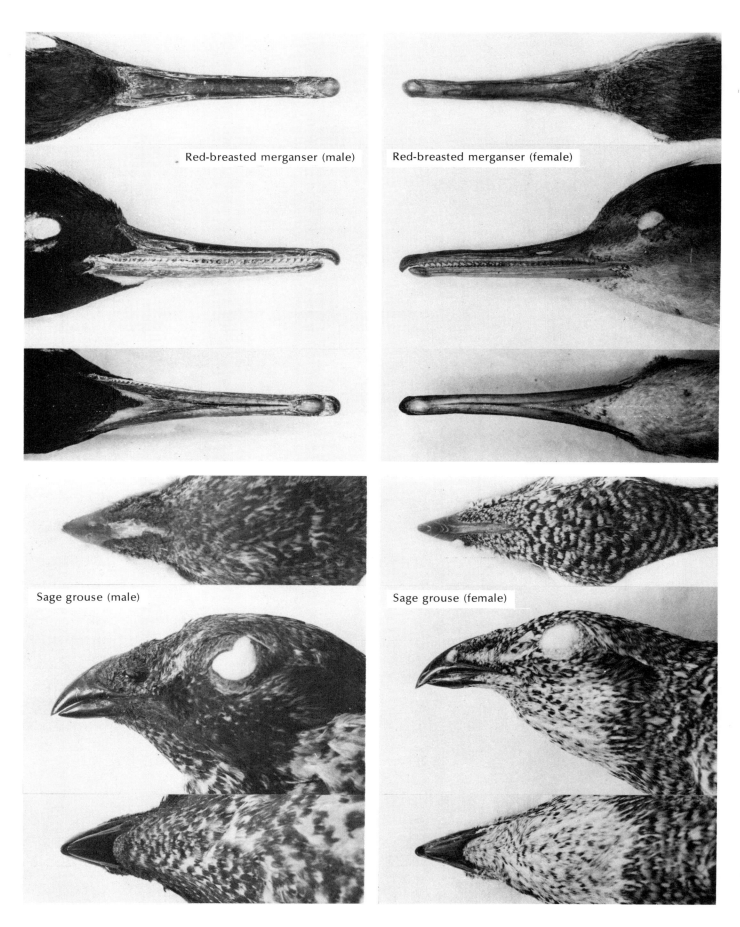

Red-breasted merganser (male)

Red-breasted merganser (female)

Sage grouse (male)

Sage grouse (female)

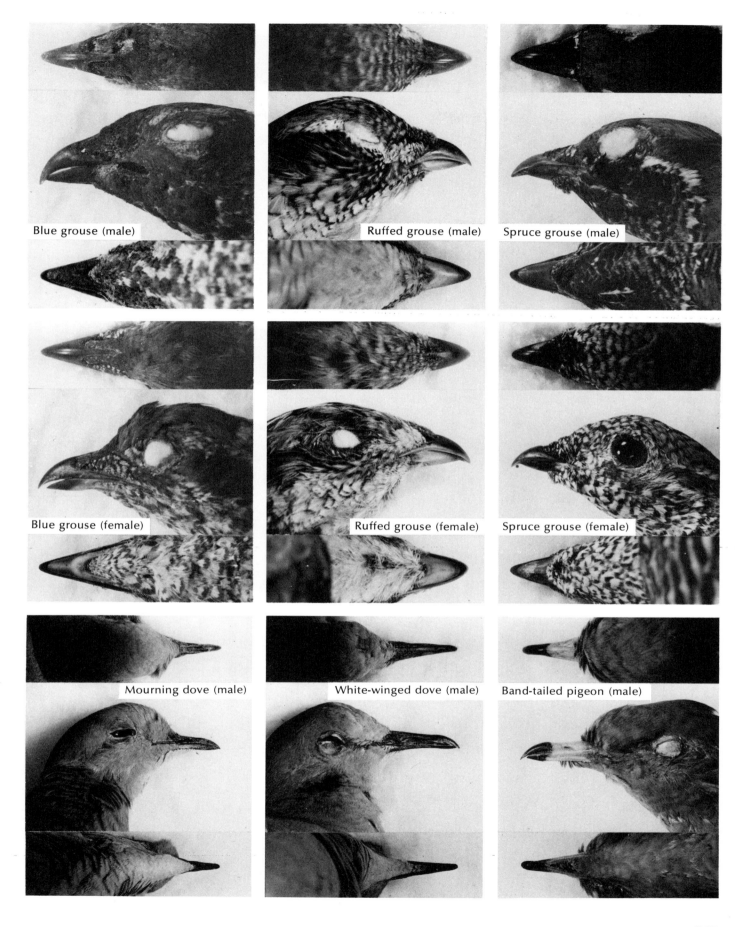

Blue grouse (male)

Ruffed grouse (male)

Spruce grouse (male)

Blue grouse (female)

Ruffed grouse (female)

Spruce grouse (female)

Mourning dove (male)

White-winged dove (male)

Band-tailed pigeon (male)

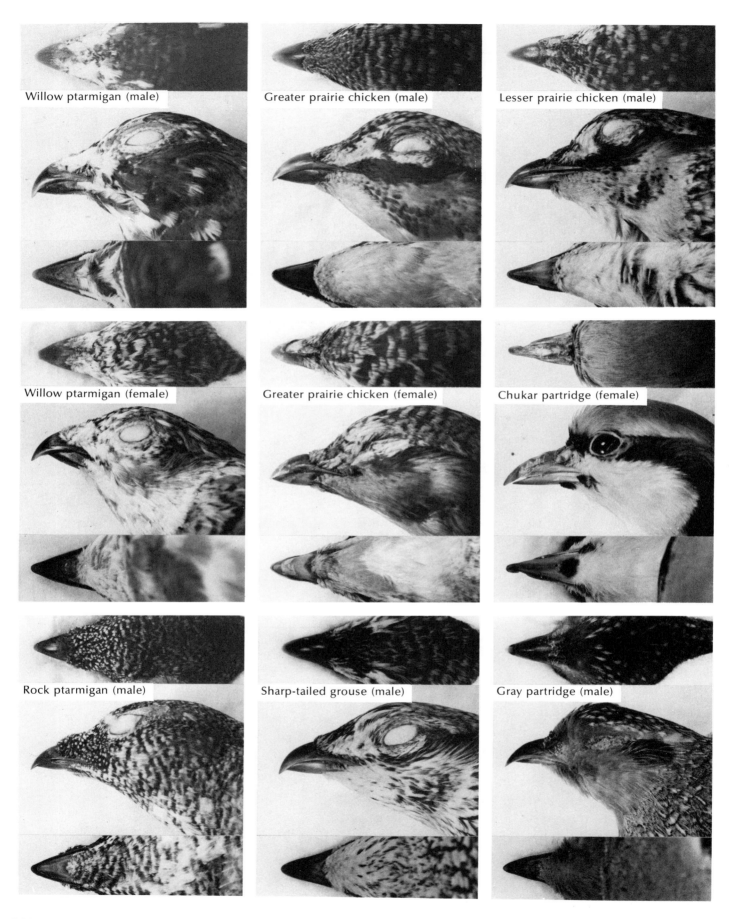

Willow ptarmigan (male)

Greater prairie chicken (male)

Lesser prairie chicken (male)

Willow ptarmigan (female)

Greater prairie chicken (female)

Chukar partridge (female)

Rock ptarmigan (male)

Sharp-tailed grouse (male)

Gray partridge (male)

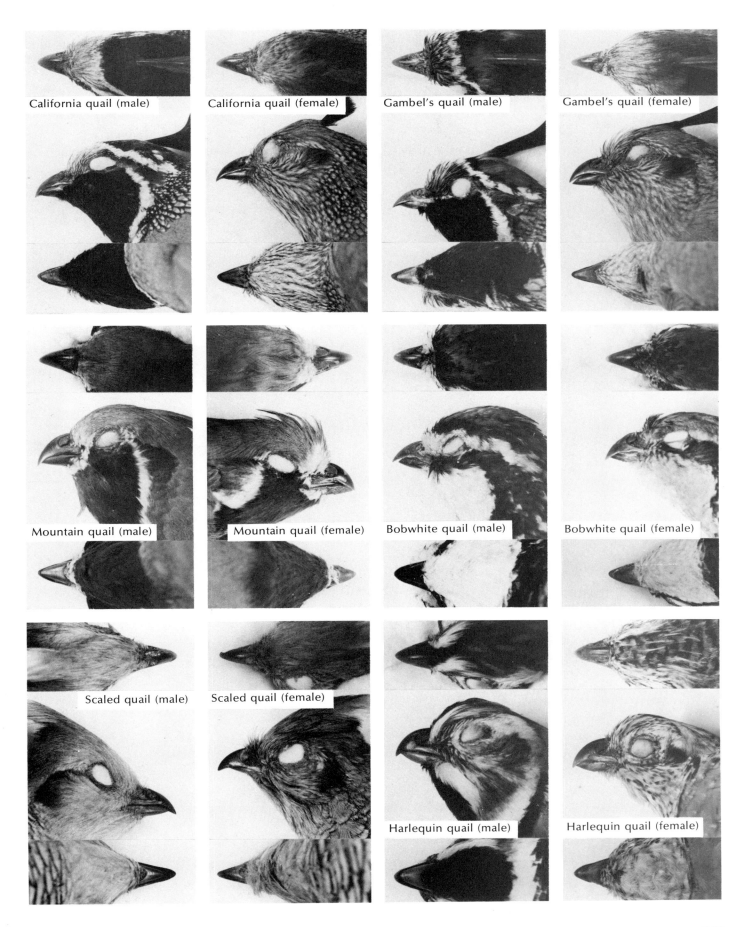

California quail (male)

California quail (female)

Gambel's quail (male)

Gambel's quail (female)

Mountain quail (male)

Mountain quail (female)

Bobwhite quail (male)

Bobwhite quail (female)

Scaled quail (male)

Scaled quail (female)

Harlequin quail (male)

Harlequin quail (female)

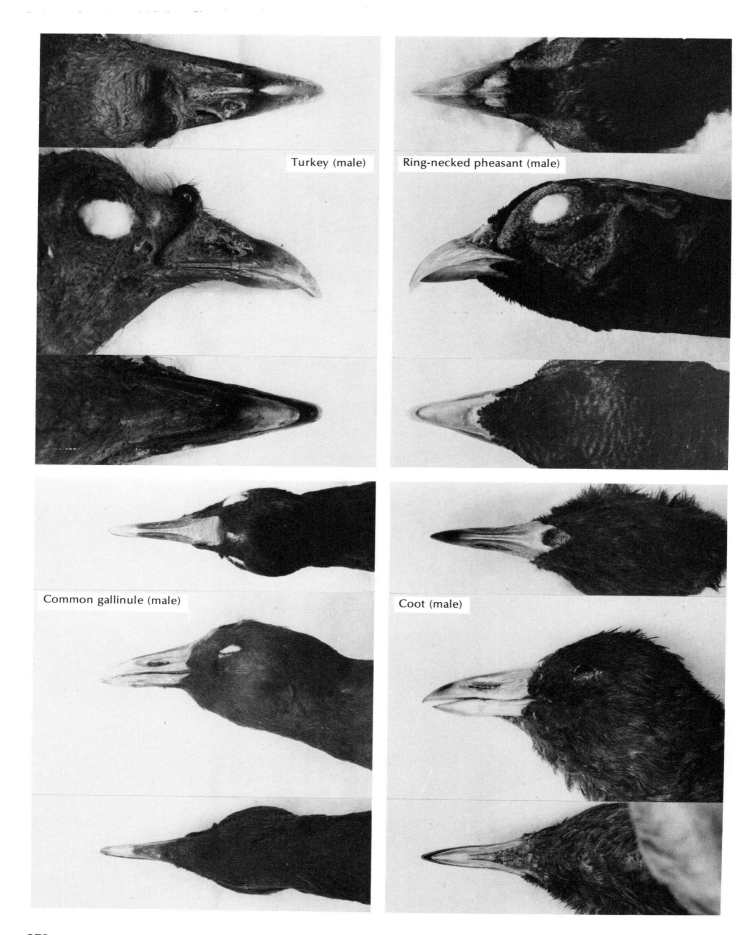

Turkey (male)

Ring-necked pheasant (male)

Common gallinule (male)

Coot (male)

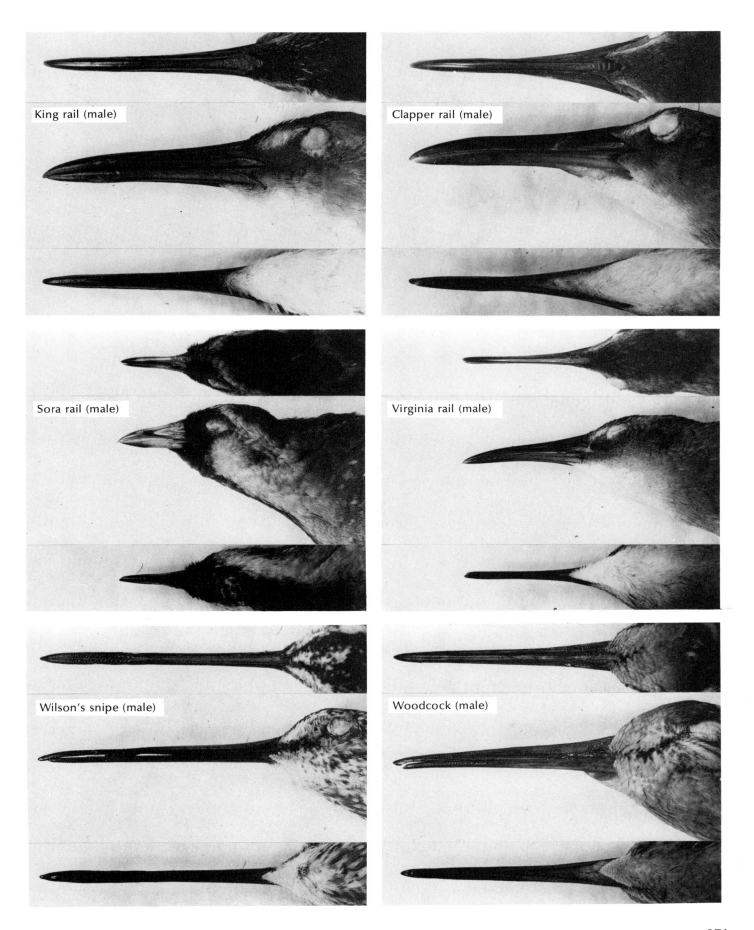

King rail (male)

Clapper rail (male)

Sora rail (male)

Virginia rail (male)

Wilson's snipe (male)

Woodcock (male)

Appendix

SOURCES OF INFORMATION

Game Bird Pictures

Allan, Arthur A. *Stalking Birds with a Color Camera*. National Geographic Society, (out of print).

———."Duck Hunting with a Color Camera." *National Geographic*, October 1951.

Audubon Magazine. National Audubon Society, 950 Third Ave., New York, N.Y. 10022.

Bauer, Erwin A. *Duck Hunter's Bible* (paperback). Doubleday, n.d.

Bellrose F. C. *Ducks, Geese, and Swans of North America*. Stackpole Books, 1976.

Breakthrough Magazine, P. O. Box 1320, Loganville, GA 30249.

Burk, Bruce. *Waterfowl Studies*. Winchester Press, 1976.

———. *Complete Waterfowl Studies*. Schiffer Publishing Ltd., 1984.
Vol. I—Dabbling & Whistling Ducks.
Vol. II—Diving Ducks.
Vol. III—Geese & Swans.

Butcher, Devereau. *Seeing America's Wildlife in Our National Refuges*. Devin-Adair, (out of print).

Clement, Roland C. *The Living World of Audubon*. Grosset and Dunlap, (out of print).

Frank, Charles W. *Anatomy of a Waterfowl*. Pelican Publishing Co., 1982.

Hanson, Harold C. *The Giant Canada Goose*. Southern Illinois University Press, 1965.

Heintzelman, Donald S. *North American Ducks, Geese, and Swans*. Winchester Press, 1978.

Hoskins, Eric. *Waders*. Pelham Books Ltd., London, 1983.

Johnsgard, Paul A. *Grouse and Quails of North America*. University of Nebraska Press, 1973.

———. *Handbook of Waterfowl Behavior*. Comstock Pub. Assoc. (Cornell University Press), 1965.

———. *North American Game Birds of Upland and Shoreline*. University of Nebraska Press, 1975.

———. *Waterfowl of North America*. Indiana University Press, 1975.

———. *Waterfowl: Their Biology and Natural History*. University of Nebraska Press, 1968.

Kortright, F.H. *The Ducks, Geese, and Swans of North America* (rev. ed.). Stackpole, 1975.

Lansdowne, James F. *Birds of the Eastern Forest*. 2 vols. Houghton Mifflin, 1968.

———. *Birds of the Northern Forest*. Houghton Mifflin, 1966.

LeMaster, R. *The Great Gallery of Ducks*. Contemporary Books, 1985.

Linduska, Joseph P., ed. *Waterfowl Tomorrow*. Washington, D.C.: U.S. Government Printing Office.

Line, Les, and Russell, Franklin. *The Audubon Society Book of Wild Birds*. Harry N. Abrams, 1976.

National Wildlife Magazine. 1412 Sixteenth St., NW, Washington, D.C. 20036.

Phillips, J. C. *A Natural History of Ducks*. Dover Publications, 1986.

Queeny, Edgar M. *Prairie Wings* (reprint of 1946 ed.). Schiffer, 1979.

Rand, Austin L. *American Water and Game Birds*. Dutton, (out of print).

Spaulding, Edward S. *The Quails*. Macmillan, (out of print).

Terres, John K. *The Audubon Society Encyclopedia of North American Birds*. Alfred A. Knopf, 1980.

Todd, Frank S. *Waterfowl: Ducks, Geese, and Swans of the World*. Harcourt Brace Jovanovich, 1979.

Van Wormer, Joe. *The World of the Canada Goose*. Lippincott, 1968.

Veasey, Tricia. *Waterfowl Illustrated*. Schiffer Publishing Ltd., 1983.

Water, Prey, and Game Birds of North America. National Geographic Society, n.d.

Wildfowl Carving and Collecting Magazine. P. O. Box 1831, Harrisburg, PA 17105.

Williams, Cecil S. *Honker*. D. Van Nostrand, (out of print).

Zim, Herbert, and Sprunt, Alexander. *Game Birds*. Western, 1961.

Bird Anatomy

Aymar, Gordon. *Bird Flight*. Dodd Mead, (out of print).

Beebe, C. William. *The Bird*. Dover, (out of print).

Darling, Lois and Louis. *Bird*. Houghton Mifflin, (out of print).

Frank, Charles W. *Anatomy of a Waterfowl*. Pelican Publishing Co., 1982.

LeMaster R. *Waterfowl, The Artist's Guide to Anatomy, Attitude and Color*. Contemporary Books, Inc., 1983.

Pettingill, Olin Sewall, Jr. *Ornithology in Laboratory and Field*. Burgess, 1970.

Bird Carving

Breakthrough Magazine. P. O. Box 1320, Loganville, GA 30249.

Bridenhagen, Keith and Patrick Spielman. *Realistic Decoys*. Sterling Publishing Co., 1984.

Chapel, C. and C. Sullivan. *Wildlife Woodcarvers*. Stackpole Books, 1986.

Chip Chats Magazine. *National Woodcarvers' Association*, 7424 Miami Ave., Cincinnati, Ohio 45243

Gilley, Wendell. *The Art of Bird Carving.* Hillcrest Publications, 190 South 100 East, Spanish Fork, Utah 84660.

Lacey, John. *How to do Wood Carving.* Fawcett, (out of print).

Le Master, Richard. *Wildlife in Wood.* Chillicothe, Ill.: Modern Technology, Inc., 1978.

LeMaster, R. *Art of the Wooden Bird.* Contemporary Books, 1985.

Murphy, Charles F. *Working Plans for Working Decoys.* Winchester Press, 1979.

Murphy, Charles F. *Working Decoy Plans: Kit 2. A Sneak Box Book-Kit.* Winchester Press, 1986.

Schroeder, Roger and James D. Sprankle. *Waterfowl Carving with J. D. Sprankle.* Stackpole Books, 1985.

Schroeder, Roger. *How to Carve Waterfowl.* Stackpole Books, 1984.
How to Carve Waterfowl, Book 2. Stackpole Books, 1986.

Small, Anne. *Masters of Decorative Bird Carving.* Winchester Press, 1981.

Starr, Jr., George Ross. *How to Make Working Decoys.* Winchester Press, 1978.

Tawes, William I. *Creative Bird Carving.* Cornell Maritime, 1969.

Veasey, Tricia and Tom Johnson. *Championship Carving.* Schiffer Publishing, Ltd., 1984.

Wildfowl Art Magazine. Ward Foundation, 655 S. Salisbury Blvd., Salisbury, MD 21801.

Wildfowl Carving and Collecting Magazine. P. O. Box 1831, Harrisburg, PA 17105.

Photography

Jacobs, Lou, Jr. *Amphoto Guide to Lighting.* Amphoto, 1979.

Oberrecht, Kenn. *The Outdoor Photographer's Handbook.* Winchester Press, 1979.

Studio Lighting for Product Photography. Kodak Professional Data Book No. 0-16.

Warham, John. *The Technique of Bird Photography.* Focal Press, 1973.

Taxidermy

Blake, Emmet R. *Preserving Birds for Study.* Chicago Natural History Museum, (out of print).

Elwood, J.W. *Lessons in Taxidermy.* Omaha, Neb.: Northwestern School of Taxidermy.

Herter, George Leonard, and Barrie, Myron E. *The Science of Modern Taxidermy.* Waseca, Minn.: Herter's Inc.

Moyer, John W. *Practical Taxidermy.* Ronald Press Co.

Pray, Leon L. *Taxidermy.* Macmillan, 1943.

———. *Bird Studies for the Taxidermist.* Greenfield Center, N.Y.: Modern Taxidermist Publication.

Books

Books Plus. P. O. Box 731, Lodi, NJ 07644.

Pattern Books

Burk Bruce. *Decorative Decoy Designs.* Winchester Press, 1986.

Godin, Patrick R. *Championship Waterfowl Patterns.* Godin Art, Inc., 1986.

Ponte, Alfred M. *26 Realistic Duck Patterns.* Lincoln Press, 1982.

Sprankle, J. D. *Waterfowl Patterns & Painting.* Greenwing Enterprises, 1986.

Chapell, C. and C. Sullivan. *Pattern Book—Drake Diving Ducks. Pattern Book—Drake Puddle Ducks.*

Clay Modeling

Kise, W. Kent, Jr. *How To Make A Wood Carving Into A Masterpiece.* Hamilton Publishing Company, P. O. Box 5087, Lancaster, PA 17601.

Video Tapes

Tape I. Carving by Pat Godin.
Tape II. Texturing by Pat Godin.
Tape III. Painting by Pat Godin. Georgetown Inc. Video Productions, P. O. Box 625, Bethel Park, PA 15102.
Tape I. Jim Sprankle Carving a Green-Winged Teal.
Tape II. Jim Sprankle Painting a Green-Winged Teal. Greenwing Enterprises, Rt. 2, Box 731B, Chester, MD 21619.

SUPPLIES

Cast Bills

Wilcut Co. 7113 Spicer Drive, Citrus Heights, CA 95610 (Oscar Johnston's Study Bills)

Cast Feet

Richard Delise, 920 Springwood Drive, West Chester, Penn. 19380.

Glass Eyes

Robert J. Smith, 14900 West 31st Ave., Golden, Col. 80401.

Tohickon Glass Eyes, P.O. Box 15, Erwinna, Penn. 18920.

West Coast Taxidermy Supply Co., 648 San Mateo Ave., San Bruno, Calif. 94066.

Carving Tools & Supplies

Craftswoods, 10921 York Road, Hunt Valley, MD 21030.

Chez la Rogue, P. O. Box 1315, Foley, Alabama 36536.

Knott's Knives, 106 South Ford Ave., Wilmington, Del. 19805.

Kulis Karvit, 725 Broadway Avenue, Bedford, OH 44146.

Nick Purdo, 27340 Jean, Warren, Mich. 48093. (Custom Knives.)

P. C. English Enterprises, Inc. RT. 1, Box 136, Fredericksburg, VA 22401.

Montana Carving Supply, Rt. 1, Box 251, Wilsall, Montana 59086.

Woodcraft, P. O. Box 4000, Woburn, MA 01888. (Very complete line of tools and supplies).

A source for the following items referred to in this book:

Foredom Power Tools	Warren Tools
PowerArm	Forstner Bits
Pantograph	Graph Paper
3-inch Leather Strop Wheel	Karbide Kutzall rotary rasps

Wood Carvers Supply, Inc. P. O. Box 8928, Norfolk, VA 23503.

Wood Gallery and Supplies, Holiday Mall Shopping Center, Morehead, MN 56560

The Power Carver. Paul H. Gesswein & Co., P. O. Box 3998, Bridgeport, CT 06605.

Burning Tools

Detail Master. Leisure Time Products, 2650 Davisson St., River Grove, IL 60171.

Hot Tools, Inc., P. O. Box 615, Marblehead, MA 01945.

Tool Sharpening

Lansky Sharpeners, P. O. Box 800, Buffalo, NY 14221.

Frank Mittermeier, 3577 E. Tremont St., Bronx, N.Y. 10465. (Catalog.).

Craftsman Illustrated Sharpening Manual. Sears, Roebuck and Co., Mail Order Catalog No. 9K2924.

Carving Woods

Albert Constantine and Sons, 2050 Eastchester, Bronx, N.Y. 10461.

Chez la Rogue, P. O. Box 1315, Foley, AL 36536.

Craft Cove, 2315 W. Glen at Route 150, Peoria, Ill. 61611.

Craftwoods, 10921 York Road, Hunt Valley, MD 21030.

Kent Courtney, Woodsman, 1413 Texas Ave., Alexandria, La. 71301.

Montana Carving Supply, Rt. 1, Box 251, Wilsall, Montana 59086.

P. C. English Enterprises, Ind., RT. 1, Box 136, Fredericksburg, VA 22401.

Reel Lumber, 454 S. Anaheim Blvd., Anaheim, Calif. 92805.

Robert M. Albrecht, 18701 Parthenia St., Northridge, Calif. 91324.

Wood Gallery and Supplies, Holiday Mall Shopping Center, Morehead, MN 56560

Wood Carvers Supply, Inc. P. O. Box 8928, Norfolk, VA 23503.

Index